ENGINEERING EQUALITY

Engineering Equality

An Essay on European Anti-discrimination Law

ALEXANDER SOMEK

OXFORD
UNIVERSITY PRESS

This book has been printed digitally and produced in a standard specification in order to ensure its continuing availability

OXFORD
UNIVERSITY PRESS

Great Clarendon Street, Oxford OX2 6DP
United Kingdom

Oxford University Press is a department of the University of Oxford. It furthers the University's objective of excellence in research, scholarship, and education by publishing worldwide.
Oxford is a registered trade mark of Oxford University Press in the UK and in certain other countries

Reprinted 2012

British Library Cataloguing in Publication Data
Data available

Library of Congress Cataloging in Publication Data
Data available

ISBN 978-0-19-969337-5

For Roland Gerlach, my most remarkable
and dearest friend

Preface

This book attempts to determine the point and the limits of anti-discrimination law. As a field of legal policy, it is put into perspective by inquiring into how successful it can be as a strategy of social policy. The book uses legal analysis in order to expose the intrinsic shortcomings of anti-discrimination law, which fails to provide adequate legal guidance and invites constant supplementation by pedagogical projects of social engineering.

I hasten to add that the book is not another conservative diatribe against what is generally taken to be a progressive idea; on the contrary, it challenges the belief that anti-discrimination law is capable of delivering social progress. The challenge is not formulated empirically, that is, with reference to one or the other statistic as regards persistent discrimination, but rather conceptually, that is, with an eye to the basic concepts governing its operation.

In the course of writing this book I have incurred many debts.

The plan to this book goes back to a workshop that I helped co-organize in 2004 with the support of the Austrian Chamber of Workers. The support provided by Christoph Klein and Neda Bei is gratefully acknowledged.

Research for this book has been generously funded by the University of Iowa College of Law. I should like to thank two of my former Deans, N. William Hines and Carolyn Jones, for their generous support. Dean Gail Agrawal spontaneously agreed to cover licensing expenses for the dust jacket illustration. Major progress on the manuscript was made during my tenure as a fellow at the Institute for Advanced Study in Berlin (2007–2008).

As always, I am particularly grateful to my dear wife Sabine, who read several drafts of the manuscript and from whose observations the book benefited throughout.

The librarians at the Law Library of the University of Iowa, in particular John Bergstrom, provided their usual exceptional assistance. My research assistant Amanda Thai updated all references to Treaty articles in order to reflect the changes brought about by the Treaty of Lisbon.

The book is dedicated to the man with whom I have had the most refreshing conversations on its topic and whose acumen as a lawyer is only surpassed by his love of classical music. As much as he and I agree on legal matters—and this includes anti-discrimination law—we sometimes disagree profoundly on truly important things, such as the rank that is to be accorded to Schönberg's *Gurrelieder* in the history of music. Even though he is sadly mistaken in this case, my life would be severely impoverished—indeed, a far less good life—if it were not for all the intermittent conversations I have with him.

Alexander Somek

Iowa City
November 2010

Contents

List of Abbreviations xii
Table of Cases xiii

Introduction 1
1. Reconciling Competitiveness with Solidarity 1
2. Practical and Intellectual Success 4
3. Europe's Social Question 6
4. The Turn to Employment 9
5. The Turn to Management 10
6. Manageable Social Policy 11
7. Equality Management: the Macro and the Micro Level 12
8. The Systematic Analysis 13
9. Triangulating the Neoliberal Left 14
10. The Normative Deficiency of Anti-discrimination Law 16
11. The Neoliberal Predicament and its Antidote 17
12. Constructivism: a Note on Legal Analysis 19

1. Social Policy: from Domestication to Disarmament **21**
1. The Social Question in a Transnational Context 21
2. The Economic is the Political 22
3. The Elusive Social Model 26
4. Domestication 29
5. Assimilation 32
6. Towards Disarmament: Monetary Union 35
7. Social and Nowhere to go: Competences 36
8. Social and Nowhere to go: the Problem-solving Gap 38
9. Explaining the Turn to Employment 40
10. The Dual Economy: Competitive Solidarity and Liberalization 43
11. The Rise of Authoritarian Liberalism 45
12. Substantive Economic Due Process 47
13. Renationalization 50
14. Conclusion: the Place of Anti-discrimination Law 51

2. From Legislation to Discourse and Mobilization **53**
1. Reviewing the History 53
2. The Technocracy of Problem-solving Interaction 55
3. The Anti-discrimination Action Programme 58
4. The Link to Employment and Broader Social Policy Objectives 59
5. The Example of the EQUAL Programme 62

6. The New *Concordantia Catholica*: Creating Self-confident Human Resources 64
7. The Transformation of the Union's Power: Discoursive Holism 68
8. The Transformation of the Union's Power: Mobilization 70
9. First-order and Second-order Discourse 73
10. Emotivism: from Rights to Attitudes 75
11. The Underlying Silence 76
12. Vague Hopes 78
13. Conclusion 82

3. Neoliberalism and Morality 83
1. Introduction 83
2. Neoliberalism 84
3. Freedom and Responsibility 87
4. Redistribution and Decommodification 88
5. Distribution by Means of Morality 89

4. Direct Discrimination 93
1. Introduction 93
2. Market Equality 93
3. The Neoliberal Left 96
4. Distributive Justice: the Internal Analysis 99
5. Yielding 100
6. How Norms Change Social Meanings 102
7. Pre-normative and Normative Intent 103
8. The Systemic Context of Direct Discrimination 105
9. Distributive Agents 106
10. Redistribution and not Attitudes 108
11. Conclusion 110

5. Normative Twist and Antinomy 113
1. Introduction 113
2. The Priority of Indirect Discrimination 113
3. Is Direct Discrimination Different or Special? 115
4. Extensional and Intensional Causation: Two Different Types of Normativity 118
5. The Demise of per se Illegality and the Relevance of Treating Like Cases Alike 122
6. The Lure of Comparability 124
7. The Inevitable Deontological Misreading 126
8. From Extensional Causation to Pre-normative Intent 128
9. The Seat of the Normative Deficiency 131
10. Without Patterns: Reasons and Derogations 132
11. Proportionality 134
12. Decommodification 136
13. Conclusion 138

6. Consequences of Normative Deficiency **141**
1. The Normative Deficiency Stated 141
2. Moralism 142
3. The Inscrutability of Intent 145
4. Conventional Understandings? 148
5. From Law to Casuistry 149
6. A Minimalist Solution: Free-market Paternalism 150
7. Groupism and Reification 153
8. The Abstention from Terror 155
9. Conclusion 157

7. Moral Re-engineering: the Neoliberal Predicament **159**
1. Introduction 159
2. The Micro-level Cousin of European Strategies 159
3. A Strong Start 161
4. The Law of Bias 164
5. Changing the Law while Leaving the Market in Place 165
6. Businesses as Correctional Facilities 167
7. From Labour to Experts 169
8. From Law to Pedagogy 171
9. Ecstatic Self-observation 172
10. Conclusion 174

8. Beyond Inclusion **177**
1. Introduction 177
2. Accommodation 178
3. Unpacking the Meaning of Discrimination 180
4. The Persistence of the Deontological Perspective 183
5. Coda: the Wrong of Discrimination 185
6. Solidarity 186
7. Reversing Reductions 189
8. The Social Question in a Transnational Context 190
9. Conclusion 194

Bibliography 197
Index 215

List of Abbreviations

ADA	Americans with Disabilities Act 1990
CEC	Confédération Européenne des Cadres
CEEP	European Centre of Employers and Enterprises
EC Treaty	Treaty establishing the European Community
ECHR	European Convention on Human Rights
ECtHR	European Court of Human Rights
ECJ	European Court of Justice
ECOFIN	Economic and Financial Affairs Council
ECR	European Court Reports
EIoP	*European Integration Online Papers*
ESF	European Social Fund
ETUC	European Trade Union Confederation
EU Treaty	Treaty on European Union
FEU Treaty	Treaty on the Functioning of the European Union
OMC	Open Method of Coordination
UEAPME	European Association of Craft, Small and Medium-sized Enterprise
UNICE	Union of Industrial Employers' Confederations of Europe

Table of Cases

US SUPREME COURT

McDonnell Douglas Corp. v. *Green*, 411 US 792 (1973). 145
Washington v. *Davis*, 426 US 229 (1976). 91
McCleskey v. *Kemp*, 481 US 279 (1987). 91
Price Waterhouse v. *Hopkins*, 490 US 228 (1989). 145

EU CASES

Goodwin v. *United Kingdom* (App. No. 28957/95) [2002] All ER (D) 158 (Jul). 121
Case C-36/74, *Walrave and Koch* v. *Union Cycliste Internationale* (1974) ECR 1405. . .49
Case C-43/75, *Gabrielle Defrenne* v. *Société anonyme belge de navigation aérienne Sabena (Defrenne II)* [1976] ECR 455 2
Case C-69/80, *Worringham* v. *Lloyds Bank Ltd* [1981] ECR 787. 104
Case C-96/80, *Jenkins* v. *Kingsgate* [1981] ECR 911 117
Case C-170/84, *Bilka-Kaufhaus GmbH* v. *Weber von Hartz* [1986] ECR 1607. 114
Case C-222/84, *Marguerite Johnston* v. *Chief Constable of the Royal Ulster Constabulary* [1986] ECR 1651. 133
Case C-248/86, *Grant* v. *South-West Trains* [1998] ECR 621 118
Case C-109/88, *Danfoss* [1989] ECR 3199 134
Case C-171/88, *Ingrid Rinner-Kühn* v. *FWW Spezial-Gebäudereinigung GmbH & Co. KG* [1989] ECR 2742 . . . . .114, 116
Case C-177/88, *Dekker* v. *Stichting Vormingscentrum voor Junge Volwassen Plus* [1990] ECR I-3941. . . . . .109, 128
Case C-179/88, *Handels- of Kontorfuntionaerernes Forbund i Danmark* v. *Dansk Arbejdsverforening* [1990] ECR I-3979 130
Case C-184/89, *Nimz* v. *Freie und Hansestadt Hamburg* [1991] ECR I-297. 101
Case C-260/89, *ERT* [1991] ECR I-2925 80
Case C-179/90, *Merci Convenzionali Porto di Genova SpA* v. *Siderurgia Gabrielli SpA* [1991] ECR I-5889 30
Case C-127/92, *Enderby* v. *Frenchay Health Authority and the Secretary for Health* [1993] ECR I-5535. 123
Case C-343/92, *Roks and others* v. *Bestuur van de Bedrijfsvereniging voor de Gezondheid, Geestelijke en Maatschappelijke Belangen and others* [1994] ECR I-571 117
Case C-444/93, *De Weerd* [1995] ECR I-4741 117
Case C-32/93, *Webb* v. *EMO Air Cargo* [1994] ECR I-3567 109
Case C-13/94, *P.* v. *S.* [1996] ECR I-2143 118
Case C-243/95, *Kathleen Hill and Ann Stapleton* v. *Revenue Commissioners and Department of Finance* [1998] ECR I-3739 118
Case C-409/95, *Hellmut Marschall* v. *Land Nordrhein-Westfalen* [1997] ECR I-6363 . 110
Case C-50/96, *Deutsche Telekom AG* v. *Lilli Schröder* [2000] ECR I-743. 34
Case C–85/96, *María Martínez Sala* v. *Freistaat Bayern* [1998] ECR I-2691 33
Case C-158/96, *Raymond Kohll* v. *Union des caisses de maladie* [1998] ECR I-19 . . .7, 34

Case C-249/96, *Grant* v. *South-West Trains Ltd* [1998] ECR I-621 128
Cases C-369/96 and C-376/96, *Arblade* [1999] ECR I-8453 32
Case C-167/97, *Regina and Secretary of State for Employment, ex parte Nicole Seymour Smith and Laura Perez* [1999] ECR I-623 . . . . 114, 117
Case C-212/97, *Centros Ltd* v. *Erhvervs- og Selskabsstyrelsen* [1999] ECR I-1459 46
Case C-249/97, *Gabriele Gruber* v. *Silhouette International Schmied GmbH & Co. KG* [1999] ECR I-5295 128
Cases C-270/97 & C-271/97, *Deutsche Post AG* v. *Elisabeth Sievers & Brundhilde Schrage* [2000] ECR I-929 2
Case C-273/97, *Sidar* v. *Secretary of State for Defence* [1999] ECR I-7403 133
Case C-281/97, *Andrea Krüger* v. *Kreiskrankenhaus Ebersberg* [1999] ECR I-5127 4
Case C-309/97, *Angestelltenbetriebsrat der Wiener Gebietskrankenkasse* v. *Wiener Gebietskrankenkasse* [1999] ECR I-2865 34
Case C-333/97, *Susanne Lewen* v. *Lothar Denda* [1999] ECR I-7243 123
Case C-281/98, *Roman Angonese* v. *Cassa di Risparmio di Bolzano SpA* [2000] ECR I-4139 49
Case C-285/98, *Tanja Kreil* v. *Bundesrepublik Deutschland* [2000] ECR I-69 134
Case C-322/98, *Kachelman* v. *Bankhaus Hermann Lampe KG* [2000] ECR I-7505 . . . 126
Case C-382/98, *The Queen and Secretary of State for Social Security ex parte: John Henry Taylor* [1999] ECR I-8955 118
Case C-79/99, *Juila Schnorbus* v. *Land Hessen* [2000] ECR I-1997 121
Case C-157/99, *B.S.M. Geraets-Smits and Stichting Ziekenfonds VGZ and between H.T.M. Peerbooms and Stichting CZ Groep Zorgverzekeringen* [2001] ECR I-5473 34
Case C-184/99, *Rudy Grzelczyk* v. *Centre public d'aide sociale d'Ottignies-Louvain-la-Neuve* [2001] ECR I-6193 33
Case C-381/99, *Brunnhofer* v. *Bank der Österreichischen Postsparkasse AG* [2001] ECR I-4961 121
Case C-385/99, *V.G. Müller-Fauré* v. *Onderlinge Waarborgmaatschappij OZ Zorgverzekeringen UA* and *E.E.M. van Riet* v. *Onderlinge Waarborgmaatschappij ZAO Zorgverzekeringen* [2003] ECR I-4509 31
Case C-438/99, *Maria Luisa Jiménez Melgar* v. *Ayuntamiento de Los Barrios* [2001] ECR I-6915 130
Case C-112/00, *Eugen Schmidberger, Internationale Transporte und Planzüge* v. *Republik Österreich* [2003] ECR I-5659 49
Case C-218/00, *Cisal di Battistello Venanzio & C. Sas* v. *Istituto nazionale per l'assicurazione* [2002] ECR I-691 30
Case C-187/00, *Helga Kutz-Bauer* v. *Freie und Hansestadt Hamburg* [2003] ECR I-2741 135
Case C-208/00, *Überseering BV* v. *Nordic Construction* [2002] ECR I-9919 46
Case C-320/00, *Lawrence* v. *Regent Office Care Ltd* [2002] ECR I-7325 108
Case C-25/01, *Rinke* v. *Ärtzekammer Hamburg* [2003] ECR I-8349 114
Case C-117/01, *K.B.* v. *National Health Service Agency* [2004] ECR I-541 120
Case C-167/01, *Kamer van Koophandel en Fabrieken voor Amsterdam* v. *Inspire Art Ltd* [2003] ECR I-10155 48
Case C-256/01, *Allonby* v. *Accrington & Rosendale College* [2004] ECR I-873 107
Case C-320/01, *Wiebke Busch* v. *Klinikum Neustadt GmbH & Co. Betriebs-KG* [2003] ECR I-2041 107

Cases C-4/02 & C-5/02, *Hilde Schönheit* v. *Stadt Frankfurt am Main* [2003] ECR I-12575 114
Case C-19/02, *Viktor Hlozek* v. *Roche Austria Gesellschaft mbH* [2004] ECR I-11491 123
Case C-36/02, *Omega Spielhallen- und Automatenaufstellungs-GmbH* v. *Oberbürgermeisterin der Bundesstadt Bonn* [2004] ECR I-9609 49
Case C-77/02, *Erika Steinicke* v. *Bundesanstalt für Arbeit*, 11 September [2003] ECR I-9027 117
Case C-138/02, *Brian Francis Collins* v. *Secretary of State for Work and Pensions* [2004] ECR I-6193. 33
Joined Cases C-184/02 & C-223/02, *Spain and Finland* v. *Parliament and Council* [2004] ECR I-7789 101
Case C-196/02, *Vasiliki Nikoloudi* v. *Organismos Tilepikinonion Ellados AE* [2005] ECR I-1789 . . . . 101, 117
Case C-220/02, *Österreichischer Gewerkschaftsbund, Gewerkschaft der Privatangestellten* v. *Wirtschaftskammer Österreich* [2004] ECR I-5907. 125
Case C-285/02, *Elsner-Lakeberg* v. *Land Nordrhein Westfalen* [2004] ECR I-5861 . . . . 122, 124
Case C-313/02, *Nicole Wippel* v. *Peek & Cloppenburg GmbH & CoKG* [2004] ECR I-9483 123
Case C-209/03, *The Queen (on the application of Dany Bidar)* v. *London Borough of Ealing and Secretary of State for Education and Skills* [2005] ECR I-2119 33
Case C-144/04, *Werner Mangold* v. *Rüdiger Helm* [2005] ECR I-9981 133
Case C-244/04, *Commission* v. *Germany* [2006] ECR I-885 31
Case C-294/04, *Carmen Sarkatzis Herrero* v. *Instituto Madrileño de Salud (Imsalud)* [2006] ECR I-1513. . . . . 107, 119
Case C-13/05, *Sonia Chacón Navas* v. *Eurest Colectividades SA* [2006] ECR I-6467 130
Case C-17/05, *B.F. Cadman* v. *Health & Safety Executive* [2006] ECR I-9583 134
Case C-341/05, *Laval un Partneri Ltd* v. *Svenska Byggnadsarbetareförbudet* [2007] ECR I-11767 . . . . 31, 192
Case C-411/05, *Félix Palacios de la Villa* v. *Cortefiel Servicios SA* [2007] ECR I-8531 . . 118
Case C-438/05, *International Transport Workers Federation, Finnish Seaman's Union* v. *Viking Line* [2007] ECR I-10779 . . . . 34, 192
Case C-267/06, *Tadao Maruko* v. *Versorgungsanstalt deutscher Bühnen* [2008] ECR I-1757. 126
Case C-300/06, *Ursula Voß* v. *Land Berlin* [2007] ECR I-10573 122
Case C-303/06, *S. Coleman* v. *Attridge Law and Steve Law* [2008] ECR I-5603 182
Case C-460/06, *Nadine Paquay* v. *Société d'architectes Hoet + Minne SPRL* [2007] ECR I-8511 119
Case C-54/07, *Centrum voor gelijkheid van kansen en voor racismebestrijding* v. *Firma Feryn NV* [2008] ECR I-5187. 105
Case C-388/07, *The Queen on the application of The Incorporated Trustees of the National Council on Aging* v. *Secretary for Business, Enterprise and Regulatory Reform* [2009] ECR I-1569. 117
Case C-555/07, *Kücükdeveci* v. *Swedex GmbH & Co. KG*, 19 January 2010. . . . 133, 135

Introduction

1. Reconciling Competitiveness with Solidarity

For at least two reasons, the international success[1] and the growing intellectual penetration of modern anti-discrimination law[2] merit sustained attention. The first reason affects the tendency of a historically fairly recent field of law to expand, gradually but steadily, its scope of application.[3] The second betrays a desire for coherence, which is amply reflected in an increasingly interdisciplinary body of academic analysis.

Both reasons in juxtaposition make it inevitable to take anti-discrimination law seriously as a type of *social legislation*.[4] Social legislation redistributes resources and opportunities against a baseline established by private transactions, thereby decreasing the dependence of people on market dealings.[5] In Europe, at any rate, the rise of this new type is closely associated with a new deal of employment relations, which is deemed to be desirable from the perspective of both economics and social justice.[6]

[1] See, for example, Protocol No. 12 to the Convention for the Protection of Human Rights and Fundamental Freedoms, signed in Rome, on 4 November 2000. It underscores that an anti-discrimination principle is part of the common European human rights standard with regards to acts of public authority. See http://conventions.coe.int/Treaty/en/Treaties/Html/177.htm accessed 22 December 2010. For an introduction to the respective international developments, see C. McCrudden and H. Kountouros, 'Human Rights and European Equality Law' 2006/8 *University of Oxford Faculty of Law Legal Studies Research Paper*, 4–8; C. McCrudden, 'Introduction', in C. McCrudden, *Anti-discrimination Law*, 2nd edn (Aldershot: Ashgate, 2004), xi–xxxii, at xii–xiii; S. Perchal, 'Equality of Treatment, Non-discrimination and Social Policy: Achievements in Three Themes' (2004) 41 *Common Market Law Review* 533–551 at 547–551.

[2] There can be little doubt that anti-discrimination law has become the darling subject of 'progressive' legal scholars and steadfast libertarians alike. There is a burgeoning literature which is developing as a result. For a highly useful overview, see C. McCrudden, 'Introduction', n. 1, xi–xxxii.

[3] See M. Bell, *Anti-discrimination Law and the European Union* (Oxford: Oxford University Press, 2002), 136–143.

[4] See G. de Búrca, 'EU Race Discrimination Law: A Hybrid Model?', in G. de Búrca and J. Scott (eds), *Law and New Governance in the EU and the US* (Oxford: Hart Publishing, 2006), 97–120 at 99, who observes that both the so-called Framework Directive and the Race Directive 'were seen by some as the first step towards a new kind of European social law'. According to Ellis, the aspirations underpinning new EU anti-discrimination legislation 'are justice and an improved quality of life for literally millions of people within the European Union'; see E. Ellis, *EU Anti-discrimination Law* (Oxford: Oxford University Press, 2005), at 1.

[5] For a more elaborate account of social legislation, see below pp. 30 n. 54, 88.

[6] It is a well-known fact that the inclusion of Article 157 FEU Treaty (ex 141 EC Treaty) into the agreement was motivated by the economic objective to prevent comparative disadvantage on the part

First, efforts are made to increase access to labour markets for former outsiders or those who are usually likely to be left out ('inclusion').[7] Second, employment relationships are supposed to become less rigidly focused on the standard full-employment situation, in particular as regards rules governing collective representation, dismissals, working time and associated benefits ('flexibilization').[8]

Both developments are associated with an alteration of Europe's basic social orientation.[9] Prior to the promotion of inclusion and flexibilization, European social legislation and industrial relations used to have their point in protection and redistribution. Benefits tended to accrue to insiders at the expense of outsiders.[10] It was protective in that a basic task of employment law, for example, was to assist people in keeping their jobs. Owing to trade union pressure, enterprises had to perform a redistributive function as to the scale of wages paid out to different tiers of the workforce. Slackers and less productive members were held in employment and subsidized by the contributions by others. By contrast, the new vision appeals to universal self-reliance, initiative, competitiveness, entrepreneurial stamina, and personal responsibility.[11] Consequently, the role of the state as the purveyor of common concern is shifting from sheltering people—mostly, the male

of businesses that have to comply with anti-discrimination objectives. It has been assumed by the ECJ, early in its jurisprudence, that Article 157 FEU Treaty (ex 141 EC Treaty) serves a twofold purpose that is both economic and social. See Case 43/75, *Defrenne* v. *Sabena* (II) [1976] ECR 455. More recently, the Court explained that the economic aim is secondary to the social aim. The Court stated that Article 157 FEU Treaty (ex 141 EC Treaty) 'constituted the expression of a social right'. See Joined Cases C-270/97 & C-271/97, *Deutsche Post AG* v. *Elisabeth Sievers & Brundhilde Schrage* [2000], ECR I-929 at para. 57.

[7] On 'inclusion' as the rationale underpinning anti-discrimination law, see H. Collins, 'Discrimination, Equality and Social Inclusion' (2003) 66 *Modern Law Review* 16–43.

[8] What such 'flexibilization' means is captured by Barnard. From the vantage point of the demand side it means numerical (e.g., fixed-term contracts), working time (e.g., switches from full- to part-time work), and functional (e.g., shifts of tasks) flexibility. Seen from the supply side this implicates the increase in temporary employment and permanent re-skilling. See C. Barnard, 'Flexibility and Social Policy', in G. de Búrca and J. Scott (eds), *Constitutional Change in the EU: From Uniformity to Flexibility?* (Oxford: Hart Publishing, 2000), 197–216 at 198. See also S. Deakin and H. Reed, 'The Contested Meaning of Labour Market Flexibility', in J. Shaw (ed.), *Social Law and Policy in an Evolving European Union* (Oxford: Hart Publishing, 2000), 71–102. Ashiagbor points out correctly that in the context of labour market regulation the term 'flexibility' by default comes to mean 'deregulation'. See D. Ashiagbor, *The European Employment Strategy: Labour Market Regulation and New Governance* (Oxford: Oxford University Press, 2005), at 69. For a discussion of different forms of flexibility, see ibid. at 154–164.

[9] On the following, see the perceptive diagnosis by W. Streeck, 'Competitive Solidarity—Rethinking the "European Social Model" ', http://www.mpifg.de/pu/workpap/wp99-8/wp99-8.html accessed 23 December 2010.

[10] This has changed. The wage structure has become increasingly in-egalitarian in European countries. See G. Esping-Andersen, *Social Foundations of Postindustrial Economies* (Oxford: Oxford University Press, 1999), 24–25.

[11] On a philosophical plane, this shift is most visibly reflected in the relation between J. Rawls' *A Theory of Justice* (Cambridge, MA: Harvard University Press, 1971), on the one hand, and B. Ackerman's and A. Alstott's *The Stakeholder Society* (New Haven, CT: Yale University Press, 1999), on the other. Comparing these two works, one cannot but agree with Hegel that philosophy is the spirit of the age articulated in thoughts. Proponents of governmentality studies, to be sure, address this transition as the emergence of a neoliberal form of governmentality. See, for example, T. Lemke, "The Birth of Bio-politics": Michel Foucault's Lectures at The Collège de France on Neoliberal Governmentality' (2001) 30 *Economy and Society* 190–207. For a very promising analysis,

breadwinner—against the peril of unemployment to coaching everybody into performing successfully in an increasingly rougher business environment. Social policy loses its protective edge. It becomes more investment-oriented, that is, calibrated to the production of human resources that are adapted to function under ever-changing and highly competitive conditions.[12]

This is consonant with one of the chief overall policy goals of the European Union to attain economic growth and prosperity on the basis of a unique combination of competitiveness and solidarity.[13] As the Commission states in the White Paper on Social Policy:[14]

> Competitiveness and solidarity have both to be taken into account in building a successful Europe for the future.

Anti-discrimination law appears to play an essential role in this context.[15] It is difficult to imagine a principle that would be better suited to reconciling solidarity and competitiveness than the principle of equality of opportunity.[16] It is intuitively plausible to assume, hence, that such a reconciliation obtains where equality of opportunity has levelled the playing field.

Anti-discrimination law espouses a certain interpretation of this reconciliatory principle.[17] It protects people who happen to bear certain characteristics—most of

see M. L. Flear, 'Neoliberalism, the Open Method of Coordination, and the Undemocratic Governance of Health' (2007, manuscript on file with the author).

[12] See Streeck, n. 9. See B. Jessop, *The Future of the Capitalist State* (Cambridge: Polity Press, 2002) for a reconstruction of the shift from a 'Keynesian Welfare State' to a 'Schumpeterian Competition State'. This tendency is amply reflected in the EU employment strategy, which is laid down in Article 148 FEU Treaty (ex 128 EC Treaty), and pursued in the context of the so-called Luxembourg strategy. For a useful overview, see Deakin and Reed, n. 8.

[13] This lay at the heart of the so-called Lisbon strategy. See Presidency Conclusions, 24 March 2000, para. 24:

> People are Europe's main asset and should be the focal point of the Union's policies. Investing in people and developing an active and dynamic welfare state will be crucial both to Europe's place in the knowledge economy and for ensuring that the emergence of this new economy does not compound the existing social problems of unemployment, social exclusion and poverty. (http://www.europarl.europa.eu/summits/lis1_en.htm#c)

[14] European Commission, *European Social Policy—A Way Forward for the Union: A White Paper*, COM(94) 333 final, 27 July 1994, para. 3. Arguably, this double objective can be traced back to Defrenne, n. 6. For this context, see C. Barnard, 'Social Policy Revisited in the Light of the Constitutional Debate', in C. Barnard (ed.), *The Fundamentals of EU Law Revisited: Assessing the Impact of the Constitutional Debate* (Oxford: Oxford University Press, 2007), 109–151 at 112–113.

[15] The growing importance of the Union's anti-discrimination policy is concomitant to the Lisbon strategy, which promises to boost the competitiveness of the European economy (http://europa.eu/scadplus/glossary/lisbon_strategy_en.htm accessed 23 December 2010). See McCrudden and Kountouros, n. 1 at 18.

[16] See S. Fredman, *Discrimination Law* (Oxford: Clarendon Press, 2002), at 14–15. For an account, see J. Roemer, *Equality of Opportunity* (Cambridge, MA: Harvard University Press, 1998). For a skeptical perspective, see J. H. Schaar, 'Equality of Opportunity—and Beyond' (1967), repr. in L. P. Pojman and R. Westmoreland (eds), *Equality: Selected Readings* (New York/Oxford: Oxford University Press, 1997), 137–147.

[17] For an interpretation of European anti-discrimination law in light of the principle of equality of opportunity, see C. Barnard, *EC Employment Law*, 3rd edn, (Oxford: Oxford University Press, 2007), at 338.

which are socially salient, for example, sex, race, religion, ethnicity—from disadvantage that involves conduct by private actors or the state in the context of the provision of goods and opportunities. Characteristically, the protection is limited to certain critical goods,[18] the precise extension of which (for example, 'pay') is subject to a great deal of litigation and casuistry. Most often, the goods in question are crucial for a person's full participation in society, such as, for example, a dwelling, a job, or some career whose progress is measurable in terms of pay raises and promotions. Only in exceptional cases, the protection from discrimination extends beyond the context of housing and employment.[19]

As a principal matter, anti-discrimination law does not alter the competitive nature of the social access to goods where it is already subject to competition. Nonetheless, it exhibits special moral concern for those who are likely to become, in a market context, the victims of bigotry and stereotypes. With regard to potential social outsiders, it is not at all implausible to stretch the panoply of discrimination beyond unequal treatment and also to include into its scope matters such as harassment or the creation of a hostile work environment.

2. Practical and Intellectual Success

As regards the scope of protection from discrimination, narrowly understood, it is well known that European anti-discrimination law was initially restricted to prohibiting, in the employment context, pay discrimination on the grounds of sex and subsequently expanded into a more general equal treatment obligation.[20] Directive

[18] See J. Gardner, 'On the Grounds of Her Sex(uality)' (1998) 18 *Oxford Journal of Legal Studies* 167–187 at 167. Needless to say that my loose reference to this type of goods could be specified in terms of 'social primary goods', 'transcendental interests', or 'conditional goods'. See, for that matter, Rawls, *A Theory of Justice*, 92; O. Höffe, 'Transzendentaler Tausch: Eine Legitimationsfigur der Menschenrechte?', in S. Gosepath and G. Lohmann (eds), *Philosophie der Menschenrechte* (Frankfurt: Suhrkamp, 1998), 29–48, at 32–33.

[19] See Article 3(1) of the Council Directive 2000/43/EC of 29 June 2000 implementing the principle of equal treatment between persons irrespective of racial or ethnic origin [2000] OJ L 180.

[20] Article 157 FEU Treaty (ex 141 EC Treaty) aside, sex discrimination has been ruled out since 1975/76 pursuant to Article 1 of Council Directive 75/117 on the approximation of the laws of the Member States relating to the application of the principle of equal pay for men and women, OJ L45, 19–20 [1975] and Article 2 of Council Directive 76/207/EEC of 9 February 1976 on the implementation of the principle of equal treatment for men and women as regards access to employment, vocational training and promotion, and working conditions, OJ L39, 40–42 [1976]. The Directives supplement the protection afforded by Article 157 FEU Treaty (ex 141 EC Treaty). See Ellis, n. 4 at 18. The Court, however, stated, that Article 157 FEU Treaty (ex 141 EC Treaty) is limited to questions of equal pay and does not extend to equal treatment cases. See, for example, Case C-281/97, *Andrea Krüger* v. *Kreiskrankenhaus Ebersberg* [1999] ECR I-5127 at para. 18. Legislation is necessary in order to give effect to protection from discrimination. Directive 78/7/EEC on the progressive implementation of equal treatment with regard to statutory social security schemes, OJ L6, 24, concluded the original set. For a brief account of the subsequent legislative history, which had been given momentum through a series of 'action programs', see Barnard, n. 17 at 300–301. Seven of the existing sex equality Directives have been consolidated into one legal instrument, namely, Directive 2006/54/EC on the implementation of the principle of equal opportunities and equal treatment of men and women in matters of employment and occupation, OJ L204, 23–36.

2000/78/EC[21] marked a major turning point, for it extended protection from discrimination to the grounds of religion or belief, disability, age and sexual orientation (Article 1). The so-called Race Directive[22] pushed the scope of application beyond the context of employment, occupation and vocational training, however, exclusively for cases of discrimination on the grounds of racial or ethnic origin. Article 1(7) of Directive 2002/73/EC[23] made it mandatory for Member States to establish 'equality bodies' that are commissioned with monitoring compliance and supporting victims of discrimination. Recently, the protection from discrimination on the grounds of sex was extended to include trade in goods and services.[24] Finally, the Fundamental Rights Charter, which is, at least as regards most Member States, part of primary law pursuant to the new Article 6 EU Treaty, extends in its Article 11(1) protection from discrimination even to colour, ethnic or social origin, genetic features, language, religion or belief, political or any other opinion, membership of a national minority, property and birth.

Current political developments[25] and theoretical discussions alike betray an increasing awareness that what once began with a focus on employment discrimination and a small set of immutable characteristics may have already borne out principles that might encompass other, not even immutable grounds, of discrimination[26] and be relevant to spheres of private conduct outside the contexts of employment or housing.[27] To be sure, extension along the scope of personal characteristics need not necessarily be followed by expansions along the context of application. Conceivably, protection from discrimination could be legitimately

[21] Council Directive 2000/78/EC of 27 November 2000 establishing a general framework for equal treatment in employment and occupation, OJ L 303, 16–22 [2000]. I should mention that in 1997, a social partner agreement on discrimination against part-time workers was subsequently adopted in the form of a Directive. See Directive 97/81 OJ L 14/9 [1988].

[22] See n. 19.

[23] Directive 2002/73/EC of the European Parliament and of the European Council of 23 September 2002 amending Council Directive 76/207/EC on the implementation of the principle of equal treatment for men and women as regards access to employment, vocational training and promotion, and working conditions, OJ L 269/15 [2002].

[24] See Council Directive 2004/113/EC of 13 December 2004 implementing the principle of equal treatment between men and women in the access to and supply of goods and services, OJ L 373/37 [2004]. Even more recently, a European Institute for Gender Equality was established. See Regulation 1922/2006 of the European Parliament and of the Council of 20 December 2006 in establishing a European Institute for Gender Equality, OJ L 403 [2006].

[25] For example, Article 1/1 of the 12th Protocol to the European Convention also sweeps broadly:

> The enjoyment of any right set forth by law shall be secured without discrimination on any ground such as sex, race, colour, language, religion, political or other opinion, national or social origin, association with a national minority, property, birth or other status.

[26] A case in point is the unequal treatment on the basis of body size or unappealing looks. See E. Kristen, 'Addressing the Problem of Weight Discrimination in Employment' (2002) 90 *California Law Review* 57–109; R. Post, 'Prejudicial Appearances: The Logic of American Anti-discrimination Law' (2000) 88 *California Law Review* 1–40.

[27] See, for example, A. Masselot, 'The State of Gender Equality Law in the European Union' (2007) 13 *European Law Journal* 152–168; on the potential use of Article 19 FEU Treaty (ex 13 EC Treaty, moved) as legal base in the area of health care services, see Bell, n. 3 at 141–142. On 'untitled' discrimination, that is, discrimination outside the sphere protected by Title VII of the Civil Rights Act, see, notably, I. Ayres, *Pervasive Prejudice? Unconventional Evidence of Race and Gender Discrimination* (Chicago, IL: University of Chicago Press, 2001).

limited to the distribution of certain critical goods.[28] Nevertheless, there seems to inhere in anti-discrimination law a generalizing momentum that might bring in the future within its scope of application even the aesthetically inept[29] or those adhering to widely detested habits.

As regards the quest for doctrinal coherence, recent work by scholars—even by those working in an Anglo-American context, where scholarship has traditionally been most indulgent of enduring fragmentation—is increasingly driven by a bid for systematicization.[30] As a result, it has become not merely difficult to maintain the traditional boundary between differential treatment and disparate impact[31] but also to draw a line between anti-discrimination and disability law[32] or anti-discrimination and affirmative action.[33] In the United States, at any rate, the drive towards systematicization is held back by a compromising judiciary which appears to recoil from drawing out the implications of innovative principles;[34] but once jurisdictional niceties and established distinctions of levels of scrutiny come to be increasingly experienced as unwelcome residues of old ways of thinking, the prevalence of this perception itself indicates that more is at stake than matching legislative provisions with constitutional powers. It seems to indicate that current judicial practice is blocking the path towards the realization of an emerging ideal of social legislation.

3. Europe's Social Question

The career of European anti-discrimination law and policy is nonetheless somewhat paradoxical. The European Union appears to have taken the lead in a field in which the integration process is otherwise deemed to have been least successful. Anti-discrimination law, arguably, is part of social policy;[35] the latter has been, undeniably, the sick man of the Union's internal policy.[36]

[28] See above n. 18.

[29] See Post, n. 26.

[30] For a noteworthy European example, see Bell, n. 3.

[31] Most prominently, L. Hamilton Krieger, 'The Content of Our Categories: A Cognitive Bias Approach to Discrimination and Equal Employment Opportunity' (1995) 47 *Stanford Law Review* 1161–1248.

[32] See, notably, C. Jolls, 'Anti-discrimination and Accommodation' (2001) 115 *Harvard Law Review* 642–699; P. S. Karlan and G. Rutherglen, 'Disabilities, Discrimination, and Reasonable Accommodation' (1996) 46 *Duke Law Journal* 1–41.

[33] See, for example, C. R. Sunstein, *Free Markets and Social Justice* (New York: Oxford University Press, 1997); L. Hamilton Krieger, 'Civil Rights Perestroika: Intergroup Relations after Affirmative Action' (1988) 86 *California Law Review* 1251–1333.

[34] See, for example, for the context of American disability law, S. R. Bagenstos, 'The Future of Disability Law' (2004) 114 *Yale Law Journal* 1–82 at 35–40; more generally, J. Rubenfeld, 'The Anti-anti-discrimination Agenda' (2002) 111 *Yale Law Journal* 1141–1178.

[35] From a formalist perspective, one might want to object that Article 19 FEU Treaty (ex 13 EC Treaty, moved) has given anti-discrimination law a more fundamental place in Union law. I shall ignore this objection for the purpose of this introduction.

[36] See M. Poiares Maduro, 'Europe's Social Self: "The Sickness Unto Death"', in J. Shaw (ed.), *Social Law and Policy in an Evolving European Union* (Oxford: Hart Publishing, 2000), 325–350;

The analysis contained in the first two chapters of this book seeks to explore this paradox against the broader context of current Union anti-discrimination policy.[37] It departs by recalling to mind the significance which 'the social question' has always had for European integration. In fact, since its inception, the integration process was accompanied by a 'not merely' mantra, according to which Europe has always been supposed to be more than a 'mere' market society.[38] Ever since their founding, the Community and Union were followed by a train of proposals and various attempts to render it more social.

The *first chapter* sketches the regulatory constraints that the law of the common market has created for the pursuit of social policy by the Member States. The impact of Union law, to be sure, has not been without ambivalence. While there is express willingness on the part of the ECJ to respect national autonomy under certain conditions, it has become exceedingly difficult for Member States to make out, in advance, whether the Court is willing to see these very conditions obtain from one case to the next.[39] Those framing national social policy have reason to be cautious when a collision with Union law is to be expected. Similarly, even though Member States have often been given leave to uphold their social policies,[40] these are increasingly maintained with the awareness that the attitude of the Union is more one of toleration than of support. I will complement the picture by pointing out how over the years the perception of national social policy has come to be *assimilated* to the mindset of the common market.

This situation is exacerbated by the well-known fact that the recreation of a welfare state on the European level appears not to present a viable option.[41] First, the jurisdictional space available to the Union is quite limited—too limited, at any rate, for such a task. Second, even if the Union had legal power to recreate a transnational equivalent to a national welfare state, the emergence of such a regime would be extremely unlikely owing to a net loss of social policy-making capacity

W. Streeck, 'Vom Binnenmarkt zum Bundesstaat? Überlegungen zur politischen Ökonomie der europäischen Sozialpolitik', in S. Leibfried and P. Pierson (eds) *Standort Europa: Europäische Sozialpolitik* (Frankfurt: Suhrkamp, 1998), 369–421.

[37] The other part of an explanation would have to dig deeper into the history and point to the fairly notorious fact that Article 157 FEU Treaty (ex 141 (then 119) EC Treaty) had been introduced on the initiative of France that did not want to suffer a competitive disadvantage in the face of widespread pay discrimination in other member states.

[38] See Barnard, n. 14 at 111.

[39] For an overview, see V. Hatzopoulos, 'Health Law and Policy: The Impact of the EU', in G. de Búrca (ed.), *EU Law and the Welfare State: In Search of Solidarity* (Oxford: Oxford University Press, 2005), 111–168. This raises a more fundamental question about the ECJ's jurisprudence. In my opinion, it bespeaks a deep crisis of normativity. See my 'Dogmatischer Pragmatismus: Über die Normativitätskrise der Europäischen Union', in S. Hammer, A. Somek, M. Stelzer, and B. Weichselbaum (eds), *Der soziale Rechtsstaat in Europa (*Festschrift *Theo Öhlinger)* (Vienna: WUV-Universitätsverlag, 2004), 41–67.

[40] The ECJ usually proclaims in its rulings that it is the preserve of the Member States to regulate certain matters of social policy, at any rate, as long as they stay within the limits set by free movement provisions. See, for example, Case C-158/96, *Raymond Kohll* v. *Union des caisses de maladie* [1998] ECR I-1931, para. 17.

[41] See S. Leibfried and H. Obinger, 'Nationale Sozialstaaten in der Europäischen Union: Zukünfte eines "sozialen Europas"', in *TranState Reprints* (Bremen: University of Bremen, 2008).

suffered by the Member States when they are acting together. Not only individually and at the national level, but also collectively and at the supranational level do the Member States lack the capacity to achieve what they could have achieved, principally, prior to European integration. It turns out, indeed, that the public policy instruments that can be used by the Member States for the purpose of economic and social stabilization necessitate a move towards the flexibilization—or rather, 'flexicuritization'[42]—of employment relationships.

The *first chapter* concludes with observations concerning a shift in the jurisprudence of the ECJ towards what can be described as, borrowing American constitutional parlance, transnational substantive economic due process. It gives rise to increasing regulatory disarmament on the part of those Member States that have an 'organized' economy (i.e., a high degree of government involvement and stakeholder participation)[43] and raises serious concerns about potentially self-subversive tendencies of economic liberalization in Europe.

Moreover, this development finally brings to the surface what the social question truly amounts to in a *transnational* context. It is not *simply* about relieving the lot of the poor or guaranteeing, in whichever form, freedom from need;[44] rather, it is about whether national welfare systems that allow for a high degree of human independence from the market mechanism can be sustained as they are forced, within a transnational federation, to interact with systems that are unlike their own. Roughly speaking, it is about how social market economies with a more coordinated form of capitalism[45] can be sustained when they coexist with liberal market economies within one system that is structurally biased in favour of the latter.[46]

Already at this point, it will emerge that European anti-discrimination law does not reply to how the social question presents itself *specifically* in a transnational context. Anti-discrimination law and policy are addressed to a transnational problem only in a weak sense, in that they help countries that have made a commitment

[42] 'Flexicurity' is the new darling token of European employment reform. It suggests a combination of little or no job security with state support for the unemployed and strong efforts to restore employability through retraining. See Council Conclusions on Flexicurity in times of crisis, 2947th Employment, Social Policy, Health and Consumer Affairs Council meeting Luxembourg, 8 June 2009.

[43] On the distinction between organized and liberal market economies, see P. A. Hall and D. Soskice, 'An Introduction to Varieties of Capitalism', in P. A. Hall and D. Soskice (eds), *Varieties of Capitalism: The Institutional Foundations of Comparative Advantage* (Oxford: Oxford University Press, 2001), 1–68.

[44] See H. Arendt, *On Revolution* (London: Pelican Books, 1977), at 59–60.

[45] Coordinated (or 'organized') capitalist systems have the state more heavily involved in creating the public infrastructure and in fostering technological innovation and professional training. The state participates in economic planning and in brokering deals between social partners. A social market economy, typically, not only provides social assistance for those who can prove to be in need but social security for all with regard to pension incomes, health care, and unemployment benefits. Ideally, it also attempts to provide services for families, children, the elderly, and disabled persons. See M. Höpner and A. Schäfer, 'Eine neue Phase der europäischen Integration: Legitimitätsdefizite europäischer Liberalisierungspolitik', in M. Höpner and A. Schäfer (eds), *Die Politische Ökonomie der europäischen Integration* (Frankfurt: Campus Verlag, 2008), 130–156 at 131.

[46] For a most recent analysis, see F. W. Scharpf, 'The Double Asymmetry of European Integration, Or: Why the EU Cannot Be a Social Market Economy' (2009) 09/12 *MPIfG Working Paper* 25–28.

to protection from discrimination not to suffer a disadvantage vis-à-vis others. However, protection from discrimination on grounds of sex or sexual orientation is not a problem that is *intrinsic* to a transnational context. By contrast, institutional differences between organized and liberal forms of capitalism (or liberal and social market economies) have the potential to unsettle a transnational system.

What is more, anti-discrimination law and policy are undoubtedly normatively very appealing. Who should be in favour of race discrimination? In this normative appeal, however, resides a danger, too. The success of the European anti-discrimination project is likely to detract from what truly is the social question in a transnational setting. Should it turn out—as the remainder of the essay will argue, indeed—that anti-discrimination law is normatively deficient, its moral appeal is even liable to disguise the Union's lack of ability to address social concerns.

4. The Turn to Employment

In the *second chapter*, I turn to anti-discrimination law and policy. It actually represents that field of Union social policy which has been steadily successful since its inception. It even survived the current reorientation of social policy towards the use of more 'soft' as opposed to 'hard' legal means. The new, 'soft' social policy is associated with the rise of employment policy (Title IX, Articles 145–150 FEU Treaty (ex Title VIII, Articles 125–130 EC Treaty)) immediately before and in the wake of the conclusion of the Amsterdam Treaty. The resulting redefinition of European social policy in terms of securing the employability of human resources and the move from 'hard' harmonizing legislation to 'softer' tools of governance (reports, plans, benchmarking) are part of one and the same process.[47] They follow through on the shift of orientation that I mentioned above.

This shift is profound. The task of social policy is no longer perceived to lie in alleviating market dependence.[48] Social policy is now directed at making dependence more sustainable through enhancing the inclusive fitness of individuals. The idea is that, unless people have sufficient means to support themselves, nobody should be able to claim an exemption from the universal need to make one's life and livelihood dependent on the interplay of supply and demand. There is no reason, for example, to protect employed insiders at the expense of more qualified outsiders. If the former are sheltered from competition due to the persistence of sexist or racist employment practices, they are likely to become the target, rather then the beneficiaries, of social policy. Consequently, the inclusive fitness of Europeans is supposed to be increased by removing obstacles to the participation in the labour market that originate from factors such as racial prejudice or the traditional domestic allocation of labour, on the one hand, or the lack of skills and insufficient

[47] See D. Ashiagbor, 'EMU and the Shift in the European Labour Law Agenda: From "Social Policy" to "Employment Policy" (2001) 7 *European Law Journal* 311–330 at 329.

[48] See G. Esping-Andersen, *The Three Worlds of Welfare Capitalism* (Princeton, NJ: Princeton University Press, 1990), at 37.

motivation, on the other. The new employment policy is conducted—evocative of the most recent, and also most curious, rendering of the Third Way[49]—with a new entrepreneurial spirit that turns away from 'social spending' and moves towards 'social investment'.[50] Not surprisingly, this strategy of creating sustainable market-dependence is backed up with the subordination of social policy to economic policy—or even an increasing degree of absorption.[51] As social policy becomes redefined with an eye to employment objectives, it is about to play an increasingly ancillary role vis-à-vis the pursuit of economic goals.

I think it is fair to say that, owing to this strong emphasis on the supply side, the reorientation is surrounded by neoliberal air. In order to appear legitimate, however, subsuming social under economic objectives needs to be presented as though it were based upon an even-handed reconciliation of social and economic concerns.[52] The claim to have thus discovered the key to an all-encompassing ('Catholic') concordance between potentially conflicting economic and social objectives is a visible trait of European neoliberalism.

5. The Turn to Management

In the *second chapter*, I also try to show how anti-discrimination law has become interconnected with the European Employment Strategy, which is in turn enveloped in the Union's overarching economic agenda, namely, the formerly so-called Lisbon strategy.[53] As a result, anti-discrimination law is part of a process[54] where the protection of the interests of employees becomes secondary to securing their

[49] See A. Giddens, *The Third Way: The Renewal of Social Democracy* (Cambridge: Polity Press, 1998); see Ashiagbor, n. 8 at 281–282.

[50] On this spirit, see C. de la Porte, 'Is the Open Method of Coordination Appropriate for Organising Activities at European Level in Sensitive Policy Areas?' (2002) 8 *European Law Journal* 38–58 at 48.

[51] See, generally, Streeck, n. 9. The subordination is actually spelled out in Article 146(2) FEU Treaty (ex 126(2) EC Treaty), where the Member States are exhorted to conduct their employment policies in 'a way consistent with the broad guidelines of the economic policies of the Member States and of the Community adopted pursuant to Article 99(2)'. That is, the economic policy guidelines laid down by the Council define the most general framework for the pursuit of social policy objectives in this field. Practically, this is played out in the 'mainstreaming' of social policy issues into the meetings of the Economic and Financial Affairs Council (ECOFIN) and the de facto incorporation of the employment strategy into the aims of the Lisbon process. See European Commission, *White Paper on Growth, Competitiveness, and Employment: The Challenges and Ways Forward into the 21st Century*, COM(93) 700 final (1993), and E. Szyszczak, 'The New Paradigm for Social Policy: A Virtuous Circle?' (2001) 38 *Common Market Law Review* 1125–1170 at 1133, 1135, 1140, 1151; K. Jacobsson, 'Soft Regulation and the Subtle Transformation of States: The Case of EU Employment Policy' (2004) 14 *Journal of European Social Policy* 355–370 at 358.

[52] See Szyszczak, n. 51 at 1152–1153.

[53] Even though the Lisbon Process has officially expired in 2010, it has substantially been carried over into the 'Europe 2020' agenda. See European Commission, 'Europe 2020: A Strategy for Smart, Sustainable and Inclusive Growth', COM(2010) 2020.

[54] On the link between the European Employment Strategy and gender mainstreaming, see Barnard, n. 17 at 304–305.

interest in employment and employability for the sake of economic stabilization.[55] As the rights associated with the status of employees, which until recently have been deemed to be associated with economic citizenship, tend to recede into the background,[56] policy discourses increasingly encourage social actors to submit 'creative' proposals to a common problem-solving project, the epitome of which are 'integrated guidelines'.[57]

Effective equality management depends on good communication. The turn to management, thus, necessarily involves the use of discourse. As is well known to proponents of critical discourse analysis, discourse creation is not an innocuous affair. Coupled with asymmetries of social power, the imagery introduced by classifications can serve as a medium for ruling others.[58] Hence, leading through talking is not an idle task. Not only are Member State governments put in the awkward position of having to redescribe their social systems in the newspeak created by the Council and Commission, the use of discourse allows these institutions to present the reconciliation of competing objectives at a *symbolic* level. Optimistic guidelines and cheerfully formulated action plans can pretend that the convergence on harmonious objectives is unlikely to encounter any fundamental resistance, for example, on the ground of a profound conflict between the life interests of ordinary people and the acceleration of production and consumption under contemporary capitalism. In fact, what can be done at that symbolic level is to stage activity by changing the description of strategies and goals.[59] The symbolic celebration of social progress is all the easier where, as is the case for transnational cooperation, the political process is blissfully insulated against collisions with potentially unruly forces.

6. Manageable Social Policy

The shift from the adoption of social legislation—the latter option is seldom available to the Union for a variety of reasons—to more open methods of voluntary coordination is congruent with experiencing the *situation* of social policy-making in

[55] For a statement to this effect, see the 'Economists for an Alternative Economic Policy in Europe', quoted in Ashiagbor, n. 8 at 171.

[56] The claim may appear to be overstated in light of the social rights contained in the Charter of Fundamental Rights. Nevertheless, the import of these rights is a question that requires more detailed analysis and cannot be, hence, subject of premature celebration. I shall return to this matter in the second chapter.

[57] So-called 'integrated guidelines' are used by the European Council in order to coordinate the economic and the employment policies of the Member States. See, for example, Council Decision 2005/600/EC of 12 July 2005.

[58] For an introduction, see R. Wodak, 'Critical Discourse Analysis', in C. Seale, G. Gobo, J. F. Gubrium, and D. Silverman (eds), *Qualitative Research Practice* (London: Sage, 2004), 197–213 at 198.

[59] On the replacement of the four original pillars of the European Employment Strategy with three overarching objectives, see K. Armstrong and C. Kilpatrick, 'Law, Governance, or New Governance? The Changing Open Method of Coordination' (2007) 13 *Columbia Journal of European Law* 649–677 at 666.

a certain way. Arguably, the facilitation of voluntary self-improvement appears to be an attractive option when the situation is marked by a number of features.

First, policy-making is imagined to be a process of common problem-solving. It is expected to work best when a high number of 'stakeholders' provide input and experts recommend options for implementation. Negatively put, this means that the situation of policy-making is not perceived to be fraught with irreconcilable conflicts between and among ideological persuasions. In a situation of conflict, by contrast, it might be best to let one party prevail over others while leaving losers the opportunity to make good in the future. Contests between or among political parties with different visions of the political economy fit the latter description. This type of situation is *not* susceptible to description in terms of common problem-solving.

Second, the situation is envisaged as a fertile ground for communicative action.[60] All agents coordinate their action plans by deliberating about common goals and reasonable means to achieve them. It is presumed that common action might be based on consent and practical convergence, not least because the pool of reasons available to the agents involved is homogenous enough to make the undistorted exchange of ideas possible.

Finally, it is assumed that the reasons in favour of voluntary compliance are at least as strong as self-interest. In fact, since compliance is equated with the readiness for voluntary improvement, the situation has to indicate that improvement is in the self-interest of the polity affected. This is the case for regulatory competition where the incentive for policy change ('improvement') originates from the motive to maintain an attractive business place.

7. Equality Management: the Macro and the Micro Level

That European anti-discrimination law is characterized by an increasing complementarity of 'hard' regulation and 'soft policy' coordination formulates no new insight, in particular not for those using the designator 'hybridity' to refer to this situation.[61] But recognizing the complementarity does not really explain the reason why 'hard' legislation is insufficient to attain anti-discimination's noble objectives and why the latter is ostensibly depended on supplementary equality management.

The explanation given in Chapters 4 to 6 of this book is that anti-discrimination law is *normatively deficient*. Put simply, it does not regulate enough. When things cannot be accomplished by playing by rules, the need arises to get things done by innovative action, which is expected to accomplish, in one way or another, what mere norms fail to deliver. This explains why the need for equality management arises in the first place.

[60] See J. Habermas, *Theory of Communicative Action*, trans. by T. McCarthy (Cambridge: Polity Press, 1984), vol. 1 at 82–101.

[61] See T. Hervey, 'Thirty Years of EU Sex Equality Law: Looking Backwards, Looking Forwards' (2005) 12 *Maastricht Journal of European and Comparative Law* at 307–327 at 322.

Moreover, the binocular perspective applied in this book will reveal that the move to equality management can be observed at two levels. At the *macro level*, it affects the 'complementary' between legislation and the pursuit of 'action programs' or 'mutual learning processes', the instigation of which has been encouraged in the European Union. For the most part, these processes are about generating a pool of new ideals in the triadic relation of the European Commission, Member State governments, and civil society. However, the very same shift to management can be observed in the manner in which scholars—in the United States—imagine anti-discrimination strategies to be reinforced at the *micro level* of workplace organization. Both the micro and macro strategy switch from legislation to management and, as regards the subjects affected, from the legality of compliance to practical training and moral improvement. Both strategies involve a high degree of 'pedagogicization' and rest their hope on changing attitudes and social understandings. Remarkably, in their focus on attitudes and social understandings, the normative deficit of anti-discrimination law *persists*.

Despite a high degree of overlap, the difference between the strategies is obvious. Whereas the macro level tries to impact on practices from the outside—that is, in a manner similar to a regulation—the micro level tries to overcome the normative deficiency of anti-discrimination law from within its sphere of application, namely, the workplace. The binocular perspective of this book will reveal that the most recent European attempts to reinforce protection from discrimination resemble closely proposals made in the context of American anti-discrimination scholarship where the narrow confines of law are imagined to be supplanted by social learning processes. It is remarkable to observe that the attitude-transforming pedagogical structures that some US American scholars would like to see realized at the workplace level are supposed to be realized in Europe in the context of joint efforts of interested actors ('stakeholders') and national administrations.

Whereas the developments at the European macro-level will be explored in Chapter 2, I shall return to the micro level in Chapter 7. Without overburdening the discussion of European developments with reflections on US American scholarship, it is necessary to examine these developments for one very important reason. The micro level reveals the pathologies inherent in the move to equality management that remain largely latent at the European macro level.

8. The Systematic Analysis

The thesis that anti-discrimination law, understood as a type of social legislation, is normatively deficient, is part of an even larger claim, namely, that the ascendancy of anti-discrimination law is not by accident concomitant to neoliberalism. There are, however, at least two ways of defending this claim. The first is presented in Chapters 1 and 2. It amounts to an exploration of the broader public policy context of the relevant legislation. In this context, the macro level of equality management plays a prominent role. The second consists of reconstructing the social policy perspective that is *systematically* articulated within the categories and principles of anti-discrimination law. From within the very terms with which anti-discrimination law tries to impact on personal relations, the association with neoliberalism is, indeed, all the more striking.

The task of such an internal reconstruction is left to the larger part of the essay. Whereas in the first two chapters the adjective 'neoliberal' is used merely to describe a historically momentous shift of orientation from status protection to employment market access, on the one hand, and from collective interest representation to investment in human capital, on the other, the *third chapter* tries to put this shift into a broader perspective. It is based on the recognition that neoliberalism is as a major historical force determinative of the spirit (*Geist*) of our age.[62] Its ascendancy does not leave social policy unaffected.

Roughly speaking, the spirit of an age is manifest in the *default account* of reasons that we take to be authoritative for the purpose of defending claims. The default account stands for what we believe to be convincing because we expect it to sound convincing to everyone. It is by no means the only account that people resort to in a historical situation, but it is the one that is not expected to be burdened with the onus of proof.

By default, neoliberalism treats the market not merely as one sphere among others but rather as the universal law governing our social existence. This is not to say that the neoliberal view of the world does not recognize anything outside markets; it is, however, the distinguishing mark of our age that any social practice is by default rendered intelligible from within the mindset of rationally calculating individuals for whom the good of life is, whatever it may amount to individually, mediated by acts of consumption.[63] It is not by accident that under the auspices of neoliberalism economics comes to take the centre stage of the social sciences.

The commitment to market rationality is not without moral constraints. In fact, it is part of the moral strength of neoliberalism to expect consumers to avail themselves of consumer goods by catering to the tastes and needs of others. While consumption is the message, market coordination is the medium. Hence, the moral principle that is *compatible* with neoliberalism has it that whoever wants to live well needs to adapt to market demand. Adaptability is the chief social virtue. It is equality of adaptability against which all allocations are subject to critical appraisal.

9. Triangulating the Neoliberal Left

The neoliberal left—in contradistinction to its more conservative laissez-faire counterpart—is committed to rectifying adverse distributive consequences that

[62] The following remarks on the spirit of an age are influenced by T. Pinkard, *Hegel's Phenomenology: The Sociality of Reason* (Cambridge: Cambridge University Press, 1994).

[63] For the transformation of the meaning of love and romance along these lines, see E. Illouz, *Consuming the Romantic Utopia: Love and the Cultural Contradictions of Capitalism* (Berkeley, CA: University of California Press, 1997).

originate from the influence of factors that seriously hamper or even prevent adaptation. Any rectification requires a modicum of intervention into markets. It is remarkable to observe, though, how compatible the commitment to intervention is with the basic neoliberal contention that all human dealings are essentially market dealings.

First, the factors that are recognized to undermine adaptability are socially salient (often 'visible') enough in order to become a factor in encounters among strangers. The social imagery relevant for the neoliberal left envisages *individuals* engaged in trade and barter and not, for example, collisions between functionally differentiated subsystems of society[64] or the threat posed by such systems to the human psyche.[65] Hence, disadvantages are taken to arise as a result of individual acts, albeit it is recognized that disadvantages arise also as the aggregate effect of such acts.

Second, the preferred method of rectification is not the replacement of the market with a different social mechanism but rather its moral purification. The ideal world envisaged by anti-discrimination law is a world inhabited by *better people*—and not, for example, a world where power differentials in the relation of capital and labour have been readjusted such as to approach evermore closely a sustainable equilibrium.

It should not go unnoticed that owing to both restrictions, the neoliberal left can only choose from among a limited set of options. First, disadvantages that are directly or indirectly linked with highly visible and immutable personal characteristics have to be the central focus of concern. It is difficult, however, to come up with a consistent list of immutable factors and to explain, for example, why discrimination on the grounds of religion or political persuasion ought not to be permitted by contrast to discrimination on the grounds of race. Why would it be unreasonable to expect flexible and adaptable employees to adhere to the political views of their bullying bosses? Moreover, anti-discrimination law promises success to those who have internalized the entrepreneurial subjectivity of self-promoting market participants. Anti-discrimination law itself discriminates systematically against those who *simply* fail or who do not conceive of life as a career or as a project for the success of which they find themselves burdened with a special responsibility. Invisible inadaptability that originates, for example, from a commitment to tradition or the fate of having a certain character does not enter the neoliberal picture. Second, market-correcting solutions are premised on the counterfactual example of a world where no actor would be tarnished with a bad attitude or unconscious bias. What for law and economics is the hypothetical world without transaction costs, which supplies the imagined background for the deduction of efficiency-optimizing rules, is for anti-discrimination law a market inhabited by morally unadulterated participants. Not even the problem of indirect discrimination

[64] See, for that matter, A. Fischer-Lescano and G. Teubner, 'Regime-collisions: The Vain Search for Legal Unity in the Fragmentation of Global Law' (2004) 25 *Michigan Journal of International Law* 999–1046.

[65] See G. Teubner, 'The Anonymous Matrix: Human Rights Violations by "Private" Transnational Actors' (2006) 69 *Modern Law Review* 327–346.

would arise for most women since an ideal counterfactual world has allocated childrearing responsibilities equally. What remains outside the purview of anti-discrimination law, then, are discretionary political measures that replace competition with sheltered practices of employment that offer opportunities to lead a decent life without the inhibitions originating from omnipresent exhortations to excel or the expectation to pursue a career.

10. The Normative Deficiency of Anti-discrimination Law

The *third chapter* offers a rough outline of the argument that is to follow in Chapters 4 to 7. In the *fourth chapter*, I defend a reading of anti-discrimination law that accords priority to the redistributive point of view. Ironically, this viewpoint also reveals its normative deficiency.

I argue that the law's most prominent category, direct discrimination, cannot be accounted for unless by appeal to its redistributive task. The law removes from individual conduct its ordinary ambivalence in that it prohibits reliance on certain grounds of distinction and entrusts distributive agents, notably employers, with the task of breaking the social cycle of systemic discrimination. Direct discrimination norms thereby constitute what counts as the agent's intent, normatively understood. With such normative intent, it is clarified that—disclaimers of agents about their 'real' pre-normative intentions notwithstanding—doing x counts as engaging in discrimination on the grounds of y.

The constitution of normative intent specifies the redistributive mandate inherent in protection from indirect discrimination for a special causal relation between an individual agent and individual effects. Since the focus comes to rest consequently on individual acts, intentions and choices, the redistributive mandate of anti-discrimination law is submitted to a deontological realization. This gives rise, necessarily, to a deontological misreading of anti-discrimination law. It appears to be, at its core, about identifying guilty minds and bad attitudes. Indeed, owing to its very constitution, anti-discrimination law becomes realized on the basis of a false understanding of its own foundation.

The *fifth chapter* draws out the implication inherent in the distributive view by explaining why the category of direct discrimination is in no manner different from indirect discrimination but rather a special case of it. Direct discrimination isolates one causal relation between market transactions and distributive outcomes. This causal relation can be given an extensional and an intensional interpretation. An extensional interpretation relies on a 'but for' analysis. What matters is whether the presence of a prohibited ground is causally involved in bringing about the difference of treatment. It therefore promises a finding of direct discrimination against various rationalizations of conduct ('Defendant did not mean to . . . '). Alas, this promise cannot be kept. The most appealing interpretation of direct discrimination is intensional, which means that it examines conceivable reasons for action and thereby opens the door to enquiries into pre-normative intent. This accounts for anti-discrimination law's inverted appearance. It is normatively twisted.

Underneath this twist lurks an antinomy, which is the essence of its normative deficiency. Indirect discrimination is more fundamental than direct discrimination. But direct discrimination is more important to the realization of anti-discrimination law, for it promises to fill the void left by the absence of distributive patterns.

However, the root of this deficiency is twofold. First, anti-discrimination law, even though distributive in its orientation, does not recognize any distributive patterns. Hence, no such patterns can direct the application of normative intent. Second, recourse to pre-normative intentions cannot provide clear guidance either, for the real intent of agents is necessarily elusive. Since, owing to the deontological misreading, anti-discrimination law nonetheless becomes thrown back to the level of pre-normative intentionality, its application is destined to become the hotbed of moral controversy. The *sixth chapter* tries to explain and to specify in which respect moralism is the consequence of its normative deficiency and a permanent feature of its practical application.

The normative deficit of anti-discrimination law also explains why the field is systematically vulnerable to be intellectually diluted into pure casuistry. By casuistry I do not mean that for legal rules and principles to become clear they ordinarily require a comparative reflection on how they are to be applied to cases. Casuistry in the sense of the term relevant here does not mitigate indeterminacy but rather exacerbates and conceals it. When principles themselves are not sufficiently clear or pull into different directions, clinging to precedents, no doubt, creates the comforting image of adhering to legal standards; however, resort to precedents offers no reprieve where principles are so muddled that the holding of a case is without further dispute only relevant to the facts that it purports to have ruled on. This experience of such pseudo-normativity is ordinarily made in the relation of two or more conflicting cases that seem to claim equal relevance to a case at hand. In such a situation, precedents do not in any manner prejudice results. Judicial reasoning has an easy time of engaging in distinguishing, thereby even further increasing, the complexity of the field.

It is to be feared, or even to be expected, that in a situation marked by pervasive casuistry, the purported reconciliation of economic and social objectives is likely to be tilted in favour of the former. Under the auspices of neoliberalism, the voice of economic rationality sounds more commonsensical than high-minded moral demands. The synthesis in the relation of competitiveness and solidarity may hence become dominated by the imperatives of flexibility, availability, self-promotion, or permanent requalification at the expense of the interests of life as it exists outside of work. In short, anti-discrimination law is not unlikely to be a blunt tool of social protection.

11. The Neoliberal Predicament and its Antidote

The *seventh chapter* pushes the matter further by studying how the normative deficiency grows into a true neoliberal predicament if attempts at reinforcing anti-discrimination law remain tied to the horizon of the pre-normative level. This predicament comes to the fore in efforts undertaken by scholars of the 'second generation' of US American anti-discrimination law. They try to imagine what it would take to overcome this deficiency.

In Chapter 7, the analysis comes to a full circle. The study of the micro-level equivalent to European macro-level policy-learning strategies further elucidates the absence of normative guidance inherent in recourse to pre-normative dealings. Not surprisingly, attempts at making progress are concerned with changing attitudes and dispositions, without, however, having a clear conception of the direction in which policy is to be moved. 'Experimentation' and 'mutual learning processes' are the euphemistic referents used in this context. Their currency indicates the persistence of impasse.

Second-generation scholarship, instead of overcoming moralism, aggravates an already existing preoccupation with attitudes, intentions, and personal biases. Worse still, social problems are deemed to originate from a lack of moral self-observation on the part of individual agents and organizations. Resolving these questions is believed to require monitoring and cleansing of the mind of inappropriate, even if unconscious, content. It is disturbing to observe how scholars advocate the implementation of hyper-competitive production models to the transformation of the souls and minds of unreconstructed employers and employees. Second-generation anti-discrimination law comes perilously close to a mind-moulding exercise short of embracing terror.

The *eighth chapter* turns to so-called accommodation requirements and argues that these do not represent one more element in the deontological toolbox of anti-discrimination law. Rather, they represent the law's very own means of drawing out its innermost aspiration. In principle, the embrace of accommodation reverses the deontological inversion of anti-discrimination law. The result of the double negation is not a mere affirmation of the distributive dimension but rather its transcendence into a broader ambition.

The limited personal scope of accommodation requirements is difficult to defend. With the recognition of accommodation, the emphasis of the protection from discrimination shifts from conduct and distribution towards decommodification, that is, making human life generally more independent of the market nexus. However, creating the conditions of a relatively more decommodified life presupposes the full range of social policy strategies whose capabilities have been impaired in Europe while anti-discrimination law was rising to new heights. While the neoliberal predicament exposes the significance of anti-discrimination law, accommodation represents its limit.

Hence, one is bound to conclude that European anti-discrimination law is a self-contradictory project. Its ascendancy is concomitant to a displacement of that full-blown social policy which would be required for its own realization. Anti-discrimination law is social policy in the state of its disempowerment by competitiveness.

Lest I be misunderstood, I hasten to add that the following essay has not been designed as a diatribe against the noble cause of protecting people from discrimination. Rather, it is meant to explore its limit. Anti-discrimination law may be very useful in targeting animus and narrow stereotypes. But it cannot supply the core of a social model.

The book concludes with an appeal to the historical horizon from within which debates over the Third Way have been conducted in Europe. These debates will have to continue. Otherwise, it is to be feared that Europe will be robbed of its social core in the future.

12. Constructivism: a Note on Legal Analysis

Chapters 1 to 3 of this book are concerned with exploring the broader context of European anti-discrimination policy. Methodologically, they might pass as descriptive political science. By contrast, Chapters 4 to 8 present a type of legal analysis that neither considers itself limited by jurisdictional bounds nor aspires to reconstruct European equality law as it stands. Evidently, it is interested in fundamental categories and associated ways of thinking. It is thereby that it wishes to make sense of the significance of a certain field of law.

For the purpose of the following analysis, intermittent reference to the US American experience is particularly useful. The academic debate has already begun to explore various options of reinforcing anti-discrimination policy. Examining these proposals helps to determine its significance. Since capturing this significance is the point of the essay, I abstain from discussing the intricacies of, for example, allocating the burden of proof for cases of direct or indirect discrimination.

The analysis to be found in Chapters 4 to 8 espouses a conception of legal scholarship that I consider to be adequate to our intellectual situation. This situation is marked by both the demise of legal positivism and the widespread reluctance to embrace natural law theory. We are aware that law cannot be treated as a *stable* possession which is fixed ('laid down') in certain positing acts. What we claim to be law is the product of arguments. Equally, we sense that law is also not the manifestation of timeless reason. What we claim to be law is very much a product of our time.

A jurisprudential position that avoids embracing legal positivism and natural law theory without retreating to the intellectual high ground of postmodernism[66] can, with a certain measure of historical accuracy, be characterized as constructivist. The constructivism practiced in this essay is, indeed, related to its nineteenth-century German predecessor. While sharing certain of its traditional central concerns, it also rejects others. With traditional constructivism the position shares the belief that legal thought is devoted to making our normative ideas clear. The point of this endeavour is to have clear ideas help us comprehend the objective normative meaning of social situations. If it were not for legal thought, it would not be authoritatively known whether or not, for example, a certain pair of utterances is a binding contract or whether, closer to the point of our analysis, an act amounts to discrimination. Since it is part of the objective meaning of legally relevant situations to carry normative implications and since modern law, at any rate, is about empowering the human will, constructivist analysis seeks to determine the rights that emerge as a

[66] See, for example, D. Patterson, *Law and Truth* (New York: Oxford University Press, 1995).

result of legally significant situations. The task of elucidating their objective meaning involves the use of legal distinctions. They ought to be as clear as possible

This is what the constructivism practiced here has in common with its predecessor. What it does not endorse is the confidence of the latter that the system of legal concepts provides the legal analyst with the intellectual resources to find the one right answer to any and every legal problem, or worse still, the contention that the authoritative source for such answers in hard cases is the conceptual system itself. The new constructivism readily concedes that the substantive construction of a system of law may in certain or even in most cases not admit of one right answer. A construction may not even be able to establish the jurisdiction of the organ that is supposed to absorb a substantive indeterminacy. One may have to conclude that the law is objectively unclear.

When situations are legally unclear, the law cannot rule. Unclear legal situations become supplanted by the interference of other media of communication, such as money and power. But even where legal institutions are marked by indeterminacy, this indeterminacy is bounded and the product of the work of a set of concepts and distinctions. Bounded indeterminacy is constituted by the interaction of a set of normative ideals. It is this type of indeterminacy which is of particular interest to the analysis that follows.

What distinguishes the new constructivism from its nineteenth-century precursor is also the key role played by an insight, which was first formulated by Hans Kelsen.[67] It continues to play a central role in social system's theory. The legal system not only uses what it takes to be authoritative legal standards in order to elucidate the objective meaning of social situations; legal acts themselves are self-referentially constituted. Such acts validate themselves by claiming to be valid legal acts. Any contractual agreement which is taken seriously by the parties is self-validating in that the parties claim to be bound by it. But also the judgments handed down by courts are self-validating in the sense that they situate themselves within a context that points to the source of their authority. Of course, validation is a cooperative social process, in the course of which legal thought is generative of a constantly evolving structure of reasoning.

Not surprisingly, the self-interpretations of legal acts are error-prone and susceptible to self-obfuscation. They are so, in particular, when the law is in the hand of courts. Courts need to decide. Owing to the permanent embarrassment by carrying a burden of justification, courts are likely to ascribe to their reasoning more solid foundations than they actually can possess. This is unavoidable. Indeed, in their case, it is particularly obvious that the raising of legal claims involves self-validation in spite of insufficient reasons. As a result, the reality of legal systems, aside from over-determination by money and power, is marked by the production of ideology.

It is the task of legal scholarship to remove from the appearance of legal materials, piece by piece, the ideological distortions that originate from overconfident justifications.

[67] See H. Kelsen, *Introduction to the Problems of Legal Theory*, first pub. 1934, trans. by B. Litschewski Paulson and S. L. Paulson (Oxford: Clarendon Press, 1992).

1

Social Policy: from Domestication to Disarmament

1. The Social Question in a Transnational Context

This chapter offers a sketch of the impact that the European Union has had on social policy in Europe. At the outset, it will be seen that even though the Union's vision remains highly indeterminate (in particular, the often-invoked 'European social model'), there is also a propensity to concentrate efforts on collective human resource management. This focus emerges in a context in which social policy has become subject to *domestication*, *assimilation* and, eventually, *disarmament*.

I speak of domestication in a twofold sense of the term. This means, first, that social policy has largely remained the domestic affair of the Member States,[1] however coordinated it may have already become in the Union. Second, social policy has been domesticated in the sense of having been tamed in a manner that makes it compatible with constraints established by the common market. While still in the hands of the Member States, social policy needs to be pursued with circumspection in order to be consistent with the demands of European Union law.

The prevalence of domestication is all the more understandable, given that in the field of social policy both the *jurisdictional* and *actual* powers of the Union are narrowly circumscribed. Not surprisingly, the rise to prominence and greater visibility of one particular area, namely, employment policy, reflects a common concern of national social welfare states. The development of employment policy is concomitant with the career of a broader European anti-discrimination agenda.

Assimilation is the process by which, owing to the application of fundamental freedoms (including European citizenship), national social benefits are extended across national bounds. Social benefits, when touched by European Union law, become likened to rights associated with economic mobility.

Monetary Union has taken away from Member States major tools of macroeconomic policy, such as currency revaluation, and seriously curtailed their leeway in matters of fiscal policy. This partial disarmament of the Member States is further enhanced by recent developments in the ECJ's case law that have gone beyond

[1] This, at any rate, has been the allocation of competence envisaged by the ordo-liberal European economic constitution. See C. Joerges, 'A New Alliance of De-legalisation and Legal Formalism? Reflections on Responses to the Social Deficit of the European Integration Project' (2008) 19 *Law and Critique* 235–253 at 239.

domestication and ushered in a new area of market liberalization. The development affects, in particular, industrial relations and systems of wage determination.

This development reveals, remarkably, the intricacy of the social question that arises in a transnational federal system. It is not simply the question of how a polity responds to the exigencies of freedom from want; rather, it is about whether the *difference* in levels of market independence that is sustained for its citizens by participating states is in the long term likely to imperil the cohesion of a transnational polity. Arguably, the uncompensated disarmament of national social policy threatens to send the economic integration project on a downwards path of self-subversion.

Against this background, the prominent role played by anti-discrimination law in the European Union is doubly significant. First, it reflects the supply-side oriented part of social policy on which all seem to be able to agree. Second, its prominence distracts, nonetheless, from what truly is the social question in a transnational federal system. To the extent that it promises to solve the problem of 'inclusion', it is also a symptom of unresolved transnational conflict.

2. The Economic is the Political

With the European Union's growing imperial expanse, the integration project has come to be surrounded by a somewhat mystical air. No longer is Europe neatly tied to a market-making agenda whose implementation gives rise to certain welcome or unwelcome 'spillover' effects.[2] Until very recently, at any rate, something else seems to have been at stake. Before the economic crisis and currency rescue efforts began taxing European self-confidence, gaining ground vis-à-vis the United States of America in defining humanity's ultimate dream appears to have become the core ambition.[3] For quite some time, Europe has enjoyed presenting itself as having a mission on the globe.[4]

[2] See E. B. Haas, 'The Study of Regional Integration: Reflections on the Joy and Anguish of Pretheorising', in L. Lindberg, S. A. Scheingold, and A. Stuart (eds), *Regional Integration* (Cambridge, MA: Harvard University Press, 1971), 3–42.

[3] See J. Rifkin, *The European Dream: How Europe's Vision of the Future is Quietly Eclipsing the American Dream* (New York: Tarcher/Penguin, 2004) and most recently, S. Hill, *Europe's Promise: Why the European Way is the Best Hope in an Insecure Age* (Berkeley, CA: University of California Press, 2010); but see also on Europe qua only option that remains in the face of the unpalatable alternative between the American dream and Chinese style authoritarian capitalism, S. Žižek, 'What Does Europe Want' http://www.lacan.com/zizekslovenia.htm accessed 23 December 2010. Clearly, some tend to be sceptical about this, raising the spectre of the impending collapse of a wimpy 'impire'. See, notably, N. Ferguson, *Collossus: The Price of America's Empire* (New York: Penguin Press, 2004), 239–258.

[4] See, notably, European Council (Presidency Conclusions): Laeken Declaration on the Future of the European Union, 15 December 2001, http://european-convention.eu.int/pdf/lknen.pdf accessed 23 December 2010. Intriguingly, American journalists who are (ostensibly) repulsed by the political course of their own country have a proclivity to celebrate Europe's ascendancy to the rank of a new 'superpower'. This may be a bit premature. See, however, T. R. Reid, *The United States of Europe: The New Superpower and the End of American Supremacy* (New York: Penguin Press, 2004). For a discussion of renewed European imperialism that is different from its American counterpart, see

In spite of recent despondency, this development remains puzzling. It does not reflect, at any rate, what one would have originally expected to be within the compass of the Union's reasons for existence. The Union began, when it was still an economic community, in a much more introverted and moderate vein. In retrospect, it appears plain that for a region reemerging from the ashes of yet another incredibly disastrous war, the creation of a common market provided the key to securing peace by promoting universal prosperity.[5] From the outset, arguably, European capitalism, which came to be endorsed in the wake of the Second World War, was the preferred tool for making existential political struggles for distant societal goals unattractive. It was to replace the emotional pull of social visions with the prospect of pleasurable rewards.[6] The core mission of European capitalism has been to make Europeans more predictable[7] by substituting the appeal of high-minded ideals with the lure of aesthetically overdetermined commodities.[8] Whether this project is sustainable still remains to be seen.[9] The current crisis has revealed how easily confidence in its long-term success can be shattered.

Ironically, the requisite affirmation of the banal and the commonplace is epitomized by the Community itself, which commended itself after unification plans had turned out to be unfeasible. The Community offered a promising way to settle for 'the second best'. European integration would be misunderstood, hence, if

P. Swan, 'American Empire or Empires? Alternative Juridifications of the New World Order', in A. Bartholomew (ed.), *Empire's Law* (London: Pluto Press, 2006), 137–160.

5 The social dimension of the Community, as envisaged in the Spaak report, rejected the idea that the Community had to play a role in the harmonization of social policy. The improvement of working conditions would have to be the effect of market integration, not its precondition. Wage differentials were expected to reflect differences in productivity. See C. Barnard, 'Social Policy Revisited in the Light of the Constitutional Debate', in C. Barnard (ed.), *The Fundamentals of EU Law Revisited: Assessing the Impact of the Constitutional Debate* (Oxford: Oxford University Press, 2007), 109–115 at 110.

6 In a sense, the capitalism of European integration is capitalism as historically reconstructed by Hirschman, that is, understood as a means to prevent the otherwise impending collapse of society. See A. O. Hirschman, *The Passions and the Interests: Political Arguments for Capitalism before its Triumph* (Princeton, NJ: Princeton University Press, 1977). Interestingly, Hirschman presents his account of the ratio of modern capitalism as an alternative to Weber's exploration of its religious roots. This is not the conclusion that needs to be drawn from his study. Quite conceivably, capitalism admits of different political rationalizations which come to the fore whenever the system appears to be in crisis. Whereas a Weber-type capitalism will forever endorse self-reliance, sacrifice, hard work, and more individual initiative, a Hirschman-type capitalism will see a greater role for the state in the event that capitalism tends to become self-subversive. See M. Weber, 'Die protestantische Ethik und der Geist des Kapitalismus', in his *Gesammelte Aufsätze zur Religionssoziologie*, vol. 1 (Tübingen: Mohr, 1920), p. 111. For a recent and fairly straightforward defence of Weber-type capitalism and its underlying virtues, see S. Huntington, *Who are We? The Challenges to America's National Identity* (Princeton, NJ: Princeton University Press, 2004).

7 See F. Nietzsche, *On the Genealogy of Morality*, trans. by C. Diethe (Cambridge: Cambridge University Press 1994), at 36.

8 This, I take it, is the plausible core of Haltern's depiction of Europe's 'post-political' state. See U. Haltern, 'Pathos and Patina: The Failure and Promise of Constitutionalism in the European Union' (2002) *European Law Journal* 19–38.

9 For a sceptical perspective, Marx aside, see J. Schumpeter, *Capitalism, Socialism and Democracy* (London: Routledge, 1992, 1st edn 1943), 121–142. The project may be sustainable as long as the losers mistake their losses for sacrifices made to the community.

one were to ignore that in Europe, more than anywhere else in the world, the economic is the political; it is and maintains to be so, at any rate, where 'functional integration' and 'technocracy' have been deployed to carve out a purportedly 'apolitical' sphere of regulatory problem-solving.[10] From its inception, European integration has been a political project precisely because the Community clearly was to be the ersatz for the fulfilment of more fanciful designs.[11] It was attractive not least because it aided 'the West' in unequivocally conveying the ideological message of capitalism across the Iron Curtain where the new (and old) enemy was seen to be set.[12]

Evidently, on the eve of the elevation of market-making to the level of the European Union, the project had already come a long way and ostensibly grown into a shape that made it eligible to be taken seriously as a political ideal in its own right.[13] Supranationality has been claimed to be about sustaining the nation state by stripping it, at the same time, of its adverse and notoriously aggressive effects.[14] It has been said that 'tolerance' is the fabric of the European constitutional bond.[15] And yet, in the course of the 'acquisition'[16] of twelve plus two new Member States, the project seems to have gone off track. Talk of the 'reunification'[17] of the European continent aside,[18] the purveyors of meaning are inclined to adopt, as their default position, the invocation of unlimited growth. This is the one value that European integration appears to be committed to today.[19] A booklet published by

[10] For the most sophisticated defence of the European 'regulatory state' along these lines, see G. Majone, 'Europe's "Democracy Deficit": The Question of Standards' (1998) 4 *European Law Journal* 5–28.

[11] What I am alluding to is, of course, the failure of the European Defence Community. See D. Dinan, *Ever Closer Union: An Introduction to European Integration*, 2nd edn (London: MacMillan, 1999), 26–28.

[12] Among the few who did not forget that the European Community is a product of the Cold War are sober conservative American commentators. See R. Kagan, 'Power and Weakness' (2002) 113 *Policy Review*, http://www.uweb.ucsb.edu/~thartman/files/127/Kagan–PowerandWeakness.pdf accessed 23 December 2010.

[13] For a remarkable scholarly document, see J. H. H. Weiler, 'The Transformation of Europe' (1991) 100 *Yale Law Journal* 2403–2483.

[14] For a brief discussion of conceptions of supranationality, see A. Somek, 'On Supranationality' (2001) 5 *European Integration online Papers* (*EIoP*); http://eiop.or.at/eiop/texte/2001-003a.htm.

[15] See J. H. H. Weiler, 'Federalism and Constitutionalism: Europe's *Sonderweg*', in K. Nicolaidis and R. Howse (eds), *The Federal Vision: Legitimacy and Levels of Governance in the United States and the European Union* (Oxford: Oxford University Press, 2000), 54–72; ibid., 'A Constitution for Europe? Some Hard Choices' (2002) 40 *Journal of Common Market Studies* 565–580 at 568.

[16] I borrow the term from N. Ferguson, 'The End of Europe?', http://www.travelbrochuregraphics.com/extra/end_of_europe.htm accessed 23 December 2010.

[17] See, for example, 'The Fall of the Soviet Union and the Reunification of Europe', http://www.thenewfederalist.eu/The-Fall-of-the-Soviet-Union-and-Reunification-of-Europe accessed 23 December 2010.

[18] In fact, if it would make sense at all then because it is reminiscent of Coudenhove-Kalergi's call for a *Wiedervereinigung Europas*, which, however, did not make much sense at the time it was articulated. R. Coudenhove-Kalergi, *Die Wiedervereinigung Europas* (Vienna: Herold, 1964). See also F. Niess, *Die europäische Idee aus dem Geist des Widerstands* (Frankfurt: Suhrkamp, 2001), at 12–16.

[19] Maybe it has always been committed to this, for 'growth' needs to be the core value of an *imperium economicum*. See S. Puntscher Riekmann, *Die kommissarische Neuordnung Europas: Das Dispositiv der Integration* (Vienna/New York: Springer, 1998), 14, 19.

the European Commission praising enlargement was quite outspoken about this: 'By its very nature, the European Union is destined to grow.'[20] With disarming innocence, this sentence insinuates that there is nothing else worth aiming at.

The question that is left unanswered in this context is what it is for the process of growth to be distinctively *European*.[21] Anti-Turkish and pro-Turkish appeals to a 'Christian Europe' aside,[22] as the European Union reaches out beyond the geographical limits of the continent[23] it clearly presents itself as adhering to values that may as well also be the values of any other regional integration project. As is well known, Article 2 EU Treaty contains a commitment to freedom, democracy, the rule of law, and fundamental rights. These are principles to which, fortunately, many nations officially subscribe.[24] In a sense, they represent even the core of America's perennial mission. Even the fallback characterization of Europe as an 'empire', albeit intriguing from a historical perspective, remains substantively thin.[25]

It cannot be denied, nonetheless, that the (continental) Western European civilization is in many ways unique, in particular when compared with the stubborn incorrigibility of American capitalism. Part of what makes Europe distinctive is the realization that 'winner-takes-all' solutions are not capable of stabilizing European societies.[26] They have turned out to be unsuccessful with regard to both the hegemonic ambitions of nations and the relation between social classes. Success depends on the construction of mediating schemes or, put less comfortably, on the patient support of unprincipled and often murky solutions. European economic systems with all their multifarious (and cumbersome) structures of cooperation and involvement of state actors rest on the endorsement of such schemes. They come in a variety of forms.[27] From their existence often results a capitalist mode of

[20] See European Commission, More Unity and More Diversity: The European Union's Biggest Enlargement (European Communities, 2003) 3 (available at http://ec.europa.eu/publications/booklets/move/41/en.pdf).

[21] Scholarship, however, is well aware of enduring divisions and cleavages that account for the fact that the integration project is driven by an insatiable hunger for reconciliation and compromise. See C. Offe, 'The European Model of "Social" Capitalism: Can it Survive European Integration?' (2003) 11 *Journal of Political Philosophy* 437–469. On the elusiveness of raising the issue of 'European-ness', see Ferguson, n. 3 at 251.

[22] For a discussion, see J. H. H. Weiler, *Ein christliches Europa* (Vienna: Anton Pustet, 2004).

[23] See, for example, 'The Fall of the Soviet Union and the Reunification of Europe', http://www.thenewfederalist.eu/The-Fall-of-the-Soviet-Union-and-Reunification-of-Europe accessed 23 December 2010.

[24] For a similar observation, see C. Offe, 'Sozialpolitik und internationale Politik: Über zwei Hürden auf dem Weg zum "Zusammenhalt" Europas' (manuscript on file with the author) (2004) at 9.

[25] See I. Zielonka, *Europe as Empire: The Nature of the Enlarged European Union* (Oxford: Oxford University Press, 2006).

[26] See Offe, n. 21 at 440.

[27] The literature studying varieties of more or less organized capitalisms identifies two, three, or five different types. See P. A. Hall and D. Soskice, 'An Introduction to Varieties of Capitalism', in P. Hall and D. Soskice (eds), *Varieties of Capitalism: Institutional Foundations of Comparative Advantage* (Oxford: Oxford University Press, 2001), 1–68; B. Amable, *The Diversity of Modern Capitalism* (Oxford: Oxford University Press, 2003). Remarkably, with the exception of the Asian type of capitalism all other types are to be found in Europe. See M. Höpner and A. Schäfer, 'Grundzüge

production that is embedded in mechanisms of collective crisis management.[28] Their preponderance has helped, until recently, to dampen capital's impact on ordinary people.

3. The Elusive Social Model

The institutional structures requisite to sustaining European capitalism have come to be known, only at a late stage of its development, under the name of the 'European social model'. While it is difficult to pin down the term's precise meaning, it seems to have been introduced by the Union with a noteworthy emphasis on the investment in human resources. Its very invocation is an attempt to extract from a variety of traditions, which clearly do not at all overlap or match up to one model in institutional terms, some common themes and objectives. Intriguingly, what is perspicuous by its absence in the relevant attempts is any emphasis on the negation of the market mechanism through strategies of decommodification.[29]

It was the former President of the European Commission, Jacques Delors, who emphasized that a particular social model is a central element of European identity.[30] The expression, 'European Economic and Social Model', is a creature of the Santer Commission.[31] As is well known, any talk of *one* single European social model in institutional terms would be misguided.[32] It has been correctly observed that, as a concept, 'the' European social model both reveals and hides. While contrasted with the United States, the social systems of *Western* European states appear to fall squarely into one category, a great deal of diversity can be seen when the contrast to the United States does not enter the picture.[33] Precisely because it is such a moving target, the European social model has become the preferred rhetorical tool designating virtually any institution or substantive achievement of the European social welfare state.[34] Consequently, it shouldn't come as a surprise that characterizations of the European social model vary with regard to the context in which it is invoked. For example, in Annex I, para. 11 of the Presidency

einer politökonomischen Perspektive auf die europäische Union', in M. Höpner and A. Schäfer (eds), *Die politische Ökonomie der europäischen Integration* (Frankfurt: Campus Verlag, 2008), 11–45 at 19.

[28] For a classical analysis, see C. Offe, *Contradictions of the Welfare State*, ed. by J. Keane (Cambridge, MA: MIT Press, 1984).

[29] On the meaning of decommodification, see below pp. 28, 88.

[30] See European Commission, *White Paper on Growth, Competitiveness, and Employment: The Challenges and Ways Forward into the 21st Century*, COM(93) 700 final (1993). As a Social Democrat Delors had to come up with a strategy to counteract the internal market project.

[31] See J. Santer, 'The State of the Union', Debate at the European Parliament, Strasbourg, 21 October 1998, http://www.lex.unict.it/cde/documenti/vari/98_99/jacquer_santer.htm.

[32] See Offe, n. 24 at 11. M. Jepsen and A. Serrano Pascual, 'The European Social Model: An Exercise in Deconstruction' (2005) 15 *Journal of European Social Policy* 231–245; J. Alber, 'Das "europäische Sozialmodell" und die USA' (2006) 34 *Leviathan* 208–241 at 226.

[33] See D. M. Trubek and J. S. Mosher, 'New Governance, EU Employment Policy, and the European Social Model' (2001) 6 *Jean Monnet Working Paper* at 2.

[34] See Jepsen and Pascual, n. 32.

Conclusions of the Nice European Council (7–9 September 2000),[35] the European Social Model is characterized with reference to: (1) systems that offer a high level of social protection; (2) the importance of social dialogue; and (3) the existence of services of the general interest covering activities vital to social cohesion. Further below, however, the European social model is taken to be 'characterised by the indissoluble link between economic performance and social progress'.[36] This is a theme that was introduced already by the Lisbon Council, which initiated the Lisbon process. The Council Conclusions of the Lisbon Council actually spoke about 'modernising' the European social model without supplying a proper definition. At the same time, the text already reveals a basic concern with the generation and regeneration of human resources:[37]

People are Europe's main asset and should be the focal point of the Union's policies. Investing in people and developing an active and dynamic welfare state will be crucial both to Europe's place in the knowledge economy and for ensuring that the emergence of this new economy does not compound the existing social problems of unemployment, social exclusion and poverty.

This narrower theme of investment in labour supply is complemented, still, in the Nice Conclusions with a reference to the broader scope of social policy in European social welfare states:[38]

Alongside employment policy, social protection has a fundamental role to play, but it is also necessary to recognise the importance of other factors such as housing, education, health, information and communication, mobility, security and justice, leisure and culture.

A slightly different approach, again, has been taken by the Commission asserting that 'quality is at the heart of the European social model'.[39] Investment in people appears to play a role here, too:[40]

Quality reflects the desire, not just to defend minimum standards, but to promote rising standards and to ensure a more equitable sharing of progress. It delivers results—embracing the economy, the workplace, the home, society at large. It links the dual goals of competitiveness and cohesion in a sustainable way, with clear economic benefits flowing from investing in people and strong, supportive, social systems.

In the same paper, the European social model is then characterized with reference to the level of public expenditure and equitable distribution of benefits by contrast

[35] http://www.consilium.europa.eu/ueDocs/cms_Data/docs/pressdata/en/ec/00400-r1.%20ann.en0.htm accessed 23 December 2010.
[36] See ibid., para. 15.
[37] See Presidency Conclusions of the Lisbon European Council (23–24 March 2000), http://www.europarl.europa.eu/summits/lis1_en.htm accessed 23 December 2010.
[38] See n. 35 at para. 23.
[39] See Communication from the Commission to the Council, the European Parliament, the Economic and Social Committee and the Committee of the Regions, Employment and Social Policies: A Framework for Investing in Quality, COM(2001) 313 final at 1.
[40] Ibid.

to the United States.[41] Investing in people, however, appears to be the one theme running consistently through later pronouncements.[42]

Even though the *European* social model cannot be defined, it is not impossible to define what a social model as such is supposed to accomplish. A social model is a society's mode of managing the risks to human life that are specifically created by modern capitalism. These risks are associated with losing access to the employment market or the ability to work in a self-employed capacity owing to sickness, accidents, old age, or downfall in the demand for one's skills. On a reflexive level, these risks are also manifest in the fact that markets cannot guarantee absorbing these risks for all in an equitable manner. A social model is the result of political action. In that a social model introduces *twofold* independence-form markets, it helps to lift human existence from the fetters of the commodity form. Social models are methods of generalized decommodification. The result can be relatively weak where what is thereby intended is merely preventing utmost deprivation; a social model is then likely to have its focus on combating poverty. The aims of a social model, however, can also be far more ambitious when increasing market independence is supposed to translate into enabling forms of life that would seem unsustainable under conditions of laissez-faire.

The policy areas that are of relevance to a social model have long played a secondary or merely supplementary role in the integration process. This may have changed, most visibly, with the conclusion of the Amsterdam Treaty, which not only incorporated the Social Policy Agreement into the Treaty but also introduced a new title on employment. The draft Constitutional Treaty, and subsequently the Lisbon Treaty, mention the 'social market economy' and thereby underscore that Europe's social dimension is a central tenet of integration.[43] Even though the identification of the European social model with the 'social market economy' is historically doubtful at best,[44] it would be inaccurate to dismiss continental (Western) Europe's association with varieties of capitalisms having a quasi-corporate organization and different commitments to the public pursuit of decommodification.[45]

[41] See ibid. at 5.

[42] On the strong supply-side orientation of the Lisbon process, see D. Ashiagbor, *The European Employment Strategy: Labour Market Regulation and New Governance* (Oxford: Oxford University Press, 2005), at 303.

[43] In the spirit of the *concordantia catholica* permeating much of current European integration rhetoric, the draft Treaty had no pain to spell out a commitment to a 'highly competitive social market economy'. See Article I-3 of the Draft Treaty establishing a Constitution for Europe, adopted by the European Council in June 2004. See http://european-convention.eu.int/docs/treaty/cv00850.en03.pdf accessed 23 December 2010. The reference to the social market economy appears again in Article 3 FEU Treaty (ex Article 2(3) EC Treaty as amended by the Lisbon Treaty).

[44] See C. Joerges and F. Rödl, 'The "Social Market Economy" as Europe's Social Model?' (2004) 8 *EUI Working Paper Law*, No. 2004/8, at http://cadmus.eui.eu/bitstream/handle/1814/2823/law04-8.pdf?sequence=1, accessed 1 January 2011; for an even more critical and utterly pessimistic analysis, see, most recently, F. W. Scharpf, 'The Double Asymmetry of European Integration; Or: Why the EU Cannot Be a Social Market Economy' (2009) 9/12 *MPIfG Working Paper*.

[45] See Offe, n. 21 at 444. I think that Weiler is mistaken in disparaging the belief in a distinct European welfare capitalism, and he underrates the value attached to it by most Europeans. See J. H. H. Weiler, 'A Constitution for Europe? Some Hard Choices' (2002) 40 *Journal of Common Market Studies* 563–580, at 569–571.

4. Domestication

As is well known, none of the types of European capitalism is replicated at the Union level. Certain exceptions aside,[46] social policy and the institutions of organized capitalism are vested in the Member States. Since the inception of integration, but in particular over the last decades, sustaining these types has been increasingly confronted with constraints that originate from Union law.

The creation of a common market has severely restricted the use by Member States of some of the most reliable tools of employment and social policy: nationalization, subsidies, bailouts for near bankrupt firms, the protectionist use of tariffs and product or service standards, and the regulation of the influx of 'guest workers'. Processes of liberalization have affected the Member States' option to use the public sector as an employment buffer.[47] As is well known, European competition law (Article 106 FEU Treaty (ex 86 EC Treaty)) confronts Member States with severe constraints with regard to the organization of public provision.[48] State-owned or state-commissioned enterprises that are entrusted with the provision of services of a general economic interest are submitted to the rigours of abuse control (Article 102 FEU Treaty (Ex 82 EC Treaty)), unless Member States are able to demonstrate that liberalization would 'obstruct' the performance of the undertaking's statutory tasks.[49] The jurisprudence of the ECJ has been wavering between asserting and relaxing control. In principle, the Court is more accommodating than the Commission with which Member States were repeatedly forced to negotiate mutually acceptable solutions. According to the Court's jurisprudence, Member States do not have to show that an obstruction of performance would be tantamount to imminent bankruptcy; nor does the burden rest on them to propose alternative forms of providing public goods that might be less restrictive than a reservation of monopoly rights to particular undertakings.[50] Moreover, the ECJ is ready to exempt certain services, pension insurance, for example, from the rigours of competition law altogether if an insurance provider is not to be classified as an undertaking. For an insurance to be an undertaking it has to engage in an economic

[46] What comes to mind, of course, is the role that Articles 154–155 FEU Treaty (ex 138–139 EC Treaty) accord to the 'social partners' in the adoption of policies.

[47] See F. W. Scharpf, 'The European Social Model: Coping with the Challenges of Diversity' (2002) 40 *Journal of Common Market Studies* 645–670 at 648.

[48] For an overview, see S. Giubboni, *Social Rights and Market Freedoms in the European Constitution: A Labour Law Perspective*, trans. by R. Inston (Cambridge: Cambridge University Press, 2006), at 183–197.

[49] On how EU competition law is applied (or disapplied) to insurance schemes with a social component law, see, e.g., S. Boni and P. Manzini, 'National Social Legislation and EC Antitrust Law' (2001) 24 *World Competition* 239–255; A. Winterstein, 'Nailing the Jellyfish: Social Security and Competition Law' (1999) 23 *European Competition Law Review* 324–333; S. Giubboni, 'Social Insurance Monopolies in Community Competition Law and the Italian Constitution: "Practical" Convergences and "Theoretical" Conflicts' (2001) 7 *European Law Journal* 69–94.

[50] For an account of the case law, see L. Hancher, 'Community, State, and the Market', in P. Craig and G. de Búrca (eds), *The Evolution of EU Law* (Oxford: Oxford University Press, 1999), 721–742, at 733.

activity. The latter is not the case where the operation of the insurance scheme applies the principle of solidarity by which the Court means, essentially, that it is subservient to the political pursuit of redistributive aims among the persons and risks insured.[51]

Despite the relaxation granted by the ECJ, it is in this sphere that the reassessment of social policy in terms of market behaviour becomes troublesome. Public undertakings and grants of state aid, which are also subject to stringent restrictions,[52] have always been an important tool for national social policy. They were used for purposes extending far beyond the provision of public goods, thereby achieving employment effects[53] (not only, but also for slackers) and cushioning the impact of collective redundancies.

It thus appears that social policy, even if only loosely and superficially understood in the sense of 'market correction'[54] does not fit comfortably with the mindset of Union law. The latter is geared, essentially, towards market creation.[55] Only those aspects of social policy are likely to become adopted by Union law whose thrust can be translated into a normative framework that endorses the mobility of factors of production.[56] It should not come as a surprise that European

[51] See Case C-218/00, *Cisal di Battistello Venanzio & C. Sas* v. *Istituto nazionale per l'assicurazione* [2002] ECR I-691, paras 41–45.

[52] See Article 107 FEU Treaty (ex 87 EC Treaty).

[53] This can be observed for the *Merci* case in which the Court deemed an exclusive right impermissible on the grounds of Articles 102 and 106 FEU Treaty (ex 82 and 86 EC Treaty) because the entrusted undertaking was 'induced' to abuse its dominant position. See Case 179/90 *Merci Convenzionali Porto di Genova SpA* v. *Siderurgia Gabrielli SpA* [1991] ECR I-5889. The exclusive right, however, had been granted to ensure the employment of the local labour force in the unloading of ships.

[54] Usually, social policy is defined following T. H. Marshall's classic formulation as the use of political power with the aim of correcting, modifying, or superseding the operation of the economic system in the pursuit of values that are not supported by market forces themselves. See T. H. Marshall, *Social Policy* (London: Heinemann, 1975), at 15; W. Streeck, 'Vom Binnenmarkt zum Bundesstaat? Überlegungen zur politischen Ökonomie der europäischen Sozialpolitik', in S. Leibfried and P. Pierson (eds), *Standort Europa. Europäische Sozialpolitik* (Frankfurt: Suhrkamp, 1998), at 379. Thus understood, social policy is always market-correcting. It comprises a whole plethora of activities ranging from facilitating universal health insurance to the provision of affordable housing, free public education, or maintaining hospitable urban environments. This understanding of social policy, however, sweeps very broadly. Any market-correcting activity can be given the appearance of 'social policy'. Subsidizing a variety of religious denominations would pass as social policy as would the provision of security by an armed police force rather than private security agencies competing in a market. Eventually, any use of political power would be tantamount to social policy. Even though, admittedly, there is no compelling reason against the use of such a broad notion, the contours and functions of social policy are more accurately captured by a more narrow conception. When it comes to this, the classical formulations by Eduard Heimann provide guidance for they anchor social policy in curing the chief ill of a capitalist economy, which is to deprive people of their freedom inasmuch as they are treated as though they were commodities. More precisely, according to Heimann, social policy is the attempt to infuse into capitalism a counter-principle that manifests itself in freedom-restoring strategies that respond to the modes with which capitalism, by preserving legal freedom, undermines the social freedom of workers. See E. Heimann, *Soziale Theorie des Kapitalismus: Theorie der Sozialpolitik*, edn 1929, new edn ed. by B. Badura (Frankfurt: Suhrkamp 1980), 121, 167.

[55] See Streeck, above n. 54 at 369–421.

[56] See, for example, the Directives on the Mutual Recognition of Diplomas 89/48/EEC and 92/51/EEC. For a comprehensive overview of legislation and case law, see A. P. van der Mei, *Free Movement of Persons within the European Community* (Oxford: Hart Publishing, 2003).

social policy is predictably one-dimensional.[57] Aside from facilitating the portability of pension insurance accounts, it is restricted, for the most part, to certain aspects of labour law that are particularly relevant to transnational businesses, such as workers' representation in transnational firms,[58] workers' rights in the case of transfers of undertakings,[59] or more generally directed at levelling the playing field.[60] Contrariwise, this means that market-correcting legislation by the Member States is perceived through a lens highlighting its actually or potentially adverse impact on transnational commerce. It is consistent with this perspective that the ECJ is disposed to attribute to market access relatively great weight, in particular when it can be combined with resolution of potentially conflicting social policy objectives. Where a tension can be observed, for example, between the locally organized workforce and posted workers, the ECJ is ready to choose a path that is consistent with facilitating mobility of services and, hence, serves the latter group.[61] It seems, therefore, as though social policy goals are readily supported by the Court as long as they come in tandem with, or are ancillary to, the competitive pursuit of economic interests.

For quite some time, the Court's jurisprudence appears to have been evenhanded.[62] Although the ECJ has taken seriously free movement provisions as a side constraint on the design of social policy, in some instances it appeared to have been also receptive to public interest justifications for obstacles to economic mobility.[63] Even

[57] As Paul Pierson puts it, European social policy has a 'hollow core'. What can be accomplished is, at best, the incremental mutual accommodation of levels of social protection, for the Union lacks the formal competence and the political capacity for central guidance. See P. Pierson, 'Social Policy and European Integration', in A. Moravcsik (ed.), *Centralisation or Fragmentation? Europe Facing the Challenges of Deepening, Diversity, and Democracy* (Washington, DC: Brookings Institution, Council on Foreign Relations, 1998), 124–158, at 144.

[58] See Council Directive 94/45/EC of September 1994 on the establishment of a European Works Council or a procedure in Community-scale undertakings and Community-scale groups of undertakings for the purposes of informing and consulting employees, OJ L 254, 1994, 0064.

[59] See Council Directive 77/187/EEC of 14 February 1977 on the approximation of the laws of the Member States relating to the safeguarding of employees' rights in the event of transfers of undertakings, businesses, or parts of businesses [1977] OJ L61/27. This Directive is, however, no longer in force.

[60] See, for example, legislation of safety standards mentioned in Barnard, n. 5 at 484.

[61] See, for that matter, Case C-341/05, *Laval un Partneri Ltd* v. *Svenska Byggnadsarbetareförbudet* [2007] ECR I-11767, para. 105.

[62] Barnard, n. 5 at 496 puts the matter much more elegantly by saying that in the area in which social regulation collides with single market policies 'the Court has shown itself to be the least surefooted'. The Court has been inclined, though, to accept requirements addressed to foreign firms to comply with substantial parts of the employment laws, in particular tariff agreements, of the host state. See Case C-244/04, *Commission* v. *Germany* [2006] ECR I-885, para. 61. For a discussion, see C. Barnard, 'Social Policy Revisited in the Light of the Constitutional Debate', in C. Barnard (ed.), *The Fundamentals of EU Law Revisited: Assessing the Impact of the Constitutional Debate* (Oxford: Oxford University Press, 2007), at 139–143.

[63] This can be observed for cases such as *Müller-Fauré* (see Case C-385/99, *V.G. Müller-Fauré* v. *Onderlinge Waarborgmaatschappij OZ Zorgverzekeringen UA* and *E.E.M. van Riet* v. *Onderlinge Waarborgmaatschappij ZAO Zorgverzekeringen* [2003] ECR I-4509), and *Collins* (Case C-138/02, *Brian Francis Collins* v. *Secretary of State for Work and Pensions* [2004] ECR I-6193). See the conclusion of a discussion of the Court's case law by Hatzopoulos: '[...] [I]t is almost impossible for an entity involved in the provision of healthcare services to know whether or not it should abide by the [criteria set out for solidarity] until before its case is actually judged by the Court of Justice.' V. Hatzopoulos,

though the Court has not shied away from encumbering national legislation with the demands of the internal market, it has also exhibited good will to relieve its strong hold on public interest grounds. This double gesture of restriction and relaxation may be owing to the Court's realization that the only social welfare regime there is in the European Union is associated with the type of state that is to be found at the national level.

Summing it up, over the last decades market-correcting national social policy has come under increasing scrutiny by the European Union. This does not mean that it has been *necessarily* on the wane. Until very recently, social policy has been largely subject to 'domestication'.[64] For the most part, it remains a national affair and is, as such, tamed by the internal market.

I would like to examine below in which respect more recent developments have pushed the relation between the Union and its Member States beyond mere domestication and more into the direction of disarmament.

5. Assimilation

Before examining the move from domestication to disarmament, I would like to invite attention to a development that can be called 'assimilation'. On the level of European Union law, social rights, at any rate, have been assimilated to the mindset of the internal market.[65] Not surprisingly, Union law has in this connection extended the idea of market access to matters of social policy.[66] When seen through the lens of free movement, social policy is simply about the delivery of, and the access to, services and benefits.[67] Put bluntly, it is government largesse. In the context of European Union law, however, its dispensation must not give rise to discrimination on the grounds of nationality. Since the Court has transferred European citizenship

'Health Law and Policy: The Impact of the EU', in G. de Búrca (ed.), *EU Law and the Welfare State: In Search of Solidarity* (Oxford: Oxford University Press, 2005), 111–168 at 157.

[64] See S. Leibfried and P. Pierson, 'Social Policy: Left to Courts and Markets?', in *Policy-making in the European Union*, 4th edn (Oxford: Oxford University Press, 2000), 267–292 at 284–286. The authors, however, would probably find my assessment overstated in light of the gradual expansion of the Union's competence in this area.

[65] In a less sceptical mood, however, but also guarded against premature optimism, Bell concludes that in the face of the dominance of 'market citizenship', the model of social citizenship has been boosted by the Amsterdam Treaty and the Fundamental Rights Charter. He concludes, though, that it is still more an aspiration than a reality for the Union. See M. Bell, *Anti-discrimination Law and the European Union* (Oxford: Oxford University Press, 2002), 16, 27–29.

[66] Ironically, this has given rise to challenges of minimum wage requirements on free movement grounds. See Cases C-369/96 and C-376/96 *Arblade* [1999] ECR I-8453. For a discussion of the social dimension of market access, see C. Barnard and S. Deakin, 'Market Access and Regulatory Competition', in C. Barnard and J. Scott (eds), *The Law of the Single European Market: Unpacking the Premises* (Oxford: Hart Publishing, 2002), 197–224.

[67] This perspective can actually clash with the self-understanding of social policy, for example, as regards the nature of in-kind provision of services. See *Müller-Fauré* n. 63.

into the most fundamental right to be free from such discrimination when enjoying transnational mobility,[68] the jurisprudence came to exhibit astounding activism as regards the extension of social benefits to European citizens.[69] Member States cannot limit the personal eligibility for benefits, such as childcare allowances and other transfer payments, to their own nationals as soon as nationals from other Member States are lawfully resident on their territory.[70] Union law can put social policy to its own service so long as it comes in the form of an economic 'service'. Its underpinning in solidarity, however, remains alien to it.[71]

Assimilation can, in turn, have a domesticating effect. The general principle brought to bear on access to social benefits by the ECJ, namely the outlawing of all discrimination on the grounds of nationality, can create pressure to level down benefits for the nationals of Member States.[72] The Austrian system of university admission, which used to be based on a fairly non-competitive standard, is a case in point, in particular with regard to medical studies.[73] Subject to the constraints of citizenship, non-competitive admission systems, such as the use of quotas for students with foreign diplomas, are deemed to be permissible only if they can be plausibly linked to maintaining a balanced high-quality medical service open to all and in so far as this contributes to achieving a high level of protection of health.[74]

[68] See notably, Case C-184/99, *Rudy Grzelczyk* v. *Centre public d'aide sociale d'Ottignies-Louvain-la-Neuve* [2001] ECR I-6193, para. 31: 'Union citizenship is destined to be the fundamental status of nationals of the Member States, enabling those who find themselves in the same situation to enjoy the same treatment in law irrespective of their nationality, subject to such exceptions as are expressly provided for.'

[69] See, for example, Case C-456/02, *Michel Trojani* v. *Centre public d'aide sociale de Bruxelles* (CPAS) [2004] I-7573 on the access to non-contributory benefits and, choosing another example, on the extension of access to job-seekers' allowances in the interaction of citizenship and free movement of workers, Case C-138/02, *Brian Francis Collins* v. *Secretary of State for Work and Pensions* [2004] ECR I-6193; Joined Cases C-22/08 & C-23/08, *Athanasios Vatsouras and Josif Koupatantze* v. *Arbeitsgemeinschaft Nürnberg* 900, paras 38–39. For a discussion of the problems posed by these developments, see M. Ferrera, 'Towards an "Open" Social Citizenship? The New Boundaries of Welfare in the European Union', in G. de Búrca (ed.), *EU Law and the Welfare State: In Search of Solidarity* (Oxford: Oxford University Press, 2005), 11–38 at 20–21, 24.

[70] See C–85/96, *María Martínez Sala* v. *Freistaat Bayern* [1998] ECR I-2691, holding that a child-raising allowance falls within the remit of the Council regulation 1408/71 EEC of 14 June 1971 *ratione materiae* Union law and ought to be granted to a non-national as soon as a national of another Member State lawfully resides in the territory of the Member State. For an even more expansive approach, see Case C-184/99, *Rudy Grzelczyk* v. *Centre public d'aide sociale d'Ottignies-Louvain-la-Neuve* [2001] ECR I-06193; Case C-209/03, *The Queen (on the application of Dany Bidar)* v. *London Borough of Ealing and Secretary of State for Education and Skills* [2005] ECR I-2119.

[71] See *Cisal*, n. 51.

[72] For example, if access to a job-seeker's allowance cannot be based on nationality but only on periods of lawful permanent residency, then Member States could have the incentive to phase out such benefits altogether. Why should their national constituency have an interest in subsidizing nationals of another Member State?

[73] For a discussion, see A. Somek, 'Solidarity Decomposed: Being and Time in European Citizenship' (2007) 32 *European Law Review* 787–818, at 816–818.

[74] See Case C-73/08, *Nicolas Bressol and Others, Céline Chaverot and Others* v. *Gouvernement de la Communauté française*, 13 April 2010 at para. 62.

How assimilation translates into domestication can also be observed for matters of health insurance.[75] Only under restrictive conditions may Member States demand that social benefits be consumed on their own territory.[76] However, the basic idea is—choosing a random example—that if the quality of health care is better in another Member State, any European citizen should be free to obtain it there. Within reasonable limits, national health care regulation is expected to adjust to competitive pressures.[77] Notwithstanding the fact that the European Court of Justice has repeatedly stated, in *dicta*, that there is an 'independent' (or even human rights-based) social justification for European social law,[78] it also made plain that the rationale for Article 157 FEU Treaty (ex 141 EC Treaty) (ruling out discrimination on the grounds of sex in the context of pay) also lies in pre-empting the competitive disadvantage of firms that are located in Member States with laws protecting against pay discrimination.[79] Not surprisingly, regulatory interaction, more precisely its self-regulation, has entered European social policy. The guarantee of freedom of establishment and of freedom to provide services, which reinforce such interaction, have recently posed a severe challenge to long-entrenched systems of industrial relations.[80] I shall return to this challenge below.

[75] For an overview, see R. R. Geyer, *Exploring European Social Policy* (Oxford: Polity Press, 2000), at 58–71; C. Barnard, *EC Employment Law*, 2nd edn (Oxford: Oxford University Press, 1999), at 1–5. On the constraints exercised by free movement rules, in particular free movement of services, on the national definition of the extent to which insurance benefits can be enjoyed by insured persons in Member States other than the State providing insurance, see M. Fuchs, 'Free Movement of Services and Social Security—*Quo Vadis*' (2002) 8 *European Law Journal* 536–555; V. G. Hatzopoulos, '*Killing* National Health and Insurance Systems but *Healing* Patients? The European Market for Health Care Services after the Judgments of the ECJ in *Vanbraekel* and *Peerbooms*' (2002) 39 *Common Market Law Review* 683–729.

[76] The *Kohll* and the *Decker* cases are the relevant authorities in this field. See Case C-158/96, *Raymond Kohll* v. *Union des caisses de maladie* [1998] ECR I-193; Case C-120/95, *Nicolas Decker* v. *Caisse de maladie des employés privés* [1998] ECR I-01831. *Kohll* deals with remunerative orthodontist work done in Germany outside a hospital by a privately established doctor. In *Decker*, a pair of glasses with corrective lenses was bought on a Luxembourg prescription from a Belgian optician. In both cases, the insurance fund initially denied reimbursement. The Court, however, applied Article 54 FEU Treaty (ex 48 EC Treaty), guaranteeing freedom to provide services, which precludes Member States from making the provision of services between Member States more difficult than the provision of services within one Member State. The opening of one major insurance system to the European market is probably just the beginning, as other cases are coming up which test the limits of welfare states' 'closed shops'. Will Member States be able to defend mandatory insurance schemes? For a discussion, see Leibfried and Pierson, n. 64 at 282–283. Later, in *Müller-Fauré* (n. 63) a regime was deemed consistent with Union law that restricted benefits to in-kind provision by contracted providers. The Court is ready to grant even more speculative arguments a certain weight where the maintenance of hospital services is concerned. See Case C-157/99, *B.S.M. Geraets-Smits and Stichting Ziekenfonds VGZ and between H.T.M. Peerbooms and Stichting CZ Groep Zorgverzekeringen* [2001] ECR I-5473, para. 106. For an analysis, see V. Hatzopoulos, 'Health Law and Policy: The Impact of the EU', in G. de Búrca (ed.), *EU Law and the Welfare State. In Search of Solidarity* (Oxford: Oxford University Press, 2005), 111–168 at 138–140.

[77] For a critical discussion, see C. Newdick, 'Citizenship, Free Movement and Health Care: Cementing Individual Rights by Corroding Social Solidarity' (2006) 43 *Common Market Law Review* 1645–1668 at 1654–1656, 1665; Fuchs, n. 75; Hatzopoulos, n. 75.

[78] See Case C-50/96, *Deutsche Telekom AG* v. *Lilli Schröder* [2000] ECR I-743, para 57.

[79] See already Case 43/75, *Defrenne* v. *Sabena* (no. 2), [1976] ECR I-455.

[80] See, aside from *Laval*, n. 61, Case C-438/05, *International Transport Workers Federation, Finnish Seaman's Union* v. *Viking Line*, [2007] ECR I-10779.

6. Towards Disarmament: Monetary Union

Any summary account on the overall context of social policy in the EU would be incomplete if it did not mention the impact of Monetary Union, not least since the recent debt crisis triggered a mushrooming of austerity programmes in various countries. The common solution found in response to Greece's deficit and public finance problem creates additional strain on the budgets of Member States whose deficits may not even yet have been excessive.[81] All over the European Union, spending on social services is in the process of being diminished at a rate that raises the concern that the reductions might have a massively recessive impact on the economy as a whole.[82]

Even aside from the current crisis, Monetary Union undeniably has had a profound impact on the national social welfare state.[83] It took away from the Member States major tools of macroeconomic control. First, Member States are no longer capable of tinkering with the currency conversion rate or of adjusting interest rates. They cannot, for example, decrease the value of their currency in order to boost their exports without forgoing revenues from production. There can also be little doubt that countries with comparatively lower levels of economic growth suffer from a high-interest rate policy pursued by the European Central Bank.[84] Second, Monetary Union is based on a tight connection between prize stability and fiscal discipline. In fact, prize stability is the prime directive of Monetary Union.[85] Fiscal policy is generally subject to the constraints of the Stability and Growth Pact,[86] which introduces a cap for the annual deficit and thus curbs the level of public expenditure.[87] As a result, Member States have little fiscal room for manoeuvre in order to influence their economic performance. This is exacerbated by the fact that Member States cannot, under conditions of regime competition, raise corporate taxes or taxes on higher incomes without risking capital flight. The brunt of taxation is borne by the immobile factors of production while mobile factors are in the position to pick and choose the most favourable

[81] The Member States decided to establish a 'European stabilisation mechanism' on the basis of Article 122(2) FEU Treaty and an intergovernmental agreement of the Euro area Member States. The latter group of Member States agreed to be ready to complement resources through a 'Special Purpose Vehicle'. See ECOFIN Council Conclusions, Brussels 9–10 May 2010.

[82] See P. Krugman, 'The Pain Caucus' *The New York Times* 31 May 2010.

[83] See, generally, F. Snyder, 'EMU Revisited: Are we Making a Constitution? What Constitution are we Making?', in P. Craig and G. de Búrca (eds), *The Evolution of EU Law* (Oxford: Oxford University Press, 1999), 417–475 at 448–449.

[84] It is one of the highly questionable assumptions of Monetary Union that Member State economies develop equally. See A. Schubert, *Der Euro: Die Krise einer Chance* (Frankfurt: Suhrkamp, 1998), at 100.

[85] See Article 127 FEU Treaty.

[86] The Stability and Growth Pact consists of a set of legal and non-legal instruments concerning the continuation of budgetary discipline in economic and Monetary Union. For a detailing of its composition, see http://europa.eu/scadplus/glossary/stability_growth_pact_en.htm accessed 23 December 2010.

[87] See Article 127(2) FEU Treaty and the Article 1 of Protocol (No 12) on the Excessive Deficit Procedure.

environment.[88] The resulting competitive downward spiral of high tax rates leads to diminishing tax revenue.[89] Third, what is left to Member States as a macro-economic policy tool is social retrenchment and depressing wages, where possible. Without monetary policy and confronted with severe shackles on deficit spending, what remains for domestic policy in order to influence international competitiveness are the stagnation of wages and the creation of a flexible business environment.[90] As a matter of fact, the Member States suffer from massive disarmament.

Most remarkably, as the current fiscal crisis has revealed, the experience of disarmament triggers greater domestication in its wake. Growing transnational competition exercises a destructive effect on the employment prospects of low-skilled workers. The transnational economy devalues work at the expense of capital since the highest revenues are expected to accrue from the least labour-intensive forms of production.[91] The pool of those whose skills are no longer in demand is steadily growing. Not surprisingly, the losers of economic integration turn to the community from which they have successfully sought reprieve in the past, that is, their national social welfare state. The need to provide access to unemployment benefits, government-assisted housing, or affordable education becomes even more pressing. Paradoxically, the demands made on the social welfare state are potentially even greater under the auspices of fiscal austerity.

Since there is no supranational alternative in sight, national clienteles loyally support their national systems and defend their scarce resources against those whom they believe to be outsiders. Instead of perceiving jointly the transnational economy as the source of their problem, they end up reasserting old national sympathies. The tension between the Greeks and the Germans is the case in point. It is by reinforcing national social cohesion at the expense of wider European sympathies that the European integration process threatens to become self-subversive.

7. Social and Nowhere to go: Competences

Given that Union law profoundly altered the context of national social legislation one might wonder why the Union should not itself make more effective forays into the social domain. But notwithstanding the fact that the scope of Union powers has been expanded over the last decades, the powers of legislation remain subject to noteworthy limitations.

Titles X–XII (Articles 151–166) FEU Treaty (ex Title XI [Articles 136–150] EC Treaty) lay down the principles for, and carve out the jurisdictional space of, Union social policy. Title XI is composed of three chapters. Whereas Articles 157 to 158 of

[88] See S. Leibfried and H. Obinger, 'Nationale Sozialstaaten in der Europäischen Union: Zukünfte eines "sozialen Europas"', in *TranState Reprints* (Bremen 2008), at 7.

[89] See Höpner and Schäfer, n. 27 at 29–30.

[90] For a more detailed analysis, see H. Enderlein, 'Wandel durch den Euro: Wie die Währungsunion die nationale Fiskal- und Lohnpolitik verändert', in M. Höpner and A. Schäfer (eds), *Die Politische Ökonomie der europäischen Integration* (Frankfurt: Campus Verlag, 2009), 415–448.

[91] See Schubert, n. 84 at 60–61, 79.

Title X in FEU Treaty (ex Articles 141–142 of Chapter One in EC Treaty) introduce basic rules for equal pay for work of equal value, Title XI (Articles 162–164) of FEU Treaty (ex Chapter Two [Articles 146–148] of EC Treaty) is devoted to the Social Fund. Title XII FEU Treaty (ex Chapter Three EC Treaty) deals with educational and vocational training. The major legal bases for powers of legislation in the field of social policy are laid down in the first provisions of Title X (Articles 151–156) of FEU Treaty (ex Chapter One Articles 136–140 of EC Treaty). Substantially, they reflect what used to be, prior to its incorporation by the Amsterdam Treaty, the Protocol on Social Policy that had been signed by all eleven Member States (with the exception of the United Kingdom) upon the conclusion of the Maastricht Treaty.[92]

The Union's competence is limited in four respects.

First, certain issues of social policy are explicitly excluded from the purview of Union competence, such as the right of association and the regulation of strikes and lockouts (Article 153[5] FEU Treaty (ex 137[5] EC Treaty)).[93] The Fundamental Rights Charter has done nothing to alter this fact.[94]

Second, most of the competences are of a complementary kind,[95] which means that the enactment of legislation is explicitly excluded and Union action restricted to encouraging cooperation among Member States or to the setting of incentive measures (Article 153[2][a] FEU Treaty (ex 137[2][a] EC Treaty)).

Third, where the Union has legislative competence, for example, as regards health and safety at work, working conditions, social security, and social protection of workers, it is restricted to laying down, by means of directives, 'minimum requirements for gradual implementation' (Article 153[2][a] FEU Treaty (ex 137[2][a] EC Treaty)).

Fourth, certain matters remain the prerogative of unanimous decision-making in the Council (e.g., protection from dismissal) unless the Council decides, unanimously again, to submit the matter to the ordinary legislative procedure. Where social security and social protection of workers are concerned, no such move is possible (Article 153[2] FEU Treaty (ex 137[2] EC Treaty)).

The social policy legislation which had been adopted on the Union level is a patchwork of regulations that were borne out of initiatives made in the 1970s and late 1980s. It is widely acknowledged that the legislation, taken as a whole, lacks a coherent design.[96] Much of the legislation bears the imprint of waves of social

[92] The incorporation process was impressively complex, to say the least. For a very helpful sketch, see C. Barnard, 'Flexibility and Social Policy', in G. de Búrca and J. Scott (eds), *Constitutional Change in the EU: From Uniformity to Flexibility?* (Oxford: Hart Publishing, 2000), 198–217.

[93] In the eyes of the ECJ, this does not mean that the exercise of the right to engage in industrial action is not subject to constraints by either freedom of establishment or freedom to provide services. See, as regards the former, *Viking*, n. 80, para. 40, and, as regards the latter, *Laval*, n. 61, para. 93.

[94] The Fundamental Rights Charter does not extend Union competence (Article 51[2] of the Charter). See also Barnard, n. 5 at 116.

[95] For a description of the nature of complementary competence, see A. von Bogdandy and J. Bast, 'The European Union's Vertical Order of Competences: The Current Law and Proposals for Its Reform' (2002) 39 *Common Market Law Review* 227–268, at 249.

[96] See C. Barnard, 'EC "Social" Policy', in P. P. Craig and G. de Búrca (eds), *The Evolution of EU Law* (Oxford: Oxford University Press, 1999), 479–511 at 496.

legislation that were set off in order to put a more social face on the Common Market.[97] The existing incoherence is aggravated by the fact that since the conclusion of the Amsterdam Treaty, new players began to occupy the field, namely, the 'social partners'[98] who have to be consulted by the Commission before they may submit a proposal (Article 154[2] FEU Treaty (ex 138[2] EC Treaty)) or on whose initiative collective agreements can be given *erga omnes* effect by a Council decision (Article 155[2] FEU Treaty (ex 139[2] EC Treaty)).[99] Evidently, in the face of diverse national social policy legislation and divergent standards of industrial relations,[100] unified social legislation is next to impossible to attain. Harmonization appears to be feasible only at the cost of numerous exceptions and a great measure of variability.[101] As a result, legal instruments have become increasingly complex and difficult to comprehend. This experience has given rise to—notably in the context of the new employment title (Title IX, Articles 145–150 FEU Treaty (ex Title VIII, Articles 125–130 EC Treaty))[102]—the use of a softer law governance mechanism.

8. Social and Nowhere to go: the Problem-solving Gap

The process of domestication exercises a well-known feedback that has been famously described, at least in part, by Scharpf as the 'joint decision trap'[103]. More generally, it means that in certain key areas, cooperation among States on the European level is likely to encounter obstacles and lead to suboptimal solutions

[97] See Barnard, n. 96 at 482–483. For a similar assessment with regard to the social legislation prior to the adoption of the Lisbon agenda, see M. Daly, 'Whither Social Policy? An Account and Assessment of Developments in the Lisbon Social Inclusion Process' (2007) 37 *Journal of Social Policy* 1–19 at 2–3.

[98] The social partners are composed of ETUC, Eurocadres/CEC on the part of labour and UNICE, CEEP and UEAPME on the part of management. On the role played by the social partners and the problems posed with regard to their 'representativity', see, for example, C. Barnard, 'The Social Partners and the Governance Agenda' (2002) 8 *European Law Journal* 80–101.

[99] The Directive on parental leave goes back to initial decision-making following this route. See Barnard, n. 96 at 485.

[100] My recognition of disparity and diversity may be tainted with optimism. According to more pessimistic observers, the systems on industrial relations are drifting everywhere into the direction of mere 'voluntarism'. See W. Streeck, 'Neo-Voluntarism: A New Social Policy Regime?' (1995) 1 *European Law Journal* 31–59.

[101] This, at any rate, seems to have been the lesson of the Working Time Directive. See Barnard, n. 96 at 488–489. The Working Time Directive has been criticized for both its rigidity and its flexibility. It is rigid in choosing 48 hours as the maximum working week, 11 hours per 24-hour period as daily rest period, and a maximum of 8 hours as setting the ceiling for night work. It is inexplicable, of course, why compliance with those particular figures should in any given context be most conducive to the protection of safety and health. Flexibility is granted with regard to the reference period for the calculation of maximum hours and, in particular, for the negotiation of special arrangements between the social partners. In addition, the Directive leaves completely open the definition of key terms, such as, 'working time'.

[102] It had been introduced by the Treaty of Amsterdam (Articles 125–130 EC Treaty).

[103] See See F. W. Scharpf, 'The Joint Decision Trap: Lessons from German Federalism and European Integration' (1988) 88 *Public Administration* 239–278; ibid., 'Die Politikverflechtungsfalle: Europäische Integration und deutscher Föderalismus im Vergleich' (1985) 26 *Politische Vierteljahresschrift* 323–356.

or even to end in an impasse. Consensus on harmonizing legislation is generally difficult to attain. Should it be restricted, as has been once suggested by the Commission, to the harmonization of labour costs that derive from social security taxation and employment regulation? This would leave unaffected the playing field for regional pay differentials which reflect different levels of productivity.[104] But in which direction should harmonization move even in such a restricted sphere? Levelling up to the standards of social protection established in affluent societies, such as Germany or Austria, would give less wealthy Member States the raw end of the deal. As Scharpf explains:[105]

> [I]f social-welfare and environmental regulations were harmonized at, say, the Danish level, the international competitiveness of economies with lower productivity would be destroyed. If exchange rates were allowed to fall accordingly, the result would be higher domestic prices and, hence, impoverished consumers. If devaluation were ruled out (e.g. in a Monetary Union), the result would be de-industrialisation and massive job losses—just as they occurred in Eastern Germany when the relatively backward GDR economy was subjected to the full range of West German regulations under a single currency.

Contrariwise, the mere possibility of 'social dumping' is highly relevant, not just for law-making in the European Union but also for decisions affecting the allocation of resources by transnational businesses.[106] It has conferred on such businesses considerable bargaining power since they can threaten to relocate production to places where labour costs are cheaper.[107]

Following Scharpf, it is possible to pin down the areas where European problem-solving capacity cannot emerge even if there were no limits to Union jurisdiction: social policy, industrial relations, and the taxation of business profits and capital incomes. More precisely, it affects industrial relations regulations that are believed to interfere with managerial prerogatives or to reduce the flexibility of the labour market; or laws that raise the costs of production or increase the reservation wages for workers, the taxation of mobile factors of production, of capital incomes, and of the income of internationally mobile professionals.[108] In these areas, European integration creates a problem-solving gap,[109] which arises as a consequence of

[104] See Barnard n. 96 at 501.

[105] See F. Scharpf, *Governing in Europe: Effective and Democratic?* (Oxford: Oxford University Press, 1999), 79.

[106] Barnard refers to the matter as 'wage dumping' in the context of private economic decision-making. See Barnard, n. 96 at 503.

[107] This is the true social reality of 'social dumping'. It is manifest in greater bargaining power. See C. Barnard, 'Regulating Competitive Federalism in the European Union? The Case of EU Social Policy', in J. Shaw (ed.), *Social Law and Policy in an Evolving European Union* (Oxford: Hart Publishing, 2000), 49–69, at 63–64.

[108] See also C. Offe, 'Demokratie und Wohlfahrtsstaat: Eine europäische Regimeform unter dem Stress der europäischen Integration', in W. Streeck (ed.), *Internationale Wirtschaft, nationale Demokratie: Herausforderungen für die Demokratietheorie* (Frankfurt: Campus Verlag, 1998), 99–136.

[109] The first to have discovered and, indeed, welcomed the problem-solving gap in a transnational context was Friedrich August von Hayek who believed that, owing to the absence of common sympathies, a federal 'suprastate' would lack the political clout to adopt market-intervening and market-correcting policies. See F. A. Hayek, *Individualism and Economic Order* (Chicago, IL: University of Chicago Press, 1948) 255–272.

profound conflicts of economic interests among national governments. I shall return to the reasons for stalemate below. It is worth noting, at this point, that the policy areas affected are also the areas essential to the existence and justification of the democratic welfare state.[110] I add that the expansion of the legislative procedure to new areas of public policy did nothing to alleviate the problem; indeed, the increasing influence of the European Parliament extends a veto power to new groups of stakeholders.[111]

Not surprisingly, the only bypass that the Union has found in order to overcome its problem-solving gap is the soft Open Method of Coordination, which is substantially often leaning towards neoliberal solutions.[112]

9. Explaining the Turn to Employment

If the observations above are correct, then social policy remains in core areas a domestic affair. At the same time, it is severely challenged by the constitutional constraints of free movement, competition law, and Monetary Union. Since the Union can neither *de jure* nor de facto take the helm, it should not come as a surprise that it basically tries to assist Member States in one area that is traditionally the focus of residual liberal social policy, namely combating poverty.[113] The issue has been addressed, however, from the perspective of facilitating participation in social life and therefore approached under the broader heading of combating social exclusion (and invigorating 'inclusion').[114]

In a similar vein, the Union has become more strongly engaged in coordinating and improving national employment policy. Overstating the point a bit, European social policy has found a new core in employment policy. Its rise is actually a symptom of the problem created by integration, in particular by the demands of fiscal discipline.[115] If neither traditional means of sheltering national industries nor deficit spending are legitimate means of public policy, then the 'flexibilization'[116] of

[110] See F. W. Scharpf, 'Democratic Legitimacy under Conditions of Regulatory Competition: Why Europe Differs from the United States', in K. Nicolaidis and R. Howse (eds), *The Federal Vision* (Oxford: Oxford University Press, 2001), pp. 355–374, at 362. Scharpf also explains, ibid. at 356, that in Europe democratic legitimacy is much more closely associated with the social welfare state than in the United States.

[111] See Scharpf, n. 110 at 361.

[112] See Leibfried and Obinger, n. 88 at 21–22.

[113] See, most recently, the announcement of a 'flagship initiative', the 'European Platform against Poverty' in European Commission, 'Europe 2020: A Strategy for Smart, Sustainable and Inclusive Growth' COM(2010) 2020 at 17–18.

[114] Remarkably, facilitating 'inclusion' has been downgraded from its rank of a central goal of the Lisbon strategy in the wake of the interim Kok report. See Daly, n. 97 at 7.

[115] For interesting observations in this respect, see D. Ashiagbor, 'EMU and the Shift in the European Labour Law Agenda: From "Social Policy" to "Employment Policy"' (2001) 7 *European Law Journal* 311–330.

[116] What such 'flexibilization' means is adequately captured by Barnard. From the vantage point of the supply side it means numerical (e.g., fixed-term contracts), work time (e.g., switches from full to part-time work), and functional (e.g., shifts of tasks) flexibility. Seen from the supply side this appears to implicate the increase in temporary employment and permanent re-skilling. See C. Barnard,

'rigid' labour markets seems to present itself as the only available alternative to decrease spending and to raise the tax yield.[117] A successful employment policy is a pressing need of every Member State. Even here, the promise seems to lie in liberalization. This is the Union's tune.[118] All that the Union had to do in this situation was to insert itself[119] and to reverse the thrust of traditional social policy, including its own, by pursuing employment policy in lieu of other social policy goals.[120] This also provided the Union with a welcome opportunity to reap a legitimacy rent. In the eyes of the public, creating more jobs for European citizens is no less, maybe even more, important than attenuating the democracy deficit.[121]

The new social policy approach of the EU emerged in the mid 1990s.[122] Its emphasis lies almost exclusively on the vexing unemployment problem.[123] The exigency of unemployment policy should not come as a surprise. Most of the Member States of the Union have been, until recently, Keynesian national welfare states.[124] As has been pointed out by Offe,[125] the social system of states of this type comprises four layers, which give rise to a feedback loop in the relation between the first and the fourth.

First, the state provides basic ground rules that facilitate access to the labour market and protects the health and safety of workers.

'Flexibility and Social Policy', in G. de Búrca and J. Scott (eds), *Constitutional Change in the EU: From Uniformity to Flexibility?* (Oxford: Hart Publishing, 2000), 197–216 at 198.

[117] Aside from the fact that lowering or abandoning corporate taxes presents a means of attracting businesses. But this, again, adversely affects the tax yield.

[118] See S. Deakin and H. Reed, 'The Contested Meaning of Labour Market Flexibility', in J. Shaw (ed.), *Social Law and Policy in an Evolving European Union* (Oxford: Hart, 2000), 71–102.

[119] I should mention that employment policy, in particular with the aim of flexibilization, has been on the agenda of the EU even prior to the Amsterdam Treaty, in fact, since the Essen European Council of 1994. It was preceded by the ominous Commission communications. See E. Szyszczak, 'The New Paradigm for Social Policy: A Virtuous Circle?' (2001) 38 *Common Market Law Review* 1125–1170 at 1134–1135; Ashiagbor, n. 115 at 322, 326.

[120] The story is more complex, of course. In a White Paper on growth (*White Paper on Growth, Competitiveness, and Employment: The Challenges and Ways Forward into the 21st Century*, COM[93] 700 final) the Commission envisaged certain demand-side measures to create more jobs, such as investments in major transport or telecommunication projects. This part of the programme was rejected by the Member States who were concerned that the necessary centralization of expenditure and competence for employment policy would impinge on their national sovereignty. Moreover, in anticipation of Monetary Union it was feared that an expansive fiscal policy would give rise to inflation. See Ashiagbor, n. 115 at 320–321. See also C. Barnard and S. Deakin, 'A Year of Living Dangerously? EC Social Rights, Employment Policy, and EMU', in B. Towers and M. Terry (eds) *Industrial Relations Journal European Annual Review 1998* (Oxford: Blackwell, 1999), 355–372 at 356. As a result, what the Member States are left with is their national employment policies, conducted under the supervision of Commission and Council within the framework created by the so-called Open Method of Coordination.

[121] See Ashiagbor, n. 115 at 314.

[122] See E. Szyszczak, 'The New Paradigm for Social Policy: A Virtuous Circle?' (2001) 38 *Common Market Law Review* 1125–1170 at 1134–1135.

[123] See Szyszczak, n. 122 at 1132–1135.

[124] For a reconstruction of this type of state from the perspective of political economy, see B. Jessop, *The Future of the Capitalist State* (Cambridge: Polity Press, 2002), at 58–61.

[125] On the following, see C. Offe, 'The European Model of "Social" Capitalism: Can it Survive European Integration?' (2003) 11 *Journal of Political Philosophy* 437–469 at 451–453.

Second, the viability of the status of employees is bolstered through arrangements concerning the security of workers outside and in the event of the loss of work. Disability, sickness, unemployment insurance, and a public pension system guarantee wage replacement in the event that the worker is unable to earn a living. A similar role is played by family allowances.

Third, a system of industrial relations, however broadly or narrowly conceived, supports workers in defending their income. It is expressive of solidarity that accounts for a more compressed wage-scale (with redistribution among different strata of the workforce).[126]

Fourth, the Keynesian welfare state adopts a set of fiscal, trade-related and monetary policies to promote and secure full employment, upon which the viability of the three preceding layers critically depends. Income earned in wages is indispensable not only to reproduce the tax revenues needed to finance 'social insurance' but also to sustain a full or high level of employment itself.[127] If it were not for a high level of employment, a critical mass of unemployed workers would undercut compromises hammered out in collective bargaining by agreeing to work for lower wages or by accepting atypical forms of employment from which little or no taxes can be siphoned off into social insurance schemes. Evidently, systemic causation is at work here. Just as much as the viability of the arrangements comprising the first three layers depends on what is accomplished on the fourth, the success of the latter turns on the accessibility of the labour market, the integrity of public insurance schemes and the reasonableness of the demands made on one another by social partners.

The limits set to European social policy by the legal structure of European economic integration explain why only the *first* and the *fourth* layer of existing national social systems can be affected by the Union.[128] As we have seen above, in a Union which is characterized not only by a variety of systems of social protection and different arrangements regarding industrial relations but also by disparities in the respective levels of social protection and productivity, no consensus can be reached over whether scaling up or scaling down national standards defines the path leading to a common Union system. There is not even the prospect of reaching a settlement on some 'middle ground', for such middle ground would be perceived as being either 'too high' or 'too low', depending on the country's perspective. All that the Union is in a position to do is to influence market access conditions and to create a moderately healthy and safe working environment,[129] in particular, as the redistributive impact of health and safety measures is not so easily perceived.[130]

[126] On the latter, see Streeck, n. 54.

[127] See Jessop, n. 124 at 79.

[128] See also Offe, n. 125 at 457–459.

[129] See F. W. Scharpf, 'Politische Optionen im vollendeten Binnenmarkt', in K. Jachtenfuchs and B. Kohler-Koch (eds), *Europäische Integration* (Stuttgart: Leske + Buderich, 1996), 109–122 at 117–119.

[130] On the (purported) redistributive neutrality of regulatory policy, see G. Majone, 'Redistributive und sozialregulative Politik', in K. Jachtenfuchs and B. Kohler-Koch (eds), *Europäische Integration* (Stuttgart: Leske + Budrich, 1996), 225–247 at 225.

Roughly stated, the Union has already 'absorbed', and is always ready to absorb more, Member State competence where the first layer of social policy is concerned. The assimilation of social policy to the mindset of market creation is part of that process (see section 4 above). Since there is next to nothing (where competence and the lack of consensus are concerned) that can be done with regard to the second and the third layer, the European integration process gives rise to an *inverse federal structure*.[131] While the regulation of market access is elevated to a transnational level, the insurance against the attendant social risks and collection of the revenues for their successful management (e.g., taxation) remains a national affair.[132] As a result, a precarious equilibrium needs to be maintained between increased competitive pressures, on the one hand, and sustaining the national welfare state, on the other. The revenues needed to that end presuppose the taxation of wages. Consequently, 'employment policy' becomes a joint European concern since raising the level of employment is indeed in the self-interest of every single Member State.[133]

This shift was reconfirmed by the mid-term review of the Lisbon Strategy, the so-called *Kok Report*, which stated clearly that: 'having more people in employment is the best way of safeguarding the social and financial sustainability and further development of European welfare systems.'[134] Paradoxically, even though the shift to employment policy presupposes the prior existence of a Keynesian welfare state and is, in this respect, path-dependent, the employment strategy is substantively not at all likely to restore a Keynesian equilibrium. Rather, it is part of a process of readjustment in whose course European social systems are recalibrated in order to be sustainable in a more competitive environment.

10. The Dual Economy: Competitive Solidarity and Liberalization

What I called, following Scharpf, the inverse structure of European federalism is, indeed welcomed, by champions of economic liberalism. They applaud overcoming the influence of national sympathy or special regional interest, for it gives rise to less government for the simple reason that there is less agreement on policy among the constituent units. No bailouts for ailing industries will be forthcoming when

[131] On the 'converse pyramid of EU social policy' see B. Fitzpatrick, 'Converse Pyramids and the EU Social Constitution', in J. Shaw (ed.), *Social law and Policy in an Evolving European Union* (Oxford: Hart Publishing, 2000), 303–324.

[132] See F. W. Scharpf, 'Democratic Legitimacy under Conditions of Regulatory Competition: Why Europe Differs from the United States', in K. Nicolaidis and R. Howse (eds), *The Federal Vision: Legitimacy and Levels of Governance in the United States and the European Union* (Oxford: Oxford University Press, 2001), 355–374 at 366–368.

[133] For a historical account of the shift of orientation from social policy to employment policy, see Ashiagbor, n. 115 at 314–326.

[134] See Report from the High Level Group chaired by Wim Kok, *Facing the Challenge: The Lisbon Strategy for Growth and Employment*, http://ec.europa.eu/research/evaluations/pdf/archive/fp6-evidence-base/evaluation_studies_and_reports/evaluation_studies_and_reports_2004/the_lisbon_ strategy _for_growth_and_employment__report_from_the_high_level_group.pdf accessed 23 December 2010.

the taxpayers do not perceive the recipients to belong to 'their' people.[135] Moreover, once national societies are embedded in an integrated market, they experience incentives to affect their comparative advantage even by downgrading their level of social protection. Before long, their respective social systems are likely to erode and to converge on a minimal and residual level.

The inverse structure of European federalism is even more clearly revealed in the case of Monetary Union. The common currency is supposed to be stabilized without backing by a central authority,[136] which, aside from enforcing the necessary fiscal discipline, would also be in the position to mitigate the unequal impact of a unified monetary policy through transfers and public investments. Ordinarily, it is widely assumed that a common currency—given its importance for the totality of social and economic policy—would presuppose some 'political' union.[137] This is not the case in the European Union, which explains the cumbersome need to coordinate concerted efforts to help Member States to help themselves.

The European economy is therefore characterized by a remarkable dualism. The Member States are responsible, invariably owing to voter reprisal, for the economic performance of the *organized national economy*[138] over which they wield traditionally a modicum of public power. They are the trustees of 'competitive solidarity'[139] on the basis of which governments support, as much as they can, their national constituencies to perform successfully in transnational environments. The commitments of competitive solidarity become all the more urgent in the face of the combined domesticating and disarming effects of both the internal market and Monetary Union. Not surprisingly, issues that could or maybe even should be a matter of partisan contest at the European level are submerged and dealt with by the groups that participate in corporatist structures at the national level. While the position of trade unions is weakened in a transnational economy they show more readiness to support their received national models of organizing capitalist production.[140] In such a situation, a political conflict marked by a significant right–left distinction does not emerge. This explains why the *liberalizing economy* associated with European Union policies does not encounter any other resistance than that which can be easily dismissed as 'nationalistic' and hence as backward-looking.

135 See Hayek, n. 109 at 262.

136 See Schubert, n. 84 at 42.

137 See, most recently, P. Krugman, 'The Euro Trap' *The New York Times* 30 April 2010.

138 I use the term 'organized economy' in the sense used by Höpner and Schäfer. It refers to three features of European market economies that are strongly embedded in various forms of social cooperation: (1) the existence of non-market based relations between businesses and stakeholders (e.g., workforce representation on corporate boards); (2) a relatively high degree of public influence on private investment or purchasing decisions; and (3) a high level of politically calibrated redistribution of market effects. See M. Höpner and A. Schäfer, 'Eine neue Phase der europäischen Integration: Legitimitätsdefizite europäischer Liberalisierungspolitik', in: M. Höpner and A. Schäfer (eds), *Die politische Ökonomie der europäischen Integration* (Frankfurt: Campus Verlag, 2008), 129–156 at 130."ll"

139 See W. Streek, 'Competitive Solidarity—Rethinking the "European Social Model"', http://www.mpi-fg-koeln.mpg.de/pu/workpap/wp99-8/wp99-8.html.

140 See Höpner and Schäfer, n. 27 at 35–37.

The liberalizing economy with its domesticating, assimilating, and disarming effects thereby steers clear of contestation on ideological grounds.

11. The Rise of Authoritarian Liberalism

One may wonder whether this dual economy is not actually endorsed by the Member States. Arguably, they have the power to affect the precarious equilibrium between competitive solidarity and increasing liberalization.

As Höpner and Schäfer have pointed out,[141] the plausibility of such an intergovernmental view on the European economy is increasingly cast into doubt by the behaviour of the main movers of the supranational project, Commission and Court. Generally, interpreting the doings of these institutions as serving the mere Member States' interests presupposes some rather sophisticated account of why it is the case that both remain, in spite of a remarkable degree of independence, the agents of the latter.[142] Usually, an account of this type involves conceiving of their powers as a *package* whose exercise *as a whole and on the whole* benefits all Member States. The work of both institutions avoids externalities and reduces decision-making costs. Respecting their agency lends credibility to a long-term commitment to cooperation, which avoids the pitfalls associated with cumbersome interstate negotiation. Commission and Court are in a position to fill in the gaps left in basic agreements and to push for Pareto improvement which would not come to pass if it were not for their delegated powers. Consequently, the partial loss of common control is deemed to be offset by efficiency gains.

For at least two reasons, the intergovernmental perspective is increasingly difficult to defend. First, the agency perspective can scarcely be sustained where the Commission acts strategically in order to secure the partisan support of some Member States against others.[143] What is more, it is next to impossible for the Member States to control the ECJ. Revising the Court's divinations of primary law (Treaties and unwritten fundamental principles) is scarcely an option in the face of the consent needed for Treaty amendments (Article 48 [6] EU Treaty). Politically, Member States show very little support for one another when countries suffer defeat before the Court. They do not, that is, join in an effort to formulate platforms of resistance.[144] The prospects for an *ex ante* control of judicial behaviour are not better. It is, in particular, difficult to influence the behaviour of judges through party affiliation since the determining factor of the Court's jurisprudence

[141] See Höpner and Schäfer, n. 138 at 130–134.

[142] See, for example, M. A. Pollack, *The Engines of European Integration: Delegation, Agency, and Agenda Setting in the EU* (Oxford: Oxford University Press, 2003).

[143] See the example of the takeover Directive, discussed in M. Höpner and A. Schäfer, 'A New Phase of European Integration: Organized Capitalism in Post-Ricardian Europe' (2007) 07/4 *MPIfG Discussion Paper* 15–17.

[144] See F. W. Scharpf, 'Individualrechte gegen nationale Solidarität', in M. Höpner and A. Schäfer (eds), *Die politische Ökonomie der europäischen Integration* (Frankfurt: Campus, 2008), 89–99 at 97.

seems to lie in an institutional ethos that embraces as its chief virtues creativity and innovation.[145]

Second, and more importantly, Court and Commission have opted substantively for policies that are clearly at odds with the institutional and moral commitments of a number of core Member States. Liberalization efforts by the Commission, such as the service or the takeover directives,[146] would have in their original form impacted negatively on countries with higher social standards and relatively more organized economies.[147] Moreover, the ECJ has in several rulings concerning company[148] and labour law[149] accorded transnational economic activity relatively greater weight than received mechanisms of protecting the interests of creditors or labour, such as collective action. In each of these cases, the Court defied conventional standards governing the exposition of law[150] and rather lent its support to liberalization on the basis of quite 'creative' readings of its own case law.[151] Against this background, it is fair to say that the Union has been witness to a cunning recrudescence of authoritarian liberalism. The designation, which was first used by the German public law scholar Hermann Heller in order to describe the ideological thrust of German legislation by emergency decree towards the end of the Weimar Republic,[152] stands for the constitutionally questionable pursuit of laissez-faire objectives from above. The pursuit of sustaining a 'healthy economy'[153] rises above the netherworld of political bickering and shifts into an authoritarian, indeed, administrative mode.[154] The result is, in the words of Höpner and Schäfer, 'administered convergence towards liberal market capitalism'.[155]

[145] See M. Höpner, 'Usurpation statt Delegation: Wie der EuGH die Binnenmarktintegration radikalisiert und warum er politischer Kontrolle bedarf' (2008) 08/12 *MPIfG Discussion Paper* at 7, 26–29; see also my 'The Emancipation of Legal Dissonance', in H. Koch, K. Hagel-Sørensen, U. Haltern, and J. H. H. Weiler (eds), Europe: The New Legal Realism (Copenhagen: DJØF Publishing, 2010), 679–713.

[146] For an account of the legislative history, see Höpner and Schäfer, n. 143 at 12–18.

[147] See Höpner and Schäfer, n. 27 at 20.

[148] See Case C-212/97, *Centros Ltd* v. *Erhvervs- og Selskabsstyrelsen* [1999] ECR I-1459; Case C-208/00, *Überseering BV* v. *Nordic Construction* [2002] ECR I-9919.

[149] See *Viking*, n. 80; *Laval*, n. 61; Case C-346/06 *Dirk Rüffert* v. *Land Niedersachsen*, 3 April 2008.

[150] For an analysis, see F. Rödl, 'Transnationale Lohnkonkurrenz: ein neuer Eckpfeiler der "sozialen" Union?', in A. Fischer-Lescano, F. Rödl, and C. U. Schmid (eds), *Europäische Gesellschaftsverfassung* (Baden-Baden: Nomos, 2009), pp. 145–160.

[151] This is manifest, for example, in how the Court turned the horizontal effect of fundamental freedoms from an instrument that was supposed to protect the interest of labour into an instrument that can be used against it. See my 'Idealization, De-politicization and Economic Due Process: System Transition in the European Union', in B. Iancu (ed.), *The Law/Politics Distinction in Contemporary Public Law Adjudication* (Utrecht: eleven international publishing, 2009), 137–167 at 148–151.

[152] See H. Heller, 'Autoritärer Liberalismus?' (1933), repr. in *Gesammelte Schriften*, vol. 2 (Leiden: A. W. Sijthoff, 1971), 643–653.

[153] See C. Schmitt, 'Starker Staat und gesunde Wirtschaft' (1932), repr. in *Staat, Großraum, Nomos: Arbeiten aus den Jahren 1916–1969*, ed. by G. Maschke (Berlin: Duncker & Humblot, 1995), 71–85.

[154] I have argued before that this authoritarian mode is not completely alien to European integration. See A. Somek, 'Authoritarian Constitutionalism: Austrian Constitutional Doctrine 1933 to 1938 and its Legacy', in C. Joerges and N. Singh Ghaleigh (eds), *Darker Legacies of Law in Europe: The Shadow of National Socialism and Fascism over Europe and its Legal Traditions* (Oxford: Hart, 2003), 361–387, 381–387.

[155] Höpner and Schäfer, n. 138 at 137.

12. Substantive Economic Due Process

From a jurisprudential perspective, the shift towards authoritarian liberalism is revealed in a certain interpretation of fundamental freedoms, in particular in the case of freedom of services or freedom of establishment.[156]

As is well known, fundamental freedoms have hitherto been constructed in two different ways. Understood as *prohibitions on discrimination on grounds of nationality*, they protect against unequal treatment by Member States pursuing protectionist goals. By contrast, as *prohibitions on obstacles to transnational mobility*, they help to remove the relative disadvantages that arise for transnational commerce as a result of the coexistence of various national regulatory regimes. Differences between and among the laws of various States are an enduring, even if not logically necessary, feature of a system of nation states. They impact adversely on commerce when goods that can be sold in one Member State cannot be marketed in another owing to a difference in product standards. The obstacle may emerge without a trace of protectionist objectives.

Traditionally, the obstacle-based approach to freedom of movement has focused on the difference between a home state and a host state, with the home state paradigmatically being the country from which a good originates. Recently, the Court has radicalized this approach in a manner which can be described as *transnational substantive economic due process.*

The expression 'substantive economic due process' is borrowed from American constitutional history. It stands for the strict protection of 'liberty' in the due process clause of the Fourteenth Amendment in support of economic rather than social objectives.[157] Substantive economic due process was the hallmark of the Supreme Court's jurisprudence during the so-called *Lochner* area, which has its name after the infamous decision by the Supreme Court in which it struck down maximum working-hour legislation on the ground of an unconstitutional interference with freedom of contract.[158]

In the European transnational context, substantive economic due process is characterized by three features.

First, burdens on an economic activity are deemed to be problematic against the baseline of wherever an economic activity can be legally initiated. The relation between home state and host state has become increasingly interchangeable in that nationals of one Member State are deemed to be entitled, as a matter of European Union law, to constitute an economic activity pursuant to the laws of another merely in order to have set aside the more stringent laws at home.[159] Once an

[156] I have attempted to sketch this development previously in the article quoted in n. 151 and in my analysis 'The Argument from Transnational Effects I: Representing Outsiders through Freedom of Movement' (2010) 16 *European Law Journal* 315–344.

[157] For an introduction, see B. Ackerman, *We the People*, vol. 1: *Foundations* (Cambridge, MA: Harvard University Press, 1991), at 62–67.

[158] See *Lochner* v. *State of New York*, 198 U.S. 45 (1905).

[159] This has been asserted as a right by the ECJ in *Centros*, n. 148 at para 26.

economic activity has been initiated legally in one Member State and encounters obstacles in another, the obstacles are subject to challenge. This is true of the establishment of companies outside of one's own Member State[160] as well as the attempt to benefit from less exacting labour standards through the reflagging of a vessel.[161] Indeed, in certain instances, the ECJ has come to read fundamental freedoms as essentially encompassing the right to create corridors for economic activities pursuant to the law of their constitution. It thereby encourages European citizens to avail themselves of the most cost-effective regulatory background.

This situation seems to give rise to regulatory competition among the Member States. But this is not what is precisely the case.

Second, once the full set of fundamental freedoms becomes recalibrated from a substantive economic due process perspective, these freedoms take aim at the full plethora of social legislation. Simplifying matters a bit, it can be said that while the paradigmatic target of the obstacle approach used to be the comparatively more restrictive product characteristic, economic due process focuses on whatever 'absorbs' markets into the 'social system'.[162] It serves, thus understood, as a disembedding mechanism. The shift of focus on the regulatory environment *as a whole* moves the interaction of the trustees of competitive solidarity evermore strongly *beyond* mere regulatory competition.

In its purest form, regulatory competition involves the price mechanism. Governments experience through product prizes whether or not their laws are advantageous for their businesses. It is through this mechanism that they learn about a need to adapt. Freedom of movement makes it possible for companies to relocate, but it does not in principle directly affect national company laws.[163] Substantive economic due process, by contrast, gives rise to regulatory disarmament through the exercise of rights. It does not operate through prizes as an information-gathering mechanism, but rather through the harder channels of litigation. It results, where it succeeds, in setting aside national laws. Member States are no longer able to sustain their own regulatory environment for transnational commerce even if they were willing to bear the costs. They are exposed to the disarming effect of transnational economic due process.

Third, substantive economic due process is holistic in its sweep. The holism is manifest in two interrelated ways. To begin with, the Court's reasoning in *Viking*[164] and *Laval*[165] revealed a radically new interpretation of fundamental free-

[160] See, for example, Case C-167/01, *Kamer van Koophandel en Fabrieken voor Amsterdam* v. *Inspire Art Ltd*, 30 September 2003.

[161] See, as is well known, *Viking*, n. 80.

[162] See K. Polanyi, *The Great Transformation: The Political and Economic Origins of our Time* (Boston, MA: Beacon Press, 2001) at 71.

[163] Quite remarkably, the Delaware effect in the United States is based upon the 'full faith and credit' clause of the US Constitution, as a result of which states outside Delaware have to recognize companies that were registered in Delaware. This—important—exception does not alter the fact that ordinarily in a federal system regulatory competition does not directly affect the applicable laws of the states involved.

[164] See *Viking*, n. 80 at 36.

[165] See *Laval*, n. 61 at para. 98

doms that reverses the traditionally labour-friendly thrust of horizontal effect. Originally, in cases such as *Defrenne*,[166] *Walrave*,[167] or *Angonese*,[168] the horizontal effect of fundamental freedoms was neatly tied to protecting the interests of workers.[169] The new cases turned the spear of horizontal effect against trade union action, which is submitted to such stringent requirements of proportionality as though acts by trade unions were acts of public power.[170] Horizontal effect has now become an instrument that can be used even against internationally concerted trade union action, such as combating the reflagging practice at issue in *Viking*.[171]

In addition, the holism of transnational substantive economic due process is also manifest in what can be usefully referred to as the 'Schmidberger trap'. The latter was prepared for the Member States in the *Schmidberger* case,[172] in which the court was confronted with the question of whether Member States may have to permit interferences with fundamental freedoms on national constitutional grounds when persons rightfully exercise fundamental rights. The ECJ conceded interferences for this reason, however, by wavering—even more so in the *Omega Spielhallen* case[173]—between recognizing the *state's* responsibility for the protection of fundamental rights vis-à-vis fundamental freedoms,[174] on the one hand, and the application of Union's *own* fundamental rights standard, on the other. While the Court merely generally conceded in *Schmidberger*[175] that the protection of fundamental rights is a legitimate ground of restriction, *Viking*[176] and *Laval*[177] made it abundantly clear that it is the Union's fundamental rights standard which matters and not the level of protection deemed to be warranted by the law of the Member States' constitution. While this may already indicate for some Member States a levelling down of the applicable standard, in particular as regards the right of association and the right to strike, the Court also took it for granted that exercises of fundamental rights need to be justified as proportionate vis-à-vis fundamental freedoms and not the other way round. This direction of justification may explain

166 Case C-43/75, *Gabrielle Defrenne* v. *Société anonyme belge de navigation aérienne Sabena* [1976] ECR 455.

167 See Case C-36/74, *Walrave and Koch* [1974] ECR 1405.

168 See C-281/98, *Roman Angonese* v. *Cassa di Risparmio di Bolzano SpA* [2000] ECR I-4139.

169 See my analysis in n. 151 at 145–151.

170 On the absurdity of this move, see R. Rebhahn, 'Grundfreiheiten versus oder vor Streikrecht' (2008) 22 *Wirtschaftspolitische Blätter* 63–69.

171 See *Viking*, n. 80 at paras 88–89.

172 See Case C-112/00, *Eugen Schmidberger, Internationale Transporte und Planzüge* v. *Republik Österreich* [2003] ECR I-5659.

173 See Case C-36/02, *Omega Spielhallen- und Automatenaufstellungs-GmbH* v. *Oberbürgermeisterin der Bundesstadt Bonn* [2004] ECR I-9609. The Court rested undecidedly between absorbing the Member States' own fundamental rights standard (para. 34) and respecting legitimate differences with regard to the national level of protection (para. 38). Apparently, the matter was not settled among the judges themselves.

174 Such a recognition does not sell supremacy of EU law short, rather, it reasserts it, for recognizing the state's obligation to protect fundamental rights as a legitimate objective to interfere with freedoms is perfectly consistent with EU law and not at all comparable with a situation where Union law is reviewed on national fundamental rights grounds.

175 See *Schmidberger*, n. 172 at para. 71.

176 See *Viking*, n. 80 at para. 46.

177 See *Laval*, n. 61 at para. 94.

why the Court has no qualms about assimilating trade union action to the exercise of public power that is backed up by the use of force. Indeed, the formalism involved in the reasoning works like a Freudian slip. In the liberal imagery created by the Court, acts by trade unions are just as inimical to economic liberty as the coercive power of the state.

13. Renationalization

From a historical perspective, cases such as *Viking*, *Laval*, and *Rüffert* are deeply disturbing. If one thing had been taken for granted by the founders of the European Economic Community then it was that transnational wage competition is to be avoided.[178] What had been just recently overcome on the national level through the establishment of social legislation and corporate cooperation was not to be undone transnationally. Of course, under the auspices of authoritarian liberalism, one may wonder whether there are good reasons of social justice to have workers from low-wage countries enjoy their competitive advantage over workers from high-wage countries, not least because the latter are more likely than the former to benefit from a more tightly knit social safety net.

Upon closer inspection, however, it turns out that this perspective is not at all as plausible as it may appear.[179] It is at least open to debate why transnational economic integration should come at the expense of the least qualified workers in high-wage economies while the larger share of the benefits goes to those with higher earnings and to the bulk of consumers at large. In addition, wage competition cannot be reconciled with the European Economic Community's original objective to bring about the approximation of wages and working conditions among Member States. If at all, it is more likely to support the levelling down that is embraced by the likes of Hayek. Finally, since wage competition leads to a redistribution of work from high earners to lower earners, it most definitely benefits businesses. The overall distributive effect is not at all in the interests of workers as a group (in old-fashioned parlance: as a 'class'), but feeds into the overall trend of widening the gap of inequality in Europe.[180]

The irony of this development is that while domestication, assimilation, and disarmament have their source in Europe's liberalizing economy, the opposition that it engenders is most likely to wear the vestiges of loyalties to national traditions. It is to be expected that instead of healthy right–left controversies over the course of the European economy this process will encourage further drift among different national cultures of production and distribution.[181] In the social policy field, at any rate, the Union has done quite a bit to invite opposition to European integration.

[178] The basic expectation had been that wage differentials would reflect productivity differentials. See Rödl, n. 150 at 147.

[179] See ibid. at 150–151.

[180] See Alber, n. 32 at 219.

[181] See M. Höpner and A. Schäfer, 'Grenzen der Integration—wie die Intensivierung der Wirtschaftsintegration zur Gefahr für die politische Integration wird' (2010) *Integration* 2–30 at 19–20.

14. Conclusion: the Place of Anti-discrimination Law

I hope that this brief sketch of the broader context of Union social policy helps to understand why European anti-discrimination law has been able to attain a prominent place. Owing to a lack of competence and a persistent problem-solving gap, there is not much else left for the Union to do. Moreover, the anti-discrimination agenda is consistent with the employment strategy.

Both reasons, however, cannot alter the fact that anti-discrimination law is of no avail when it comes to resolving the social question that arises *specifically* in a transnational context. It is the question whether the antagonism between countries with higher and lower degrees of market independence—an antagonism that is fuelled by increasing disarmament—might jeopardize the cohesion of a transnational system. Simply put, anti-discrimination policies do not solve the problem that is *intrinsic* to transnational integration with an inverse federal structure. It merely addresses a problem that exists in more than one national system *and* removes the potential disadvantages suffered by states that adopt anti-discrimination legislation vis-à-vis others that do not. It is to be expected, indeed, that the prominent place occupied by anti-discrimination laws and policies detracts attention from the reproduction of divisions along national lines. Viewed from this perspective, they seem more like *idols* of supranationality rather than recipes for long-term success.

With an eye to the analysis that follows in the subsequent chapters, I would like to summarize the major points of the preceding discussion.

First, against the backdrop of domestication, anti-discrimination law represents the one area of social policy where the Union clearly has the power to adopt legislation. In fact, it is the one field where Union law does not run up against divergent national traditions and where it is likely to instigate progress.

Second, anti-discrimination law is congruent with the Union's more general commitment to bring about integration by means of market access. Anti-discrimination law extends the idea of market access from the transnational level of fundamental freedoms to the national level of horizontally effective fundamental rights. It creates opportunities for those who would have none owing to the persistence of widespread prejudice and stereotypes. The commitment to market access[182] explains how anti-discrimination law can be assimilated to the mindset of Union law.

Third, anti-discrimination law obviously lends itself to an amalgamation with the employment strategy. It is clearly congruent with the attainment of employment objectives.

Fourth, anti-discrimination policy can without difficulty accommodate other ways of attaining public policy objectives in addition to legislation. The mixing of 'hard' and 'soft' measures has recently become a more general feature of Union

[182] For an articulation in the context of free movement of goods, see S. Weatherill, 'After *Keck*: Some Thoughts on how to Clarify the Clarification', (1996) 33 *Common Market Law Review*, 885–906; for a more general perspective, see Barnard and Deakin, n. 66.

policy. In the next chapter, I would like to explain how anti-discrimination law became enlisted to the pursuit of voluntary and communicative coordination strategies.

Fifth, the situation of the social welfare state in the European Union is characterized by an increasing shift from domestication to disarmament. It is associated with the rise of substantive economic due process at the transnational level.

Sixth, this shift explains the nature and the exigency of the social question in a transnational context. While at its most elementary level, the social question concerns freedom from want on the basis of reliable insurance against the risk of losing one's place in society, in a transnational context it concerns the antagonism that arises between and among national states owing to the impact of economic liberalization. It has its most visible manifestation in the challenge whether wage competition between employees located in different Member States should be embraced as part of the federal social agenda. From an egalitarian perspective, at any rate, there are strong reasons counselling against it. Moreover, endorsing antagonism between and among the national employees is likely to reinforce centrifugal forces and, hence, likely to undermine the integration project itself.

Seventh, anti-discrimination law is remarkably irrelevant to what is truly the social question in a transnational setting. On the contrary, it is consistent, even if not complicit, with the agenda of authoritarian liberalism to facilitate unimpeded market access.[183] Owing to its morally appealing outlook—who should be in favour of discriminating against Muslims or homosexuals?—it is likely to find widespread support. This appeal may distract attention from, and even conceal, deeper structural problems. It would, indeed, play an ideological role if anti-discrimination law turned out to be normatively deficient.

The latter is, however, what the remaining chapters set out to prove.

[183] See M. Höpner, 'Warum betreibt der Europäische Gerichtshof Rechtsfortbildung? Die Politisierungshypothese' (2010) 10/2 *MPIfG Working Paper* at 6.

2

From Legislation to Discourse and Mobilization

1. Reviewing the History

Undoubtedly, the Union deserves credit for having advanced an approach to social policy that, had it not been for the Union, would have remained only of partial significance in Europe. For a long period of time, employment discrimination law has been the 'lonesome hero' of social policy in the EU.[1] Building on the relative success of sex discrimination law,[2] the Amsterdam Treaty introduced Article 19 FEU Treaty (ex 13 EC Treaty moved), laying the foundation to attain more comprehensive protection from discrimination in the future.[3] The Treaty of Nice supplied the Union with a special legal basis for the adoption of 'incentive measures' on the basis of the co-decision procedure (ex 251 EC Treaty) instead of unanimity in the Council, which is still needed for the adoption of new legislation. As an originally legally inconsequential document, the Fundamental Rights Charter had a great time of coming up with a more bountiful, however motley, assembly of

[1] For such a characterization of Article 157 FEU Treaty (ex 141 EC Treaty), see M. Poiares Maduro, 'Europe's Social Self: "The Sickness Unto Death"', in Jo Shaw (ed.), *Social Law and Policy in an Evolving European Union* (Oxford: Hart Publishing, 2000), 325–350; see also his 'We still Have not Found what we Have Been Looking for: The Balance between Economic Freedom and Social Rights in the EU', in P. Alston (ed.), *The EU and Human Rights* (Oxford: Oxford University Press, 1999), at 455.

[2] See Council Directive 75/117/EEC on equal pay for male and female workers [1975] OJ L 45/19; Council Directive 76/207/EEC on equal treatment with regard to access to employment, vocational training, promotion, and working conditions [1976] OJ L 39/40; Council Directive 97/80/EC on the burden of proof in cases of discrimination based on sex [1980] OJ L 14/6 amended by Directive 98/52/EC [1998] OJ L 205/66. For a more comprehensive overview, see C. Barnard, *EC Employment Law*, 3rd edn (Oxford: Oxford University Press, 2007), at 300–303. See also nn. 19–24 of the Introduction chapter of this book.

[3] For a careful construction of Article 19 FEU Treaty (ex 13 EC Treaty) which explains that the wording ('without prejudice to the other provisions of this Treaty and within the limits of the powers conferred by it upon the Community') indicates that Article 19 FEU Treaty (ex 13 EC Treaty) neither derogates from more special anti-discrimination provisions nor exceeds the material scope of the application of the Treaty, see M. Bell, *Anti-discrimination Law and the European Union* (Oxford: Oxford University Press, 2002), at 129–132. It should be borne in mind, in this context, that the 'scope' of negative integration, that is, the cases of discrimination relevant to Union law, may be broader than the competence to enact legislation ('positive integration').

forbidden grounds.[4] Finally, the now buried draft Constitutional Treaty listed in its Article 3 among the Union's major goals measures combating discrimination.

Article 19 FEU Treaty (ex 13 EC Treaty moved) provides Union anti-discrimination policy with a broad legal base.[5] Not only was it the basis for the adoption of the Framework,[6] the Race Directive,[7] and the Equal Treatment in Services Directive,[8] but it also helped to launch the supplementary action programme to combat discrimination.[9] The Race Directive, even though inheriting many concepts from the toolbox of sex equality, provided some inspiration for another reform in the gender discrimination area, namely, the so-called Equal Treatment Amendment Directive,[10] which introduced 'equality bodies'. In 2008, the Commission presented a proposal for legislation that would, in the eyes of the Commission, complete the legislative agenda.[11] This latest Directive would, by complementing the Framework Directive, prohibit all forms of discrimination and harassment on the grounds of religion or belief, disability, age, or sexual orientation beyond the workplace.[12]

The equality bodies introduced by the Amendment Directive are supposed to monitor compliance and to support victims of discrimination.[13] In a more recent

[4] Article 21(1) of the Charter of Fundamental Rights of the European Union states that any discrimination based on grounds such as sex, race, colour, ethnic or social origin, genetic features, language, religion or belief, political or any other opinion, membership of a national minority, property, birth, disability, age, or sexual orientation shall be prohibited. See OJ 2000 C 364/1.

[5] See M. Bell, 'Equality and Diversity: Anti-discrimination Law after Amsterdam', in J. Shaw (ed.), *Social Law and Policy in an Evolving European Union* (Oxford: Hart Publishing, 2000), 157–170.

[6] See Council Directive 2000/78/EC of 27 November 2000 establishing a general framework for equal treatment in employment and occupation [2000] OJ L 303. This directive is comprehensive. Not only does it include definitions of 'direct' and 'indirect' discrimination (Article 2/2), it also incorporates the basic principles governing age discrimination (Article 6) and the 'reasonable' accommodation of disabled persons (Article 5), matters that are dealt with in separate statutes in the United States.

[7] See Council Directive 2000/43/EC of 29 June 2000 implementing the principle of equal treatment between persons irrespective of racial or ethnic origin [2000] OL L 180. The scope of application of this Directive extends beyond the employment context into areas such as social advantages, education, and 'access to and supply of goods and services which are available to the public, including housing' (Article 3/1). This is not so say, however, that public housing needs to be made available to, for example, African migrant workers now. Article 3/2 allows Member States to continue to discriminate on the grounds of nationality.

[8] See Council Directive 2004/113/EC of 13 December 2004 implementing the principle of equal treatment between men and women in the access to and supply of goods and services, OJ L 373.

[9] See 2000/750/EC, Council Decision of 27 November 2000 establishing a Union action programme to combat discrimination, OJ L 303.

[10] Directive 2002/73/EC of the European Parliament and of the European Council of 23 September 2002 amending Council Directive 76/207/EC on the implementation of the principle of equal treatment for men and women as regards access to employment, vocational training and promotion, and working conditions, OJ L 269/15.

[11] See European Commission, Proposal for a Council Directive on implementing the principle of equal treatment between persons irrespective of religion or belief, disability, or sexual orientation, COM(2008) 426 final.

[12] See Article 3 *leg. cit.*

[13] See Article 1/7 Directive 2002/73/EC, which introduced a new Article 8a. These bodies do not affect the work of associations engaged in public action. See Article 1(2) *leg. cit.* that amends Article 2. So-called 'bodies for the promotion of equal treatment' had been introduced by Article 13 of the

Green Paper,[14] the Commission leaves little doubt that it would be pleased to see more of these bodies or, at any rate, better information gathering, in the future.[15] Their operation could even merge the promotion of gender equality with combating all other forms of discrimination into one consolidated equal treatment task force (an 'equality police', as it were). The relevant vision is referred to as a new 'integrated approach' to non-discrimination.[16] The Commission also explicitly states that equality bodies would be the 'key partners' in the future development of the anti-discrimination policy of the Union.[17] The completion of the legislative programme aside, new initiatives in the field of anti-discrimination are likely to take the form of 'incentive measures'.[18] They are likely, hence, to be concerned with managing cooperative efforts at improvement.[19]

2. The Technocracy of Problem-solving Interaction

Anti-discrimination policy is an instance of how what has come to be known as 'new governance'[20] is combined or mingled with the implementation and enforcement of legal norms.

New governance stands for a bundle of management strategies, the aim of which is to facilitate cooperative problem-solving.[21] I shall leave aside the question of which type of combination or coalescence of norm enforcement and management is to be observed in the context of anti-discrimination law.[22] I would like to

Race Directive (note 7). The tasks performed by these bodies have to comprise helping victims of discrimination to pursue their complaints, empirical research regarding the occurrence of discriminatory acts, the making of recommendations to national parliaments, etc.

[14] See European Commission, *Green Paper—Equality and Non-discrimination in an Enlarged European Union* (June 2004), COM(2004) 379, http://eur-lex.europa.eu/LexUriServ/site/en/com/2004/com2004_0379en01.pdf accessed 23 December 2010.

[15] See European Commission, 'Non-discrimination and Equal Opportunities: A Renewed Commitment', COM(2008) 420 final, at 7.

[16] See Green Paper, n. 14 at 29; see also European Commission, 'Equality and Non-discrimination: Annual Report 2004', http://ec.europa.eu/social/BlobServlet?docId=1664&langId=en accessed 23 December 2010.

[17] See Green Paper, n. 14 at 26.

[18] See G. de Búrca, 'EU Race Discrimination Law: A Hybrid Model?', in G. de Búrca and J. Scott (eds), *Law and New Governance in the EU and the US* (Oxford: Hart Publishing, 2006), 97–120 at 104.

[19] Some of these are outlined in the 'Renewed Commitment', n. 15 at 7–9.

[20] Within a few years only, the exploration of new governance has grown into an intellectual field of its own. It is closely associated with the introduction of the Open Method of Coordination in the employment context. See C. Kilpatrick, 'New EU Employment Governance and Constitutionalism', in G. de Búrca and J. Scott (eds), *Law and New Governance in the EU and the US* (Oxford: Hart Publishing, 2006), 121–151 at 122–123. J. Scott and D. M. Trubek, 'Mind the Gap: Law and New Approaches to Governance in the European Union' (2002) 8 *European Law Journal* 1–18.

[21] It is worth noting that the rise of managed problem-solving, which is increasingly taking the place of regulation, can also be observed on an international level. See M. Koskenniemi, 'The Fate of Public International Law: Between Technique and Politics' (2007) 70 *Modern Law Review* 1–30 at 9–15.

[22] I should like to mention, though, that according to de Búrca, the measures surrounding the implementation of the Race Directive amount to a successful 'hybrid' model. See de Búrca, n. 18 at 118–120. Generally, various relations are observed between and among different forms of engaging

underscore, nonetheless, the major respects in which new governance strategies differ from a legal regime for the protection of rights.[23] I do not want to insinuate, though, that the relevant aspects are all equally salient in each instance of new governance.

First, in contrast to the legislative formulation and judicial protection of rights, governance arrangements are less hierarchical and based upon voluntary compliance. In fact, they invite positive initiative with regard to the development of new standards and strategies. They are systematically directed towards innovation. For this end, new governance seeks to mobilize the actors involved, who are expected to make creative contributions to a common cause. Governance regimes do not rest content with laying down norms and having addressees comply for whatever reason they may see fit. Governance defies legality. The addressees of governance efforts are rather expected to make the respective governance agenda their own and to develop an appetite for recognition that accrues from working towards a common end.[24] Consequently, new governance needs to incite enthusiasm or to tap on already existing zeal. When it comes to accountability and goal-attainment, what matters, instead of legal sanctions for non-compliance, are peer review and reputational accountability. To a large extent, then, new governance is about creating *competitive laboratories* for the purpose of permanent policy readjustment.[25]

Second, the pursuit of public policy is supposed to be both an interactive and an adaptive process. It is interactive in that it involves input from local administrators and potential addressees. This 'local knowledge' becomes filtered from within the more 'panoramic view' that emerges from the application of a comparative perspective.[26]

'hard' and 'soft' law, such as complementarity, rivalry, and transformation (hybridity). See D. M. Trubek and L. G. Trubek, 'New Governance and Legal Regulation: Complementarity, Rivalry, and Transformation' (2007) 13 *Columbia Journal of European Law* 539–564 at 544–545; see also D. M. Trubek, P. Cottrell, and M. Nance, '"Soft Law," "Hard Law" and EU Integration', in G. de Búrca and J. Scott (eds), *Law and New Governance in the EU and the US* (Oxford: Hart Publishing, 2006), 65–94. For a different formulation, according to which there is either an unbridgeable gulf between law and new governance (the 'gap thesis') or hybrid combinations or even a transformation of law by the latter, see G. de Búrca and J. Scott, 'Introduction: New Governance, Law and Constitutionalism', in ibid., 1–12 at 4–10; C. F. Sabel and W. H. Simon, 'Epilogue: Accountability without Sovereignty', in ibid., 395–411 at 394–395.

[23] For a highly useful set of contrasts, on which I draw in the text, see de Búrca, n. 18 at 98.

[24] See D. Ashiagbor, *The European Employment Strategy: Labour Market Regulation and New Governance* (Oxford: Oxford University Press, 2005), at 207–208, who observes that convergence among the Member States results from this process.

[25] See Sabel and Simon, n. 22 at 400:

> It is correct, then, that new governance repudiates the rule of law in its principal-agent variation, mostly fundamentally by disrespecting the distinction between enforcement and enactment. On the other hand, it suggests an alternative discipline that could be seen as a reinterpretation of the basic rule-of-law ideal of accountability. The alternative, instead of looking backward to a prior enactment and upward toward a central sovereign, looks forward and sideways: forward to the ongoing efforts at implementation, sideways to the efforts and views of peer institutions.

[26] See C. F. Sabel, 'Beyond Principal-agent Governance: Experimentalist Organizations, Learning, and Accountability', http://www2.law.columbia.edu/sabel/papers/Sabel.definitief.doc at 9.

The idea is not, however, to stabilize the results of co-variation (or 'concurrent production'); rather, standards are meant to be changed from one situation to the next. What one is supposed to arrive at, then, are not stable but 'rolling rules'.[27] They are subject to adaptation and revision in the process of implementation.[28] Ultimately, administrative agencies, drawing on the experience and the variation generated in a multilevel system are expected to restrict or to expand the scope of application of rules.

If it is correct to label any system of rule 'technocratic'[29] by which its claim to authority rests on embodying superior expertise, it is not inaccurate to say that new governance wishes to supersede, or at least to complement, the juristocracy of reviewing courts with the technocracy of problem-solving interaction.[30] Directly deliberative participation by the addressees of administrative regimes may be essential to improving the quality of regulation; it is, however, not intended to honour the will of thinking subjects.[31]

Since the generation of superior expertise involves permanent experimentation and interaction among horizontally and vertically aligned problem-solving units, the shift towards new governance marks the step *from the regulation of action towards action itself.* The meta-task left to governing agencies consists of managing the processes whereby legislation and application coalesce into one overall scheme of intelligent adaptation. The obvious loss of separation of powers is counter-balanced by the more or less voluntary nature of cooperation.

The move from law to management—and from compliance with decisions to the flexible adaptation to unforeseen challenges—is one instance of how the rationality of adaptive economic behaviour becomes absorbed by political and legal institutions. It is indicative, indeed, of how the legal system becomes colonized by the demands of flexible economic agency.

27 See W. H. Simon, 'Toyota Jurisprudence: Legal Theory and Rolling Rule Regimes', in G. de Búrca and J. Scott (eds), *Law and New Governance in the EU and the US* (Oxford: Hart Publishing, 2006), 37–64 at 58.

28 See, for example, Sabel and Simon, n. 22 at 405; Sabel, n. 26 at 15.

29 Interestingly, in its beginning, 'technocracy' was associated with a social vision, that is, the vision of a society with great abundance of goods and more leisure owing to the superior productivity brought about by technology. Also, it was believed that a technocratic society should be able to dispense with the merit principle. Wealth would make its application superfluous. For a reconstruction of the beginnings, which are associated with the business plans and the political adventures of H. Scott, see A. Mohler, 'Der Weg der "Technokratie" von Amerika nach Frankreich', in H. Barion, E. W. Böckenförde, and E. Forsthoff (eds), *Epirrhosis. Festgabe für Carl Schmitt*, 2nd edn (Berlin: Duncker & Humblot, 2002), 579–596 at 590–591. From its inception, however, technology was marked by a deep distrust of all ideology. Only after it had become blended with the elitist self-understanding of the Napoleonic *Grandes Ecoles* of France, did it come to accrue the elements that are associated with it to this day: a preference for the scientific exploration of necessities over democratic bickering and the strengthening of the executive branch, which includes increasing consultation by experts (see ibid. at 595–596). See also E. Forsthoff, *Der Staat der Industriegesellschaft: Dargestellt am Beispiel der Bundesrepublik Deutschland* (Munich: C.H. Beck, 1971), at 36–40.

30 See Sabel and Simon, n. 22 at 407.

31 For an ambiguous statement, see J. Cohen and C. F. Sabel, 'Directly-deliberative Polyarchy' (1997) 3 *European Law Journal* 313–342 at 314.

3. The Anti-discrimination Action Programme

The anti-discrimination action programme ran from 2001 to 2006[32] and was superseded by the more encompassing Union Programme for Employment and Social Solidarity ('PROGRESS').[33] The action programme had been designed to combat all forms of direct and indirect discrimination, which were all explicitly considered to be 'equally intolerable'.[34] To this end, the action programme aimed at improving the understanding of issues related to discrimination, strengthening organizations' means of action, supporting the exchange of information and good practice, tightening networking on the European level, and, finally, promoting and disseminating the values and practices underlying the effort to combat discrimination (this includes 'awareness-raising campaigns').[35] Access to the programme was granted, among others, to local and regional authorities, NGOs, national statistical offices, and the media.[36] The Commission was required to cooperate both with NGOs and the social partners. The measures were supported by a budget that totalled €98.4 million. They were divided up into three different strands.[37]

The first strand was mainly devoted to the development of methods regarding the gathering and evaluation of information concerning discrimination. The second strand, 'capacity building', made funding available for all agents who were engaged in transnational cooperation and who had a stake in information exchange or mutual learning with regard to best practice. It also promised support to 'relevant European-level non-governmental organisations with experience in fighting discrimination and acting as advocates of people exposed to discrimination in order to promote the development of an integrated and coordinated approach to the fight against discrimination'. Finally, under the heading 'awareness-raising',[38] the third strand offered funding for the organization of conferences, seminars and events at a European level, the organization of seminars by Member States on the implementation of the anti-discrimination Directives, media events dealing with the international exchange of best practice, and, finally, 'the publication of materials to disseminate the results of the programme, including through the construction of an Internet Site providing examples of good practice, a forum for the exchange of ideas and a database of potential partners for transnational exchange actions'.

[32] For a more detailed reconstruction, see de Búrca, n. 18 at 104–111.

[33] See http://ec.europa.eu/social/main.jsp?langId=en&catId=327 accessed 23 December 2010.

[34] See recital 5 of the preamble. In recital 7, sex discrimination is, however, excluded from the programme because it is 'dealt with by specific Community action'. Hence, the target is discrimination based on racial or ethnic origin, religion or belief, disability, age, or sexual orientation (Article 1). On the gender equality programme, see http://ec.europa.eu/social/main.jsp?catId=418 accessed 23 December 2010.

[35] Article 2 of the Council Decision.

[36] See Annex *leg. cit.*

[37] See Annex *leg. cit.* According to the Green Paper, n. 14 at 13, about 100 initiatives receive support from this programme every year.

[38] Awareness-raising continues in that the Commission supports anti-discrimination and diversity training seminars. See http://ec.europa.eu/social/main.jsp?catId=667&langId=en accessed 23 December 2010.

Ostensibly, the engineering of learning processes is now part and parcel of the Commission's policy strategies. The Framework Strategy for non-discrimination[39] now claims to take account of comments and reactions to the Green Paper published earlier.[40] More than 1,500 contributions were received from national authorities, specialized equality bodies, regional and local authorities, social partners, experts, and NGOs.[41]

4. The Link to Employment and Broader Social Policy Objectives

I tried to explain in the previous chapter how domestication, assimilation, and disarmament indirectly account for the importance attained by anti-discrimination in the context of the Union's social policy. Owing to its formidable fit with the European Employment Strategy, which has also come to occupy the central stage, it is not by accident that social policy governance becomes evermore deeply permeated with the anti-discrimination theme.[42] Anti-discrimination and social inclusion are essential components of the PROGRESS programme.[43] It has been established to support financially the implementation of the objectives of the European Union in the fields of employment and social affairs.[44]

Already the Green Paper[45] attributes to anti-discrimination policy considerable importance with regard to the future development of social policy in general. It unequivocally asserts that 'the principles of equal treatment and non-discrimination are at the heart of the European Social Model'[46] and identifies major policy objectives for the future.[47]

[39] See 'Communication from the Commission to the Council, the European Parliament, the European Economic and Social Committee and the Committee of the Region: Non-discrimination and Equal Opportunities for All—A Framework Strategy', COM(2005) 224 final.

[40] See n. 14.

[41] See Framework Strategy, n. 39 at 3.

[42] On the association of the employment strategy and anti-discrimination policy, see also Barnard, n. 2 at 305, 311, 384, 390.

[43] See European Commission, General Guidelines for the Implementation of the Community Action Programme for Employment and Social Solidarity—PROGRESS (2007–2013), 01/FB D(2006) at 3:

> PROGRESS brings together previous Community programmes and budget lines under an integrated framework. It is centred on issues related to specific areas (employment, working conditions, and social protection and inclusion) and on issues related to specific target groups (gender equality and non-discrimination).

[44] The other components are social protection and inclusion, employment and working conditions. As the official website explains, PROGRESS is the EU's new employment and social solidarity programme. Working alongside the European Social Fund (ESF), it is scheduled to run from 2007 to 2013. It replaces the four previous ones that ended in 2006 covering actions against discrimination, supporting equality between men and women, employment measures, and the fight against social exclusion. See http://ec.europa.eu/social/main.jsp?langId=en&catId=327 accessed 23 December 2010.

[45] See n. 14.

[46] Green Paper, n. 14 at 3; the Commission, evidently, has a great time of presenting the Union as the vanguard of anti-discrimination law. See Green Paper, ibid. at 11; ibid., at 18: 'There has also been considerable international interest in recent developments within the EU, whose anti-discrimination legislation is among the most advanced in the world and is widely regarded as an effective model.'

[47] I shall leave aside the objective that has already been attained, namely, the extension of protection from sex discrimination into the field of services.

The first objective is backward-looking. Even though most of the Member States have done something at the end of the period set for implementation of the two major Directives,[48] it is not clear whether, in all cases, they have also done enough.[49] In the Green Paper and in the subsequently adopted Framework Strategy,[50] the Commission expresses its concern that there have been delays in the transposition of the Directives. Moreover, it is noted that it is not clear whether the Directives may have not been badly implemented in some instances.[51] Whereas the Commission left no doubt in the Green Paper that it would use the traditional 226 EC Treaty (now Article 258 FEU Treaty) procedure to deal with defaulting or sluggish Member States, the Framework Strategy envisages also training and capacity building actions for specialized equality bodies, judges, lawyers, NGOs and social partners, networking, and information exchange and awareness-raising.[52]

Second, the Commission expressed concern that minorities in the newly acquired Member States, in particular the large number of Roma, might continue to suffer exclusion and harassment in those and other Member States of the Union.[53] As planned, the Commission established a high-level advisory group[54] for what it describes to pose a 'multi-dimensional problem'.[55] In a similar vein, the Commission is aware that problems encountered by asylum seekers also merit sustained attention.[56]

Finally, the Commission sets out more broadly defined goals. Aside from integrating—possibly even mainstreaming[57]—anti-discrimination into other policy areas of the Union,[58] the Commission is also explicitly interested in intensifying

[48] The newly acquired Member States had to have their legislation ready by the time they entered the Union, the old Member States were given time until July and December 2003, respectively.

[49] See Commission, DG for Employment and Social Affairs, Equality and Non-discrimination. 'Annual Report', n. 16 at 9–16 for a useful overview. See 'Non-discrimination and Equal Opportunities', n. 15 at 3.

[50] See Framework Strategy, n. 39 at 3.

[51] See Green Paper, n. 14 at 21.

[52] See Framework Strategy, n. 39. 6.

[53] See Green Paper, n. 14 at 3, 20; see also Framework Strategy, n. 39 at 10–11; see also Non-discrimination and Equal Opportunities, n. 15 at 9–10.

[54] See Framework Strategy, n. 39 at 10. See http://ec.europa.eu/social/main.jsp?catId=423&langId=en&newsId=458&furtherNews=yes accessed July 2009.

[55] See ibid. The Commission also points out that in the new Member States, where the unemployment rates of older workers are particularly high, the notion of age discrimination is not rapidly taking hold. The Commission would, however, like to see the number of employed older workers increase.

[56] See Green Paper, n. 14 at 27.

[57] See Non-discrimination and Equal Opportunities, n. 15 at 6–7. 'Mainstreaming' is the major approach with regard to gender issues. Accordingly, all general policies and measures ought to be mobilized 'specifically for the purpose of achieving equality by actively and openly taking into account at the planning state their possible effects on the respective situation of men and women (gender perspective)'. See European Commission, Incorporating Equal Opportunities for Women and Men into all Community Policies and Activities, COM(96) 67 final. Generally, the idea of mainstreaming is that a certain public policy issue should not be treated as a compartmentalized problem but rather be dealt with as an integral component of other policies. See de Búrca, n. 18 at 117. The Commission contemplated the future mainstreaming of anti-discrimination policy in its Framework Strategy, n. 39 at 7.

[58] See Green Paper, n. 14 at 27.

exchanges with 'stakeholders' and stimulating mutual learning from the exchange and emulation of good practice.[59]

The Commission leaves no doubt that the ultimate emphasis of anti-discrimination policy rests on changing attitudes and behaviour.[60] Anti-discrimination policy is also likely to be on the agenda of the European Fundamental Rights Agency.[61] The Commission would like to ensure that 'a range of funding instruments' is used to promote 'exchanges of good practice, co-operation and networking between national authorities, specialised equality bodies, organisations working with victims of discrimination, and other stakeholders'.[62] The PROGRESS programme[63] is supposed to play an important part in creating a pool of information that policy-makers might draw on in the future.[64]

Anti-discrimination law has become a part of the package of policies that comprise issues of employment and social inclusion.[65] The Green Paper expresses confidence that the implementation of anti-discrimination law will reinforce the European Employment Strategy (the so-called Luxembourg process)[66] and efforts in the field of social inclusion. More remarkably, still, the former 'EQUAL' initiative, which used to be financed through the Social Fund,[67] quite clearly relied on anti-discrimination strategies to pursue employment objectives. Moreover, it is

59 See Green Paper, n. 14 at 24; Framework Strategy, n. 39 at 7–8.

60 See Green Paper, n. 14 at 28–29; Non-discrimination and Equal Opportunities, n. 15 at 8–9.

61 See Council Regulation (CE) No 168/2007 of 15 February 2007 establishing a European Union Agency for Fundamental Rights (FRA), OJ L 053, 22/02/2007, 1–14. According to Article 2 of the Regulation, the Agency shall have as its task:

> to provide the relevant institutions, bodies, offices and agencies of the Union and its Member States when implementing Union law with assistance and expertise relating to fundamental rights in order to support them when they take measures or formulate courses of action within their respective spheres of competence to fully respect fundamental rights.

Since the Agency superseded the European Monitoring Centre on Racism and Xenophobia (Article 29 [1] *leg.cit.*) it will evidently have to deal with matters of discrimination. See also de Brúca, n. 18 at 111–115.

62 Framework Strategy, n. 39 at 7. See also de Brúca, n. 18 at 115–117.

63 See above n. 44.

64 See Framework Strategy, n. 39 at 8.

65 Indeed, in the Green Paper, n. 14 at 13 the Commission boasts that 'in a relatively short space of time, anti-discrimination has become one of the most widely known areas of EU employment and social policy'.

66 The Luxembourg Jobs Summit of the European Council of November 1997 launched the European Employment Strategy. As a consequence of the new *concordantia catholica*, the European Employment Strategy has become a sub-element of the Lisbon Strategy. The substance of the so-called 'Luxembourg process' (for a documentation by the Commission, see http://europa.eu/legislation_summaries/employment_and_social_policy/community_employment_policies/c11318_en.htm accessed 23 December 2010) is principled upon flexibility, lifelong learning, entrepreneurship, adaptability, that is, virtues typically associated with the *Weltanschauung* of economic liberalism. For a succinct critique, see S. Deakin and H. Reed, 'The Contested Meaning of Labour Market Flexibility', in J. Shaw (ed.), *Social Law and Policy in an Evolving European Union* (Oxford: Hart Publishing, 2000), 71–102 at 95. This *Weltanschauung* is consonant with the idea of market-making and market-creation. It does not pose other values in opposition to it. I shall return to this shift of orientation shortly.

67 The EQUAL initiative was implemented until 2008 and expired in the framework of the new ESF regulations. See Regulation (EC) No 1081/2006 of the European Parliament and of the Council of 5 July 2006 on the European Social Fund and repealing Regulation (EC) No 1784/1999. See http://ec.europa.eu/employment_social/equal/about/key-doc_en.cfm accessed 23 December 2010.

understood, from the outset, that EQUAL 'constitutes a permanent laboratory for experimentation in developing and disseminating new approaches for implementing employment policies to combat all manners of discrimination and inequalities, including those suffered by asylum seekers'.[68]

5. The Example of the EQUAL Programme

The European Employment Strategy[69] initially rested on four labour-supply oriented guidelines that were designed to ensure better access to the labour market, the creation of lasting jobs,[70] and of opportunities for self-employed occupations. The four guidelines came under the headings of 'employability', 'entrepreneurship', 'adaptability', and 'equal opportunity'.[71] In the context of the EQUAL programme, which expired in 2008, anti-discrimination was consistently addressed as a tool serving goals set out by the guidelines.[72] Even though the substance of EQUAL has been integrated into the more encompassing PROGRESS programme, a look at its design serves to illustrate how new governance is supposed to operate in the context of employment.

The first Commission Communication introducing the EQUAL Initiative[73] stated that the goal of the initiative was 'to promote new means of combating all forms of discrimination and inequalities in connection with the labour market, through transnational co-operation'.[74] The remainder of the Communication left little doubt that protection from discrimination was supposed to play the role of a means to an end, with the end being defined by the Employment Strategy. Accordingly, combating racism and xenophobia with regard to the labour market was presented as a strategy to enhance 'employability'.[75] The promotion of lifelong learning and 'inclusive work practices which encourage the retention of those suffering discrimination and inequality' were to foster overall adaptability.[76] In

[68] First Communication by the Commission to the Member States regarding the EQUAL programme, COM(2000) 852, 14 April 2000 at 2.

[69] http://ec.europa.eu/social/main.jsp?catId=101&langId=en accessed 23 December 2010.

[70] The first Communication regarding the EQUAL initiative (see n. 68) speaks about 'quality jobs with a future' (p. 4).

[71] See, e.g., Council Resolution of 22 February 1999 on the 1999 Employment Guidelines, OJC 69/02 1999. There is a constitutional basis, as it were, for these labour supply-side strategies. Article 145 FEU Treaty (ex 125 EC Treaty) commits the Member States and the Union toward developing a coordinated strategy for promoting a 'skilled, trained and adaptable workforce and labour markets responsive to economic change'.

[72] It is thus that the fourth pillar is mainstreamed into the first three pillars. Mind that this is reflected in the simplification brought about in 2003. The four pillars were replaced with 'three overarching objectives': (1) full employment; (2) quality and productivity; and (3) cohesion and inclusion. See Future of the Employment Strategy, n. 127 at 9–10. See K. Armstrong and C. Kilpatrick, 'Law, Governance, or New Governance? The Changing Open Method of Coordination' (2007) 13 *Columbia Journal of European Law* 649–677 at 666.

[73] See n. 70. [74] Ibid., para. 3. [75] Ibid., 16.

[76] Ibid. It cannot be denied that not all that the Commission says in this paper is equally plausible, and the example above suggests that anti-discrimination objectives apparently had to be 'squeezed into' the framework of the European Employment Strategy's guidelines.

any event, in the context of EQUAL, it was understood that anti-discrimination law is a key factor in providing equal access to jobs.[77]

The second Commission Communication emphasized even more strongly that the programme, taken as such, was a 'learning platform' which was aimed at discovering 'new ways of achieving the policy objectives of the European Employment Strategy and the Social Inclusion Process'.[78] Indeed, EQUAL was described as a 'laboratory' for experiments with alternative ways of 'tackling discrimination and inequality in the labour market'. Its aim was to 'test innovative approaches to policy delivery' either by wholesale or by more piecemeal transnational borrowings.[79] To that end, EQUAL had been created to fund the development of innovative solutions in order to have them 'analysed, benchmarked and disseminated both within Member States and across the Union'.[80] The Member States were encouraged to stimulate the creation of transnational 'Development Partnerships' which were supposed to be the nodes in emerging networks for the dissemination and mainstreaming of good practice.[81] For the internal structure of such partnerships, the principle of 'empowerment' was declared to be essential. It was taken to mean that the potential beneficiaries of the implementation of programmes had to have a say in the allocation of project funds.

The thrust underlying the social policy approach came even more explicitly to the fore in the Second Communication, which even celebrated the success of the first four years of the initiative's operation.[82] The holistic grip of the initiative was visible in the way in which EQUAL was presented as thematically intertwined with the employment and social inclusion strategies.[83] Access and return to the labour market, encouraging lifelong learning, reducing gender gaps, combating racism and xenophobia recurred on the list of topics, and so did increasing the adaptability of firms and workers and finding better ways at reconciling family and professional life.[84] One was seen in conjunction with the other. The practices of interest were indeed referred to as 'holistic approaches',[85] the 'mainstreaming' of which in the policies on the national and European level is a stated goal of the programme.[86] The policy strategies that were part of such *holistic sets* and identified as promising by the Commission already indicated that *mobilization* was required to make them succeed:[87] training and consultancy services targeted at employers in order to assist

[77] See the Second Communication from the Commission establishing guidelines for the second round of the EQUAL initiative, COM(2003) 840, 30 December 2003.

[78] See Second Communication, n. 77 at 1.

[79] See First Communication, n. 68 at 7, para. 28.

[80] See ibid. para. 30.

[81] Ibid. at 3, para. 11. 'Mainstreaming' is defined in the Second Communication at 14 as 'the integration and incorporation of new ideas and approaches to policy and practice'.

[82] See Second Communication, n. 77 at 2.

[83] I add in passing that the overlap and interconnection of multiple policy areas was to become a pitfall of the Lisbon Agenda. See European Commission, 'Lisbon Strategy evaluation document' SEC (2010) 114 final at 6 (with critical remarks on the use of the integrated guidelines).

[84] See Second Communication, n. 77 at 5. [85] See ibid. at 2. [86] See ibid. at 4.

[87] On the following, see Second Communication, n. 77 at 8–11. It should not go unmentioned that a major part of the initiative is concerned with the integration of asylum seekers into the labour market. See ibid. at 6–8.

them to hire disabled persons; awareness-raising regarding disability; public TV campaigns that inform men about their duties as primary caregivers and encourage them to take a paternity leave; strategies for helping older workers to be motivated as a result of which they are more likely to stay employed; development of award criteria for 'Equal Opportunity Employers'; showcasing of model employers; drafting of 'innovative curricula for primary and secondary schools which challenge traditional gender roles'; creating incentives for small enterprises to hire a more diverse workforce (through facilitating personal encounters); and helping former prison inmates in finding a job, to name but a few.

Even a quick glance at the Second Communication leaves no doubt that the mobilization of potentially all social actors involved was the preferred modality of shaping and implementing policy objectives. The Commission stated, almost cunningly, that good governance 'requires the active participation of all interested stakeholders'. In principle, the process was open to all. The participants ranged from the social partners, public bureaucracies, and non-profit private organizations, all the way down to much more loosely associated groups.[88] One gains the impression that the initiative had been designed, at least in part, to transpire into an immense brainstorming event not least owing to the Commission's emphasis that EQUAL was to be about innovation and generating new ideas.[89] The Commission, the Member States, and the Development partners were finally allocated responsibility for 'mainstreaming' best practice.[90]

I should like to return to exploring holism and mobilization as features of governance below. In what follows, I would like to examine the substantive thrust of the integrated strategies.

6. The New *Concordantia Catholica*: Creating Self-confident Human Resources

The spirit of current Union social policy is amply reflected in the Social Policy Agenda[91] and in subsequent papers,[92] such as a more recent Communication on the Social Agenda[93] and the Renewed Social Agenda.[94]

First, the global competitive economy is taken for granted. It cannot be altered. Social policy is the method of keeping pace with changing realities.[95] The economy

[88] See ibid. at 3. [89] See ibid. at 4. [90] See ibid. at 14.

[91] See Communication from the Commission to the Council, the European Parliament, the Economic and Social Committee and the Committee of the Regions: Social Policy Agenda, COM (2000) 379 final. The Agenda set out an ambitious and utterly comprehensive five-year programme. For an assessment, see Ashiagbor, n. 24 at 173–178.

[92] See, for example, Communication from the Commission to the Council, the European Parliament, the Economic and Social Committee and the Committee of the Regions: Employment and Social Policies: A Framework for Investing in Quality, COM(2001) 313 final.

[93] See European Commission, Communication from the Commission on the Social Agenda, COM (2005) 33 final.

[94] See European Commission, Renewed Social Agenda: Opportunities, access and solidarity in 21st Century Europe, COM(2008) 412 final.

[95] See ibid. at 3.

is beyond human design. It gives rise to new challenges, such as offshoring, outsourcing, and deindustrialization.[96] Social policy is meant to encourage and to accompany restructuring.[97]

Second, there is not merely complementarity[98] perceived in the relation of social and economic policy but rather instrumentality of the former with regard to the latter.[99] Good social policy, it is stated in the Social Policy Agenda and repeated in the more recent Communication, is a 'productive factor' that promises an output of overall better human resources.[100] This is spelled out clearly in the Renewed Social Agenda:[101]

The focus needs to be on **empowering and enabling** individuals to realise their potential while at the same time helping those who are unable to do so.

Indeed, according to the Commission, the interaction of social policy to economic objectives is not rife with conflict;[102] on the contrary, social policy is seen to be perfectly congruent with the attainment of economic objectives. Anti-discrimination policy is approached with the same attitude. More inclusive labour markets are welcomed because they help broaden the base of the active workforce.[103]
Indeed, ever since the launching,[104] relaunching,[105] and recent transformation[106] of the Lisbon Strategy, which used to be about transforming Europe into the world's

[96] See Communication on the Social Policy Agenda, n. 93 at 6. [97] Ibid.

[98] This is the language of the Framework for Investing in Quality. See Communication from the Commission to the Council, the European Parliament, the Economic and Social Committee and the Committee of the Regions, Employment and Social Policies: A Framework for Investing in Quality, COM(2001) 313 final, at 3.

[99] With regard to health and safety at work this is spelled out in the Communication on the Social Policy Agenda, n. 93 at 7, as follows: 'Prevention pays off: less work-related accidents and diseases push up productivity, contain costs, strengthen quality in work and hence valorize Europe's human potential.'

[100] See Social Policy Agenda, n. 91 at 5. The Commission is always quick at pointing out the systemic interaction between economic and social policy, for example, by stating that a sound social policy is essential for coping with change on the basis of a well-trained workforce (ibid. 6). See also Communication on the Social Policy Agenda, n. 93 at 5.

[101] Renewed Social Agenda, n. 94 at 3; emphasis in original.

[102] The Renewed Social Agenda, n. 94 at 3, is more nuanced: 'The reality is that economic and social actions at EU and national levels are mutually reinforcing and complementary.'

[103] See Social Policy Agenda, n. 91 at 21; Framework Strategy, n. 39 at 1.

[104] See Presidency Conclusions of the Lisbon European Council, 23 and 24 March 2000, http://www.europarl.europa.eu/summits/lis1_en.htm, para. 5, accessed 23 December 2010. It is the same Council that introduced the name 'Open Method of Coordination' for the mode of bringing about convergence among the employment policies of the Member States. See K. Jacobsson, 'Soft Regulation and the Subtle Transformation of States: The Case of EU Employment Policy' (2004) 14 *Journal of European Social Policy* 355–370 at 357. Ashiagbor, n. 24 at 328, notes succinctly that the Treaty base for the OMC:

> is modeled closely on the convergence arrangements of national economic policies, with two exceptions: first, the common employment guidelines do not advocate measures to harmonise national provisions, although they do have an indirect impact on Member State's policy. Second, in contrast to the provisions on EMU, Title VIII does not prescribe any macroeconomic objectives to be achieved, along the lines of the convergence criteria.

[105] The Lisbon strategy did not really get off the ground owing to a downturn of the Member States' economies. See European Commission, 'Communication to the Spring European Council: Working Together for Growth and Jobs: A New Start for the Lisbon Strategy', COM(2005) 24 at 4. In the face of the current economic crisis, the tone has become more modest.

[106] See European Commission, 'Europe 2020: A Strategy for Smart, Sustainable and Inclusive Growth', COM(2010) 2020. The basic thrust of the Lisbon strategy (knowledged-based economy, innovation, and social cohesion) is retained therein, however, it has been disaggregated in the three

most dynamic and competitive economy, European economic and social policy appears to be committed to what might be called, with an eye to Cusanus' classic treatise,[107] a new *concordantia catholica*. In the mediaeval intellectual world of Nicholas of Cusa, the church was envisaged as being permeated and animated by 'a sweet spiritual harmony of agreement'.[108] It was thus taken to partake of the concordance of God's eternal existence and creation. Where there is *eternal life*, according to Cusanus, there cannot be contradiction, for otherwise instability and conflict would threaten such life with extinction. But since concordance, nevertheless, presupposes difference, he concludes that 'the less opposition there is among these differences, the greater the concordance and the longer the life'.[109] Concordance thus accounts for the ontological dignity of things: the more concordance, the more similarity to God.

In a like manner, in the age in which there seems to be nothing outside, and no more alternative to, the market economy, the Commission perceives the Common Market as being ruled by a basic concordance of its elements.[110] Unity and concord are perceived to prevail in the relation of economic and social objectives. The European Union does not even perceive a tension, let alone a contradiction, between transforming the Union into the most competitive and dynamic knowledge-based market economy, on the one hand, and the promotion of social cohesion and social inclusion, on the other.[111] Indeed, it claims that promoting diversity through anti-discrimination is particularly beneficial for it enhances the competitiveness of firms.[112]

Social policy is supposed to assist people into becoming successful market participants.[113] Since in a highly competitive context only self-confident human resources are likely to succeed, the emphasis lies on building up the confidence that accrues from skills and the absence of hostile social environments. This is reflected in two strategies advocated by the Commission.

The strategy called 'quality of work' embraces the creation of more and better jobs.[114] The emphasis is on the 'quality' of work which is seen to require, not

priorities 'smart growth', 'sustainable growth', and 'inclusive growth'. The overall idea is, however, to present a vision for Europe's 'social market economy for the 21st century' (ibid. at 8).

107 See N. of Cusa, *De Concordantia Catholica* (*The Catholic Concordance*) (1443), trans. by P. E. Sigmund (Cambridge: Cambridge University Press, 1991).

108 Ibid., I.I.4. (p. 5).

109 Ibid., I.I.6. (p. 6).

110 Most generally speaking, European social policy is committed to both competitiveness and social justice. See Kilpatrick, n. 20 at 127–128, 141. See also Ashiagbor, n. 24 at 172–173.

111 See Presidency Conclusions of the Lisbon European Council, 23 and 24 March 2000, http://europa.eu.int/comm/off/index_en.htm, para. 5. Yet, there is a recognition that established European social welfare states are necessary to sustain 'the transformation to the knowledge economy' and they also 'need to be adapted [...] to ensure that work pays, to secure [...] long-term sustainability in the face of an ageing population, to promote social inclusion and gender equality, and to provide quality health services', ibid., para. 31.

112 See European Commission, 'The Costs and Benefits of Diversity', http://www.stop-discrimination.info/fileadmin/pdfs/CostsBenefExSumEN.pdf.

113 See Ashiagbor, n. 24 at 303.

114 See Social Policy Agenda, n. 91 at 15. The emphasis on the 'quality' of jobs is the attempt to arrive at an employment policy that is more attractive than the job creation in the United States. See

exclusively, but still,[115] heightened mobility,[116] more adaptability, and lifelong learning to ensure employability. Remarkably, the responsibility for creating a 'quality job' is in large part shifted from the employer to the adaptable and lifelong learning employee.[117] Almost by default, the bendiness of the latter appears to be prerequisite for experiencing the quality of work. In the more recent Communication on the Social Policy Agenda, the Commission emphasizes the role that is to be played by social policy 'to enable citizens to gain confidence in their own ability to effectively manage' the changes wrought by 'increased competition in a global context, technological development and population ageing'.[118]

The strategy called 'quality in social policy' urges the Member States to 'modernise' their systems of social protection.[119] Anti-discrimination law makes its appearance here embedded in a cluster of values that are different, but not entirely different, from equality, such as 'social cohesion' and 'social inclusion'.[120] There is an overarching finality, however, with regard to the attainment of employment objectives, which, in the eyes of the Commission, does not merely have an economic but also a 'social' dimension because employment contributes to the Union's goal of improving the quality of life.[121] Being employed in a 'quality job'

E. Szyszczak, 'The New Paradigm for Social Policy: A Virtuous Circle?' (2001) 38 *Common Market Law Review* 1125–1170 at 1154.

[115] More fully stated, it means, to achieve also to arrive at 'more balanced ways of combining working life with personal life'. See Framework for Investing in Quality, n. 98 at 2. See Ashiagbor, n. 24 at 180–185.

[116] See Renewed Social Agenda, n. 94 at 4.

[117] This is also to be observed for the Communication on the Social Policy Agenda, n. 93 at 6, even though the 'quality' aspect has come to be de-emphasized. I should grant that this is overstated and that in the Employment Guidelines which have been published by the European Council a much greater emphasis lies on the cooperation of social partners and on making life easier for employees with child-rearing obligations. Nevertheless, the core of the guidelines is defined in supply-side terms: improving employability, developing entrepreneurship (qua means to create jobs and means to become self-employed), encouraging adaptability (in particular at the workplace), aside from strengthening policies for equal opportunities. See already the 1998 Employment Guidelines, Council Resolution of 15 December 1997, Council document 13200/97. These core guidelines have not changed since they have been amended, however, and now also include aspects of the 'quality of work' strategy. For example, the Guidelines for the employment policies of the Member States, 2003/578/EC, Council Decision of 22 July 2003, OJ L 197, 13, which also lists making work pay through incentives to enhance work attractiveness, the development of human capital and lifelong learning, increasing labour supply and 'active ageing' (e.g., raising retirement age), and specifies the equal opportunity component by addressing explicitly gender equality and combating the discrimination against people at a disadvantage in the labour market. Interestingly, over the years, the Commission and Council have condensed more policy strategies with an anti-discrimination component into a guideline that calls for 'attracting more people to enter and remain on the labour market'. See Annex 1 of the Commission Proposal for a Council Decision on guidelines for the employment policies of the Member States, COM(2004) 239 final at 10. The same Communication introduces as a new guideline 'ensuring effective implementation of reforms through better governance'.

[118] See Communication on the Social Policy Agenda, n. 93 at 3.

[119] See Social Policy Agenda, n. 91 at 11, 20.

[120] I should mention that one strategy constantly flows into the other in Commission Communications so that one finds the reinforcement of anti-discrimination law also as a means of promoting 'quality of work'; which makes some sense, indeed, for the quality of work increases for women dramatically when they are free from harassment. See Framework for Investing in Quality, n. 98 at 3, 11–13.

[121] See Framework for Investing in Quality, n. 98 at 4.

means not merely being given satisfactory tasks, having a cooperative working environment, or a flexible work schedule respecting child-rearing obligations; it also means, quite plausibly, to be free from harassment and degradation by others.

7. The Transformation of the Union's Power: Discoursive Holism

In the shadow of the master Lisbon strategy, Union policies have necessarily attained a holistic orientation. They reflect the fact that they contribute to the larger project of seeing the European economy succeed in a global context. Consequently, Union power, for the most part managerial, also becomes exercised in a holistic way.[122]

In the context of the European Employment Strategy, the use of managerial authority is not restricted to one area of public policy, but encompasses several areas comprehensively.[123] The relevant processes escape jurisdictional control[124] and allow for the cross-jurisdictional integration of several policies, such as labour market policy, unemployment, pensions, taxation, vocational training, and local development.[125] In the case of pension reform and social exclusion, managed cooperation has been introduced without any express basis in the Treaty.[126] The holism of Union power has been well understood by the Working Group of the European Convention that prepared the report on Social Europe. The report recognizes that the Lisbon Strategy is about concordance: 'The balance between economic, employment and social policies and environmental policy is central to the Lisbon strategy.'[127] As is well known, the Convention nonetheless failed to constitutionalize the relevant processes[128] which have found their crystallization in the Open Method of Coordination. I shall return to the latter below.

[122] A similar development is to be observed for the hard core of Union competence in the legislative field, a development that I prefer to describe as 'market holism'. See A. Somek, *Individualism: An Essay on the Authority of the European Union* (Oxford: Oxford University Press, 2008).

[123] Hence, there is the constant intersection of funding for either the employment or the anti-discrimination related strategies. The PROGRESS funds are an example for that. See http://ec.europa.eu/social/main.jsp?catId=86&langId=en accessed 23 December 2010.

[124] See J. A. Mosher and D. M. Trubek, 'Alternative Approaches to Governance in the EU: EU Social Policy and the European Employment Strategy' (2003) 41 *Journal of Common Market Studies* 63–88 at 80. This is welcomed by J. Zeitlin, 'Social Europe and Experimentalist Governance: Towards a New Constitutional Compromise?', in G. de Búrca (ed.), *EU Law and the Welfare State: In Search of Solidarity* (Oxford: Oxford University Press, 2005), 213–241 at 220.

[125] See Zeitlin, n. 124 at 231. See also Communication from the Commission to the Council, the European Parliament, the European Economic and Social Committee and the Committee of the Regions establishing the guidelines for the second round of the Community initiative EQUAL (henceforth, 'Second Communication'), COM(2003) 840 final, 6–8.

[126] More precisely, the Open Method of Coordination is used for these policy areas even though there is no explicit Treaty base for this. See Scott and Trubek, n. 20 at 7.

[127] See the preliminary draft report of the Working Group XI 'Social Europe', Convention Working Document 38 REV 1, section II, para. 3. The Commission recently described the European Employment Strategy as a 'key component' of the Lisbon Agenda. See European Commission, 'The Future of the European Employment Strategy', COM(2003) 6 final at 4.

[128] See Zeitlin, n. 124 at 239–240.

Not surprisingly, this holism is most visible in the confluence of the 'processes' launched in the wake of European Council summits. The goals set out by one European Council meeting are constantly incorporated or 'mainstreamed' into the goals pursued by another 'process', so that at the end of the day, all Union policies have been simultaneously brought under the *chapeau* of the (former) Lisbon master strategy.[129] The resulting diffusion of Union policy across jurisdictional bounds[130] is reinforced through the voluntariness of common action. Since matters are pursued increasingly through the much hailed Open Method of Coordination (OMC),[131] the chief instrument of governance is discourse.[132] It appears even as though the various reporting and benchmarking processes that have been established in the sphere of social policy are in the process of being merged into one overarching Social Protection and Social Inclusion process.[133]

With the prevalence of discourse, Member States find themselves forced to redescribe and to restructure their social world along the lines of the imagery of meaning generated in Commission and Council documents.[134] Euphemistically put, this means that the Union creates 'a common language and categorical framework to discuss and to evaluate different solutions to similar problems'.[135] In order to attain that objective, the Union imposes on the Member States a linguistic framework that affects the representation of their political world, not just in part, but as a whole. According to the apt observation by Daly, the Europeanization of national agendas 'relies heavily on the power of cognitive mechanisms to effect both normative convergence and the emergence of an epistemic community'.[136] The outcome is a world which is all of a sudden inhabited by

[129] For example, social protection is 'mainstreamed' into the European Employment Strategy. See Szyszczak, n. 114 at 1132–4, 1146.

[130] See ibid. at 1134.

[131] As a method of policy-making, the OMC is a bypass strategy with which the Member States wish to overcome either the lack of power to adopt legislation or the lack of support for binding measures. Its development has taken its cue from methods of coordination that had been practiced already in the context of the OECD or the International Monetary Fund. See S. Leibfried and H. Obinger, 'Nationale Sozialstaaten in der Europäischen Union: Zukünfte eines "sozialen Europa"' in *TranState Reprints* (Bremen: University of Bremen, 2008), at 20. The OMC process is based on an agreement on non-binding common objectives. The Member States prepare national action plans in order to attain these objectives. The plans are evaluated by the Commission and published in joint Commission and Council reports. A set of indicators is supposed to facilitate evaluation and potential convergence. The idea is that benchmarking by indicators and the identification of best practice help to develop new policy instruments against a background of experimentation. First forms of this method were used in the context of the Economic and Monetary Union. It then came to play a role for the coordination of employment policies and attained prominence as a key tool of pursing the Lisbon strategy. The Open Method of Coordination was then also used in the areas of social inclusion, pensions, and healthcare. See Armstrong and Kilpatrick, n. 72 at 650; Ashiagbor, n. 24 at 198–208.

[132] For a related observation, see M. Daly, 'Whither EU Social Policy? An Account and Assessment of Developments in the Lisbon Social Inclusion Process' (2007) 37 *Journal of Social Policy* 1–19 at 10.

[133] See Armstrong and Kilpatrick, n. 72 at 650, 670.

[134] For excellent observations along these lines, see Jacobsson, n. 104 at 360, who identifies three 'discoursive regulatory mechanisms': joint language (key concepts), common classifications and operationalizations, and building of a common knowledge base. For a more cheerful attitude towards 'diffusion through discourse', see Trubek, Cottrell, and Nance, n. 22 at 79.

[135] Zeitlin, n. 124 at 231.

[136] See Daly, n. 132 at 14.

'quality jobs' or 'equality bodies', notions and institutions that one would be ordinarily inclined to dismiss as ludicrous if it were not for the discursive power of the leading agency. Moreover, it is a world to which continental European Social Welfare States with a more corporatist social system encounter difficulties to adjust, since the guidelines formulated and the recommendations made by the Union are not at all ideologically neutral. They are potentially more inclusive where the labour market is concerned, but more residual with regard to the level of social protection.[137]

Owing to Article 4(3) EU Treaty and Article 2(3) FEU Treaty,[138] Member States are under an indefinite obligation to integrate, reformulate, and represent issues relating to taxes, childcare, social benefits, etc. in the newspeak and classifications emanating from the European Employment Strategy.[139] But the discursive power of the Union affects not only the way in which national policy is formulated.[140] It may instil in the agents involved the belief that once a cooperative process has been instituted, there also is a mode of common action. The existence of the institution builds up confidence in its own problem-solving capacity.

8. The Transformation of the Union's Power: Mobilization

The other feature defining the transformation of power of the Union is mobilization.[141] It is brought about in a variety of ways.[142] As we have seen, from nongovernmental organizations via regional legislators and social partners[143] all the way up to the level of central governments, a number of actors is called upon to do their bit for the realization of the objectives of the employment (and social inclusion) mission.[144]

137 See C. de la Porte, 'Is the Open Method of Coordination Appropriate for Organising Activities at the European Level in Sensitive Policy Areas?' (2002) 8 *European Law Journal* 38–58 at 49–50.

138 Ashiagbor, n. 24 at 233, argues that owing to additional obligations to comply with guidelines, 'elements of the open method are indeed quite "hard" or coercive'.

139 See Szyszczak, n. 114 at 1144.

140 See Szyszczak, n. 114 at 1139.

141 See also de la Porte, n. 137 at 53. This mobilization should not be mistaken for what Roberto Mangabeira Unger would call 'high energy politics', that is, periods of sustained mass mobilization that lead up to profound political and economic changes. See his *Democracy Realized: The Progressive Alternative* (London: Verso, 1998) at 218–219.

142 For example, the Year for People with Disabilities was also the year in which the Council displayed symbolic agency by admonishing the Member States to be more active where the social integration of people with disabilities is concerned. See Council Resolution of 5 May 2003 on equal opportunities for pupils and students with disabilities in education and training [2003] OJ C 134; Council Resolution of 6 May 2003 on accessibility of cultural infrastructure and cultural activities for people with disabilities [2003] OJ C 134; Council Resolution of 15 July 2003 on promoting the employment and social integration of people with disabilities, OJ C 175.

143 The hope is, of course, that enlisting them would result in 'wage moderation'. See Social Policy Agenda, n. 91 at 7. The social partners were included into the European Employment Strategy as part of the OMC even though their cooperation had not been envisaged by the EC Treaty. See Szyszczak, n. 114 at 1148–1150.

144 See Social Policy Agenda, n. 91 at 14–15. See also Future of the European Employment Strategy, n. 127 at 18. See generally, Kilpatrick, n. 20 at 134–142, on the interaction of both public and private actors.

The selective mobilization of stakeholders and experts[145] is mostly restricted to the funding of data collection, reporting and other initiatives that result in communication. From a Habermasian perspective, the efforts at coordination lend themselves to an idealized description in terms of communicative action.[146] What one encounters in practice, however, is a great variety of machinations by governments that refer to European processes for the purpose of blame-avoidance, thereby either overstating or understating the impact of Europe.[147]

Mobilization is the energizing momentum underlying the OMC, which is widely expected to be capable of *both* 'Europeanising' public policy problems[148] and overcoming future integration obstacles.[149] It introduces into the overall communicative context of new governance a competitive element as a result of which participants experience peer pressure—via guidelines, benchmarks, and recommendations prepared by the Commission or adopted by the Council—to excel in policy innovation.[150] This is congruent with the economic reconfiguration of normativity that is inherent to new governance methods: non-compliance is tantamount to the unwillingness to improve.[151]

The OMC can be usefully contrasted[152] with the classical Community Method, which is based on Commission initiative, legislation by the Council (and Parliament), Member State implementation (in the case of Directives), and the monitoring of compliance.[153] The pragmatic principle underpinning the use of the OMC has been most clearly formulated by Zeitlin.[154] The Union resorts to it where, first,

[145] The lack of involvement of the local authorities and people with experience 'on the ground' is criticized by Zeitlin, n. 124 at 236.

[146] See above p. 12.

[147] See Zeitlin, n. 124 at 230.

[148] See Daly, n. 132 at 8.

[149] For a short description, see Jacobsson, n. 104 at 357–358; Ashiagbor, n. 24 at 208–215. This method opens the door for the Union to creep into areas of policy-making regardless of whether it has competence for legislation or not. Nevertheless, looking at the substance of the open coordination process that has been introduced under Title IX FEU Treaty (ex Title VIII EC Treaty), one might wonder whether the tendency to assimilate social policy to the functional requirements of transnational capitalism does not prevail even in this context. See, in particular, Presidency Conclusions of the Lisbon European Council, 23–24 March 2000, paras 7, 28–34, 37–40. C. Offe, 'The European Model of "Social" Capitalism: Can it Survive European Integration?' (2003) 11 *Journal of Political Philosophy* 437–46 at 467, quite perceptibly points out that the OMC is not a method of coordination at all, rather it is a method of cooperation. In the event that mere cooperation is sought by a group of agents, what is desired is a convention regardless of its content. Cooperation is the more difficult social process for it encompasses the process of debating over the merits of a rule and negotiating compliance costs. For useful assessments of the efficacy of this method, see Mosher and Trubek, n. 124; de la Porte, n. 137, 38–58.

[150] See, generally, Sabel, n. 26 at 15.

[151] See ibid. at 12.

[152] See Trubek and Trubek, n. 22 at 550. This contrast is drawn particularly starkly by Zeitlin who insinuates that the launching of the Lisbon strategy marked a watershed in the pursuit of European integration, that is, the shift from the traditional Community method to the increasing use of the OMC. However, he also claims that the OMC in a certain respect is continuous with and, indeed, a 'renewal' of the Community Method in that it builds upon a 'permanent deliberative disequilibrium' that excludes selfish outcomes without giving rise to results that are 'transcendently public-regarding'. See Zeitlin, n. 124 at 213–214, 222.

[153] See the *White Paper on Governance*. See European Commission, European Governance. A White Paper, COM(2001) 428 final at 8–9, 22.

[154] See Zeitlin, n. 124 at 219, 221.

the diversity of national traditions precludes harmonization and, second, inaction would be nonetheless inacceptable. The principle reiterates a paradox. First, the OMC comes into play precisely where Scharpf diagnosed the lack not merely of Union competence, but of political power owing to a sharp discrepancy of Member State interest.[155] The OMC thus represents action without power or, more precisely, action without the ability to leave an imprint. Second, even though there cannot be action, there must not be inaction either. Just as the middle between a norm and its non-existence is what Hegel once derided as 'empty ought',[156] the middle between action and inaction is mere activity. The OMC materializes in recursive activity. Positively speaking, it introduces activity into a domain marked by powerlessness, hoping that *something* might come from bustling interaction as the result of a miraculous collective bootstrapping exercise.[157]

The OMC employs iterative benchmarking of national policies with regard to European objectives. It rests its hope on mutual learning in order to stimulate and to facilitate reform in areas with highly diverse national traditions, such as employment and social policy.[158] However, it has been correctly observed that the method can also be used to complement existing legislation and thus to create 'hybrid' regimes.[159] Hence, the OMC comes in a variety of forms and has undergone modifications in specific areas of public policy.[160] The use of the OMC has been extended from the employment context (the so-called Luxembourg process or the European Employment Strategy)[161] to efforts to combat social exclusion and to matters such as pension reform.[162] Nevertheless, it is fair to say[163] that it is based upon certain general principles, such as participation across several levels, decentralized information-gathering, flexible revisability, and peer review.[164] In contrast

[155] See above p. 39.

[156] See G. W. F. Hegel, *Science of Logic*, trans. by A. V. Miller (London: George Allen & Unwin Ltd, 1969), at 133–136.

[157] For an appropriately sceptical assessment of the effectiveness of the OMC, see Daly, n. 132 at 8, 12; M. Höpner and A. Schäfer, 'Grundzüge einer politökonomischen Perspektive auf die europäische Union', in M. Höpner and A. Schäfer (eds), *Die politische Ökonomie der europäischen Integration* (Frankfurt: Campus Verlag, 2008), 11–45 at 13, 22.

[158] See Trubek, Cottrell, and Nance, n. 22 at 77.

[159] Kilpatrick, n. 20 at 131 goes even so far as to claim that the OMC, the European Social Fund and employment law have already coalesced into one hybrid regime. See also Trubek, Cottrell, and Nance, n. 22 at 82.

[160] For example, whereas the pursuit of the European Employment Strategy involves the production of national action plans, the latter are not part of the OMC used in the sphere of social inclusion. See Armstrong and Kilpatrick, n. 72 at 648, 657, 673.

[161] See below p. 75.

[162] See D. Natali and C. de la Porte, 'Participation through the Lisbon Strategy: Comparing the European Employment Strategy and Pensions OMC' (2009) 15 *European Review of Labour and Research* 71–91. See also Scott and Trubek, n. 20 at 4–9; Offe, n. 149 at 461. See also Council Conclusions of the Stockholm Council 2001. Zeitlin, n. 124 at 216, predicts the extension of the OMC to a great variety of policy areas in the future.

[163] It is claimed, however, that any generalization of the OMC amounts to a reckless simplification. See Armstrong and Kilpatrick, n. 72 at 654.

[164] For a more thorough characterization, see Trubek, Cottrell, and Nance, n. 22 at 77–79.

to Union legislation, the OMC trusts softer methods, such as emulation, mutual learning, shaming of underachievers, and, above all, voluntary convergence.[165]

For two reasons, at the least, it is an open question whether the OMC can indeed give rise to remarkable transformations in the context of employment.[166]

First, against the background of the diversity of European systems of social protection, the identification of 'best practice' cannot make much sense.[167] It would make sense only if, for example, the continental European welfare states were de facto pressured into adopting more residual solutions or a more inclusive approach to labour market policy. But when Member States experience pressure to react to economic necessity, come what may, it becomes difficult to attribute reform to learning from peers. The results that one has seen of the use of the OMC seem to support such a sceptical conclusion. Member States shift from withdrawing people from the labour market (for example, through incentives for early retirement) to assisting them to adapt (for example, encourage lifelong learning).[168] The change of orientation might have originated from the confluence of increasing regulatory interaction and heightened strains of the national budget. It is difficult to attribute the efforts of the omnipresent neoliberal readjustment of systems of social protection to the success of the OMC. It is not conceivable that they could have come about without that formidable tool or, alternatively, that learning from others offers clues as to how best to 'neoliberalize'.

Second, in a field that is marked by high public vigilance and heavily entrenched interests on the part of domestic stakeholders, it is not quite clear why a national government should have incentives to comply with non-binding Council recommendations if doing so would trigger retribution by the national electorate. It may well be the case, thus, that voluntary participation merely signals 'good faith' and loyalty to European integration,[169] while labour markets and social protection systems remain in limbo. For purposes of integration, this would be a perfectly sufficient achievement if it were indeed the ultimate aim of integration to create the appearance of activity and to celebrate its own growth.

9. First-order and Second-order Discourse

The pragmatic limitations inherent in what is celebrated, by some, as a 'new form of pragmatic constitutionalism'[170] do not alter the fact that the OMC is an

165 There is, however, not much evidence that these processes do actually take place. See Zeitlin, n. 124 at 233–234. It also uses 'benchmarking' as a means of comparison, which is a typical management tool. See Szyszczak, n. 114 at 1145.

166 On the following, see also Offe, n. 149 at 465–467. Jacobsson, n. 104 at 358 arrives at a much more optimistic assessment of the efficacy of the OMC and attributes it to high-level political participation, 'which entails more mutual commitments and peer-pressure mechanism than the ad hoc and weak procedures of previous soft law mechanisms'.

167 A 'lack of fit' is even brought up in national reports. See Mosher and Trubek, n. 124 at 74.

168 See Zeitlin, n. 124 at 229.

169 For that possibility, see ibid. at 229–230; Daly, n. 132 at 13.

170 See Zeitlin, n. 124 at 222–223.

altogether exceptional communicative feat. Not only does it involve the use of discourse in the form of reporting, recommending, and shaming, it has also given rise to a whole cottage industry of scholarship that is devoted to explaining what the OMC *truly* is[171] or why it has attained the status of the preferred tool for the new 'experimentalist' governance of the European Union.[172] This development suggests that second-order discourse is an integral legitimating factor. Not by accident, the production of the relevant scholarship has been encouraged and even funded by the European Union itself.[173]

Social science discourse creates a political surplus, incidentally, for it cannot easily address the desirability of results. Above all, this would be overtly political. What is more, the results of the OMC do not lend themselves to a direct impact evaluation simply because of its reflexive manner of operation.[174] Recognition of failure is success. The method cannot fail on its own terms as long as the goal of the process is to redefine goals in the event of underachievement. Hence, one can always attribute bad performance to the mischaracterizations of goals and emerge victorious from learning. With the OMC, the Union and the learning Member States always win.

Social science research is hence drawn to examining methods and processes rather than results. It is even likely to react with enthusiasm where the instrumentality of policy-making appears to be a replica of the international scholarly community itself owing to the presence of factors such as paper production, exchange of ideas, 'ranking' (benchmarking), and peer review. The social science community is inclined to signal even greater approbation when real-world problem-solving appears to reflect the spirit of Deweyan pragmatism. Suddenly, the grey world of bureaucratic paper production can be perceived as clad in a decorous philosophical garb.[175] The resulting celebration of new governance on the discursive level reinforces the belief that discourse and mobilization actually accomplish something.

What is achieved, in any event, is the self-referential reproduction of discourse. It has been suggested, indeed, that should the OMC encounter difficulties or even resistance in the course of its operation, it ought to be applied reflexively to itself through the creation of benchmarks with regard to the working of the benchmarking process.[176]

[171] For a highly illuminating discussion of four conceivable models, see Ashiagbor, n. 24 at 215–235. For a perspective that is skeptical of all generalizations, see Armstrong and Kilpatrick, n. 72. For a general overview and analysis, see N. Walker and G. de Búrca, 'Reconceiving Law and New Governance' (2007) 13 *Columbia Journal of European Law* 519–537.

[172] For a most comprehensive and most pronounced instance of this scholarship, see C. F. Sabel and J. Zeitlin, 'Learning from Difference: The New Architecture of Experimentalist Governance in the European Union' (2007) C-07-02 *European Governance Papers* at 22–25.

[173] See, for example, the Connex Network, http://www.connex-network.org accessed 7 February 2011.

[174] For similar but less pointed observations, see Zeitlin, n. 124 at 228. On the OMC qua 'reflexive harmonization', see Ashiagbor, n. 24 at 220–226.

[175] See Sabel, n. 26.

[176] See Zeitlin, n. 124 at 226.

10. Emotivism: from Rights to Attitudes

Holism and mobilization eclipse what would otherwise be noticed for its pointed silence. The message implicit in the Employment Strategy is that creative ideas and institutional innovations are needed because what is currently in place has become untenable.[177] What is in place is, evidently, nothing short of the traditional rights associated with the status of a regular worker or an employee. Over the last decades these rights have become 'uncool'.[178] They had to take the blame for 'rigidity', lack of access for outsiders, high expenditures, and the competitive disadvantages resulting thereof. Consequently, status-related rights are absent in this discourse.[179] They do not matter. In their absence, the only material that the law or political initiatives can work with is the *attitudes* of actors. Governance defies legality. This explains the *emotivism*[180] pervading the new social policy.[181] It is about changing the attitudes and qualifications of persons on the basis of a variety of means, increasingly, however, through 'awareness-raising', personal encounters, re-skilling, that is, through the application of correctional techniques, and other methods of creating adaptable human resources. While employees are expected to become more success-oriented, employers need to overcome their sexism, racism, homophobia, xenophobia, religious intolerance, patriotism, or parochialism.

Not surprisingly, the talk of cooperative efforts at awareness-raising and again, strategies of mobilization, occupy ample space in sketches of the future anti-discrimination agenda.[182] In its 2004 report, for example, the Commission publicly applauded, among other things,[183] the following initiatives taken by the Member States: the introduction by France of a new sanction that forces discriminators to attend a 'citizenship course' (*stage de citoyenneté*) inculcating in them the importance of diversity, tolerance of others, and respect for human rights;[184] the sending of those found guilty of discrimination to correctional facilities; the adoption of codes of practice at the inter- and supra-firm level against racism and other forms of discrimination; the encouragement of people to report cases of discrimination they

[177] See S. Deakin, 'The Many Futures of the Contract of Employment', in J. Conaghan, R. M. Fischl, and K. Klare (eds), *Labour Law in the Age of Globalisation* (Oxford: Oxford University Press, 2002), 177–196.

[178] For succinct observations, see R. Gerlach, 'Wozu noch Arbeitsrecht?' (2003) 2 *Juridikum* 103–106.

[179] An obstacle to such a debate, ironically, is the existence of the Charter. On its role, see Ashiagbor, n. 24 at 172–178.

[180] The term is borrowed from moral theory. Emotivism is a theory of morality claiming that the point of moral argument is to change the attitude of its addressee. See C. L. Stevenson, *Facts and Values* (New Haven, CT: Yale University Press, 1963), at 10–31.

[181] Foucauldians, to be sure, would at this point sense the presence of 'neoliberal governmentality'. See T. Lemke, '"The Birth of Bio-politics": Michel Foucault's Lectures at The Collège de France on Neoliberal Governmentality' (2001) 30 *Economy and Society* 190–207.

[182] See Green Paper, n. 14 at 26.

[183] For example, conciliation procedures for the settlement of discrimination issues, involvement of trade unions and NGOs to support victims of discrimination.

[184] See 'Annual Report', n. 16 at 19.

happen to observe via a telephone hotline (which smacks of snitching, to be sure); the organization of a competition for students aged 10 to 19 to come up with creative ideas for combating discrimination.[185]

The Commission leaves no doubt that in its opinion awareness-raising is indispensable for success.[186] Already in 2004, it launched a website with the URL http://www.stop-discrimination.info,[187] and conducted an advertisement campaign with a 'Stop Discrimination' Truck. Among other things, 'run for diversity' T-shirts were given out to marathon runners across Europe to wear during city marathons.[188]

11. The Underlying Silence

Should the silence of mobilizational policy with regard to existing status rights really be a reason for concern? If nothing is accomplished in this process, nothing is destroyed either.

However, something is rendered obscure in the course of the discursive overdetermination of the individual and collective rights of employees. Aside from its lack of transparency, accountability, and the absence of normative standards addressing matters of fair participation,[189] the communicative celebration of restructuring puts into question the core of the 'old' systems of social protection. Somewhat misleadingly, the point of these systems was often explained with reference to 'social and economic citizenship'.[190] It means, merely, that access to certain goods ought to be insulated from the market nexus and guaranteed by the state, broadly understood. This insulating effort pertains, in particular, to health insurance, pension payments, or educational facilities and extends all the way down to the social position that often provides access to social insurance schemes, namely employment ('the job').

Within a Bismarck-style social welfare regime, at any rate, enjoying the rights associated with social citizenship presupposes employment. Paradoxically, the attenuation of market dependency implicates its exacerbation. The key to resolving the conflict between independence and dependency has been thought to lie in making employment sustainable. For employment to be sustainable it has to be stable and free from depersonalization and humiliation. This explains the existence

[185] See ibid. at 25, 30–31.

[186] See ibid. at 26. Part of this process was an advertisement campaign.

[187] The Web address is now http://ec.europa.eu/employment_social/fdad/cms/stopdiscrimination?langid=en accessed 22 December 2010. See also http://www.age-platform.org/ accessed 23 December 2010.

[188] See 'Annual Report', n. 16 at 29.

[189] This is correctly highlighted by Szyszczak, n. 114 at 1141, 1170; see also Zeitlin, n. 124 at 226, 232, 236.

[190] See, for example, J. Wickham, 'The End of the European Social Model: Before it Began?', http://www.tcd.ie/ERC/observatorydownloads/Social%20Model.pdf, 1–5 accessed 23 December 2010. See, more generally, M. Roche, *Rethinking Citizenship: Welfare, Ideology and Change in Modern Society* (Cambridge: Polity Press, 1992).

of labour law and why its existence makes a difference with regard to a *mere* employment strategy that is aimed at making human resources more perfectly adapted to fluctuant markets. On the basis of labour law, work can be understood, by employees, as a mere means that is needed to attain ends which lie outside employment itself. What is more, the relative job security associated with sustainable employment gives rise to a more casual work ethic. Workers who are protected against the loss of their jobs and whose interests are represented at the enterprise level need not transfigure their dependence on a dull task into the meaning of life. They can take it easier because they can accept that what they do does not matter to them. Conversely, work becomes all the more important the more individuals are exposed to the omnipresent competitive maxim to improve in order to succeed. When self-improvement and self-management vis-à-vis the job attain overwhelming importance, life itself becomes transformed into a perennial ('lifelong') run for perfection.[191]

It goes without saying that the core components of social citizenship, thus understood, are the protection from unjustified dismissal, mutually coordinated, and socially cushioned redundancies, a state-funded backup system that protects employees against the consequences of the employer's bankruptcy, minimum wage, or collective wage determination, working hours regulations, rights to a maternity or paternity leave, paid sick leaves (for a certain period, at any rate), paid vacations, and, finally, the predominance of a regular employment relationship that pays a wage sufficient to earn a living. Employees' representatives are necessary in order to secure these rights and to humanize the execution of tasks that are defined from above. In the context of the workplace, at any rate, economic citizenship encompasses not only the right to a healthy and safe workplace but also the right to have a say, or at least to be regularly informed, where the conduct of business is concerned. The most developed form of such rights are rights to codetermination at both the workplace and the board of supervisors' level.

Existing regimes of social citizenship have been chastised for their 'rigidity'[192] (and 'flexicurity' is presented as the cure).[193] I am inclined to believe that the obsession with 'rigidity'[194] is myopic because it overlooks the overall systemically

[191] Viewed from this angle, neoliberalism is, indeed, illiberal, for it makes it indispensible for people to adopt a more or less perfectionist lifestyle. It should not surprise us to see that those who are left of the left begin to rediscover basic liberal values, such as the value of legality. See, for example, M. Koskenniemi, 'Constitutionalism as Mindset: Reflections on Kantian Themes About International Law and Globalization' (2007) 8 *Theoretical Inquires in Law* 9–36.

[192] See Wickham, n. 190 at 4. See also S. Deakin and H. Reed, 'The Contested Meaning of Labour Market Flexibility', in J. Shaw (ed.), *Social Law and Policy in an Evolving European Union* (Oxford: Hart, 2000), 71–102 at 76.

[193] It suggests a combination of little or no job security with state support for the unemployed and strong effects to restore employability through retraining. See Council Conclusions on Flexicurity in times of crisis, 2947th Employment, Social Policy, Health and Consumer Affairs Council meeting Luxembourg, 8 June 2009; European Commission, Towards Common Principles of Flexicurity: More and Better Jobs through Flexibility and Security, COM(2007) 359 final.

[194] For an overview of the debate and the difficulties faced by European Social Democrats, see J. Handler, 'The "Third Way" or the Old Way?' (2000) 48 *Kansas Law Review* 765–800 at 771–778.

beneficial effects of social and economic citizenship.[195] The cooperative structure in which it is embedded secures collective rationality for it makes trade unions, which are organized at a trans-enterprise level, more other-regarding in their behaviour, and enlists both capital and labour to the long-term project of joint economic success—a responsibility that invites moderation in times of crisis.[196] Indeed, what happens to this core of European social regimes in the course of European integration is that they become recast in 'softer' formats—for example, the format of nice and high-minded glossy brochures that deal with corporate responsibility.[197] What used to be treated as a matter of right is in the process of becoming transformed into a matter of appropriate or congenial governance style.

12. Vague Hopes

It is not the case, to be sure, that social and economic citizenship rights are likely to be dismantled in one fell swoop. There is simply no European political debate. The absence of debate is intertwined with the persistence of the diffuse hope that the direct application of the Fundamental Rights Charter on the output of competitive and interactive policy generation[198] would push the process in the right direction. As a fallback position, there is confidence, too, that the very process itself might serve as a bulwark against the neoliberal tide.

With the entry into force of the Lisbon Treaty, the essential parts of the Charter have officially attained direct effect.[199] This prospect makes it all the more reasonable

[195] Evidently, I couldn't agree more with Handler, n. 194 at 800, who concludes that 'one of the few bright spots in the twentieth century was the European social democratic welfare state in the post World War II period' and that it needs to be defended.

[196] See C. Offe, 'The European Model of "Social" Capitalism: Can it Survive European Integration?' (2003) 11 *Journal of Political Philosophy* 437–469 at 444. Offe also adds that high wages are conducive to innovation. He concludes that

> taken together, economic status rights will not only *protect* economic actors (employees, farmers, artisans, small and medium-sized businesses, banks, the professions etc.) from adverse impacts; they can also *contribute* to overall and long-term (economic as well as non-economic) outcomes that are superior to pure market transaction with its blindness to the interest of others, to externalities and to the past or future. If there is anything distinctive about the 'European' model of capitalism, it is the insight, congealed in a myriad of economic institutions and regulatory arrangements, that the interest of 'all of us' will be served well if the pursuit of the interest of 'each of us' is to some extent constrained by categorical status rights.

[197] For example, 'softer' initiatives have been made with regard to strengthening corporate social responsibility on a purely voluntary basis. See the Green Paper by the European Commission on Promoting a European Framework for Corporate Responsibility, COM (2001) 366, which clearly seeks to replace regulation with habitualization. See also the Communication from the Commission concerning 'Corporate Social Responsibility: A Business Contribution to Sustainable Development', COM (2002) 347; see Council Resolution of 6 February 2003 on corporate social responsibility, OJ 2003/C 39/02.

[198] See B. Hepple, *Rights at Work: Global, European and British Perspectives* (London: Sweet & Maxwell, 2006), at 36–37; S. Giubboni, *Social Rights and Market Freedoms in the European Constitution: A Labour Law Perspective*, trans. by R. Inston (Cambridge: Cambridge University Press, 2006), at 145–149.

[199] See Article 6(1) EU Treaty.

to presume the rights contained in the Charter to have an impact on the interpretation of Union law.[200] Aside from enshrining a number of social rights in its Titles III ('Equality') and IV ('Solidarity'), the Charter guarantees freedom of association (Article 12) and prohibits slavery and forced labour (Article 5). Among the core social rights that are protected figure prominently the right of workers to consultation (Article 27) and to collective bargaining (Article 28), the right to protection from unjustified dismissal (Article 30), and the right to a free placement service (Article 29). Some provisions, though, are devoid of normative import, for example, the 'recognition' on the part of the Union of access to services of general economic interest (Article 34).

The application of the rights is limited, however, in three important respects.

First, in several instances, the Charter contains a *default deference* to protection afforded 'in accordance with the rules laid down by Union law and national laws and practices'. For example, the right protecting against unjustified dismissal and the rights associated with maternity, illness, or industrial accidents are subject to this proviso (Articles 30 and 34). It has to mean more than merely the requirement that any restriction needs to be based on law. Otherwise, the relevant provision of Article 52 would be rendered superfluous.[201]

Since the Charter only applies within the scope of application of Union law it is clear that the proviso contains a default reference to the national standard of protection. Conceivably, it means that unless there is Union legislation, the level of protection does not exceed the scope of protection granted by national laws. This is not to say that the Charter rights are empty. It may mean that national provisions can be held against the Member State without regard to the nationality of the person affected. Such a reading of the default reference would be consonant with the Charter's explicit claim not to expand the scope of application of Union law and to be applicable only within that scope. When read in conjunction with Article 52, however, the Charter rights can be given even more bite. Article 52 says that any limitation on the exercise of the rights and freedoms recognized by the Charter must be provided for by law and respect the essence of those rights and freedoms. Since the history of German fundamental rights jurisprudence taught that this alleged 'essence' can only be determined on the basis of the application of the proportionality principle,[202] it is fair to say that national provisions, even though

[200] Not, of course, for the United Kingdom and Poland. Both countries decided to stick to the existing fundamental rights *acquis*, even though it may be very difficult to distinguish extensions of existing rights to new situations from applications of Charter rights proper. As regards the social rights laid down in Title IV of the Charter, it is clear, however, that the relevant provisions remain inapplicable. See Article 1(2) of the Protocol on the Application of the Charter of Fundamental Rights of the European Union to Poland and to the United Kingdom.

[201] Article 52 of the Charter provides that any limitation on the exercise of the rights and freedoms recognized by this Charter must be provided for by law.

[202] See M. Stelzer, *Das Wesensgehaltsargument und der Grundsatz der Verhältnismäßigkeit* (Vienna/New York: Springer, 1991).

introducing a default level, must not fall below what is necessary to protect these rights in a meaningful way. The same holds true, but without default deference, of rights that are guaranteed without the proviso. They are also susceptible to infringement on proportionate grounds (Article 59 FEU Treaty (ex 52 EC Treaty)).

Second, consonant with the default deference, the Charter explicitly intends not to extend the scope of Union competence (Article 58[2] FEU Treaty (ex 51[2] EC Treaty)). Hence, even though the Charter merrily promises the right to strike, this is a promise that it cannot keep simply because Article 153[5] FEU Treaty (ex 137 [5] EC Treaty) categorically excludes Union jurisdiction on this issue.[203]

Third, the Charter applies only to acts of the Union and to those acts where the Member States are to be considered as its agent ('when implementing Union law').[204] There can be little doubt that when the Member States make attempts to comply with recommendations they do not implement *law* and are hence not confronted with the responsibility for their potential failure to comply through improvement.[205] It may be objected that, thus understood, Member State agency is far too narrowly construed. Alternatively, the actors involved in the European Employment Strategy could be viewed as partners in a common Union enterprise. Hence, the Charter would be relevant to all national laws, e.g. labour legislation, enacted by Member States owing to their membership in the modernization team. Owing to the holistic grip of new governance, however, the pedigree of national legislation would remain profoundly unclear. Legislation against the background of informal policy coordination is not, at any rate, tantamount to the implementation of a Directive or the application of a Regulation. It could be argued that since the European Employment Strategy is merely part of the broader Lisbon process, in the final event all Member State acts would have to be seen as 'implementations' of European Union policy. Such an interpretation would rob Article 51(2) of its normative import. Hence, the Charter simply cannot apply to voluntary compliance by Member States with benchmarks or recommendations.

This sobering insight might explain why some are disposed to rest their hopes on the process of competitive creative policy interaction itself. Perhaps the 'values' enshrined in the Charter are best realized on the basis of the OMC processes themselves.[206]

[203] I am following C. Barnard, 'Social Policy Revisited in the Light of the Constitutional Debate', in C. Barnard (ed.), *The Fundamentals of EU Law Revisited: Assessing the Impact of the Constitutional Debate* (Oxford: Oxford University Press, 2007), 109–151 at 116, while being aware that a different interpretation might be possible.

[204] Article 51(1) of the Charter. Hence, the Charter is narrower than existing jurisprudence which also extends the scope of application to instances where Member States derogate from fundamental freedoms. See Case C-260/89, *ERT* [1991] ECR I-2925.

[205] See Sabel, n. 26 at 12.

[206] For a proposal to use the OMC for the purpose of fundamental rights realization, see O. de Schutter, 'The Implementation of the EU Charter of Fundamental Rights through the Open Method of Coordination' (2004) 7/04 *Jean Monnet Working Paper*, http://www.jeanmonnetprogram.org/papers/04/040701.html. For a critical perspective, see K. A. Armstrong, 'The Open Method of Cooperation and Fundamental Rights: A Critical Appraisal', http://eucenter.wisc.edu/OMC/Papers/Rights/armstrong.pdf.

The wellspring of creative ideas may deliver feasible solutions to problems of health and elder care.[207]

Even advocates of the method fear, however, that as a result of its operation the concordance in the relation of social and economic objectives will not necessarily materialize. In particular, the Member States have apparently fallen short when it comes to realizing labour market activation *plus* social inclusion, flexibility *plus* security, better pay *plus* flexible work organization, or the inclusion of the younger generation *plus* active ageing.[208] Regardless of what the future might hold, one should not be surprised that the experimentalist method does not automatically deliver results. The experimentalist ethos underlying new governance works best in a context where technological innovation accounts for the competitive edge. Techological optimization is in large part self-explanatory. The 120 GB iPod is superior to its 80 GB predecessor. The impression of apparent self-evidence does not come about for politically sensitive issues such as employment policy. Current EU policy reflects a strong tendency to equate the enhancement of flexibility/adaptability and the inclusion into the labour market with a successful employment strategy.[209] But this begs the question. Employment policy cannot be severed from larger questions of social policy that are deeply political. They affect the question of how Europeans want to live.

Lest we forget, political institutions are human inventions that help people to extricate themselves from the impression of false necessity.[210] Any politicization of the Employment Strategy, however, is avoided by the OMC. It should not come as a surprise, then, that the Green Paper and the Communications regarding the EQUAL programme are revealing also from a governance perspective. They read as though they had been compiled in a manner faithful to the strategies set out in the White Paper on Governance.[211] They invite the deliberate bypassing of traditional national constituencies by claiming the direct support of public opinion and transnational civil society. Consequently, the Commission points out that Eurobarometer polls indicate strong popular support in favour of anti-discrimination policy.[212] This is cheap. Who would, if asked, not be in favour of protection from discrimination? The EQUAL Programme also mobilizes civil society. Again, from the perspective of a well-meaning bureaucracy, one may believe that this is all it takes to bring the Union closer to its citizens. Moreover, the Commission prides

207 See Zeitlin, n. 124 at 241.

208 For a list of desiderata, see Future of the European Employment Strategy, n. 127.

209 See ibid. at 10; Report from the High Level Group chaired by Wim Kok, 'Facing the Challenge: The Lisbon strategy for growth and employment', http://europa.eu.int/comm/lisbon_strategy/index_en.html at 31 at 31–34.

210 See H. Arendt, *The Human Condition* (Chicago, IL: University of Chicago Press, 1959); R. M. Unger, *False Necessity* (Cambridge: Cambridge University Press, 1987).

211 European Commission, *European Governance: A White Paper*, COM (2001) 428 final, http://europa.eu.int/eur-lex/en/com/cnc/2001/com2001_0428en01.pdf.

212 It is the kind of popular support claimed for the adoption of a constitution. The invocation of such support is shabby propaganda, to say the least. Constitutions are by their very nature considered good things. If you ask a person on the street whether he would be in favour of a constitution, his reply would be a resounding 'Yes.' Similarly, if one were asked whether he or she would support efforts to combat discrimination he or she would not say no.

itself on its cooperation with nongovernmental actors. But these are, *pace* champions of deliberative democracy,[213] questionable sources of democratic legitimacy. They do not occupy the centre of national political debates, at any rate, not in a way that would match up with the central significance of political parties and government coalitions. It is definitely convenient for the Commission to tap such inputs, not least because they can be presented as 'democratic support'.[214] Upon closer inspection, however, this turns out to be a questionable invocation of democratic ideals. Democracy is *not* just about communication. It is also and vitally about the exercise of *power* by popular constituencies.

13. Conclusion

The last sections of this chapter seem to have led us far afield from anti-discrimination policy proper. Nonetheless, they were supposed to elucidate in which respect the latter is part of a complex web of policies that share a mobilizing and holistic productivist orientation. As a consequence, much responsibility is perceived to rest on the shoulders of employees. They are expected to adapt, to become more entrepreneurial and to subject their life to the discipline of lifelong learning. There is, on the other side, also an ever-increasing responsibility attributed to the employer to abstain from discrimination. Moreover, the emphasis on awareness-raising and on educating people about what is deemed to be normal in a diverse society indicates that policies are eventually targeted at changing the attitudes of market participants.

The puzzling moralism that emerges at this point will be explored in the following chapter, where I attempt to explain how it is concomitant with the rise of neoliberalism. Whereas this chapter tried to sketch a historical association, it is the systematic connection that I would like to explore next.

In subsequent chapters, it will be seen also how efforts at reinforcing the efficacy of anti-discrimination policy tend to rely on governance strategies that are strikingly similar to the move towards holism and mobilization that was to be observed for common European policy formation.

[213] See, in particular, J. S. Drysek, *Deliberative Democracy and Beyond: Liberals, Critics, Contestations* (Oxford: Oxford University Press, 2000).
[214] See *White Paper on Governance*, n. 211 at 11–16.

3

Neoliberalism and Morality

1. Introduction

The previous chapters examined the career of anti-discrimination law in the broader context of European social policy. I tried to point out that in light of both the formal legal powers and the actual capacities of Union legislation, the protection from discrimination does not collide with divergent national traditions and promises to bring about real progress. Substantively, anti-discrimination law is congruent with the Union's commitment to promote integration through market access. It commends itself, indeed, for a Union for which social policy is supposed to arrive at some appealing combination of competitiveness and solidarity (instead of merely mitigating the effect of the former on the latter). The most straightforward candidate for such a synthesis is equality of opportunity. Where the overall project is to improve the performance of markets, realizing equality becomes translated into facilitating non-discriminatory access to opportunities that have been generated by markets.

Remarkably, the pursuit of anti-discrimination objectives involves a turn from legislation to management. Legislation is increasingly complemented by, or embedded into, collaborative attempts at improving its effectiveness. At the macro level of institutional interaction, which is expected to reap the rewards of mutual learning, this is part of how the European Union aspires to make progress at the level of policy definition. By contrast, recent American anti-discrimination scholarship proposes to substitute abiding by laws with intra- and inter-firm training efforts at personal transformation—a matter to which I would like to return in section 8 in Chapter 7. In both cases, however, the maxim to strive for *constant improvement*, which is the prime directive of competition, displaces compliance with norms. The distinction between any given rule and its correct application becomes superseded by the distinction between the state prior and the state after improvement. What leads from one state to the other is either a learning or a training process. The application of norms begins to look old. It is apparently overcome by the intelligent engineering of version 2.0 from version 1.0. Not surprisingly, these new processes defy legality and target directly the attitudes of persons. In aiming at attitudes, they are remarkably moralistic.

In the previous chapter, I studied the move from law to management and training from an external point of view. In no manner, that is, did I examine whether there is something intrinsic to anti-discrimination law that might explain this move. In the chapters that follow, I would like to argue that the turn from 'hard' to 'soft' measures or, more accurately put, from legality to relentless improvement, is congruent with principles that govern the internal constitution of anti-discrimination law. It may not come as a surprise that the concern with attitudes, which takes centre stage in training efforts, bespeaks the utmost relevance of morality. This relevance is, in turn, an effect of what I would like to call the normative deficiency of anti-discrimination law.

This deficiency and the significance of morality do not emerge from an ideological vacuum. I speculate that they are deeply associated with the predominance (also known as 'hegemony' in Gramsci Marxist circles) of neoliberalism. In the pages that follow, I would like to enter a complex field with an emphasis on how morality and moralism are not by accident concomitant to the ascendancy of a set of beliefs that is ordinarily allied with neoliberal ideology.

The purpose of this chapter is to prepare the ground for further analysis. More precisely, it is through the lens of neoliberalism that I would like to hint at the themes that will be explored subsequently in the chapters that follow.

2. Neoliberalism

Using the protean term 'neoliberalism' for explanatory purposes may raise the spectre of intellectual shallowness. More than anything else, 'neoliberalism' has become the darling token of residual protest—the battle cry of last resort used by those who bemoan the demise of economic alternatives to global capitalism. The rhetoric of disempowered protest aside, however, the term can also be used with conceptual and historical accuracy[1] and thus help to locate the still predominant perspective on the human condition in a broader ideological setting.

With an eye to Foucault[2] and those who developed his late work on governance techniques into 'governmentality' studies,[3] I would like to characterize

[1] See, for example, D. Harvey, *A Brief History of Neoliberalism* (Oxford: Oxford University Press, 2005), 2–3, who introduces a very useful characterization of the common denominator of neoliberal policies. Accordingly, neoliberalism sees human well-being best advanced by 'liberating individual entrepreneurial freedoms and skills within an institutional framework characterised by strong private property rights, free markets, and free trade' (ibid., p. 2).

[2] See M. Foucault, *Ethics: Subjectivity and Truth*, ed. by P. Rabinow (New York: New Press, 1994), 76–78.

[3] See T. Lemke, '"The Birth of Bio-politics": Michel Foucault's Lectures at The Collège de France on Neoliberal Governmentality' (2001) 30 *Economy and Society* 190–207; A. Hunt and G. Wickham, *Foucault and Law: Towards a Sociology of Law as Governance* (London: Pluto Press, 1994); N. Rose, *Powers of Freedom: Reframing Political Thought* (Cambridge: Cambridge University Press, 1999); M. Dean, *Governmentality: Power and Rule in Modern Society* (New York: Sage Publications, 1999); G. Burchell, C. Gordon, and P. Miller (eds), *The Foucault Effect: Studies in Governmentality* (Chicago, IL: University of Chicago Press, 1991); W. Brown, 'Neoliberalism and the End of Liberal Democracy', in *Edgework: Critical Essays on Knowledge and Politics* (Princeton, NJ: Princeton University Press, 2005), 37–59. Most recently, U. Bröckling, *Das unternehmerische Selbst: Soziologie einer Subjektivierungsform* (Frankfurt: Suhrkamp, 2007).

neoliberalism—by contrast to classical liberalism—as the belief that the market is not merely one social sphere amongst others (which needs to be sheltered against state intrusion), but rather the universal law governing our social existence. At their deepest level, all of our relations are taken to be essentially market dealings—a matter over which adherents to a neoliberal social philosophy desire to enlighten people since, in their opinion, endorsing this view holds out the promise of material rewards.[4] Consequently—and again in contrast to classical liberalism—neoliberalism recognizes only one form of practical rationality, that is, the rationality of market participants. On the surface, of course, various social spheres exhibit commitments to different values and a multiplicity of ways of thinking. As a social institution, the family, for example, seems to be based on love and affection. However, according to the enlightened neoliberal view, the essence of even this type of social relation becomes intelligible only once it has been recast in terms of market conduct.[5] The pursuit of such a purportedly enlightening reexamination is extended, in particular, to politics.[6]

Neoliberalism, I hasten to add, is not merely an explanatory view *of* what motivates human conduct, namely, the pursuit of self-interest. It is more than a theory among others. Rather, as I tried to point out in the Introduction, it is part of the spirit of our age (see above p. 14). It is manifest in the widely shared belief that reflexive accounts of our conduct are likely to be successful, and not met with unrelenting contestation, when they are cast in terms of market rationality. This reveals their normative force. Appeals to the rationality of market participants are likely to be silently condoned—without, however, for that reason eliciting moral approbation—when obligations of loyalty towards family or colleagues become compromised or even sacrificed for the sake of personal advancement. We do not expect, at any rate, reflexive accounts in terms of market rationality to be morally appealing. They are likely to succeed, nonetheless, because everyone takes for granted that received moral conventions are relatively powerless vis-à-vis market rationality. Pursuant to a cognitive convention, reasons associated with market conduct are counted as motivationally *stronger* than reasons of morality. We mutually understand ourselves to be vulnerable to their overriding force. This expectation and the readiness to accommodate moral disillusionment are constitutive of the experience that market dealings are the *essence* of social life.

Substantively, neoliberalism represents a remarkable departure from its classical predecessor.[7] In fact, the departure is so radical that the composite

[4] See Brown, n. 3 at 40.

[5] See G. Becker, *A Treatise on the Family* (Cambridge, MA: Harvard University Press, 1991).

[6] For an orthodox introduction, see D. Mueller, *Public Choice III* (Cambridge: Cambridge University Press, 2003); for a critical introduction, see D. P. Green and I. Shapiro, *Pathologies of Rational Choice Theory: A Critique of Applications in Political Science* (New Haven, CT: Yale University Press, 1994).

[7] It is difficult to establish what classical liberalism was. There can be no doubt, however, that intellectual figures such as Wilhelm von Humbolt, Jakob Burckhardt or John Stuart Mill would figure prominently in such an account. See, for example, A. S. Kahan, *Aristocratic Liberalism: The Social and Political Thought of Jacob Burckhardt, John Stuart Mill and Alexis de Tocqueville*, 2nd edn (New Brunswick, NJ: Transaction Publishers, 2001), 167–177.

term 'liberalism' may even be a misnomer. Whereas liberals traditionally regarded the exercise of political rights amongst a people as crucial to the thriving of a free society, neoliberalism no longer conceives of social life in political terms.[8]

First, neoliberalism does not recognize political boundaries. More precisely, the neoliberal world no longer is a world composed of self-governing peoples divided along national lines.[9] Indeed, nation states come to be perceived of as sources of troublesome obstacles to the realization of economic objectives. Their existence is deemed to be justified provided that they submit themselves to some supranational discipline of harmonization and take it as a given that the ultimate rationale for regulation is competition among a variety of contending sites of regulation.[10]

Second, neoliberalism is apolitical in that it no longer sees the existence of common sympathies amongst a people as an indispensable prerequisite of freedom.[11] In fact, from a neoliberal perspective, political activity is said to be an extension of the rational pursuit of self-interest, which is, owing to the necessity to cooperate with others, time-consuming, costly, and fraught with difficulties or even irrationality. Neoliberalism is apolitical in that it treats the political as essentially continuous with the private pursuit of goals, and favours, where possible, the delegation of the correction of market failure to the bureaucratic state.[12] Hence, it makes societies systematically and drastically vulnerable to the rise of its own breed of administrative authoritarianism.[13] Not surprisingly, neoliberalism is compatible with individualism, as it had once been characterized by Tocqueville, namely as 'a sentiment [...] which disposes each citizen to isolate himself from the mass of his fellows and to retire in separation with his family and his friends; in such a way that, after having thus created for himself a little society for his own use, he freely abandons the larger society to itself'.[14]

[8] And if it does, it undoubtedly has an authoritarian slant. See, for example, the anti-democratic precautions that Hayek would have taken in his ideal constitution through the establishment of a small body of representatives in his *Law, Legislation, and Liberty*, vol. 3 (Chicago, IL: Chicago University Press, 1979), at 113.

[9] See, for example, L. von Mises, 'Liberalismus', in E. Becherath, H. Bente, and C. Brinkmann (eds), *Handwörterbuch der Sozialwissenschaften*, vol. 6 (Stuttgart: G. Fischer, 1959) 596–603.

[10] On the latter, see Brown, n. 3 at 41, 44.

[11] See J. S. Mill, *Considerations on Representative Government*, orig. edn 1861 (Amherst/New York: Prometheus Books, 1991, repr.), 310–311.

[12] This position is epitomized by G. Majone, 'Europe's "Democracy Deficit": A Question of Standards' (1998) 4 *European Law Journal* 5–28.

[13] On the tacit link between neoliberalism and authoritarianism, see W. E. Scheuerman, 'The Unholy Alliance of Carl Schmitt and Friedrich A. Hayek', (1997) 4 *Constellations* 172–188; see also A. Gamble, *Hayek: The Iron Cage of Liberty* (Cambridge: Polity Press, 1996).

[14] A. de Tocqueville, *Democracy in America*, trans. by H. C. Mansfield and D. Winthrop (Chicago, IL: Chicago University Press, 2000), at 482.

3. Freedom and Responsibility

The social generalization of individualism explains why, as soon as society at large[15] is asked to come to the rescue of some, the burden of proof rests on those who would like to benefit from so-called government largesse. In order to be publicly persuasive,[16] nonetheless, neoliberal justifications need to rationalize inaction. As Max Weber was well aware,[17] the key term of such a justification is 'responsibility'. He sensed that, as a means of rationalization, it serves consistently the interest of those who are too avaricious to give. The importance attributed to responsibility affects the understanding of human freedom.

Neoliberalism is highly sceptical of any purported collective human ability to influence human well-being for the better.[18] Consequently, it highlights individual responsibility for prudent adaptation. Society at large does not act. Hence, it cannot be held responsible. But individuals act, and they can incur responsibility for what they do, in particular for their own mismanaged life.[19]

Political freedom is an empty concept for neoliberals. All freedom is exercised in the private sphere. This truncation concerns nothing short of the *meaning* of freedom itself.[20] Whereas liberals ordinarily recognize the necessity to resort to political action in order to defend what gives value to their freedom, neoliberalism, owing to the disappearance of the former, reduces all freedom to the individual ability of adaptation. Freedom is considered valuable only inasmuch as it helps people to adjust to social conventions and shifting demands.[21] Hence, neoliberal morality may concede that political intervention becomes unavoidable where individual adaptation is impossible owing to circumstances that are beyond a person's control.[22] However, these circumstances are considered evil only if they can be traced back to the evil attitudes of persons. Society at large cannot do wrong, for it does not exist as a collective body. All evil originates from individual acts, which are manifestations of attitudes.

[15] True adherents to neoliberalism do not even recognize the existence of an entity called 'society'. See F. A. Hayek, *The Fatal Conceit: The Errors of Socialism* (Chicago, IL: Chicago University Press, 1988), at 112–113.

[16] For an attempt to come up with an account of authority that actually avoids moralization and straightforwardly endorses the rights of the more powerful in a manner reminiscent of ancient sophists, see J. Buchanan, *The Limits of Liberty* (Chicago, IL: University of Chicago Press, 1985).

[17] M. Weber, *Economy and Society: An Outline of Interpretive Sociology*, trans. by E. Fischoff et al. (New York: Bedminster Press 1968), vol. 2 at 46.

[18] See F. A. Hayek, *The Road to Serfdom*, new edn (London: Routledge, 2007).

[19] See Brown, n. 3 at 42.

[20] This is quite evident in one revealing essay by Hayek. See F. A. Hayek, 'Individualism: True and False', in *Individualism and Economic Order* (Chicago, IL: University of Chicago Press, 1948), 1–32. It makes sense, indeed, to insist on the mutual dependence of political and private freedom. See J. Habermas, *Between Facts and Norms: Contributions to a Discourse Theory of Law and Democracy*, trans. by W. Rehg (Cambridge: Polity Press, 1996).

[21] See Hayek, n. 20, at 22, 24.

[22] On the resulting assimilationist bias, which is the belief that protection from discrimination is unnecessary as long as it does not affect immutable characteristics, see K. Yoshino, 'Covering' (2002) 111 *Yale Law Journal* 769–939 at 772.

The individual responsibility for one's own lot is thus complemented by the reduction of moral questions to the morality (i.e., right or wrong motivation) of conduct.

4. Redistribution and Decommodification

It needs to be conceded that an association with neoliberalism, thus understood, is not written on the face of anti-discrimination law. To assume that it obtains may even appear to be counterintuitive. I am confident, nonetheless, that the association becomes clearer when anti-discrimination law is considered to be an exemplar of social legislation.

Trivial characterizations of social policy in terms of 'market-correction' aside,[23] I depart from a minimal formulation according to which social legislation, regardless of its ultimate goals, pursues at least two objectives: *redistribution*, on the one hand, and *decommodification*, on the other. Whereas the aim of the former is to correct the market-based distribution of wealth and opportunities, the latter seeks to rescue human life from the relentless grasp of the market.[24]

A characterization of anti-discrimination law against the backdrop of this alternative may strike one as narrow. Ordinarily, the anti-discrimination principle is given a variety of conflicting and seemingly more appealing interpretations.[25] Understood as an 'anti-differentiation principle', for example, it is taken to prohibit the use of certain factors for purposes of classification (with full symmetry between ins and outs, such as whites and blacks, men and women). This understanding is notoriously popular with courts.[26] Alternatively, qua 'anti-oppression principle', it is seen as ruling out the use of relevant distinctions for the purpose of oppression. Hence, the symmetry in the relation of oppressed and dominant groups (for example, women and men) disappears. Similarly, interpreted as 'anti-subordination' or 'anti-caste' principle, anti-discrimination law is aimed at overcoming the subordination of one group under another. Anti-discrimination law would hence serve the purpose of ending status hierarchies among groups in

[23] See T. H. Marshall, *Social Policy* (London: Heinemann, 1975).

[24] See, generally, G. Esping-Andersen, *The Three Worlds of Welfare Capitalism* (Princeton, NJ: Princeton University Press, 1990), 21–22; for a critical assessment of Esping-Andersen's use of the concept from a feminist perspective, see A. Shola Orloff, 'Gender and Social Rights of Citizenship: The Comparative Analysis of Gender Relations and Welfare States' (1993) 58 *American Sociological Review* 303–328 at 311–314. I take it, however, that the critique does not detract from the usefulness of the notion itself.

[25] For an integral account that sees several conceptions of equality relevant to anti-discrimination law, see C. McCrudden, 'The New Concept of Equality' (2003) 3 *ERA-Forum* 9–29. For a highly illuminating interpretation of the equality principle and the values, with which it may compete, such as dignity or liberty, see S. Fredman, *Discrimination Law* (Oxford: Clarendon Press, 2002), at 15–24.

[26] On this and what follows, see J. Hasnas, 'Equal Opportunity, Affirmative Action, and the Anti-discrimination Principle: The Philosophical Basis for the Legal Prohibition of Discrimination' (2002) 71 *Fordham Law Review* 424–542 at 428, 431–438, 513.

society and not merely the narrower goal of avoiding the use of group-specific classifications.[27]

Preferring the duality of redistribution and decommodification over these alternatives is warranted for two reasons. The first reason is contingent. It is the interest underlying this essay to examine what anti-discrimination law offers as a type of social legislation. This reason does not deny that European equality law can be usefully conceptualized also from a different angle,[28] in particular from the perspective concerning the conditions of leading an autonomous life.[29] The second reason[30] is internal to anti-discrimination law and less accommodating as regards alternative approaches. It claims that anti-discrimination law is *best* understood in redistributive terms. In the next chapter, when exploring the concept of direct discrimination, it will be seen that there are very good, if not compelling, reasons for adopting the redistributive perspective. Once this perspective is in place, it will become clear why morality matters to the resolution of distributive questions and why this relevance is not by accident congruent with a neoliberal take on the social world.

5. Distribution by Means of Morality

The association of anti-discrimination law with the redistribution of resources and opportunities may still appear to be intuitively plausible, at any rate, more plausible than its relation with decommodification. Arguably, protection from discrimination exercises the relevant salutary effect, for example, when securing employment

[27] The anti-subordination principle has been the darling of the neoliberal left. See, for example, C. R. Sunstein, *Our Partial Constitution* (Cambridge, MA: Harvard University Press, 1993) at 339:

> The motivating idea behind an anticaste principle is that differences that are irrelevant from the moral point of view ought not without good reason to be turned by social and legal structures into social disadvantages. They certainly should not be permitted to do so if the disadvantage is systemic. A systemic disadvantage is one that operates along standard and predictable lines in multiple important spheres of social life, and applies in realms that relate to basic participation as a citizen in a democracy. These realms include education, freedom from private and public violence, wealth, political representation, and political influence. The anticaste principle might suggest that with respect to basic human capabilities and functionings, one group ought not to be systematically below the other.

For similar articulations of the anti-subordination principle, see, for example, J. Balkin, 'The Constitution of Status' (1997) 106 *Yale Law Journal* 2313–2374; J. Balkin and R. Siegel, 'The American Civil Rights Tradition: Anticlassification or Antisubordination' (2003) 58 *University of Miami Law Review* 9–33 at 13; R. Siegel, 'Equality Talk: Antisubordination and Anticlassification Values in Constitutional Struggles over Brown' (2004) 117 *Harvard Law Review* 1470–1547 at 1477; D. G. Reaumé, 'Discrimination and Dignity' (2003) 63 *Louisiana Law Review* 645–695.

[28] According to McCrudden, the European equality directives pursue anti-subordination aims in that they seek to remedy 'status harms'. See C. McCrudden, n. 25 at 13–17; C. McCrudden and H. Kountouros, 'Human Rights and European Equality Law' 2006/8 *University of Oxford Faculty of Law Legal Studies Research Paper*, 4–8 at 4–5.

[29] See J. Gardner, 'On the Grounds of Her Sex(uality)' (1998) 18 *Oxford Journal of Legal Studies* 167–187 at 170–171.

[30] In Chapter 4, this second reason will be further developed into two different reasons. See below pp. 99–100.

and participation in social life for those who would otherwise remain unemployed.[31] The contribution to decommodification, by contrast, is far less salient; it is less salient than, for example, in the case of a social health insurance system. Universal health insurance that covers citizens regardless of their contributions or category of risk attains a high level of decommodification. People at the receiving end of cross-subsidization live their life with a safety cushion they would scarcely avail of under market conditions. Anti-discrimination law does not, and maybe even should not, exercise a similarly strong effect. Anti-discrimination does not offer an employment or housing guarantee to the protected groups. Consequently, the discussion that follows will initially highlight the redistributive effect of anti-discrimination law and only later assess its contribution to decommodification.

What is remarkable, still, is the manner in which anti-discrimination law pursues the redistributive aim, for the analysis will reveal that it is deeply invested with a moral view of the world. In order to be precise, at this point, I draw on Hegel's analysis of moral consciousness.[32] Hegel believed that morality is, indeed, a one-sided expression of practical reason, and, as a result of its one-sidedness, also deficient. As shall be explored below, the deficiencies of anti-discrimination law arise from an inescapable, however often disclaimed, concern with the intent of the agent, the indeterminacy of obligation and the indeterminacy of the distributive goal that protection from discrimination is supposed to achieve.[33] I address these matters as the *normative deficiency* of anti-discrimination law.

It might strike one as odd to view one field of law, in particular, as invested with a moral point of view. One might have expected the law to be the technique of social coordination that, owing to the use of coercive threats, is altogether different from morality; or, alternatively, one may find it impossible to dissociate how the law thinks from the moral point of view, since legal thought appears to be an application of moral reasoning to a special problem, namely, the authorization of coercion.[34] Both objections, which need to be taken seriously in their own right, have no bearing on the analysis below. What matters is that it makes a difference

[31] It has rightly been stated, hence, that anti-discrimination law secures the inclusion into society. See H. Collins, 'Social Inclusion: A Better Approach to Equality Issues' (2005) 14 *Transnational Law and Contemporary Problems* 897–918.

[32] The term 'moral view of the world' plays a major role in Hegel's analysis of morality. See G. W. F. Hegel, *Phenomenology of the Spirit*, trans. by A. V. Miller (Oxford: Oxford University Press, 1977), at 365–373.

[33] Morality is understood here, in Hegelian vein, as a certain mode of accounting for human action. Morality is different from, say, psychoanalysis. Morality is a specific way of making sense of, defending and influencing human behaviour, a way that relies on pinning down intention, assessing responsibility, identifying choice, eliciting remorse, etc. The interpretation of dreams does not loom large in morality. A theory of morality is a reconstruction of the way in which the application of a certain point of view on human action is reflected in human practice. This is, without doubt, the way in which 'morality' was conceived of by Hegel in his *Elements of the Philosophy of Right*, trans. by H. B. Nisbeth (Cambridge: Cambridge University Press, 1991). See H. Schnädelbach, *Hegels Praktische Philosophie: Ein Kommentar der Texte in der Reihenfolge ihrer Entstehung* (Frankfurt aM: Suhrkamp, 2000), at 220. The law is replete with morality, thus understood, and it was no less a figure than Holmes who despaired of it. See O. W. Holmes, 'The Path of the Law', repr. in (1997) 110 *Harvard Law Review* 991–1009 (first published in 1897).

[34] This would be a Kantian perspective.

whether or not the determination of legal obligations *more or less* involves essentially moral issues, such as good or ill will or, more precisely, human will manifest in actions for either good or bad reasons.[35] The degree of entanglement is high in the case of criminal law, it is low for the application of constitutional procedures. Cast in somewhat more familiar terms, there is a difference between more or less *formal* legal systems.[36] Formal legal systems depend for their application on ascertainable external facts. They do not presuppose routinely an inquiry into the state of mind of the norm-addressees.

The close association with morality bespeaks the lack of *formal qualities* of anti-discrimination law. This lack of formality, in turn, is part of what undercuts its potential for decommodification. Anti-discrimination law, I will conclude, falls short of providing an attractive type of social legislation.

This failure becomes unwittingly revealed in scholarly proposals aimed at re-inforcing its thrust.[37] Indeed, it is in these proposals that the normative deficit of anti-discrimination law becomes fully revealed.[38] Attempts at giving it a more radical twist, without thereby transcending the limits of morality, lay bare its neoliberal soul. It is manifest in a deontological perspective on legal relations.[39] What matters, accordingly, are responsibility, diligence, attitudes, intentions, and,

[35] See C. M. Korsgaard, *Creating the Kingdom of Ends* (Cambridge: Cambridge University Press, 1996), at 55.

[36] See Weber, n. 17 at 884–885. See also R. M. Unger, *Law in Modern Society: Towards a Criticism of Social Theory* (New York: Free Press, 1976), at 204.

[37] There can be little doubt that anti-discrimination law as practiced in the United States by the judiciary is expressive of the moral point of view. This is true, in particular, of the US Supreme Court's restriction of the application of the strict scrutiny test to cases of intentional or purposive discrimination. See *Washington* v. *Davis*, 426 US 229 (1976). According to this doctrine, a plaintiff has to prove that an official actor, which may also be a legislature, acted with the invidious intent to discriminate. The 'intent' at stake is meant to be a state of mind in which the actor acted 'because of' and not merely 'in spite of' adverse effects on a certain group or members of such a group. See *McCleskey* v. *Kemp*, 481 US 279 (1987). As was pointed out by LaRue, this understanding of intent likens the pertinent state of mind triggering the strict scrutiny test to what is meant by 'malice' in criminal law and sets the threshold higher than what is required to be convicted of homicide. LaRue also points out that this high threshold may be a precaution against premature attempts to attribute to a legislature, which is, after all, a collective body, a state of mind that was not shared by its members. See L. H. LaRue, 'Discriminatory Intent' (1995) 1 *Race and Ethnic Ancestry Law Digest* 17–20. See also E. Schnapper, 'Two Categories of Discriminatory Intent' (1982) 17 *Harvard Civil Rights and Civil Liberties Law Review* 31–59, 41, who makes clear that what the Court had in mind in *Davis* was ends-discrimination and not means-discrimination. Only the ends-means-distinction can explain why in the eyes of the Court a legislature taking the incidental adverse effect of a group into account would not intentionally discriminate against this group. For an explanation of the persistence of the intent requirement in the jurisprudence of the Supreme Court, see B. J. Flagg, '"Was Blind, But Now I See": White Race Consciousness and the Requirement of Discriminatory Intent' (1993) 91 *Michigan Law Review* 953–1017 at 968–970.

[38] In a superb article, Bagenstos examines these very same proposals and concludes that they reveal the point at which the anti-discrimination paradigm reaches its limit. See S. R. Bagenstos, 'The Structural Turn and the Limits of Anti-discrimination Law' (2006) 94 *California Law Review* 1–47 at 40. The dialectical argument offered here goes to the heart of the matter. The limits observed by Bagenstos define the very *essence* of anti-discrimination law.

[39] See A. Somek, 'Neoliberale Gerechtigkeit: Die Problematik des Antidiskriminierungsrechts' (2003) 51 *Deutsche Zeitschrift für Philosophie* 45–59. Its application is wedded to a world inhabited by intending individual agents inflicting harm (stigma) on singular victims.

above all, acts.[40] Overstating my point a bit, as a result of the application of that perspective, the point and purpose of social policy is recast in a chillingly Puritanical way. Social problems are perceived as though they originated from a lack of self-observation on the part of an agent or organization. Consequently, their solution is thought to require heightening self-control and the cleansing of the mind of what is believed to be morally inappropriate content.[41]

With a brief consideration of attempts made in American scholarship to give bite to anti-discrimination law at the micro level of organizations through the re-socialization of potentially guilty minds the analysis will come to a full circle. It will arrive at the substitution of legislation with management and of legality of conduct with training that was to be observed in the previous chapter for the macro level of policy definition in Europe.

[40] Hence, it should not come as a surprise that judges are notoriously inclined to treat cases of alleged disparate impact or indirect discrimination as though they involved tacit disparate treatment. For the ECJ see, famously, Case 96/80, *Jenkins* [1981] ECR 911 at para. 14. See T. E. Higgins and L. A. Rosenbury, 'Agency, Equality, and Anti-discrimination Law' (2000) 85 *Cornell Law Review* 1194–1220, at 1204–1207; E. W. Shoben, 'Disparate Impact Theory in Employment Discrimination: What's *Griggs* still Good for? What not?' (2004) 42 *Brandeis Law Journal* 597–622 at 597. The point has been usefully summarized by Bagenstos, n. 38 at 45, as follows:

> Courts are hostile to disparate impact law for precisely the same reason that they hesitate to read disparate treatment doctrine as embracing implicit bias—because actions taken without a conscious intent to discriminate do not fit the paradigm of a fault-based understanding of 'discrimination.' To remit claims involving structural discrimination to disparate impact doctrine, then, does not solve the problem so much as to highlight it.

[41] This has already been observed by M. Weber, *Gesammelte Aufsätze zur Religionssoziologie*, vol. 1, 7th edn (Tübingen: Mohr & Siebeck, 1978), at p. 117–118.

4

Direct Discrimination

1. Introduction

In this chapter, I would like to defend an understanding of anti-discrimination law that highlights its redistributive dimension. The defence does not appeal to what one might fancy to be the overall aggregative effect of the correct implementation of its norms; rather, it involves a construction of its core category, direct discrimination, which would remain quite inexplicable if it were not for the distributive view.

Paradoxically, the redistributive view is both the most appealing interpretation of anti-discrimination law, in the sense of providing the best fit between principles and norms, and the key to understanding its normative deficiency. Insight into the latter, therefore, is not the upshot of cheap polemic but mediated by an attempt to present the field in a most plausible form.

It is not difficult to pin down the root of the normative deficiency. Anti-discrimination law is a project that tries to accomplish redistributive objectives by deontological means. Deontology focuses on agents, their responsibilities, their failures, and intentions. As will be seen in subsequent chapters, the translation of distribution into deontology systematically invites misreading the law's redistributive thrust. Quite remarkably, anti-discrimination law is a field of law whose mode of realization is also the cause of self-obfuscation.

I would like to introduce and defend the redistributive reading after recounting certain contextual presuppositions of anti-discrimination law that are consistent with a neoliberal perspective on distributive justice.

2. Market Equality

Anti-discrimination law most uncontroversially presupposes that members of protected groups participate in market transactions. Generally, as market participants, we are all at liberty to act as though we were the faceless agents of unexamined wants. Inasmuch as we in our capacity as market participants are to respect one another, motives or reasons do not matter. What you want is what you get. No questions asked. What you have is rightfully yours once you came to possess it pursuant to rules governing original appropriation and voluntary transactions.[1]

[1] See R. Nozick, *Anarchy, State, and Utopia* (New York: Basic Books, 1974).

In a market society, the consumer epitomizes what it means to be a free person.[2] By definition—at any rate, according to law and economics orthodoxy—the consumer can do no wrong. Consumers, viz., persons, are entitled to their wants even regardless of whether they are possessed by their wants wantonly.[3] In markets the consumers rule.

All consumers are equally independent. In order to have their wants satisfied they do not go to war against one another. They submit themselves to the web of private transactions and undertake to earn their income by catering to the tastes and needs of others. Each sovereign consumer thus becomes equally exposed to the aggregate effect of the whims of all others. Accordingly, everyone is under stress to adapt to preferences (including one's own). Market participants make the fulfilment of their own desires conditional upon the fulfilment of those of others. Market equality is premised upon mutual interdependence.

Market equality is not merely a norm, whose practical consequence is spelled out in the maxim—ill-conceived, but nonetheless still popular—that hard work undertaken in anticipation of the wants of others will pay a proportionate, or even disproportionaly greater, reward;[4] we are all under the spell of market equality precisely because it is *not* restricted to the realm of the counterfactual (as is, for example, gender-neutrality or colour-blindness).[5] It extends all the way down to who we are to one another. We expect, on a cognitive plane, others and ourselves to be nothing but faceless agents of morally unexamined wants. This *is* our collective identity. As soon as a new gadget comes out, we expect others, as we expect ourselves, to develop a craving for it.

A consumer society remits us to leading a life in the state of commodification.[6] What matters about us is whether or not what we do is marketable to others.

[2] In a similar vein, E. Heimann, *Soziale Theorie des Kapitalismus: Theorie der Sozialpolitik*, 1st edn 1929, new edn ed. by B. Badura (Frankfurt: Suhrkamp, 1980), at 167, characterized capitalism as a system that favours the consumer.

[3] The allusion is, of course, to H. G. Frankfurt, who uses the term 'wanton' in order to refer to a person without second-order desires with which to endorse or to reject desires that one finds oneself to have. See H. G. Frankfurt, *The Importance of What we Care About: Philosophical Essays* (Cambridge: Cambridge University Press, 1988), at 16–17.

[4] According to Hayek, the function of prices is 'not so much to reward people for what they *have* done as to tell them what in their own as well as in general interest they *ought* to do'. F. A. Hayek, *Law Legislation, and Liberty*, vol. 2 (London: Routledge, 1976), 71–72. The market, thus understood, does not reward past efforts per se, it does so only subject to the condition that past effort meets a current demand.

[5] It is not, in other words, merely a normative precept. It is plausible to see social life as a realization of this precept. See G. W. F. Hegel, *Elements of the Philosophy of Right*, trans. by H. B. Nisbeth (Cambridge: Cambridge University Press, 1991), at 163, para. 135.

[6] According to Polanyi, a commodity is that which is produced in order to be sold on a market. See K. Polanyi, *The Great Transformation: The Political Origins of our Time*, 2nd edn (Boston, MA: Beacon Press, 2001), at 75. Labour, he goes on to explain, is a fictitious commodity, for it is a human activity 'which goes with life itself, which is in turn not produced for sale but for entirely different reasons, nor can this activity be detached from the rest of life, be stored or mobilised'. What I have in mind when speaking of 'commodification' is that in a market society, pending strategies of 'decommodification' even 'the rest' of a person's life and thus, the whole life of a person, is conducted in view of the selling of one's skills and abilities. The life of a person is thus transformed into an enterprise.

Consumer sovereignty exacts a price. We have to direct ourselves in wary anticipation of the expectations of others. The control over one's life devolves to the cash nexus towards which all individual attention becomes therefore directed. The market is the place where the combined sovereignty of consumers is transsubstantiated into constraints that originate from anonymous webs of transaction. In order to be able to consume, everyone, in principle, is forced to adjust to demand. The market demotes self-reliant agents of morally unexamined wants into creatures busying themselves with permanent adaptations and readjustments.

Therein lays a remarkable dialectic. As persons we are free to behave as though we were the faceless agents of unexamined wants. Assuming that we all want to be such persons, we are, at the same time, collectively *determined to be* universally adaptive and—including our wants—adjustable to shifting opportunities. Being one is the price exacted by market equality for being the other. Consequently, market equality requires conceiving of ourselves as being endowed with potentially indefinite adaptability. It can keep its promise of optimal want satisfaction only if people are capable of ridding themselves of their idiosyncrasies and calibrating their wants in light of satisfactions that can be reasonably expected to obtain.[7] Hence, the wants capable of satisfaction in a society that is based on market equality are subject to an important specification. They have to be substitutable wants, that is, wants that one may have chosen to have even if the wants themselves are experienced as though they were groundless afflictions. The basis of choice is a commonly shared abstract vision of happiness. The reasonable consumer deliberately chooses to be affected by wants that are not likely to be frustrated. This is the ground of choice. When someone who feels passionate about the study of history realizes that there is no market for historians he may well choose to become a specialist in the field of, say, antitrust law. One chooses to be affected by wants in light of their satisfactability.

The ascription of adaptabilty is just as liberating about market equality as the liberty to give free reign to unexamined wants. As long as you can pay it does not matter who you are. Ideally, the same holds true for supply. It does not matter who you were before you arrived at the scene of transactions as long as you can provide what others demand. In principle, particularity does not matter. It is irrelevant whether you arrive as a Serb or a Bosnian, black or white, as a man or a woman, brilliant or dumb, pretty or ugly. The tolerance that emanates from indifference emancipates people from their pedigree.[8] What matters about them is how they perform, a matter depending vitally on their 'wealth talent', that is, the ability to earn a living by catering to the tastes of others.[9]

[7] See Hegel, n. 5 at 154, para. 126. For a useful commentary, see C. Menke, *Tragödie im Sittlichen: Gerechtigkeit und Freiheit nach Hegel* (Frankfurt: Suhrkamp, 1996), at 259, 295.

[8] The freedom guaranteed by the market is the reverse side of universal indifference. See G. Lohmann, *Indifferenz und Gesellschaft: Eine kritische Auseinandersetzung mit Marx* (Frankfurt: Suhrkamp, 1991).

[9] See R. Dworkin, *Sovereign Virtue: The Theory and Practice of Equality* (Cambridge, MA: Harvard University Press, 2000), at 323.

This is the world of Gary Becker,[10] Richard Epstein,[11] and more recently also of Mark Kelman.[12] This is the world where prejudice is eventually rooted out by greed. Performance is key to success. Particularity is relevant, if at all, only at a remove, that is, inasmuch as it contributes to heightening the abundance of already over-abundant supply. In this world, multiculturalism is celebrated for enriching the spectacle of life and increasing the diversity of food.

The appreciation of diversity comes in commodified form. What really matters is how people manage to plan their lives regardless of whether it is part of their life to conceive of life as something that has a plan.[13] A market society is the world in which people, provided they want to succeed, find themselves constrained to conceive of their lives as projects, in which they invest tireless efforts at self-improvement[14] against the unrelenting alternative to 'improve or [to] die'.[15] In a sphere that determines everyone who wishes to have wants satisfied to be indefinitely flexible the losers are, by default, suspect of being indolent and feckless.[16] Inaction is imputed to them as their choice and responsibility.

3. The Neoliberal Left

It is a build-in feature of a market society to regard the care for one's own well-being as falling within the scope of one's own responsibility.[17] A noteworthy difference

[10] See notably, G. Becker, *The Economics of Discrimination*, 2nd edn (Chicago, IL: Chicago University Press, 1971).

[11] See R. Epstein, *Forbidden Grounds: The Case Against Employment Discrimination Laws* (Cambridge, MA: Harvard University Press, 1992). For such neoliberal hardliners it was notoriously difficult to account for the fact that a laissez-faire economy historically failed to rule out discrimination. The explanation that was found for the enigma was not particularly surprising: state intervention was to blame. For a powerful critique, see I. Ayres, 'Alternative Grounds: Epstein's Discrimination Analysis in other Market Settings' (1994) 31 *San Diego Law Review* 67–87. For a critique of Epstein's claim that the social costs of anti-discrimination laws are greater than the social benefits, see J. J. Donohue III, 'Advocacy versus Analysis in Assessing Employment Discrimination Law' (1992) 44 *Stanford Law Review* 1583–1614.

[12] Having read Kelman's work from the 1980s (see, in particular, his *A Guide to Critical Legal Studies* (Cambridge, MA: Harvard University Press, 1987)), I wonder whether this is a tongue-in-cheek remark. His recent celebration of market rationality, however, is astounding. See M. Kelman, 'Market Discrimination and Groups' (2001) 53 *Stanford Law Review* 833–896. For a similar observation regarding Kelman's prior work and his current approach to anti-discrimination law, see S. R. Bagenstos, '"Rational Discrimination," Accommodation, and the Politics of (Disability) Civil Rights' (2003) 89 *Virginia Law Review* 825–923, at 875 n. 165, 918–919. Bagenstos explains that Kelman, representing the more traditional left, has an axe to grind with the cultural left and with advocates of identity politics. This agenda supposedly explains his apparently neoliberal stance.

[13] See C. Menke, *Reflections of Equality*, trans. by H. Rouse and A. Denejkine (Stanford, CA: Stanford University Press 2006), at 143–149.

[14] For highly perceptive observations, see M. Walzer, *Thick and Thin: Moral Argument at Home and Abroad* (Notre Dame, IN: Notre Dame University Press, 1994), at 23–24.

[15] See R. Bork, *The Antitrust Paradox: A Policy at War with itself*, 2nd edn (New York: Free Press, 1993), at 95.

[16] See M. B. Katz, *The Undeserving Poor: From the War on Poverty to the War on Welfare* (New York: Pantheon Books, 1989).

[17] Consequently, Dworkin takes it to be an elementary feature of commonsense morality that needs to be accommodated by philosophical theory. See n. 9 at 323.

of attitude exists, however, with regard to the threat of exclusion.[18] Whereas the neoliberal right does not accept any societal responsibility to come to the aid of those who have been unlucky,[19] the neoliberal left accepts that people deserve to be indemnified against certain adverse conditions that originate from circumstances beyond their control. Characteristics that are deemed to be 'immutable', such as race or gender, are usually included among those circumstances. In a sense, this is consistent with the ethos of a market society, for those characteristics say something about who people have been before entering the market sphere. It flies in the face of market equality when people are treated differently on the sole ground of what they happen to be outside of markets.[20] People should be rewarded for what they do and not punished for what they were born with or the private situation in which they have come to this world. Particularity is backward-looking. It is about what market participants have been before they arrived on the scene of oblivion. We all have a family name. Most of us are nationals of a state, and national citizenship is something that is primarily acquired by birth. From birth onwards we belong to a race, socially understood, and we are also very likely to belong to either of the sexes. We do not have the power to eradicate this past. It cannot be undone. If anything, it is part of our circumstances.[21]

What distinguishes the neoliberal left from the neoliberal right emerges clearly enough. The left takes market equality seriously from a normative point of view. For the neoliberal right it is merely a descriptive feature that markets may or may not possess. Anti-discrimination law is the darling of the neoliberal left, for it promises to restore equality[22] to those whose adaptability has been impaired because of a lack of 'evasive power'[23] to extricate themselves from

[18] In its extreme form, exclusion creates a situation where one's communications do not matter any more, that is, in which human beings are socially reduced to their sheer corporal existence. See N. Luhmann, 'Inklusion und Exklusion', in *Soziologische Aufklärung*, vol. 6: *Die Soziologie und der Mensch* (Opladen: Westdeutscher Verlag, 1995), 265–274, at 250.

[19] See D. Schmidtz, 'Taking Responsibility', in D. Schmidtz and R. Goodin, *Social Welfare and Individual Responsibility* (Cambridge: Cambridge University Press, 1998), 1–95 at 78. This would not exclude, of course, voluntary insurance. In cases of 'pre-existing conditions', of course, such insurance is impossible to come by for those who need it. See my 'This is about ourselves, Or: What Makes Genetic Discrimination Interesting', in N. Stehr (ed.), *Biotechnology: Between Commerce and Civil Society* (New Brunswick, NJ: Transaction Publishers, 2004), 195–216.

[20] It is not the case that adherents of the neoliberal right believe that discrimination is a morally neutral matter. They do not. They believe in the superiority of competitive solutions over government interference. Government interference is deemed either unnecessary because market forces are supposed to eliminate discriminatory conduct in the long term; or it is held to be counterproductive owing to its tendency to prohibit efficient forms of discrimination. See Epstein, n. 11 at 43, 76–77.

[21] See Dworkin, n. 9 at 323.

[22] One might at this point cunningly observe with R. Post, 'Prejudicial Appearances: The Logic of American Anti-discrimination Law' (2000) 88 *California Law Review* 1–40 at 20, that the purported concern with the individual is overshadowed by the abstractness of instrumental reason:

> Under the influence of the dominant conception, courts have interpreted the statutory focus on 'individuals' as requiring the creation of legal subjects whose capacities bypass gender conventions and attach directly to the 'context-free' logic of instrumental reason. Judicial rhetoric envisions "individuals" who exist entirely outside of the historical contingencies of received gender norms.

[23] See K. Yoshino, 'The Assimilationist Bias in Equal Protection: The Visibility Presumption and the Case of "Don't Ask, Don't Tell"' (1998) 108 *Yale Law Journal* 485–571 at 508.

social disadvantage. It is merely a seemingly paradoxical step to require that the neutralization of difference be also conscious of difference. The recognition of identity may be a necessary means for counteracting practices of 'cultural imperialism'.[24] It protects from more than just one's past self.[25] It constitutes everyone's liberty to be anyone. Market equality is equality in the eyes of which everyone counts as anyone.[26]

It should not go unnoticed, at this point, that the source of disadvantage can be twofold. It can originate from attitudes and views held by others that are directly or indirectly related to immutable characteristics.[27] Social inequality may also be caused by handicaps that people possess in relation to the market structure itself. These handicaps are usually referred to as a lack of 'talent' or 'native endowments'.[28] What society needs to do about their handicap has been the subject of an amazingly extensive philosophical debate. It does not have to concern us here, for only the first source of disadvantage is the major target of anti-discrimination law.

Thus understood, anti-discrimination law endorses market equality's commitment to adaptability, thereby indirectly accepting the market as a medium of distributive justice.[29] Indeed, by removing mostly 'immutable' characteristics from the schedule of permissible grounds of unequal treatment it restores adaptability to those who are threatened with suffering disadvantages owing to the persistence of socially created handicaps.[30] This is consistent with market society understood as a sphere of distribution. The market should not take a person's particularity into account but rather treat each person pursuant to standards of economic rationality.[31]

[24] See S. Choudhry, 'Distribution vs. Recognition: The Case of Anti-Discrimination Laws' (2000) 9 *George Mason Law Review* 145–178 at 159.

[25] See M. Minow, *Not only for myself: Identity, Politics, and the Law* (New York: New Press, 1997), at 53–58.

[26] See Menke, n. 7 at 256.

[27] See A. Somek, *Rationalität und Diskriminierung: Zur Bindung der Gesetzgebung an das Gleichheitsrecht* (Vienna/New York: Springer, 2001), at 396. On the 'assimilationist impulse' of equal protection, see also R. M. Unger, *What Should Legal Analysis Become?* (London: Verso, 1996), at 93.

[28] See Dworkin, n. 9.

[29] For a description of the neoliberal left's commitment to market efficiency minus discrimination, see the highly perceptive observations by W. Benn Michaels, *The Trouble with Diversity: How We Learned to Love Identity and Ignore Inequality* (New York: Metropolitan Books, 2006), at 75–76. Benn Michaels very aptly describes the current ideological division of the US American society between 'right' and 'left' as a division between 'reactionaries' and 'conservatives' (ibid., at 106):

> The reactionaries are the ones who attack diversity, the conservatives the ones who defend it; the reactionaries are the ones who think our inequalities are justified, the conservatives are the ones who think we don't have any or, more precisely, that the ones we do have are the products of prejudice, of treating people as if they were worse than we are.

[30] This is the explanation why, from the perspective of market equality, anti-discrimination law permissibly focuses on members of groups who are arguably marked with some social stigma. Single instances of discrimination would be combated by the market. See Kelman n. 12 at 893–894.

[31] More narrowly understood, the good of anti-discrimination law can be seen in reinstating market rationality where it is absent owing to irrational prejudice. See Kelman n. 12 at 848.

4. Distributive Justice: the Internal Analysis

I characterize anti-discrimination law deliberately with an eye to distributive justice. Above (at p. 88), however, I mentioned different readings of the anti-discrimination principle that do not emphasize its distributive dimension. It needs to be clarified, at this point, whether the redistributive perspective, to be defended here, can coexist with these interpretations or how potential conflicts can be resolved.

The distributive—or redistributive—perspective commends itself for three reasons.[32] The first reason does not at all exclude rival interpretations, which may even be treated as entirely complementary. Redistribution is of relevance since it is explicitly in the interest of this analysis to examine anti-discrimination law as a type of social legislation.

Second, there is reason to believe that other approaches would be implausible if they neglected the distributive dimension persistently. Since it would be too tiresome to prove this point by going through one account after the other, I should like to choose as one example a recent exposition that appears to be the farthest removed from the question of redistribution. According to Hellman, discrimination is wrong if an unequal treatment demeans people.[33] An act counts as demeaning if a higher authority signals through the use of a distinction that members of a certain group are not fully human and less worthy than others.[34] Not every unequal treatment or classification is capable of carrying such a signal. Historical conventions determine under which condition a treatment demeans.[35] It seems as though this account can dispense with the distributive perspective entirely. For example, a law requiring women to walk at least two meters behind their husbands in order to exhibit deference would demean women no matter what their social class. And yet, the distributive perspective would immediately enter the picture if the question were asked what women would have to do in order to avoid such a social ordeal. If women had a choice to live the promiscuous life of bachelors without for that reason facing economic and social segregation, the demeaning nature of such a rule would no longer be self-evident. Hellman's discussion of a private rental policy that distinguishes on the basis of sex or age is even more revealing. In her opinion, the policy's demeaning appearance would disappear if there were plenty of other apartments to rent for members of these groups.[36] Interestingly, Hellman also does not believe it to be demeaning when the poor spit into the face of the rich. I conclude from these examples that a theory of discrimination that is concerned with the symbolically expressive effects of legally

[32] For reasons of convenience of exposition I mentioned only two reasons above at p. 89 and did not differentiate between the second and the third.

[33] See D. Hellman, *When is Discrimination Wrong?* (Cambridge, MA: Harvard University Press, 2008), at 31, 33, 35.

[34] See ibid. at 57: 'Demeaning actions are those that put the other down. To demean is to express that the other is less worthy of concern and respect and to do so in a manner that has power.'

[35] See ibid. at 55. Remarkably, it does not even have to be an unequal treatment. See ibid. at 47.

[36] See ibid. at 37.

mediated acts cannot avoid incorporating the distributive dimension. I am confident, therefore, that accounts in which the basic principle of anti-discrimination law is internally linked to overcoming caste or oppression are even less likely to neglect it.

The most important reason in favour of the redistributive view, however, is the third. Interpretations of the anti-discrimination principle mentioned above share an external perspective. They treat anti-discrimination norms, such as provision protecting from direct or indirect discrimination, as though they were instruments for attaining a policy goal. What these approaches fail to accomplish, therefore, is to reconstruct the normative significance of anti-discrimination law from within, that is, through a close analysis of its core norms. It is on the basis of such an internal analysis that the relevance of the redistributive perspective becomes overwhelmingly clear.

5. Yielding

When viewed in juxtaposition with general private law, it is quite obvious that anti-discrimination law plays a redistributive role.[37] It redirects the flow of assets and resources, such as jobs, remunerations, perks, promotions, or dwellings,[38] to persons who would be left without any of these had voluntary transactions taken their course. Moreover, its apparently most elementary category, namely, direct discrimination, could not be accounted for without taking the redistributive dimension into account.[39]

[37] See also Choudhry, n. 24 at 152. For a related observation, see Kelman, n. 12 at 840–844. Kelman sees the redistributive dimension of anti-discrimination law restricted to measures requiring reasonable accommodation and subject to a broad balancing test. Of course, not all would agree with my contention that anti-discrimination law is first and foremost a means of redistribution. For some, anti-discrimination law protects from unjust social devaluation. See A. Koppelman, *Anti-discrimination Law and Social Equality* (New Haven, CT: Yale University Press, 1996); for others it is a practice to modify the social identities of persons as they are conveyed and reproduced through stereotypes. See Post, n. 22 at 31. Very close to Koppelman's approach is Hellman's. Strangely enough, this proximity is not acknowledged in Hellman's book. See n. 33 at 54–57 where she discusses closely related accounts without mentioning Koppelman's.

[38] On viewing jobs as assets, see P. von Parijs, *Real Freedom for All: What (if Anything) Can Justify Capitalism?* (Oxford: Oxford University Press, 1995), 110–111.

[39] Similarly, the 'inferential leap' identified by Krieger in the context of so-called 'pretext analysis' points to this redistributive orientation. (See L. Hamilton Krieger, 'The Content of our Categories: A Cognitive Bias Approach to Discrimination and Equal Employment Opportunity' (1995) 47 *Stanford Law Review* 1161–1248 at 1181.) In the context of such an analysis, where no reason can be found that would make the conduct of the employer appear to be based on any other but the prohibited ground, a discriminatory intent is attributed to her or him. Such an imputation, however, should not be understood as a judgement about the defendant's state of mind but rather as an instruction to grant the job to the member of the relevant group, for no reason can be found that would release the agent from the prima facie obligation to (re-)distribute. For the ('anti-subordinationist') view that anti-discrimination law is not first and foremost about changing attitudes but only insofar as they affect the entrenched subordination of particular groups, see Bagenstos, n. 12 at 846–847.

The Framework Directive, the Race Directive, and the Consolidated Sex Directive lay down that 'direct discrimination shall be taken to occur where one person is treated less favourably than another is, has been or would be treated in a comparable situation on grounds of [. . .]' one of the prohibited social categories.[40] The equal treatment principle laid down in those Directives declares direct (and indirect) discrimination illegal. I should like to note, in passing, that in this context, the equal treatment principle is more narrowly circumscribed than the general principle of equality, which surfaces occasionally in the European Court of Justice's case law.[41] This broader principle articulates the idea that 'like cases should be treated alike'.[42] Neither the merits nor the demerits[43] of this broader idea need to detain us here.

In order to explain in the sections that follow why the redistributive dimension is essential for the legal construction of direct discrimination I should like to invite readers to consider the following simple example.[44] Assume that the owner of a pub refuses to hire a gay waiter out of fear that her patrons would have a great time of making fun of the 'sissy'. She wishes to spare herself and her staff the embarrassment and discomfort of having to work in an environment infected with omnipresent smutty jokes. The owner does not refuse to hire the homosexual person because of animus towards homosexuals but out of concern for work atmosphere. She takes the sexual orientation of the job applicants into account only because it bears, at a remove, upon what really matters to her choice. In the words of Gardner,[45] the sexual orientation merely serves as an *auxiliary* premise, for it simply provides *information* about the applicant. The *operative* premise, which *motivates* her conduct,[46] is her anticipation of consequences on the working environment.

Creating a comfortable working environment is a neutral concern. Despite this neutral aim, however, the employer's behaviour does *not* constitute *indirect* discrimination, for indirect discrimination involves the application of a neutral criterion.[47] This

[40] See Article 2(2)(a) Directive 2000/78/EC; Article 2(2)(a) Directive 2000/43/EC; Article 2(1)(a) Directive 2006/54/EC. The ECJ made clear that the prohibition of direct discrimination does not prohibit classification on the basis of one of the forbidden grounds. The use of a classification is discriminatory only if coupled with subsequent disadvantageous treatment. See Case C-196/02, *Vasiliki Nikoloudi* v. *Organismos Tilepikinonion Ellados AE* [2005] ECR I-1789 para. 34.

[41] See C. Barnard, *EC Employment Law*, 3rd edn (Oxford: Oxford University Press, 2007), at 314.

[42] See, for example, Joined Cases C-184/02 & C-223/02, *Spain and Finland* v. *Parliament and Council* [2004] ECR I-7789, para. 64.

[43] See A. Somek, 'Equality as Reasonableness: Constitutional Normativity in Demise', in A. Sajó (ed.), *The Dark Side of Fundamental Rights* (Utrecht: eleven international publishing, 2006), 191–215.

[44] The example is also used by J. Gardner, 'On the Grounds of her Sex(uality)' (1998) 18 *Oxford Journal of Legal Studies* 167–187 at 179–181.

[45] See ibid. at 180. I shall explain below why Gardner does not see the matter that way.

[46] Raz, from whom Gardner seems to have borrowed the distinction between operative and auxiliary reasons, explains that operative reasons are either values or desires or interests. See J. Raz, *Practical Reason and Norms*, 2nd edn (Princeton, NJ: Princeton University Press, 1990), at 34.

[47] Pay discrimination with an adverse impact on women, for example, is a clear case of indirect discrimination as long as the lower wage matters and the employer does not select women merely in order to pay them less. Indirect discrimination focuses on a distributive pattern, irrespective of how the pattern is brought about. See A. Christensen, 'Structural Aspects of Anti-discriminatory Legislation and Processes of Normative Change', in A. Numhauser-Henning (ed.), *Legal Perspectives of Equal Treatment and Non-discrimination* (Amsterdam: Kluwer, 2001), 31–60 at 42.

is, at any rate, what has been unequivocally laid down in the relevant Directives. Indirect discrimination occurs whenever an apparently neutral provision, criterion, or practice would put persons bearing a certain characteristic at a particular disadvantage compared with others.[48] While 'workplace atmosphere' is a legitimate concern, the exclusion of homosexuals cannot pass muster owing to the existence of an anti-discrimination norm, such as Article 1 of Directive 2000/78/EC, which declares 'sexual orientation' to be a prohibited ground. The validity of the norm alters social meanings. Using the prohibited ground is no longer an innocent proxy for applying a neutral criterion.

6. How Norms Change Social Meanings

The alteration of social meanings is best understood when exploring the significance of the pub-owner's act by bracketing, for a moment, how the validity of an anti-discrimination norm creates a different situation. The employer *yields* to existing consumer prejudice.[49] She thereby relies on the most effective instrumental *specification* of the neutral criterion ('work atmosphere') *in her context of action*. The act of yielding, however, does not leave the meaning of her acts unaffected. Relying on sexual orientation as means conducive to an agreeable working environment allows customer and co-worker prejudice to invade the type of workplace she wishes to create. It taints the neutrality of her concern. In that sense, yielding to the expectations of others *colours* her aims. Whoever does not hire homosexuals is not *only* concerned about running a peaceful pub in the abstract, but *also* about maintaining a pub whose tranquility, should it ever come about, is made possible by accommodating homophobia. Whoever refuses to hire Africans to sell goods to customers is not merely concerned about business performance but about the revenues that accrue from serving racists. Generally, what employers yielding to customer prejudice *also* do is to create or to sustain a work environment that is receptive to prejudice and hence inimical to members of certain groups. They even create or sustain a social good—the straight guy's pub, the racist shop—whose existence affects adversely the distribution of resources and opportunities.

Correctly understood, the employer's conduct is an instance of indirect indirect discrimination.[50] Discrimination is indirect because the aim is neutral and the act in no manner motivated by animus. The neutral criterion matters not directly, but

[48] See Article 2(2)(b) Directive 2000/78/EC. Article 2(2)(b) Directive 2000/43/EC. On the pedigree of the category in the jurisprudence of the ECJ, which may have taken its cue from the American conception of 'disparate impact discrimination', see S. Fredman, *Discrimination Law* (Oxford: Clarendon Press, 2002), at 106–107.

[49] Anti-discrimination law, owing to its deontological realization (see below p. 106), has a proclivity to focus on the state of mind of the agent at the moment at which he or she reaches a decision. For a forceful analysis, see Krieger, n. 39 at 1183–1184.

[50] See A. Somek, 'Neoliberale Gerechtigkeit: Die Problematik des Antidiskriminierungsrechts' (2003) 51 *Deutsche Zeitschrift für Philosophie* 45–59 at 52–53. In the literature, such cases are usually presented as instances of 'rational discrimination'. See, for example, Bagenstos, n. 12 at 849–859, who also convincingly demonstrates that rational discrimination cannot be recast as based on hidden

indirectly through the use of another criterion whose use is revealed in yielding to bias. As a result, the neutral criterion is no longer untainted. The causal chain leading up to the desired good working environment reveals that the belief of what the latter is supposedly to be about is actually infected with bias.[51] No gay person (or no black person, for that matter) would enter the vision maintained about what it takes to have a 'good working environment'.

Against this background, it should clearly emerge what a protection from direct discrimination *does* with regard to social meanings. It taps the pre-normative colouring of social meanings that emerges from indirect indirect discrimination and cuts the Gordian knot of ambivalence. The anti-discrimination norm, qua 'scheme of interpretation',[52] authoritatively declares what the relevant acts *really* are. It allows observers to take the step from 'also' to 'truly'.

It would be mistaken to believe that any such clarification of social meanings would be possible without a norm. The prohibition of direct discrimination says, first and foremost, how a certain conduct *ought* to be understood for purposes of legal interpretation. When employers select employees by taking test scores into account, the social meaning of their conduct is not 'discrimination on the grounds of test scores' but rather that of hiring employees according to what they believe to be their abilities. Indeed, employers use test scores as a specification of 'ability'. The meaning of their conduct is thereby coloured. Their conduct may even bring about a social world where test scores come to predominate the social meaning of achievement, which would be the equivalent of a racist shop in the sphere of personal accomplishments; but we cannot say that what they *truly* do is to discriminate on the grounds of test scores unless there is a norm that prevents them from doing so.

7. Pre-normative and Normative Intent

The tangled constitution of direct vis-à-vis indirect indirect discrimination explains why the relevance of animus or other conceivable states of discriminatory intent remains *necessarily* elusive. I shall return to the matter *in extenso* below; however, already at this stage of the analysis I would like to clarify why the matter is seemingly intractable. The explanation is that intent is relevant at both the pre-normative and the normative level.

At the *pre-normative level*, conduct comes in a coloured form. It is quite clear that from this perspective, intent, in the sense of aiming at putting people down,[53]

animus or a lack of sympathy. I agree, for the important task of the anti-discrimination principle lies in curbing the legitimate scope of rational action.

[51] See E. Ellis, *EU Anti-discrimination Law* (Oxford: Oxford University Press, 2005), at 103, 112.

[52] See H. Kelsen, *Introduction to the Problems of Legal Theory*, trans. by S. Paulson and B. Litschewksi Paulson (Oxford: Clarendon Press, 1987) at 10–11.

[53] See Hellman, n. 33 at 140.

cannot be decisive,[54] for it is always possible to claim that employers do what they do out of concern for something else. If what is going on at the normative level—i.e., the use or neglect of implication of the forbidden ground—is perceived from the pre-normative level of indirect indirect discrimination, it is always possible to claim that the employer did not *really* intend to discriminate.

By contrast, at the *normative level* it is established by a norm what an act by the employer means for the purpose of juridical classification. Ideally, a prohibition of direct discrimination establishes which conduct *counts as* discrimination. If someone engages in that conduct, the act of discrimination is taken to be intentional. If the employer wants to do x and from the normative perspective doing x means doing y then she, normatively, intends to do y.[55]

We shall see below (pp. 126–131) how a normative weakness of anti-discrimination law is revealed at this point, for it is left unclear, in this context, how we are to know when doing x really means doing y. It will be seen that the lack of clarity at the normative level invariably gives rise to recourse to pre-normative intentionality.

This clarification of the notorious obscurity shows, however, that for the identification of discrimination it is quite irrelevant whether the discriminator intends to put a group down. This is not to deny that boorish animus may be encountered in cases of 'simple discrimination'.[56] Some people simply dislike those who are not of their own kind (some even dislike those who are). But the best account, paradoxically, of discrimination with animus is, in my opinion, to regard employers, paradigmatically, yielding to their own aversions. After all, they have to internalize the economic cost. Such yielding to one's own dislike of people is only wrong, of course, if it counts normatively as discrimination. For example, an employer may abhor the sheer thought of hiring men because she considers them to be ugly creatures. As long as her not hiring men does not raise any distributive concerns, she is free to discriminate legally with utmost hatred and animus; or this is what I would like to argue below.

Nevertheless, the fact that the prohibited ground coincides with a context-dependent specification of the neutral criterion explains why direct discrimination is a puzzling category. According to Gardner,[57] a case of direct discrimination is established when, for example, the sexual orientation of the applicant serves as an operative premise in the discriminator's reasoning. The sexual orientation becomes an operative (motivating) premise because the choice not to hire people with a certain sexual orientation is a conclusion drawn from, first, the original operative premise to create a good work atmosphere and, second, the auxiliary premises that co-workers and customers would make life hell for homosexuals. The

[54] See Case C-69/80, *Worringham* v. *Lloyds Bank* [1981] ECR 767.

[55] For very perceptive comments on the erroneous view that intentions are 'mental duplicates' of action, see C. M. Korsgaard, *Self-Constitution: Agency, Identity, and Integrity* (Oxford: Oxford University Press, 2009), at 96–98, 125.

[56] Kelman, n. 12 at 840, 892, refers to these latter cases as cases of 'simple discrimination'. Were the ambition of protection from discrimination limited to these cases, anti-discrimination law would not merit any analytical effort.

[57] Gardner, n. 44 at 180.

conclusion serves as the operative premise not to hire a homosexual. This is what, according to Gardner, makes discrimination 'direct'; or it explains, rather, why direct discrimination is indirect indirect discrimination, that is, the pursuit of a non-discriminatory objective mediated by a conclusion that contains the prohibited ground.[58]

Gardner's exposition of the meaning of direct discrimination is most elegant. Nevertheless, I respectfully disagree, for I believe that the matter needs to be put differently. What distinguishes an operative from an auxiliary premise is that it motivates action. Gardner characterizes auxiliary premises as in themselves 'motivationally inert'. The mere fact that someone is homosexual does not motivate the discriminator's actions; nor does the homophobic attitude of his workforce move him to act. The pub owner concludes that she had better not hire homosexuals out of concern for business performance. But the conclusion that purportedly serves as operative reason would not motivate if it were not for the original premise. The conclusion would have never been drawn had it not been for the latter. Therefore, from a pre-normative perspective, one would come up with a *false* account of the discriminator's action by looking at the conclusion alone.

8. The Systemic Context of Direct Discrimination

It is the intervention of the anti-discrimination norm that makes us perceive the conclusion ('I should not hire homosexuals') as if it were the operative premise. Isolating the conclusion from its original premises thereby assimilates her act to a manifestation of homophobia. Indeed, it is made to count as such. This explains why perceiving acts as being 'truly' acts of illicit discrimination involves falsehood. The richness and ambivalence of social meanings becomes absorbed by the normatively mandated interpretation. Anti-discrimination norms have the same deadening effect on the perception of social reality as moralistic attributions of evil schemes ('Don't you lie to me, I know what you were really up to').

Mere moralistic stultification of human conduct is not an appealing candidate for a principle of law. There must be an explanation why legal institutions tolerate this effect. I assume that the best explanation is that protection from direct discrimination is a means of breaking the systemic cycle of indirect discrimination. In fact, it is not at all unlikely that universal yielding to what people *take* to be existing aversions, prejudices, or stereotypes gives rise to pervasive exclusionary effects.[59] Employers do not hire foreigners out of fear that customers would not enter their business premises. They believe that customers expect not to be able to have an entertaining conversation with the salesperson. Consequently, all salespersons are fully conversant in the customer's vernacular. Customers experience this situation as normal. They would find exposure to foreign accents disturbing

[58] This type of situation is clearly reflected in the facts underlying Case C-54/07, *Centrum voor gelijkheid van kansen en voor racismebestrijding* v. *Firma Feryn NV* [2008] ECR I-5187.
[59] See C. Sunstein, *Free Markets and Social Justice* (New York: Oxford University Press, 1997).

and wonder whether there is something wrong with a business that decides to hire foreigners. Employers studiously avoid hiring foreigners out of concern for their business' reputation.

In a sense, the discrimination combated by anti-discrimination law, beyond catching simple animus, is always *systemic*. Nobody wants to discriminate, but everyone does because the economic rationality of market participants moves everyone to do so.[60] Even discrimination with animus is systemic, at least as long as employers believe to be able to get away with it. People live out their aversions only if they expect this to be tolerated by their social environment. Protection from direct discrimination is the attempt to break the circle at a point where a person or an institution is in charge of distributing particularly important resources or goods. These persons are told by anti-discrimination norms what their conduct 'truly' means.

9. Distributive Agents

It is by creating responsibilities for distributive agents[61] that the overall distributive thrust of anti-discrimination law becomes translated into the deontological idiom of individual responsibilities.[62] Deontology is not merely about what ought to happen somehow but about that real person who has to do or to omit something and to put his or her mind to that task.[63] In the case of employment discrimination law, the employer is cast in a position decisive for breaking the systemic circle of discrimination.[64] The employers' acts of yielding to the prejudice of others (or his own) are deemed to be particularly troublesome since employers make important allocative choices.[65] The relevance of the redistributive perspective comes to the fore

[60] The universal attitude of yielding to what one takes to be the attitude of others also casts doubt on the distinction between operative and auxiliary reasons. The distinction is burdened with the difficulty that it is unclear how operative reasons would motivate action without the co-presence of auxiliary reasons. No one would discriminate if the victims were not around.

[61] I borrow the notion 'distributive agent' from John Gardner who may in turn have borrowed it from Hugh Collins. See J. Gardner, 'Liberals and Unlawful Discrimination' (1989) 9 *Oxford Journal of Legal Studies* 1–21.

[62] In *Feryn*, n. 58 at para. 28, the Court found that even a mere public statement that is sufficiently dissuasive for a group of applicants (who owing to its existence conceivably abstain from submitting job applications) constitutes direct discrimination. The redistributive orientation of anti-discrimination law is given full force here even though nobody has actually become the victim of an act of unequal treatment.

[63] See T. Nagel, *The View from Nowhere* (New York: Oxford University Press, 1986), at 177, 180–181.

[64] Patterns of discrimination are reproduced in systemic processes. In the example at hand: the employer yields to what she believes to be consumer prejudice as a result of which existing consumer expectations become reconfirmed and re-entrenched. See Sunstein, n. 59.

[65] In fact, this is also the view held by Gardner, n. 44 at 185, however, from a deontological perspective:

> I do not mean that the employer can be regarded as morally exonerated of his employees's sins. On the contrary: when his employees do discriminate against co-workers on grounds of sex by stereotyping or otherwise, he bears vicarious moral responsibility for it; what is more, other things being equal, he should take pre-emptive action by sacking the bigots on his team as soon as he can.

here. Anti-discrimination law has no choice but to cling to employers. According to the most fundamental principle of market equality, the consumer can do no wrong. The responsible employer is the *reverse image* of the exculpated consumer.

Interestingly, no other agent—for example, the workforce—is relevant in this normative universe. The law looks towards private property owners or those in control of private resources. They are the key figures of distribution. If the state comes in then it is only because it acts as one employer among others. The acts regulated by anti-discrimination law are essentially *private* acts.[66]

The deontological focus on a responsible distributive agent does not disappear in the context of indirect discrimination. Indeed, for the purpose of establishing a case of *relevant* disparate impact, it cannot be claimed that employees working for E are worse off than employees working for F, unless it is the effect of legislation that is applicable to both.[67] Not only does the work, in cases of pay discrimination, have to be 'the same' or of 'equal value', the ECJ accommodates restricting indirect discrimination claims to cases where equal work is carried out 'in the same establishment or service'.[68] Even though the wording of Article 157(1) FEU Treaty (ex 141(1) EC Treaty) nowhere suggests that protection from discrimination is necessarily limited to situations where persons work for the same employer, the ECJ made it abundantly clear that anti-discrimination law is of no avail where there is no distributive agent. The Court said in *Lawrence* that if 'the differences identified in the pay conditions of workers performing equal work of equal value cannot be attributed to a single source, there is no body which is responsible for the inequality and which could restore equal treatment'.[69] The Court actually claims that a situation of this type is outside the scope of application of Article 157(1) FEU Treaty (ex 141(1) EC Treaty). It should not come as a surprise that the question of what it takes to identify a 'single source' invites further references.[70]

This apodictic statement of the *Lawrence* Court may indeed go too far inasmuch as it is conceivable to arrive at a similar conclusion with a more transparent appeal to the proportionality principle. It might be argued that employers may well be overburdened in their role as distributive agents when asked to step in as soon as a cross-business or even cross-sectional comparison reveals that some employees receive higher remuneration than others. Such an obligation, undoubtedly, would rob businesses of a part of their competitive edge. As soon as reasons of

[66] In certain instances, the responsibilities of distributive agents are taken quite seriously. For example, when a woman decides to return from paternal leave ahead of time then the employer has to bear the relevant adjustment costs even if the woman cannot be employed in her previous capacity because of her pregnancy. The obligation on the part of the employer is also not affected by the fact that the woman decides to return to work merely in order to benefit from the maternity allowance. See Case C-320/01, *Wiebke Busch* v. *Klinikum Neustadt GmbH & Co. Betriebs-KG* [2003] ECR I-2041 paras 39, 41, 44; for a similarly strong protection of women on maternity leave who apply during the leave period for a new position, see Case C-294/04, *Carmen Sarkatzis Herrero* v. *Instituto Madrileño de Salud (Imsalud)* [2006] ECR I-1513 paras 39, 41, 45 (inclusion of maternity leave into the determination of seniority towards the new job).

[67] Case C-256/01 *Debra Allonby* v. *Accrington & Rossendale College* [2004] ECR I-873 at para. 84.

[68] Case C-43/75 *Defrenne* v. *Sabena II* [1976] ECR I-455

[69] C-320 *Lawrence* v. *Regent Office Care Ltd* [2002] ECR I-7325, para. 17; *Allonby*, n. 67 at 46

[70] See, for example, *Allonby*, n. 67.

this type would have to be laid on the table, certain inequities could be openly addressed, too, for example, the fact that former employees who work through a new employer for less pay in the same position as before are clearly disadvantaged vis-à-vis those who were lucky enough to keep their jobs.[71] The fact that, as a matter of legal form, different employers are involved is indeed part of the systemic discrimination that arises when an incentive is created for employers to resort, in competitive markets, to more flexible and less costly employment strategies.

Ending the debate by attributing without anything further to Article 157(1) FEU Treaty (ex 141(1) EC Treaty) a restricted scope of application reveals the power that the deontological idiom wields over the legal imagination.[72] In fact, the deontological realization of anti-discrimination law systematically invites reinterpreting its redistributive core in deontological terms. Its mode of realization invites its own misreading. To be sure, there are elements of modern anti-discrimination law, such as prohibitions of harassment,[73] which are explicable only in deontological terms.[74] Thou shalt not put your fellow humans down, no matter whether they are rich or poor. But the addition of these deontological elements does in no manner affect its elementary redistributive constitution.

10. Redistribution and not Attitudes

I suspect that Gardner wishes to take the deontological appearance of anti-discrimination law seriously—its ostensible preoccupation with bad acts—and is therefore led to identify a reprehensible reason for action. The true reason explaining what is wrong with using the conclusion qua 'operative' reason is thereby rendered obscure. It can be made intelligible, as I suggested above, when concentrating on the function played by such conclusions in the systemic operation of a market society. Universal market rationality gives rise to distributive effects that are caused by acts of yielding to what are believed to be forceful negative attitudes.[75] Anti-discrimination norms are targeted at eliminating these effects.

We have already seen that the major point of anti-discrimination law consists in treating a purely instrumental use of the forbidden ground or classification, its use *without* animus, as evidence of direct discrimination.[76] This observation

[71] See *Allonby*, n. 67, paras 18, 46.

[72] For a critique (with further references), see Barnard, n. 41 at 354.

[73] See, for example, Article 2(1)(c) of the Consolidate Sex Discrimination Directive, which defines harassment as 'unwanted conduct related to the sex of a person with the purpose or effect of violating the dignity of a person, and of creating an intimidating, hostile, degrading, humiliating or offensive environment.'

[74] It makes much sense to associate them with human dignity. See S. Fredman, *Discrimination Law* (Oxford: Clarendon Press, 2002), at 120.

[75] Otherwise, the concept of direct discrimination would have to be seen as being based on a fiction. Regardless of whether the forbidden ground is used out of aversion or for instrumental considerations, it is treated as though the former were the case.

[76] See, for example, D. A. Strauss, 'The Law and Economics of Racial Discrimination in Employment: The Case for Numerical Standards' (1991) 79 *Georgetown Law Journal* 1619–1657 at 1623.

underscores the merit of a redistributive perspective on anti-discrimination law. The purpose of protection from direct discrimination cannot be to root out prejudice or a bad attitude.[77] There may be no bad attitude to begin with, but rather only the *belief* on the part of the discriminator that it is rational to accommodate potentially aversive attitudes. Anti-discrimination law also need not be aimed at overcoming prejudice on the part of those whose potential reactions are taken into account by the agent.[78] Anti-discrimination law makes sense even when the agent is completely mistaken about beliefs held by others. The reason for treating indirect indirect discrimination as a case of direct discrimination can only lie in protecting certain persons from suffering a disadvantage whenever economically prudent agents take anticipated attitudes of others or statistics into account in making their choices.[79] These others do not even have to be possessed by these attitudes. Anti-discrimination protects from the adverse systemic effects of rational behaviour.[80] They result from mutual attitude ascription. The point is, hence, to correct the aggregate effect of individual market rationality and thereby to restore market equality.[81]

Thus understood, anti-discrimination law commissions distributive agents with a task from which they are allowed to rescind themselves, if at all,[82] only if their

[77] In this connection, 'prejudice' is generally understood to be 'aversion to certain physically inscribed characteristics of people, or unwarranted belief about the negative consequences of such characteristics for the capacities of individuals'. Unger, n. 27 at 88.

[78] The contrary view is widely held, however, it is also more far-fetched and hence not relevant to the construction of anti-discrimination law. See, for example, Koppelman n. 37 at 9, 58–62, who sees the major point of the anti-discrimination project in combating stigmatization. Treatment is to be eradicated that signals that the person so treated is not quite human. See also Hellman, n. 33 at 35. In a similar vein, Alexander and Reaumé share the proclivity to search for the wrong of discrimination in a certain type of act or treatment by others. See L. Alexander, 'What Makes Wrongful Discrimination Wrong? Biases, Preferences, Stereotypes, and Proxies' (1992) 141 *University of Pennsylvania Law Review* 149–219, at 153, where he explains that he would examine discrimination 'as an expression of various types of preferences'. Reaumé wishes to make a fresh start and lend coherence to an incoherent field of law. Nevertheless, she makes it difficult for herself to succeed. First, she resorts to a Court's hapless rationalization of its own case law in order to introduce 'dignity' as the central principle of anti-discrimination law. Second, she draws out, following the reasoning by the Court, the explanatory import of 'dignity' by defining the content of the latter with reference to the explanandum, that is, instances for which one would have expected an explanation why they are tantamount to a violation of 'dignity'. At this point, the whole project becomes circular. See D.G. Reaumé, 'Discrimination and Dignity' (2003) 63 *Lousiana Law Review* 645–695 at 666–669, 672.

[79] In fact, it would not even be clear what kind of attitude is the target of anti-discrimination law. Discrimination need not be based on aversion. It can also stem from the attempt to avoid a status-damaging association with out-group members vis-à-vis in-group members.

[80] It protects, for example, from 'statistical discrimination', that is, the reliance on a stereotype for an assessment of productivity (e.g., Italians shirk, while Poles do not). See I. Ayres, *Pervasive Prejudice? Unconventional Evidence of Race and Gender Discrimination* (Chicago, IL: Chicago University Press, 2001), at 73–75.

[81] In a similar vein, Bagenstos, n. 12 at 899, asserts that virtually all discrimination is rational, for it takes place in the context of attaining a goal.

[82] According to what might be termed the 'orthodox' perspective on direct discrimination, any discrimination on the grounds of sex is per se illegal in the EU. See Case C-177/88, *Dekker* v. *Stichting Vormingscentrum voor Junge Volwassen Plus* [1990] ECR 3941, para. 12. This may have changed in more recent case law. See, for example, Case C-32/93, *Webb* v. *EMO Air Cargo* [1994] ECR I-3567. I shall return to this question below when discussing the distinction between direct and indirect discrimination.

conduct is based on what is called 'objective factors'. Unless there are 'objective factors' to the contrary, the mandate is to correct market distributions in a manner that favours the protected group.[83] Seen from this angle, the line dividing anti-discrimination law from the use of tie-breaking quotas[84] is almost imperceptibly thin. Anti-discrimination law permits to include into a justification of unequal treatment *any factor* unrelated to the prohibited ground, such as family situation, unless this would give rise to significant disparate impact, and even where there is equal qualification among candidates; tie-breaking quotas, by contrast, make it mandatory, at any rate in the latter scenario, to decide in favour of the patrons of affirmative action.[85]

11. Conclusion

Anti-discrimination norms lend expression to a normative endorsement of market equality. They typically protect people against disadvantages suffered for reasons of their particularity. From the perspective of market equality, persons are faceless bearers of unexamined wants and capable of adapting to circumstances of their satisfaction. Anti-discrimination norms remove socially created obstacles to adaptation and thereby redistribute access to resources and opportunities.

The most appealing explanation of anti-discrimination law recognizes the priority of this redistributive dimension. Such an explanation is not least consistent with one of its core normative categories, namely, direct discrimination.

The social meaning of direct discrimination is constituted by prohibitions of discriminatory treatment. Reading conduct in light of an anti-discrimination norm removes from the actor's pre-normative intent the ambiguity of meaning. The normative reading constitutes the 'true' significance of conduct.

The justification for constituting social meanings lies in creating distributive responsibilities for whomever anti-discrimination law chooses to serve as an agent. Employers, typically, are in the position to break pervasive cycles of systemic discrimination even where no actual adverse attitudes or bad intents can be encountered. All protection from discrimination is protection from systemic discrimination.

Anti-discrimination law essentially involves a translation of the pursuit of redistributive objectives into a deontological idiom. In the context of this idiom, agents are cast as though they were acting on certain prohibited grounds. The translation

[83] Interestingly, the deontological dimension of anti-discrimination law has attracted a great deal of scholarly discussion of matters such as discriminatory intent, animus, stereotypes; however, the major question of this field of law is what constitutes an objective factor. For a similar observation, see S. R. Bagenstos, 'The Structural Turn and the Limits of Anti-discrimination Law' (2006) 94 *California Law Review* 1–47 at 34–35.

[84] Tie-breaking quotas presuppose equal qualification among candidates.

[85] It is clear that, thus understood, *Marschall* was wrongly decided by the ECJ for it requires the tie-breaking task of the quota to be overruled whenever certain factors, unrelated to qualifications, tilt the balance in favour of the male candidate. See Case C-409/95, *Hellmut Marschall* v. *Land Nordrhein-Westfalen* [1997] ECR I-6363.

effort gives rise to a systematically induced misreading as soon as the normative intent of the agent cannot be established with resort to a norm that decrees that doing x counts as discrimination on the grounds of y. In such a case, owing to its deontological appearance, anti-discrimination law systematically invites recourse to pre-normative intentions. Hence, the ambiguity of social meaning re-enters a sphere where one would have expected normative clarification.

This is the first major manifestation of the normative deficiency of anti-discrimination law.

5

Normative Twist and Antinomy

1. Introduction

This chapter draws out the implications inherent in recognizing the explanatory appeal of the redistributive perspective. The analysis of the meaning of direct discrimination in the previous chapter revealed that systemic discrimination is the core concern of anti-discrimination law. In the parlance of this type of law, the observable impact of systemic discrimination is called 'indirect' or 'disparate impact' discrimination. Some groups end up worse off than others. The causal mechanisms may remain difficult to untangle.

Arguably, the normative relevance of redistribution has to be manifest in the priority of indirect discrimination over its direct counterpart. It is argued below that direct discrimination is in fact best understood to be a special case of indirect discrimination. It isolates one causal relation between agents and distributive outcomes. This causal relation can be given an extensional and an intensional interpretation. The extensional interpretation promises to isolate normative intent ('x ought to count as y') vis-à-vis an invasion of pre-normative ambiguity. Alas, this promise cannot be kept. The most appealing interpretation of direct discrimination is intensional. It examines *conceivable reasons* for action and thereby has to open the door to the consideration of pre-normative intent. This accounts for anti-discrimination law's inverted appearance. It is normatively twisted. Underneath this twist lurks an antinomy, which is the essence of its normative deficiency. Indirect discrimination is more fundamental than direct discrimination. Direct discrimination, however, is more important to anti-discrimination law, for it promises to fill a distributive void that is involved in its constitution.

The chapter concludes on a more positive note with a few remarks concerning decommodification.

2. The Priority of Indirect Discrimination

If the observation made in the previous chapter is correct that protection from direct discrimination is supposed to help break the cycle of systemic discrimination, the core situation to which anti-discrimination law formulates a response is not direct but indirect discrimination[1] or, in American parlance, 'disparate impact' discrimination.[2] Ordinarily, however, anti-discrimination norms are presented in reverse order. Protection from direct discrimination is set out first and seen as supplemented with the more erratic protection from indirect discrimination.[3] Without much more analysis, I would now like to explain why this view is misleading.

An instance of indirect discrimination is encountered when the use of a neutral criterion puts, or might put, members of one group at a particular disadvantage.[4] Prior to the adoption of the new Directives, the ECJ expected to be presented with statistical proof of discrimination.[5] The language contained in the new Directives no longer seems to require statistical evidence.[6] What matters is that the use of the neutral criterion *may* give rise to 'considerable', 'statistically significant', or 'relatively constant' distributive disparity.[7] The causes may be various, what counts is that they affect a significant number of the protected group. For example, the unequal distribution might bespeak the group's lack of bargaining power. The absence of effective representation may explain why part-time workers receive less

[1] The *locus classicus* for this in European employment discrimination law is Case 170/84, *Bilka-Kaufhaus GmbH* v. *Weber von Hartz* [1986] ECR 1607 at para. 31:

> The answer to the first question referred to by the national court must therefore be that Article 119 of the EEC Treaty is infringed by a department store company which excludes part-time employees from its occupational pension scheme, where that exclusion affects a far greater number of women than men, unless the undertaking shows that the exclusion is based on objectively justified factors unrelated to any discrimination on grounds of sex.

[2] On the acceptance of the notion of 'disparate impact' discrimination under the name of indirect discrimination by the European Court of Justice, see R. C. Hunter and E. W. Shoben, 'Disparate Impact Discrimination: American Oddity or Internationally Accepted Concept?' (1998) 19 *Berkeley Journal of Employment and Labour Law* 108–153 at 121–122; T. Loenen, 'Indirect Discrimination: Oscillating between Containment and Revolution', in T. Loenen and P. R. Rodrigues (eds), *Non-discrimination Law: Comparative Perspectives* (Amsterdam: Kluwer, 1999), 195–211 at 196. It may bear emphasis, though, that indirect discrimination analysis is not limited to the employment context in EU law (see ibid. at 208). See also J. Haskovec, 'A Beast of a Burden? The New EU Burden-of-proof Arrangement in Cases of Employment Discrimination Compared to Existing U.S. Law' (2005) 14 *Journal of Transnational Law and Contemporary Problems* 1069–1106 at 1084–1085.

[3] See, for example, L. Waddington and A. Hendriks, 'The Expanding Concept of Employment Discrimination in Europe: From Direct and Indirect Discrimination to Reasonable Accommodation Discrimination' (2002) 18 *International Journal of Comparative Labour Law and Industrial Relations* 403–427.

[4] See Article 2(2)(b) of the Framework Directive. See also Loenen, n. 2 at 206–208. On the pedigree of the category with regard to the American conception of 'disparate impact discrimination', see S. Fredman, *Discrimination Law* (Oxford: Clarendon Press, 2002), at 106–107.

[5] See Case C-322/98, *Kachelman* v. *Bankhaus Hermann Lampe KG* [2000] ECR I-7505, para. 23.

[6] See C. Barnard, *EC Employment Law*, 3rd edn (Oxford: Oxford University Press, 2007), at 326.

[7] See Case C-171/88, *Ingrid Rinner-Kühn* v. *FWW Spezial-Gebäudereinigung GmbH & Co. KG* [1989] ECR 2742, para. 15; Cases C-4/02 & C-5/02, *Hilde Schönheit* v. *Stadt Frankfurt am Main* [2003] ECR I-12575, para. 82. On the shifting characterizations within the Case C-25/01, *Rinke* v. *Ärtzekammer Hamburg* [2003] ECR I-8349, see Barnard, n. 6 at 329–330. In Case C-167/97, *Regina and Secretary of State for Employment, ex parte Nicole Seymour Smith* v. *Laura Perez* [1999] ECR I-623 at paras 60–61, the Court indicated that a lesser but persistent and relatively constant disparity over a long period between men and women would be equivalent to statistics that indicate a considerably small percentage of the protected group.

than full-time employees. Alternatively, a different employment history, which stems from a differential social allocation of child-rearing obligations, may translate into a difference of seniority-based salary increments. As long as women are disproportionately affected by these inequalities, a prima facie case of indirect discrimination can be made. In other instances, the unequal distribution may result from reliance on stereotypes. In any case, the work done by discrimination is embedded in a broader context of social conventions and beliefs that accounts for its emergence. In the worst case, under the impression of low expectations, victims choose their own disadvantage. They drop out of the race even before it has begun.

With regard to the causal mechanism, direct discrimination is special, for it *constitutes and identifies a cause* by removing from the acts of the distributive agent any ambivalence. The reason underpinning this normative act is that distributive agents are likely to yield to, to draw on, or to give free rein to stereotypical beliefs about others in systemic contexts of action. If the conduct of agents would have had a different outcome had it not been for the presence of the prohibited ground, the law says that it amounts to direct discrimination. Direct discrimination thereby comes out as a special case of indirect discrimination. It is special because the distributive consequences of systemic discrimination are presented as outcomes of the individual act of distributive agents; and it is special because no proof or projection of disadvantage across group members needs to be adduced.

Such a specification must not be mistaken for a separation. What makes direct discrimination special is the deontological focus on the effect of an act. But this explains also why it is not severed from the broader distributive context. The causally identified single instance does not require any projection of aggregate adverse effects, for if the discriminatory conduct were practiced consistently, group disadvantage would invariably arise. It is the very *normative* point of direct discrimination to let, without any further enquiry, doing x count as doing y.

By according, as a matter of the law's self-presentation, direct discrimination priority over its indirect parent, the field attains a normatively twisted appearance. The latter, however, is merely a manifestation of a deeper reversal that actually gives rise to an *antinomy* with regard to the law's source of normativity. While the distributive perspective, which is epitomized by indirect discrimination, is more fundamental, pre-normative intent[8] turns out to be indispensable in order to ascertain the meaning of anti-discrimination norms.

3. Is Direct Discrimination Different or Special?

At least two objections may be raised against classifying direct discrimination as a causally specified case of indirect discrimination.

[8] From the American experience, Krieger reports 'intent' to mean 'a subjective desire or wish' to bring about a discriminatory result. See L. Hamilton Krieger, 'Civil Rights Perestroika: Intergroup Relations after Affirmative Action' (1998) 86 *California Law Review* 1251–1333 at 1326.

The first objection invokes a deontological rationale that conceivably underpins protection from direct discrimination. An employer yielding to, or even captive of, prejudice is closer to the evil combated by anti-discrimination law than an employer who merely has a hand at bringing about an unequal distribution in the course of applying neutral criteria. I surmise that it is this perceived greater proximity to the evil attitude, indeed, that explains why anti-discrimination law is usually presented upside down. It is consonant, for example, with how the deontological viewpoint is presented in Bagenstos' superb work. Bagenstos perceives the justification for banning rational discrimination in the employer's participation in market transactions that reproduce systemic disadvantage. In his view, employers never come with clean hands unless they rescind their resources from the systemic cycle of discrimination. Their negligent contribution to this system justifies interference with their freedom.[9]

The difficulty that besets the deontological interpretation is that it would have to explain why it is more severe to put people down because of their religion than, choosing the obvious example, because of their looks. In fact, the deontological position cannot explain why it is not insidious to discriminate on the grounds of abilities (or test scores) rather than of race. Abilities are just as undeserved as membership to a race. The difference of protection for one rather than another ground can only be accounted for when distributive objectives are taken into account, for example, Rawls' difference principle, which permits rewarding talents so long as through their incentivized extraction everyone is made better off.[10]

The lack of grounding, however, does not translate into a lack of force. The view of proximity gives rise to a certain *deontological misreading* of anti-discrimination law, which is part of its intellectual fabric. Law does not come into existence without being known, as law. The law may develop false conceptions of itself that effectively enter into its operation.

The second objection goes to the heart of the difference and claims that seeing direct discrimination as a specification of indirect discrimination ignores the major difference between these categories. In principle, and contrary to indirect discrimination, direct discrimination does not admit of any justifications for reasons of 'a real need on the part of the undertaking'[11] or other objective factors.[12] In cases of

[9] He maintains this view of the employer's fault even though he also conceives of employers as distributive agents who have been chosen to play a critical role in the distribution of primary goods, such as jobs. See S. R. Bagenstos, '"Rational Discrimination," Accommodation, and the Politics of (Disability) Civil Rights' (2003) 89 *Virginia Law Review* 825–923, at 858. Bagenstos, however, brings a narrow understanding of redistribution to bear on the issue. He sees it restricted to monetary transfers (ibid. at 841). But this is far too narrow. A job is an asset, whose value by far exceeds the salary that it pays, for it provides access to social networks and varieties of services, such as health and pension insurance.

[10] See J. Rawls, *A Theory of Justice* (Cambridge, MA: Harvard University Press, 1971), at 65–67.

[11] See *Bilka*, n. 1 at para. 36.

[12] The basic test established in the *Rinner-Kühn* case has it that if a Member State can show that the means chosen meet a necessary aim of social policy and are suitable and requisite for attaining that aim, the mere fact that legislation affects a far greater proportion of women than men does not constitute discrimination. See Case C-171/88 *Ingrid Rinner-Kühn* v. *FFW Spezial-Gebäudereinigung*

indirect discrimination,[13] by contrast, such a justification can succeed when the means chosen to pursue a legitimate objective are suitable and necessary.[14] The level of judicial scrutiny varies considerably in cases of indirect discrimination.[15] Remarkably, the Court appears to be reluctant to answer questions with regard to whether a more stringent or a more relaxed test applies.[16] By and large, the legislature has a smaller range of justification available than employers, since it is less vulnerable to market forces.[17] Both the legislature and employers, however, are barred from invoking mere budgetary reasons as an objective factor justifying differential impact on men and women.[18] Nor are they in a position to justify

GmbH & Co. KG [1989] ECR 2743, para. 13. *Bilka* had earlier introduced the same type of test for private employers. See n. 1. See E. Ellis, *EU Anti-discrimination Law* (Oxford: Oxford University Press, 2005), at 112. Strangely enough, however, the Court recently stayed the official course and sustained the distinction between direct and indirect discrimination without taking case law into account that points into a different direction (of which more below). See Case 388/07, *The Queen on the application of The Incorporated Trustees of the National Council on Aging* v. *Secretary for Business, Enterprise and Regulatory Reform* [2009] ECR I-1569. One major exception to the exclusionary rule concerns, of course, occupational requirements, which rule grants Member States the power to allow the use of a forbidden characteristic if 'by reason of the nature of the particular occupational activities concerned or of the context in which they are carried out, such a characteristic constitutes a genuine and determining occupational requirement, provided that the objective is legitimate and the requirement is proportionate'. (Article 4[1] of the Framework Directive). The other major exception concerns public security, public order, and health (Article 2[5] of the Framework Directive). American anti-discrimination law recognizes the same type of exception. An employer incurs no liability where she successfully invokes a 'bona fide occupational qualification reasonably necessary to the normal operation of that particular business or enterprise'. This avenue of defence is available to the employer both under Title VII of the Civil Rights Act and under the Age Discrimination in Employment Act. See 42 USC, sec. 2000e *et seq.*; 24 USC, sec. 621 *et seq.* Invocation of such a requirement necessarily introduces a justification that removes from behaviour the taint of association with a discriminatory attitude. (I agree with Sedler on this point. See R. A. Sedler, 'The Role of "Intent" in Discrimination Analysis', in T. Loenen and P. R. Rodrigues (eds), *Non-Discrimination Law: Comparative Perspectives* (Amsterdam: Kluwer, 1999), 91–103 at 97). If, for example, an employer decides to hire a man rather than a women to perform the role of John F. Kennedy in a movie he uses sex as a distinction, however, he does not, so it seems, with discriminatory intent.

13 Disparate impact, in other words, is not per se illegal. This was made clear by the Court in Case C-96/80, *Jenkins* v. *Kingsgate* [1981] ECR 911, para. 10.

14 See *Schönheit*, n. 7.

15 For a clear statement of all elements of the proportionality principle, see *Rinner-Kühn*, n. 12; for a less stringent test, see, for example, Case C-444/93 *De Weerd* [1995] ECR I-4741 at para. 30. See also P. Craig and G. de Búrca, *EU Law: Text Case and Materials*, 4th edn (Oxford: Oxford University Press, 2008), at 895.

16 See Case C-167/97, *Seymour Smith* [1999] ECR I-623, paras 75–76.

17 See *Council on Ageing*, n. 12 at para. 46.

18 See, for example, *Schönheit*, n. 7 at 84–85 (with references to the prior case law); the Court repeats the same mantra all over. See Case C-77/02, *Erika Steinicke* v. *Bundesanstalt für Arbeit*, 11 September [2003] ECR I-9027, para. 67:

> However, to concede that budgetary considerations may justify a difference in treatment between men and women which would otherwise constitute indirect discrimination on the grounds of sex would mean that the application and scope of a rule of Community law as fundamental as that of equal treatment between men and women might vary in time and place according to the state of the public finances of the Member States.

The relevant precedent is *Roks and others* v. *Bestuur van de Bedrijfsvereniging voor de Gezondheid, Geestelijke en Maatschappelijke Belangen and others* [1994] ECR I-571; see also Case C-196/02, *Vasiliki Nikoloudi* v. *Organismos Tilepikinonion Ellados AE* [2005] ECR I-1789, para. 53. In the case of permissible derogations from direct discrimination, the Court is also highly suspicious of arguments discrimination by claiming that guaranteeing equality would be too costly.[19] The Court is ready to apply a less demanding standard of fit, even in cases where direct discrimination is permissible, and to concede the national legislature a great leeway of discretion when it comes to justifying why mandatory retirement age is capable of pursuing legitimate social policy objectives.[20] In any event, direct discrimination consists of adverse treatment that is caused by the relevance of the prohibited ground, whereas the root cause of indirect discrimination is an open question. In the latter case, the potential discriminator may invoke conceivable[21] objective factors[22] in order to dissipate the notion that the prohibited ground has been the determining factor.[23]

A reply to the second objection requires further elaboration of what it means to say that unequal treatment is caused by a prohibited ground.

4. Extensional and Intensional Causation: Two Different Types of Normativity

Apparently, a finding of direct discrimination hinges on determining the causal link between the prohibited ground and adverse treatment. *Grant* is the case in point.[24] Is it a case of discrimination on the grounds of sex when the partner of a homosexual employee is not eligible for travel concessions while partners of heterosexual employees are? The causal analysis is straightforward.[25] Neither female nor male homosexual partners are eligible, even though they would be if they were in a heterosexual relationship. Hence, sex is not the determining factor, but rather sexual orientation. Prior to the adoption of Directive 2000/78/EC, employees were free to discriminate on this ground. *P.* v. *S.* can be read as continuing in this type of causal analysis.[26] After she had undergone a sex change a formerly male employee was dismissed. Had it not been for the sex reassignment she would have stayed employed. In contrast to *Grant,* this was a case of direct discrimination. Sex was the cause.

invoking financial constraints. For example, a financial equilibrium argument is rejected when it comes to non-contributory schemes. See Case C-382/98, *The Queen and Secretary of State for Social Security ex parte: John Henry Taylor* [1999] ECR I-8955, paras 29–30.

[19] See Case C-243/95, *Kathleen Hill and Ann Stapleton* v. *Revenue Commissioners and Department of Finance* [1998] ECR I-3739, para. 40: 'So far as justification on economic grounds is concerned, it should be noted that an employer cannot justify discrimination arising from a job-sharing scheme solely on the ground that avoidance of such discrimination would involve increased cost.'

[20] See Case C-411/05, *Félix Palacios de la Villa* v. *Cortefiel Servicios SA* [2007] ECR I-8531, paras 56, 72.

[21] The legislature is not restricted to the reasons actually used. See *Schönheit,* n. 7 at 86.

[22] See ibid. at para. 91; *Steinicke,* n. 18 at 57.

[23] See Ellis, n. 12 at 112.

[24] See Case C-248/86, *Grant* v. *South West Trains* [1998] ECR 621.

[25] I find myself in disagreement with Barnard, n. 6 at 347, who suggests that the Court randomly switched comparators.

[26] See Case C-13/94, *P.* v. *S.* [1996] ECR I-2143.

One may want to characterize the interpretation of direct discrimination that prefers the causal 'but for' criterion as purely *extensional*. It does not take the contextual meaning of the act into account, in particular *not* whether the inequality is between a man and a woman. What matters is whether the presence of the ground is causally involved in bringing about a difference of treatment. Even an inequality that affects only women can count as direct discrimination on the grounds of sex.[27]

As has been argued above, the isolation of a causal relationship between individual acts and a social disadvantage is the distinguishing mark of direct discrimination. It accounts for its normative force. The extensional reading of causation—if the prohibited ground were absent the result would be different—represents a certain interpretation of it. It can be called the *extensional understanding of normativity*. This understanding sometimes comes to the fore in cases affecting pregnancy. No matter how reasonable the actions of employers may appear, the distributive burden falls on them when pregnancy is a causal factor.[28]

The extensional interpretation of causality and the attendant conception of normativity stem from an attempt to make sense of what I called above (p. 104) normative intent. Extensional causation is a mode of determining when doing x means doing y, for example, by finding that firing an employee after he had undergone a sex change means discrimination on the grounds of sex.

It would appear, then, that the line distinguishing direct and indirect discrimination is the line separating strict causation, on the one hand, from causation by reasons for action, on the other. Whereas the suspicion of direct discrimination can be dispelled only by demonstrating the absence of any causal link, the charge of indirect discrimination can be rebutted by pointing to the relevance of non-discriminatory reasons for action.

As shall be seen presently, the line drawn by 'but for' causation is more elusive than it seems to be.[29] Hence, the alternative *intensional* reading of causality perceives the cause to be part of the reasoning process. Indeed, a cause enters the domain of imputable human action only if it could count as a reason for action.[30]

[27] See, for example, Case C-460/06, *Nadine Paquay* v. *Société d'architectes Hoet + Minne SPRL* [2007] ECR I-8511, para. 29.

[28] For example, when a woman decides to return from parental leave ahead of time then the employer has to bear the relevant adjustment costs even if the woman cannot be employed in her previous capacity because of another pregnancy. The obligation on the part of the employer is also not affected by the fact that the woman decides to return to work merely in order to benefit from the maternity allowance. See Case C-320/01, *Wiebke Busch* v. *Klinikum Neustadt GmbH & Co. Betriebs-KG* [2003] ECR I-2041, paras 39, 41, 44; for a similarly strong protection of women on maternity leave who apply during the leave period for a new position, see Case C-294/04, *Carmen Sarkatzis Herrero* v. *Instituto Madrileño de Salud* (Imsalud) [2006] ECR I-1513, paras 39, 41, 45 (inclusion of maternity leave into the determination of seniority towards the new job).

[29] On the following, see the apt analysis by J. Gardner, 'On the Grounds of her Sex(uality)' (1998) 18 *Oxford Journal of Legal Studies* 167–187 at 185.

[30] This is also true for cases of negligent conduct. The actor could have taken a cause into account as a reason for abstaining from certain conduct. The philosophical theory that approaches intention from the perspective of the conclusion in practical reasoning finds a most elaborate expression in the work of Donald Davidson. See his *Essays on Actions and Events* (Oxford: Oxford University Press, 1980). For a useful introduction, see M. E. Bratman, *Faces of Intention: Selected Essays on Intention and Agency* (Cambridge: Cambridge University Press, 1999), at 209–215.

The normativity of the direct discrimination norm is drawn out, hence, not in the course of the application of a 'but for' criterion, but in the scrutiny that is brought to bear on reasons for action. From this perspective, the point of the extensional analysis becomes reconceived in the form of the maxim of having to avoid diligently acting for the wrong reasons. If, for example, nobody can find another reason why women are paid less than their male colleagues but the fact that they are women there is reason to believe that women are worse off because they are women. Their sex must have been part of the employer's reasons for action, even if only in the form of an auxiliary reason saying that hiring women helps saving on salaries. Even on an intensional interpretation of the normativity of direct discrimination, which eliminates certain grounds from the schedule of permissible reasons for action, the attribution of intent remains in principle *normative* and does not without anything further revert to the pre-normative level. What matters is the social meaning, constituted by the anti-discrimination norm, which should have occurred to the actor.[31] This social meaning, however, it not determined in the mechanical manner envisaged by the extensional reading of direct discrimination. The intensional reading of causality does not easily assimilate instances of discrimination on the grounds of transsexuality to sex discrimination, as the Court did in *P.* v. *S.*[32] Direct discrimination has to be traceable to the discriminator's *conceivable* reasoning process.[33] The idea is, at any rate, that it should have occurred to the discriminator that acting for a prohibited reason is attributable to him owing to the validity of the anti-discrimination norm.

The case of *K.B.*[34] demonstrates quite clearly that the ECJ does not—or not always—rely on an extensional reading of causality. A man, after he had undergone a sex change from female to male was ineligible to receive a widower's pension from his female partner pursuant to British laws for the reason that marriage was not an option for people whose birth records showed the same sex. The case reveals the weakness of the extensional causal criterion. Had his birth sex been male he would have been eligible for marriage and, a fortiori, the widower's pension. One would have been inclined to conclude that this case is therefore a case of sex discrimination. But the Court reasoned differently, alleging that the result of the 'but for' test is negative, for had he stayed female the widower's pension would not have been available to him either. Moreover, the Court found that sex was inapposite to the pension question since what mattered was marital status.[35] Sex was not related

[31] As Charles Fried put it so elegantly, the concept of intention closes the gap between states of the world and the agent's state of mind. This gap is closed only if we realize that judgements of right and wrong speak to individuals and are supposed to guide their actions. Moreover, these judgements are not merely about outcomes *or* states of mind but about how the link between both is manifest in the agents action. See C. Fried, *Right and Wrong* (Cambridge, MA: Harvard University Press, 1978), at 25–26.

[32] See above n. 26.

[33] See Gardner, n. 29 at 186: 'There is no other "causative" process in play but the causative process of the discriminator's reasoning, the list of considerations which affected him in what he did.'

[34] Case C-117/01, *K.B.* v. *National Health Service Agency* [2004] ECR I-541.

[35] Even more remarkably, in the *Schnorbus* case the ECJ did not apply a causal analysis. For a finding of direct discrimination the Court required the use of sex as a classification even though it was

to the widower's pension *directly* but only to a necessary condition of eligibility.[36] Of course, from a causal perspective that is heeded of this condition the applicant would have been in a different position had he been born male. Had it not been for his birth sex he would have been better off. However, for a perception of causation that merely takes into account how the alternative between male and female plays out in the present, his position vis-à-vis the pension entitlement would not have been better had he stayed female. The causal analysis does not yield a determinate result, for its result varies with regard to its scope. The causal analysis would matter only if it clarified which part of the causal chain is *relevant* to the case. Relevance concerns reasons. A selective focus on the relevant cause reveals an *intensional* understanding of normativity. In this case, the Court did not deploy an extensional reading of direct discrimination. In fact, it took, covertly, pre-normative intent into account.

The matter became subsequently resolved rather bravely. After referring to a recent decision by the European Court of Human Rights (ECtHR), according to which the impossibility of marriage to a gender-reassigned person violated the right to privacy (Article 12 ECHR),[37] the Court went on to intuit the following consequence for EU law:[38]

> Legislation, such as that at issue in the main proceedings, which, in breach of the ECHR, prevents a couple [...] from fulfilling the marriage requirement which must be met for one of them to be able to benefit from part of the pay of the other must be regarded as being, in principle, incompatible with the requirements of Article 141 EC.

And that's that. Nothing further.

From the intensional causation perspective, it follows that in order to rule out that the forbidden ground (or category) has been causally involved in effecting a certain result, it must be possible to adduce reasons that are *good enough* to dispel doubts about reliance on that ground.[39] Otherwise it could never be clarified whether someone has been discriminated against 'on the grounds of...'.[40]

The inquiry into overriding good reasons is plainly unavoidable in cases where the discriminatory treatment is diachronic and the 'but for' test of no avail. An employer replaces a man with a woman to whom he pays a lower salary.[41] How can it be known whether he discriminates 'on the grounds of sex'? It would simply be wrong to engage in counterfactual assessments of responsibility ('I bet he would have paid more

clear in the case at hand that only men were able to benefit from a neutrally formulated rule of admission. See Case C-79/99, *Juila Schnorbus* v. *Land Hessen* [2000] ECR I-1997 at para. 33.

[36] See ibid., para. at 28–30.

[37] Judgment of 11 July 2002, *Goodwin* v. *United Kingdom.*

[38] Ibid., para. 34.

[39] Gardner, n. 29 at 186, concedes that even what he terms 'auxiliary' reasons may figure among the reasons for action that are of relevance here.

[40] See Article 2(2) of the Framework Directive.

[41] This is a reversal and a variation of the facts underlying the *Brunnhofer* case. See Case C-381/99, *Brunnhofer* v. *Bank der Österreichischen Postsparkasse AG* [2001] ECR I-4961.

to a man').[42] One can only rule out sex discrimination by examining the schedule of reasons.

An intensional reading of causation, however, cannot embrace the per se illegality of direct discrimination unless the semantics of the anti-discrimination norm would leave no doubt that doing x counts as doing y in context z. It is difficult to imagine how that could be the case. The tacit embrace of intensional normativity may therefore explain why the ECJ arrived at the following result in a case where it did not specify whether discrimination was direct or indirect:[43]

> The fundamental principle laid down in Article [141] of the Treaty [. . .] precludes unequal pay as between men and women for the same job or work of equal value, whatever the mechanism which produces such inequality [. . .] unless the difference in pay is justified by objective factors unrelated to any discrimination linked to the difference in sex.

Put differently, the ECJ stated the overarching principle[44] that all distributive agents are liable to have the unequal treatment of persons imputed to them as discrimination unless they can show that they acted for good reasons. Obviously, the mechanism of how discrimination is brought about—'directly'[45] or 'indirectly'—does not matter.[46]

5. The Demise of per se Illegality and the Relevance of Treating Like Cases Alike

Upon closer inspection, it turns out that the jurisprudence of the ECJ is actually characterized by casual neglect of the distinction. In equal pay cases, the ECJ developed a three-stage model for the determination of discrimination, which may have been originally designed for cases of indirect discrimination, but this is not entirely clear.[47] The first stage involves finding the relevant comparator. Euphemistically stated, this matter requires good judgement and a great deal of patience on the part of litigants.[48] As shall be seen below, the justification of equal treatment is often tacitly and implicitly addressed when pondering the right comparator. The second stage requires determining whether both types of employees

[42] See S. L. Hurley, *Justice, Luck, and Knowledge* (Cambridge, MA: Harvard University Press, 2003), at 159–160.

[43] See *Brunnhofer*, n. 41 at para. 20.

[44] See Case C-285/02, *Elsner-Lakeberg* v. *Land Nordrhein Westfalen* [2004] ECR I-5861, para. 12.

[45] It is clear, from the outset, that 'direct' and 'indirect' do not translate into 'overt' and 'disguised', since direct discrimination will often be disguised (the hiring of a white rather than a black person because of allegedly better social skills) and indirect discrimination be quite overt (the use of an onerous and unnecessary job qualification requirement). See Ellis, n. 12 at 89.

[46] The mechanism may be quite subtle, as is the case of relatively lower pay rates for overtime work that give rise to unequal pay in the relation between full-time workers and part-time workers who work overtime and end up working the same number of hours. See Case C-300/06, *Ursula Voß* v. *Land Berlin* [2007] ECR I-10573, paras 21–22.

[47] See the very instructive exposition in Barnard, n. 6 at 345–354. Fredman discusses first the type of analysis employed in pay discrimination cases and then turns to indirect discrimination. See Fredman, n. 4 at 103.

[48] See ibid. at 8, 96–100 (reporting that the relevant litigation may take many years).

are engaged in equal work or work of equal value. In this context, job classification and job evaluation schemes are relevant. Finally, at the third stage, it has to be shown that both employees or groups of employees belong to the same employer. *Enderby* is an authority in point.[49] Speech therapists, a job predominantely carried out by women, were paid less than clinical psychologists and pharmacists, jobs almost exclusively occupied by men. Without addressing the question of whether this is a case of either direct or indirect discrimination, the ECJ simply said that lower remuneration raises a prima facie case of sex discrimination and that the burden of proof shifts to the employer to show the legitimate influence of objectively justified factors.[50] One may speculate how that matter would have appeared had it been fit into the mould of direct discrimination. Presumably, one would have had to demonstrate that had the applicant been a man, she would have been hired as a clinical psychologist. The example shows why the category of direct discrimination, taken as a per se principle, is far too crude to address the issue. It isolates a narrow segment of the conceivable reasoning process that becomes expanded when one turns to indirect discrimination. There is no fundamental discontinuity.[51]

Indeed, a recent more theoretical pronouncement in the case law notwithstanding,[52] the ECJ has worked around the per se quality of the prohibition on direct discrimination[53] by reading anti-discrimination laws as expressive of the general principle of equality, which is alleged to require treating only like cases alike.[54] Hence, the ECJ makes a finding of direct discrimination conditional upon the likeness or comparability of cases. An investigation into comparability at a stage before direct discrimination is even considered to be relevant is the equivalent of a weak objective justification requirement.[55] After all, the objective factors explaining an unequal treatment or unequal result often explain why it is reasonable to assume that differences are at stake that are reasonable enough to support inequality.

Presupposing likeness of cases as a condition for the application of direct discrimination is a less stringent constraint than a proportionality test, which

[49] See Case C-127/92, *Enderby* v. *Frenchay Health Authority and the Secretary for Health* [1993] ECR I-5535.

[50] See ibid. at para. 16.

[51] That there is no fundamental discontinuity is revealed in cases where the Court applies a strict proportionality test to legislation that avails itself of explicit derogations from the principle of non-discrimination. See as regards Article 7 Council Directive 79/7/EEC of 19 December 1978 on the progressive implementation of the principle of equal treatment for men and women in matters of social security, OJ 1979 L 6/24, Case C-382/98, *The Queen and Secretary of State for Social Security ex parte: John Henry Taylor* [1999] ECR I-8955, para. 28. On the derogation available with regard to certain occupational activities pursuant to Article 2(2) Council Directive 76/207/EEC of 9 February 1976 on the implementation of the principle of equal treatment for men and women as regards access to employment, vocational training and promotion and working conditions, OJ 1976 L 39/40, see Case C-285/98, *Tanja Kreil* v. *Bundesrepublik Deutschland* [2000] ECR I-69, paras 23, 31.

[52] See *Council on Ageing*, n. 12 at para. 59.

[53] For a curious case in which the ECJ treats a case of indirect discrimination as though it were per se illegal, see Case C-281/97, *Andrea Krüger* v. *Kreiskrankenhaus Ebersberg* [1999] ECR I-5127, para. 30.

[54] See, for example, Case C-333/97, *Susanne Lewen* v. *Lothar Denda* [1999], ECR I-7243, para. 36; Case C-19/02, *Viktor Hlozek* v. *Roche Austria Gesellschaft mbH* [2004] ECR I-11491, paras 44, 48; Case C-313/02, *Nicole Wippel* v. *Peek & Cloppenburg GmbH & CoKG* [2004] ECR I-9483, para. 56.

[55] See *Nikoloudi*, n. 18, paras 30, 36.

would call for an explanation why in light of certain objective factors certain situations do not have to be treated equally. This explains why the finding of comparability or likeness invests the ECJ with broad discretion to determine the issue. This discretion, however, is the reverse side of the ECJ accepting reasons for unequal treatment without any further inquiry into the proportionality of their application. For example, in the eyes of the ECJ it does not constitute any discrimination if Christmas bonuses are withheld from women who are on maternity leave 'where the award of that allowance is subject only to the condition that the worker is in active employment when it is awarded'.[56] The situations between those at work and those on leave are deemed to be 'incomparable'. In the *Hlozek* case, it is quite obvious that the ECJ accepted direct unequal treatment on the grounds of sex for the reason that it served as a means to bring about equal situations for men and women in a context where collective agreements and social legislation interacted. The Court thereby accepted a sound reason for unequal treatment, however, by calling the situations 'incomparable'.[57] By contrast, when comparing the situation of full-time workers and part-time workers whose income is a composite of normal and overtime pay, the Court stated that the overall pay for the same amount of hours worked is the relevant criterion. It thereby created comparability in the relation between full-time workers and those part-time workers who work the same number of hours but receive lower compensation because the remuneration for overtime hours is lower.[58]

6. The Lure of Comparability

Linking protection from discrimination to the maxim of treating like cases alike may appear to be a grand systematic consolidation of European equality law. In fact, however, it turns out to be a dangerous softening of its power to constrain. Instead of asking for an explanation why two different groups of employees are treated differently because of a difference in their employment situation, the ECJ rests content with asserting a lack of comparability.[59] This leads to a remarkable reversal in the relation of the stringency between direct and indirect discrimination. Whereas in cases of indirect discrimination objective factors are considered in the course of a more or less rigorous application of a proportionality test, cases of direct discrimination can be disposed of by invoking one special, and highly diffuse, objective factor, namely the difference in the situations. The derogating reason is thus presented as though it resided in the facts themselves.

The latter strategy is most remarkably revealed in a case in which the ECJ relied on the incomparability of situations in order to quell doubts about *indirect*

[56] *Lewen*, n. 54 at 38.
[57] See *Hlozek*, n. 54 at 48.
[58] See *Voß*, n. 46 at paras 21–22, 29, 32–33; see also Case C-285/02, *Elsner-Lakeberg* [2004] ECR I-5861, para. 17.
[59] Most remarkably in *Wippel*, n. 54 at 62–64.

discrimination.[60] The question concerned the calculation of termination payments. The relevant law required taking years of mandatory compulsory military service into account for the calculation of years of service. Periods of parental leave were not to be included. The first rule applied to men, the exclusion of parental leave time overwhelmingly affected women (98 per cent). Had the Court reasoned in a manner appropriate to cases of indirect discrimination, it would have had to accept qua objective factor that compensating men for mandatory military service is an objective factor unrelated to sex that justifies the disadvantaging of women who take time off in order to take care of their offspring. Obviously, this is not an easy position to defend. What the Court did, instead, was to present procreation and child-rearing as an essentially private affair whereas military service was seen as fulfilling a civic legal obligation.[61] Indeed, the Court concluded that given that the reasons for the suspension of employment were 'of a different nature', the employees affected were in no comparable situation.[62] This is a concealed way of saying, of course, that the difference of situations was an objective factor justifying inequality in a context where the objectivity of the factor was far from self-evident. Saying that two groups of persons are not in the same situation is tantamount to saying that there is an objective factor justifying unequal treatment.

In this case and in others, casting matters as though they raised the question of comparability is a convenient way of avoiding normative questions of responsibility. For example, full termination payments were paid out to employees who decided to leave their employment for 'important reasons' whereas only half the amount was paid out to those who left employment because of parenthood.[63] While several provisions of the relevant national legislation indicated that most 'important reasons' are associated with failures on the part of the employer to create a decent working environment, it did not appear inconceivable to link the important reason 'damage to health or moral welfare' with the pressing need to look after children, in particular in cases where the employee had no choice but to terminate employment owing to the unavailability of day care facilities. Given that the legislative list of 'important' reasons was meant to be illustrative only, it was not at all impossible to argue that awarding parents—overwhelmingly women—only half the amount constituted indirect discrimination on the grounds of sex. Of course, had the argument been successful, the employer would have borne the responsibility to compensate employees for the lack of daycare facilities. The ECJ was evidently not comfortable with reaching this *distributive* conclusion and decided that 'important reasons' are in 'substance and origin different'[64] from reasons of parental responsibility.

Most disturbingly, the contemplation of comparability is carried over to cases involving sexual orientation. Whether or not persons living in a long-term

[60] See Case C-220/02, *Österreichischer Gewerkschaftsbund, Gewerkschaft der Privatangestellten* v. *Wirtschaftskammer Österreich* [2004] ECR I-5907.
[61] See ibid. at paras 60–61.
[62] See ibid. at para. 64.
[63] See Case C-249/97, *Gabriele Gruber* v. *Silhouette International Schmied GmbH & Co. KG* [1999] ECR I-5295 paras 8, 9, 23, 29–30.
[64] Ibid. 33.

homosexual relationship can benefit, for purposes of occupational pension payments, from the protection afforded by Directive 2000/78 depends on whether the national court finds that those couples have been brought by national legislation into a situation that is sufficiently comparable to spouses.[65] This is tantamount to saying that Member States are free to discriminate on the grounds of sexual orientation so long as they do not create the institution of a life partnership.

Nonetheless, in one rare case, the Court even recognized that a finding of incomparability may in effect give rise to indirect discrimination.[66] Consequently, the Court ended up applying reflexively the anti-discrimination principle to its own jurisprudence. The reasoning was thus officially brought back within the purview of anti-discrimination analysis proper with the result, however, that in the extant case the Court was able to perceive various objective factors that may have legitimately been drawn upon by legislation.[67]

7. The Inevitable Deontological Misreading

I am confident that the analysis of the previous sections is sufficient to refute the objection that the difference between direct discrimination and indirect discrimination is manifest in the difference between per se illegality, on the one hand, and the availability of justifications, on the other. Indeed, the last examples may have shown that a strict application of direct discrimination is in some instances even tacitly avoided for redistributive reasons, for example, owing to an uneasiness about letting the distributive agent pay for the lack of public service provision.

I need to recount, at this juncture, how far we have advanced in our analysis. I argued that it is impossible to arrive at an adequate juridical construction of direct discrimination, as a normative category, unless the redistributive dimension of anti-discrimination law is accorded priority. The norm that protects from direct discrimination constitutes normative intent with the aim of perforating the web of systemic discrimination in situations where the distribution of resources and opportunities is crucial for being an equal market participant. The norm of direct discrimination thereby isolates a chain of causation that leads from acts of a distributive agent to disadvantage suffered by a victim.

The meaning of this normative intent ('doing x counts as doing y') can be drawn out in two different ways. According to the extensional reading of causality, the presence of normative intent is to be determined on the basis of a 'but for' test.[68] By

[65] See Case C-267/06, *Tadao Maruko* v. *Versorgungsanstalt deutscher Bühnen* [2008] ECR I-1757, paras 66, 69, 73.

[66] See Case C-322/98, *Bärbel Kachelmann* v. *Bankhaus Hermann Lampe KG* [2000] ECR I-7505, para. 28.

[67] See ibid., paras 33–34.

[68] How it works is beautifully demonstrated in the *Nikoloudi* case, n. 18 at 40. If the two categories are neutrally defined but the causal analysis of the regulatory history shows that one category can only be composed of members of one sex, then discrimination occurs on the grounds of sex.

contrast, the intensional interpretation examines causes inasmuch as they figure as potential reasons for action.

The extensional view of causation is internally linked to an understanding of direct discrimination that conceives of it, explicit derogations notwithstanding, as per se illegal. As soon as the forbidden ground is causally involved in the agent's conduct, the agent engages in direct discrimination. By contrast, the intensional interpretation examines causes as conceivable reasons for action that should have occurred to the agent. The spectre of discrimination disappears as soon as actors can plausibly claim that their conduct was *responsive to good reasons.*

Above I already expressed doubts with regard to the accuracy of the extensional view. As per my analysis below, it will be seen that there is good reason to distrust it. Before arriving, however, at such a negative result, one should take note of why it has great appeal. Protection from direct discrimination is a distributive norm. It can provide guidance in this capacity only if it is sufficiently insulated against sabotage by rationalizations. In other words, normative intent needs to be kept distinct from the netherworld of pre-normative ambivalence. Protection from direct discrimination is only strong if it is in a position to reply to an 'I did not mean to' defence by the agent with 'But you did'. Hence, there is reason to clinch to the extensional view. This reason goes to the heart of the normativity of anti-discrimination law.

Indeed, in the eyes of some authors, European anti-discrimination law may legitimately pride itself, in contradistinction to the American counterpart, in having stayed clear of any inquiry into a matter that is as elusive as intention.[69] What matters is causation. In the words of Ellis':[70]

> '[B]ut for' the sex of the victim, the person would have been treated more favourably, and therefore the discrimination is 'on the grounds of sex': questions of intention and motivation are quite irrelevant to such a test.

The demise of per se illegality, studied above, already indicates that this may not be the full story.

So far, I have presented the extensional and intensional readings as though they were equally plausible alternatives. The analysis has now reached the point at which insight into the indeterminacy of the extensional interpretation opens the gate to exploring more generally the profound normative deficiency of anti-discrimination law. For if the extensional interpretation does not supply protection from direct discrimination with normative force, the equation inherent in normative intent and its distributive mandate needs to be stabilized differently. When distributive patterns are of no avail—and they are not in the case of anti-discrimination law—recourse needs to be had to pre-normative intent. But pre-normative intent is a treacherous ground of normativity. It reintroduces the colouring of action with various motives. What is more, it opens the door for morality to enter the purview of law. Anti-discriminaton law that relies on the analysing of pre-normative intent is normatively deficient. Indeed, if pre-normative intent were sufficient to sustain the equation ('doing x counts as doing y'), specific anti-discrimination norms would not have had to be introduced in the first place.

[69] See Loenen, n. 2 at 201. [70] See Ellis n. 12 at 103.

8. From Extensional Causation to Pre-normative Intent

The major question of any interpretation of direct discrimination is under which circumstances one is doing y by doing x. I would like to argue that the indeterminacy of the extensional view prompts recourse to the pre-normative understanding of intent in the sense of what actors have in mind when they are doing x.

It may help to begin with a slight variation of *Grant*[71] (and *Dekker*).[72] A woman is not promoted because she lives in a same-sex partnership. Her employer dislikes women who openly endorse their lesbian sexual orientation. Another woman is promoted. The lesbian woman, however, would have been promoted had she been a man. Is this a case of direct discrimination on the grounds of sex? She is not promoted, indeed, because she is a woman. Extensionally understood, this is arguably a case of discrimination on the grounds of 'sex'. However, the causation argument is vulnerable to the reasoning applied in *Grant*. The lesbian woman would have been promoted had she had, as a woman, a different sexual orientation. This is the 'true' cause. Hence, the causality argument yields indeterminacy, which reveals why it is implausible to say that this is discrimination on the grounds of 'sex'. What *really* matters, from an intensional point of view, is the person's sexual orientation. The association of the discriminatory act with the difference between men and women ('sex') is merely contingent. Of course, taking a person's sexual orientation into account may be part of the more general prevalence of sexual stereotypes.[73] But this would stretch the concept of 'sex' beyond the elementary biological level.[74]

The example not only reveals the weakness of the extensional understanding. It also shows that owing to the deontological realization of anti-discrimination law doubts about the meaning of normative intention ('doing x is doing y') invite recourse to the pre-normative level of intentionality. Extensional accounts of normative intent yield indeterminacy, at best. From one perspective, no discrimination on the grounds of sex is involved in hiring the handsome man instead of the ugly guy. The latter would not have been hired had he been a woman. From another perspective, sex matters, even extensionally understood, owing to the connotation of sexuality with attractiveness. Had both men been looked upon as asexual human resources, the ugly fellow would have had at least a chance of being successful.

The indeterminacy of causality arguments can only be addressed by seeing causes as reasons for action, which requires moving from the extensional to the intensional interpretation. It needs to be known what agents have been aiming at, for only then can it be determined whether their doings of x count as doings of y. If y means

[71] See Case C-249/96, *Grant* v. *South-West Trains Ltd* [1998] ECR I-621.

[72] See Case C-177/88, *Dekker* v. *Stichting Vormingscentrum voor Junge Volwassen Plus* [1990] ECR I-3941.

[73] For a useful discussion, see Gardner, n. 29 at 183–186. The conclusion that discrimination on the grounds of sexual orientation is part of sex discrimination appears to be supported in the jurisprudence of the ECtHR. See *Salguieri de Silva Mouta* v. *Portugal*, reported in Fredman, n. 4 at 73.

[74] I sense that admirers of Judith Butler's work would despair of this remark.

discrimination between *different sexes*, the employer in the above example did not discriminate on the grounds of sex by hiring a man because of his handsomeness.

The extensional reading, by contrast, contributes nothing to settling questions of interpretation. Whether 'sex' discrimination needs to be narrowly or more broadly construed cannot be read off the relevant anti-discrimination provision. Potential reasons for action need to be taken into account and the question discussed whether these reasons are indeed defensible.[75] For example, even though courts may go to some length inquiring whether Sikhs or Rastafarians are objectively to be considered ethnic groups, what matters truly, from an intensional perspective on direct discrimination, is whether they are perceived by the discriminator as 'alien' elements in the people's body. From a historical point of view, the social standing of groups as 'ethnic' groups is often elusive. From a pragmatic perspective, however, it is paradoxically the very fact that persons are discriminated against that actually accounts for their standing as members of an ethnicity. As a category that denotes a risk of discrimination, the significance of 'ethnicity' arises from adverse acts and attitudes of perpetrators. Pre-normative intent claims its normative relevance. Thus understood, discrimination on the grounds of a certain factor is a self-(ful)filling category. Discrimination indicates the relevance of the ground. Discrimination is what extends the scope of application and not the other way around.

This observation suggests that whoever desires to apply anti-discrimination law *correctly* is bound to take pre-normative intentions into account. What is more, whoever is concerned about the narrowness of an existing list of prohibited grounds and not ready to resort to dubious causality arguments in order to fit new cases into old vessels has to amend the existing list as soon as one encounters bad intentions.

From the deontological perspective, which focuses on actions, limiting the focus on bad intentions only if these are linked to protected grounds appears itself to raise the spectre of discrimination. Whoever is mean to others for whichever reason is a discriminator. Hence, owing to the deontological realization of anti-discrimination law, the list of prohibited grounds becomes constantly amended in practice, and pre-normative intentions become relevant in the course of their application.[76]

Both the interpretation of norms with an eye to pre-normative intent and the extension or tacit amendment of prohibited grounds promise to avoid arbitrariness. The apparent arbitrariness of questionable causality arguments[77] is prevented by asking whether doing x intentionally really does come within the purview of doing y. The arbitrariness inherent in limiting the law's scope of application to prohibited grounds can be prevented by paying attention to *all kinds of bad intentions*.

The *Schnorbus*[78] case epitomizes how pre-normative intentions may trump normative intention, extensionally understood, in the case law of the ECJ. Julia

[75] For perceptive observations that in the construction of the concept of 'intent' a balance can be struck between competing interests, see D. R. Oritz, 'The Myth of Intent in Equal Protection' (1989) 41 *Stanford Law Review* 1105–1151 at 1149.

[76] At the same time, pre-normative intentions are a source also for various good reasons that may counsel in favour of restricting the scope of prohibited grounds.

[77] Fredman, n. 4 at 74, addresses the matter as 'manipulation'.

[78] See *Schnorbus*, n. 35.

Schnorbus wanted to be admitted to practical legal training, but preference was given to applicants who had completed their compulsory military or civilian service. Since only men were subject to the compulsory service obligation, a causal analysis with a broader horizon would have revealed a clear case of direct discrimination on the grounds of sex. The ECJ, however, reasoned that since sex was not used as a classification this was merely a prima facie case of indirect discrimination.[79] It thereby opened the door to taking the pre-normative intention into account of compensating those whose career had been delayed for reasons of public service. From there it was only a small step to conclude that the preferential admission practice would not constitute illicit indirect discrimination on the grounds of sex.[80]

Perhaps even more intriguingly is the interference of pre-normative intent revealed in *Dekker*.[81] A job was given to another woman because her contender was pregnant. There were no male applicants. The causality argument is again inconclusive. Had the pregnant woman been a man she would, arguably, have been appointed to the post. But the same would have been the case had she been, as she was, a woman, but not pregnant. The ECJ had to specify, rather, what it is about the pre-normative intention that makes this case invidious. The pregnant woman is not hired because the employer did not want to have to pay for maternity benefits. This is not right; and it is associated with a state that the woman is in owing to her sexuality. Moreover, only women can be pregnant. Hence, this is discrimination on the grounds of sex.[82] The comparative dimension disappears. Women endure sex discrimination on the grounds of pregnancy[83] even if the unequal treatment affects members of the same sex. The list of forbidden grounds becomes thereby tacitly amended.[84] The scope of application of the prohibited grounds becomes more encompassing simply because an already existing ground can in some way be associated with the manifestation of bad attitudes.

More recently, the ECJ extended the application of discrimination on the grounds of disability in favour of a person who, without being disabled herself, may have suffered discrimination owing to the disability of her child.[85] The protection from discrimination was thereby extended beyond the scope of disabled persons proper.[86] Again, the presence of a wrong attitude must have been the

[79] Ibid. at paras 38–39. [80] Ibid. at paras 34, 44. [81] See above n. 72.

[82] See *Dekker*, n. 72 para. 17. Remarkably, the Court did not continue with this questionable mode of reasoning in a case affecting an illness to which only one sex is susceptible. See Case C-179/88, *Handels- og Kontorfuntionaerernes Forbund i Danmark* v. *Dansk Arbejdsverforening* [1990] ECR I-3979, para. 14.

[83] See ibid., para. 12: '[. . .] [O]nly women can be refused employment on grounds of pregnancy and such a refusal therefore constitutes discrimination on the grounds of sex.'

[84] This amendment is reflected in Article 2(2)(c) of the Consolidated Sex Discrimination Directive. Beyond that, it is now taken for granted that refusal of employment (even non-renewal of a fixed-term contract) for the reason of pregnancy is sex discrimination. See Case C-438/99, *Maria Luisa Jiménez Melgar* v. *Ayuntamiento de Los Barrios* [2001] ECR I-6915, paras 46–47.

[85] See Case C-303/06, *S. Coleman* v. *Attridge Law and Steve Law*, Judgment of 17 July 2008, paras 33, 38.

[86] For a restrictive understanding of disability as 'a limitation which results in particular from physical, mental or psychological impairments and which hinders the participation of the person concerned in professional life', an understanding which excludes sickness, see Case C-13/05, *Sonia Chacón Navas* v. *Eurest Colectividades SA* [2006] ECR I-6467, paras 43, 54–55.

motivating factor. According to the ECJ, the reason for the extension was reliance on the disability in the context of employment.[87] But this begs the question. Not only pre-normative intent,[88] but the evilness inherent in it, must have made the extension appear plausible, for the facts of the case indicated clearly that there was reason to believe that certain benefits available to other employers had been denied to that women out of fear that the disability of her child might give rise to frequent absences and everlasting 'accommodation' requests.[89] Paradoxically, the ECJ immediately took away what it had first conceded, namely, accommodations that the woman would have actually required to be employed while also looking after her disabled child. The Court stated, without adducing any further reasons, that accommodation requirements in favour of disabled persons are the preserve of those persons alone and cannot be claimed by those who, for example, are burdened with special caregiving obligations. Hence, this seemingly generous extension of protection from discrimination was bound to remain without any real consequence in that case.

The desire to prevent arbitrariness in targeting evil acts explains why discriminatory intent, pre-normatively understood, necessarily is an essential concept of anti-discrimination law. In fact, it epitomizes how this field of law involves the forgetting of its constitution in the course of its own realization. As a normative principle, indirect discrimination is more *fundamental* than direct discrimination. Direct discrimination, however, plays a much more *important* role, for it helps to fill a normative void that is left in the process of the constitution of anti-discrimination law.

9. The Seat of the Normative Deficiency

This inversion[90] in the relation of indirect and direct discrimination reveals in which respect anti-discrimination law is inexorably twisted. The pursuit of distributive objectives[91] is relegated to the application of the deontological idiom of the law.[92] Redistribution is supposed to follow from eliminating discriminatory acts or

[87] Ibid., para. 38: 'The principle of equal treatment enshrined in the directive in that area applies not to a particular category of persons but by reference to the grounds mentioned in Article 1 [of Directive 2000/78].'

[88] See para. 50: 'Although [. . .] the person who is subject to direct discrimination on grounds of disability is not herself disabled, the fact remains that it is the disability which, according to Ms Coleman, is the ground for the less favourable treatment which she claims to have suffered.'

[89] See ibid., para. 26.

[90] On the alleged primacy of direct discrimination, see Gardner, n. 29 at 182.

[91] Bagenstos, n. 9 at 841, would object that anti-discrimination law is a very blunt tool of redistribution for it does not accomplish much. This objection goes wrong because Bagenstos relies on a very narrow understanding of redistribution which sees it limited to monetary transfers. Jobs, however, are important assets, primary goods, indeed, that people want whatever else it is that they happen to want. See J. Rawls, *A Theory of Justice* (Cambridge, MA: Harvard University Press, 1971), at 92.

[92] It is understood, that the law, for the most part, thinks deontologically in that consequences only appear on the screen of the legal system if causation can be attributed to an agent whose action was in

practices. Not surprisingly, the redistributive aim pursued by anti-discrimination law is *not patterned*.[93] It merely says that inequalities, where they exist, must not be discriminatory. This is not enough to create a pattern.

Rather, the functional equivalent of plotting a pattern is delegated to protection against conduct. With the weakness inherent in the extensional reading of causality there is nothing to seal normative intent against the influx of pre-normative ambivalence. No distributive pattern stops the rampage of the deontological idiom of law. *Schnorbus* is a good example. Had there been a distributive norm mandating that either sex of applicants had to be taken into account in proportion to their numbers in the pool, the ECJ would not have had easy recourse to pre-normative intent for the purpose of determining the scope of the principle of sex discrimination. The meaning of the principle would have been informed by a distributive norm. Such a norm would not have had to be translated into a deontological idiom.

My favourite hypothetical example for what working with patterns might come to is unfortunately next to absurd. If an orchestra, after holding screened auditions, were still only to hire men rather than women for the position of violinists, the deontological perspective would be inclined to release the orchestra of all redistributive responsibilities. There would be a good reason. Men appear to play better. However, if the proportional representation of women were the norm, it would have been established, *normatively*, that the orchestra's hiring committee is captive of a sexist bias of appreciating musical performances. Remarkably, the extensional 'but for' test would indirectly warrant the same conclusion.

10. Without Patterns: Reasons and Derogations

I mentioned above (see p. 119) that an extensional reading of causality would have insulated normative intent against the influx of pre-normative ambivalence. With the unavailability of distributive patterns, which would attain a similar effect, anti-discrimination is most plausibly applied from within the mindset of the intensional understanding of causality (and, a fortiori, of normativity). Consequently,

some way 'aimed at' or at least condoning these consequences. Accordingly, from a deontological point of view, what is morally or legally wrong is defined, first, by what, according to some objective measure, is bad for persons and, second, by acts, mostly commissions, that are in some way considered to be under the control of the agent. Accordingly, systemic collective consequences of conduct the avoidance of which is deemed to lie outside the purview of individual control are usually irrelevant from a legal point of view. For a fuller and more sophisticated exploration of this issue, see L. Katz, *Ill-gotten Gains: Evasion, Blackmail, Fraud, and Kindred Puzzles of the Law* (Chicago, IL: University of Chicago Press, 1996); T. Nagel, *The View from Nowhere* (New York: Oxford University Press, 1986), 182. For a similar observation where anti-discrimination law is concerned, see already A. Freeman, 'Anti-discrimination Law: A Critical Review', in D. Kairys (ed.), *The Politics of Law: A Progressive Critique* (New York: Pantheon Books, 1982), 96–116, at 98–99; A. Freeman, 'Racism, Rights and the Quest for Equality of Opportunity: A Critical Legal Essay' (1988) 23 *Harvard Civil Rights and Civil Liberties Review* 295–392; A. Freeman, 'Anti-discrimination Law: The View from 1989' (1990) 64 *Tulane Law Review* 1407–1441.

[93] See R. Nozick, *Anarchy, State, and Utopia* (New York: Basic Books, 1974), at 156.

protection from discrimination needs to inquire into the reasons of conduct and ask whether there are good reasons in order to dispel the impression that an act or a distribution is actually a case of discrimination.

This is congruent with equality's way of addressing distributive questions. Distributive agents may rescind themselves from fulfilling equal treatment obligations when legitimate factors would make this for them too onerous or in any other way appear unreasonable. Anti-discrimination law accommodates this approach to distributive questions by recognizing factors that may legitimately influence legislative or entrepreneurial choice.

As is well known, officially at any rate (see above p. 188), instances of permissible direct discrimination need to be based on legislative derogations, the observance of which is principally subject to proportionality scrutiny.[94] The Framework Directive contains a mop-up clause in Article 2(5), specifying public health, public security, and public order derogations.[95] Age discrimination is considered to be a special case[96] simply because people who were once young have already had a number of opportunities earlier in life. It may make sense, therefore, to restrict their access to resources. The broadly phrased derogations contained in Article 6 of Directive 2000/78EC reflect the accommodation of intuitive concerns regarding distributive justice.[97] Similarly, Article 7 of Directive 79/7[98] contains broad grounds of exception regarding differential retirement arrangements for men and women.[99] Article 14(2) of the Consolidated Directive 2006/54[100] permits the use of a sex-based characteristic if 'such a characteristic constitutes a genuine and determining occupational requirement, provided that its objective is legitimate and the requirement is proportionate'. It has been doubted that the ECJ is determined to uncover sex stereotyping in cases affecting situations of military service[101] or the use of firearms[102] and is rather predisposed to yield to, and thereby to condone, entrenched attitudes.[103] The requirement that

[94] See, for example, Article 4(1) Directive 2000/78, saying that a prohibited ground may be used where the relevant characteristic 'constitutes a genuine and determining occupational requirement'.

[95] According to Barnard, n. 6 at 414, the provision was included in order to prevent members of harmful cults, paedophiles, and people with dangerous diseases from gaining protection under the Directive.

[96] See Barnard, n. 6 at 391.

[97] The derogations may be based on 'legitimate employment policy, labour market and vocational training objectives' (Article 6 leg. cit.). It is all the more remarkable, in this context, that the ECJ ascribed to protection from age discrimination the rank of a general principle of Union law in the curious *Mangold* case. See Case C-144/04, *Werner Mangold* v. *Rüdiger Helm* [2005] ECR I-9981, para. 75. For a reconfirmation, see Case C-555/07, *Seda Kücükdeveci v. Swedex GmbH & C. KG*, Judgment of January 19, 2010, paras. 21–22.

[98] Council Directive 79/7/EEC of 19 December 1978 on the progressive implementation of the principle of equal treatment for men and women in matters of social security, OJ L 6, 24–25.

[99] See, for an introduction, Craig and de Búrca, n. 15 at 939–944.

[100] Directive 2006/54/EC of the European Parliament and the Council of 5 July 2006 on the implementation of the principle of equal opportunities and equal treatment of men and women in matters of employment and occupation, OJ L 204, 23–36 [2006].

[101] See Case C-273/97, *Sidar* v. *Secretary of State for Defence* [1999] ECR I-7403.

[102] See Case C-222/84, *Marguerite Johnston* v. *Chief Constable of the Royal Ulster Constabulary* [1986] ECR 1651.

[103] For a critical commentary, see Barnard, n. 6 at 410.

derogations stay within the limits of what is appropriate and necessary in order to achieve a legitimate aim was more strictly applied in the *Kreil* case where it was found that women cannot be barred from all military service positions involving the use of firearms.[104]

The justifications available for indirect discrimination are manifold. Reliance on them does not require an explicit legislative base. Their scope is not unlimited, however, since the ECJ persistently held that mere budgetary considerations are not strong enough to override sex equality.[105] In cases of age discrimination, the range of justifications available for employers is, again, broader than for the legislature and may include matters such as cost reduction and improving competitiveness.[106] With regard to employers, the ECJ recognized already in *Bilka* that employers may take, inasmuch as is appropriate and necessary, 'real needs on the part of the undertaking' into account.[107] In the case of unequal pay, a number of personal factors may be considered. For example, seniority may be used as a rough proxy for knowledge and experience.[108] Rewarding flexibility and adaptability with regard to variable working hours, by contrast, is only permissible when these qualities are indeed important to the task entrusted to the employee. Any wholesale reward of the disregard for one's private life would likely impact adversely on women.[109] Objective justifications may indeed be heeded of the market situation. In fact, the ECJ regarded paying full-time workers proportionately higher wages than part-time workers as justified so long as this creates an incentive to choose full-time work.[110] Market supply may justify paying unequal wages.[111] Generally, the Court is less reluctant to accept unequal pay claims by employers than by the state.[112]

11. Proportionality

The case law gives rise to casuistry. It does so for a reason. Distributive agents are market participants. It would be unfair to cut off their recourse to all market based justifications. This creates a predicament. As we have seen, breaking the circle of systemic discrimination presupposes drawing a line vis-à-vis market rationality. But anti-discrimination law does not set out distributive patterns. It remains undecided,

[104] See Case C-285/98, *Tanja Kreil* v. *Bundesrepublik Deutschland*, 11 January 2000, para. 31.

[105] See the cases mentioned in n. 18 above.

[106] See *Council on Aging*, n. 12 at para. 46.

[107] See *Bilka*, n. 1 at para. 36

[108] See Case C-109/88, *Danfoss* [1989] ECR 3199. In Case C-17/05, *B.F. Cadman* v. *Health & Safety Executive* [2006] ECR I-9583, paras 36–38, the Court stated that the employer is free to reward length of service without establishing the importance of specific tasks entrusted to the employee, in particular not where a job evaluation system was used. The length of service may then serve as a useful proxy for the experience and knowledge of the individual employee. For a more stringent view, see the earlier Case C-184/89, *Nimz* v. *Freie und Hansestadt Hamburg* [1991] ECR I-297, para. 14.

[109] See Case C-309/97, *Angestelltenbetriebsrat der Wiener Gebietskrankenkasse* v. *Wiener Gebietskrankenkasse* [1999] ECR I-2865, para. 19.

[110] See *Bilka*, n. 1; *Jenkins*, n. 13 at para. 12.

[111] See *Enderby*, n. 49.

[112] See Barnard, n. 6 at 366.

hence, where the line needs to be drawn with regard to the pursuit of economic objectives. The real critical work is often done, if at all, by the proportionality principle.[113] Where the legislature is concerned, for example, the Court, while heeded of the margin of discretion left to the Member States,[114] is often disinclined to accept 'mere generalisations' regarding the impact of certain measures on the pursuit of social objectives.[115] The Court examines the alleged means–ends relationships closely and may find that the legislature has not chosen an 'apt or suitable' means.[116]

Contrary to its appearance, the fact that the central critical role is played by the strict rationality requirement is not good news for anti-discrimination law. The normative force of protection from discrimination only comes to the fore in its capacity to exercise a stronger constraint than the maxim to use least onerous means in the pursuit of valid objectives. Anti-discrimination law's normative thrust would evaporate if it turned out that the same results can be achieved by the proportionality principle in juxtaposition with a general mandate to optimize human well-being. All that protection from indirect discrimination would require, then, were to attain objectives on the basis of narrowly tailored, least intrusive means. Returning to my favourite, alas absurd, example of the orchestra with a sexist sonoric bias, it might be argued that the orchestral sound is part of a competitive advantage. Changing the sound would adversely affect its market performance. Anti-discrimination law is bound to be silent at this point. It is indeterminate. It could either be argued that this situation marks the point at which the pursuit of market rationality has to come to an end, or it might be conceded that consumer preferences have revealed that men are better musicians than women. Neither conclusion can be based upon a principle of anti-discrimination law, but involves, rather, a choice for or against equality.

I can merely sketch here why, in my opinion, this normative deficiency, whose conditions of possibility I tried to reconstruct conceptually, is not by accident encountered in the context of the anti-discrimination principle. I take it that the most appealing interpretation of this principle perceives it as a shield against

[113] See, for example, *Schönheit*, n. 7 at para. 93. A remarkable case in which the proportionality principle does the work is *Kücükdeveci*. The ECJ recognized a lack of fit in the relation of the policy objective and an unequal treatment by attributing to the legislature an objective that it did not pursue. See Case C-555/07, *Seda Kücükdeveci v. Swedex GmbH & Co. KG*, 19 January 2010, at paras. 34, 41. The Court did so after stating explicitly that in Member States have wide discretion as regards the choice of means and ends of social policy (para. 38).

[114] The broad margin of discretion is recognized, in particular, for matters of social policy. See *Seymour-Smith*, n. 7 at para. 74; Case C-187/00, *Helga Kutz-Bauer* v. *Freie und Hansestadt Hamburg* [2003] ECR I-2741, para. 57.

[115] See, for example, with regard to the encouragement of recruitment and limiting compensation for the violation of the right against unfair dismissal employment relationships of a certain period of time, *Regina*, n. 7 at 76. See also Case C-167/97, *Seymour-Smith and Perez* [1999] ECR I-623, paras 75–76; *Council on Aging*, n. 12, para. 51; *Kutz-Bauer*, n. 114 at 58.

[116] See *Steinicke*, n. 18 at para. 65. How this works is quite impressively demonstrated in a case affecting a disadvantage involved in converting from 'job-sharing' to full-time employment. See *Hill and Stapleton*, n. 19 at 38.

self-denial.[117] More precisely, it promises protection against the loss of dignity involved in having to deny who one is in order to avoid social disadvantage. Blacks become socially white, women behave like tough guys in order to escape unequal treatment. Transsexuals conceal their identity. Communists do not dare to express their political views. Most drastically, some no longer compete for jobs because they sense that given who they are they are likely not to be given a chance. They decide to deny their self an opportunity to be present in this world.

The core perplexity of protection from discrimination is the question of which instances of self-denial are relevant to protection from discrimination. The answer is not written on the face of the equality principle. Indeed, avoiding self-denial is itself an act of self-assertion. Making certain practices socially visible as discrimination presupposes activity on the part of those whom this principle protects against disempowerment.

I speculate, but cannot prove here, that this perplexity is the ultimate source of the normative deficiency. The disempowered need to present powerfully their case of disempowerment in order to be recognized as victims of discrimination. Not by accident, law has a history. It is part of this history that women, hopefully, would regard my orchestra example, if it were not for its absurdity, as a clear instance of discrimination.

The absence of collective empowerment against market rationality is the predicament of anti-discrimination law. In fact, the law partakes of this powerlessness.

12. Decommodification

But I should not conclude on such a negative note. Before returning to the normative deficieny in the next chapter, I should like to point out, briefly, that in its actual operation anti-discrimination law is not restricted to the redistribution of resources or opportunities once people have become victims of circumstances beyond their control. In its application it *spills over* into the pursuit of decommodification.[118] In it resides, therefore, a moment of market negation.

On its surface, decommodification is based on the realization that the liberty guaranteed by market equality amounts, for most people, to 'freedom behind prison walls'.[119] Persons, that is, experience themselves as 'captive to powers beyond their control'.[120] The distinction between choice and circumstance, which animates much neoliberal social philosophy, cannot be applied *within* markets.[121] Market

[117] See my *Rationalität und Diskriminierung: Zur Bindung der Gesetzgebung an das Gleichheitsrecht* (Vienna/New York: Springer, 2001).

[118] For a first instalment, see A. Somek, 'Anti-discrimination and Decommodification', in D. Cinar (ed.), *Doing Justice to Diversity: Challenges and Visions* (Aldershot: Ashgate, 2011) (forthcoming; see http://www.euro.centre.org/data/1122641524_50805.pdf).

[119] G. Esping-Andersen, *The Three Worlds of Welfare Capitalism* (Princeton, NJ: Princeton University Press, 1990), at p. 37.

[120] Ibid.

[121] See R. Dworkin, *Sovereign Virtue: The Theory and Practice of Equality* (Cambridge, MA: Harvard University Press, 2000), at 322–324.

mechanisms *as such* are circumstances beyond human control. People would be able to endorse attributions of personal responsibility only if these were mediated by their own political choices.[122]

From the perspective of decommodification, market equality is a threat to freedom. When push comes to shove—which is still *far* from the worst case—one needs to accept *any* employment, no matter how degrading, in order to get by. In response to such a loss of control over one's own life, which is arguably a loss of freedom,[123] 'decommodification' stands for the degree to which someone is able to uphold a decent standard of living independent of the unconstrained operation of the market. Admittedly, the high degree of decommodification that goes along with leading the life of a gentleman is generally out of reach.[124]

Anti-discrimination law, to be sure, is not primarily *directed* at decommodification. In other words, it is different from a type of social legislation that aims at backing up the provision of goods with some market-defying or market-bypassing distributive mechanism. Indeed, the very point of anti-discrimination law is to facilitate market access[125] and not to exempt a certain sphere from the operation of the market. But anti-discrimination law interferes indirectly with the persona of persons by mitigating the impact of consumer sovereignty. The costs of prejudice are shifted from the victim to whomever anti-discrimination law designates to be the distributive agent (for the most part, the employer). The resulting redistribution of resources has a 'de-alienating' effect. For example, consumers are no longer in the position to avoid having to deal with persons whom they would have shunned otherwise. When they need plumbing services, Turks or Arabs will unplug their sewers. The relevant encounters politicize consumption no less than they politicize the workplace. Consumers are taught a lesson about the social world they inhabit and thereby reconciled with the sphere of production. Put differently, they are forced to confront the *Entzweiung* or schizophrenia of market society which splits people into two different halves, that is, the non-competing beneficiary of competition, on the one hand, and the economically vulnerable contender, on the other. The politicization of consumption[126] has the potential to reconcile the

[122] See K. Günther, 'Zwischen Ermächtigung und Disziplinierung: Verantwortung im gegenwärtigen Kapitalismus', in A. Honneth (ed.), *Befreiung aus der Mündigkeit: Paradoxien des gegenwärtigen Kapitalismus* (Frankfurt: Campus Verlag, 2002), at 117–139.

[123] This is a point on which, for example, both G. A. Cohen and Harry Frankfurt would agree, albeit for different reasons. According to Cohen, the amount of resources, in particular, the amount of money that we command determines our level of autonomy, whereas for Frankfurt the need to compromise what we really care about in situations of need detracts from our freedom. See G. A. Cohen, *Self-Ownership, Freedom, and Equality* (Cambridge: Cambridge University Press, 1995), 58–59; H. G. Frankfurt, *The Importance of What we Care About: Philosophical Essays* (Cambridge: Cambridge University Press, 1988), 109–110. See also J. Raz, *The Morality of Freedom* (Oxford: Clarendon Press, 1985), 372–373.

[124] See, for example, G. S. Wood, *The Radicalism of the American Revolution* (New York: Vintage Books, 1991), 36–38.

[125] See M. Bell, *Anti-discrimination Law and the European Union* (Oxford: Oxford University Press, 2002), at 136–143, 197–199.

[126] The politicization of consumption has its limits, to be sure, for it usually stops short of affecting gendered appearance norms affecting dress codes or grooming. They are accepted by American Courts as long as they conform to prevailing social norms. For an overview, see R. Post, 'Prejudicial

two spheres, for it makes people realize that everyone has to make himself or herself vulnerable in one sphere in order to enjoy freedom of choice in the other. More importantly, the degree of vulnerability depends vitally on the whimsicality of wants. The more entitled consumers are to their expectations, the less free are employees to have it their way, for example, when a court finds that employers do not unduly discriminate on the grounds of sex when they cater to gender stereotypes harboured by consumers regarding a gendered demeanour.[127] Where it is understood that limiting the scope of one's wants is essential to sustaining fair job competition for others, it becomes possible to single out wants that are inappropriate because their satisfaction would threaten to force certain groups of employees into self-denial. This decommodifying momentum is all the more remarkable for it elevates the exploration of wants over the blind operation of the price mechanism. By filtering out certain wants, it compensates for a lack of deliberation in the relation between entrepreneurs and consumers.

Anti-discrimination law also compensates for a lack of solidarity among members of the workforce. If employees were to cooperate across groups in order to bring about an equitable distribution of jobs, salaries or job-related benefits then the need for anti-discrimination law would not arise. The situations targeted by anti-discrimination law are just as much brought about by an unsolidaristic (sexist, racist, xenophobic, religiously intolerant) workforce as they are by employers. Anti-discrimination law can be understood as an attempt to eliminate certain effects of competition among segments of the workforce.

I believe it emerges clearly that, owing to its distributive effects, the particularity neutralizing thrust of anti-discrimination law becomes, at any rate rudimentarily, relevant to decommodification. Redistribution is the angle linking one to the other. Market equality reaches out beyond itself.

13. Conclusion

Since the next chapter commences with a summary statement of the normative deficiency, I would like to conclude here with a brief reconsideration of the argument's conceptual structure. Protection from direct discrimination is a distributive norm that focuses on the causal relation between acts of agents and their impact on victims. Its normative force depends on the stability of normative intent, which determines under which circumstances—remonstrations about actual intent by the agent notwithstanding—the doing of x counts as y (i.e., an act of discrimination).

Normative intent can be given an extensional interpretation. Then, it is deemed to be manifest whenever the presence of the prohibited factor makes a difference. The extensional interpretation explains which x counts as y. The extensional

Appearances: The Logic of American Anti-discrimination Law' (2000) 88 *California Law Review* 1–40 at 29–34.

[127] See Post, n. 126 at 25–27.

interpretation renders direct discrimination categorically prohibited. No justification is available. In this manner, it promises to insulate normative intent against incursions by pre-normative intentionality. The latter opens the gate for justifications and, hence, also for rationalizations. The extensional interpretation is unsustainable. This has an adverse effect on the redistributive task of anti-discrimination law. According to the intensional interpretation, the determination of normative intent submits reasons for action to scrutiny in order to determine whether a prima facie case of discrimination can be refuted owing to the prevalence of good reasons in the context of action.

The distributive aim of anti-discrimination law needs to be pursued by examining whether the reasons for unequal treatment are strong enough to allow distributive agents to extricate themselves from the burdens of their responsibility. Apparently, the major critical work is done by the proportionality principle. The intensional interpretation, in order to avoid arbitrariness, needs to be receptive to considerations of pre-normative intent. This explains why grounds of discrimination become reinterpreted with reference to encounters with bad attitudes and also gradually amended in the course of their application. With pre-normative intent occupying the field, anti-discrimination law falls prey to morality.

6

Consequences of Normative Deficiency

1. The Normative Deficiency Stated

The analysis has reached a stage at which the normative deficiency can be presented in a seemingly deductive manner. This mode of demonstration reverses the path that we have travelled so far.

The redistributive perspective is intrinsic to anti-discrimination law. It accounts for the meaning of its most fundamental norms, namely, the prohibitions of direct and indirect discrimination.

Indirect discrimination is the fundamental category. Protection from indirect discrimination, however, is not patterned. Anti-discrimination norms do not, for example, require the proportional representation of social groups. Therein manifests itself the normative deficiency. Rather than stating what it takes to realize equality, anti-discrimination norms merely exclude single acts or cumulative practices that impact unequally on members of different groups.

Owing to this core normative deficiency, neither indirect nor direct discrimination avail of clear normative guidance. Indirect discrimination is susceptible to justification on the ground of the proportionate pursuit of legitimate objectives. Determining the scope of legitimate objectives is not constrained by any distributive norm. Likewise, a case of direct discrimination cannot be established where the anti-discrimination norm does not declare a certain act to be an act of discrimination. The absence of a distributive norm comes to the fore, in this context, as a problem of identification. Ideally, a norm prohibiting direct discrimination would have to clarify authoritatively under which circumstances doing x means discriminating on the grounds of y.

The indeterminacy of this norm is concealed through the extensional understanding of causation. It is epitomized by the application of the 'but for' analysis. But this type of analysis gives rise to results that are either indeterminate or counterintuitive. The need arises, therefore, to calibrate and to amend anti-discrimination norms on the basis of an intensional reading of causation.

The indeterminacy of the direct discrimination norms is the equivalent of the indeterminacy to be encountered in the context of the indirect discrimination norm, which does not clarify when the proportionate pursuit of economic objective needs to yield to equality.

The indeterminacy of the direct discrimination norm can be addressed only with recourse to pre-normative interpretations of intent. The normative deficiency is thereby not eliminated. It persists.

Anti-discrimination law's twisted appearance—the alleged priority of direct over indirect discrimination—lends expression to a latent normative antinomy. Not only is indirect discrimination the more fundamental category vis-à-vis direct discrimination, the distributive dimension associated with the former is more important than the identification of discriminatory intent. Nonetheless, intent comes to play a central role, for it is needed, in its pre-normative form, to compensate for the normative deficiency that arises at the fundamental level. The moral evaluation of human conduct is supposed to do all the normative work that originally would have had to be done by a distributive principle.

This is the antinomy of anti-discrimination law. It remains latent—and is therefore sustainable—because of the absence of a distributive pattern. It is not possible, in other words, to confront findings of intent with pre-established distributive results.

The reference to bad intent and evil attitudes is expected to provide normative guidance. Unfortunately, as I will try to explain below, this cannot be done. Rather, the moral view of the world that is reflected in anti-discrimination law is part of the powerlessness that this field of law is supposed to overcome.

The central importance attributed to intent reveals this moralism. It is most openly manifest in American anti-discrimination law, to which our discussion will therefore briefly turn.

Moralism, in turn, explains why pre-normative intent is—or, indeed, *ought* to be—inscrutable. From the inscrutability of intent it is only a small step to the indeterminacy of obligation. Under the reversed conditions of the deontological realization of anti-discrimination law, the substantive obligation is expected to follow from intent. Put bluntly, whoever is mean to someone is a potential discriminator.

2. Moralism

I am not the first to observe that anti-discrimination law, in particular in the United States, is a manifestation of the moral view of the world[1] or, in other words, 'moralistic'.[2] But it is not easy to pin down what such a finding actually means.

Bagenstos, for one, uses this attribute very broadly. He argues that 'anti-discrimination law is plainly moralistic' and goes on to explain that 'its moralism inheres not in an effort to punish individuals who act on bad thoughts, but in the large-scale project of eliminating subordination and segregation and of enforcing a principle of equal membership in society'.[3] I suspect that such a use of the term 'moralistic' is neither accurate nor illuminating. It merely states that the point of anti-discrimination law is to give effect to an important moral principle. Taking a principle of that kind seriously is not in and of itself 'moralistic'. The moralism of a

[1] See T. Pinkard, *Hegel's Phenomenology: The Sociality of Reason* (Cambridge: Cambridge University Press, 1994), 202–207. The scope of the 'moral worldview' is broader than the two senses of moralism distinguished below. It also involves a commitment to moral self-legislation and ascribing a prominent role to individual conscience.

[2] See S. R. Bagenstos, '"Rational Discrimination," Accommodation, and the Politics of (Disability) Civil Rights' (2003) 89 *Virginia Law Review* 825–923 at 839, 857.

[3] Bagenstos, n. 2 at 839.

commitment is revealed, by contrast, in the *manner* in which it is taken seriously. Intuitively, two modalities come to mind. Both are, I add in passing, within the scope of what Hegel calls the moral view of the world.[4]

Moralism can be manifest in the belief that the amelioration of society depends vitally on the formation of *better people*. Whether a society is good or not is to be ascertained on the basis of individual acts, motives, and attitudes. Since exploring other minds is perplexing, moralists resort to simplifications. They are typically inclined to regard people as morally bad, whose acts are part of a causal chain that leads up to bad effects. In a moralistic society, one should not be surprised to encounter talk about 'vile industries' (alcohol, gambling, tobacco, firearms, and junk food). Wherever there is some*thing* bad, some*one* bad must have brought it about. Moralists believe remote consequences to be within the scope of an individual's responsibility.[5] When confronted with collapsing bridges, declining health, or increasing crime rates, they take comfort from talking about big government, the tobacco industry, and the indolent poor. In their world, a structural bad that is independent of individual action does not exist.[6] From the perspective of a moralist, thus understood, the major avenues leading to the amelioration of society are, besides rebuke, techniques of observation, training, re-education, self-improvement along with charity, consumer protest, punishment, and, should none of these work, prayer.

Alternatively, moralism is also manifest in the propagation of *overbearing postulates*. A typical moralist condemns a society as entirely evil and dreams up a better future without taking into account why ordinary people are disinclined to act on this dream and prefer to remain locked into a seemingly wicked world.

Evidently, these different understandings of moralism do not overlap. Implementing a sweeping utilitarian redistributive policy which resolutely took from the rich and gave to the poor would not have to be moralistic in the first sense of the term, for it could be brought about by a well-meaning enlightened elite.[7] But as long as good postulates do not engage existing desires and motives, utilitarianism may well remain to be moralistic in the second sense of the term.

I conjectured above about reasons why anti-discrimination law is usually cast in a reverse order and thereby subject to deontological self-obfuscation (see p. 126). First, norms are addressed to distributive agents for whom certain acts are made to count as acts of discrimination. Second, their doings appear to be in close proximity

[4] See G. W. F. Hegel, *Elements of the Philosophy of Right*, trans. by H. B. Nisbeth (Cambridge: Cambridge University Press, 1991), at 146, 170–171, paras 119, 140.

[5] For example, Thomas Pogge believes that the existing world order with its soaring inequalities is indeed upheld by each individual agent. See T. Pogge, *World Poverty and Human Rights: Cosmopolitan Responsibilities and Reforms* (Cambridge: Polity Press, 2002), at 197, according to whom each and every one of us fails to fulfil our negative duty not to uphold a world order that permits extreme deprivation for a large number of people.

[6] See A. Honneth, *Leiden an Unbestimmtheit. Eine Reaktualisierung der Hegelschen Rechtsphilosophie* (Stuttgart: Reklam, 2001), 81.

[7] See, for example, P. Singer, *Practical Ethics*, 2nd edn (Cambridge: Cambridge University Press, 1993), 218–246; R. Goodin, *Utilitarianism as a Public Philosophy* (Cambridge: Cambridge University Press, 1995), 219.

to the combated evil. The closer someone is seen to be to the actual use of an impugned category, the more it makes sense to regard that someone as also *responsible* to abstain from its use.

It is consistent with these two reasons to classify American anti-discrimination law,[8] at any rate, as moralistic in the first sense of the term identified above, according to which better people would make for a better social world.[9] This is noticeable in the imprint left on doctrine by the paradigm of a guilty mind denying others proper respect. In fact, the development of the so-called Title VII jurisprudence,[10] in marked contrast to age discrimination law,[11] confirms this point.[12] According to Krieger, Title VII jurisprudence builds on the standard assumption that discrimination, firstly, is an individual act that, secondly, results from a discriminatory motive or intent.[13] If her analysis is correct, then most of American jurisprudence rests on the reduction of causality to pre-normative intent.[14] The former becomes dissolved, indeed, in light of the latter. Disparate treatment plaintiffs do not merely have to prove causation, that is, that their status 'made a difference' with regard to hiring decisions but that '[. . .] such treatment was caused by purposeful or intentional discrimination'.[15] In most cases, 'the concepts of

[8] The matter is not so clear for European anti-discrimination law.

[9] It is usually claimed that European anti-discrimination law prohibits direct discrimination regardless of intent. See E. Ellis, *EU Anti-discrimination Law* (Oxford: Oxford University Press, 2005) at 103. However, it is clear from the case law that direct discrimination is the case where it is noticeable that it is men and women who are treated differently. See Case C-69/80, *Worringham* v. *Lloyds Bank Ltd* [1981] ECR 787 at 792.

[10] Section 703(a) of Title VII of the Civil Rights Act provides that it shall be unlawful for an employer to fail or refuse to hire or to discharge any individual, or otherwise to discriminate against any individual with respect to his compensation, terms, conditions, or privileges of employment, because of such individual's race, colour, religion, sex, or national origin.

[11] See R. A. Sedler, 'The Role of "Intent" in Discrimination Analysis', in T. Loenen and P. R. Rodrigues (eds), *Non-Discrimination Law: Comparative Perspectives* (Amsterdam: Kluwer, 1999), 91–103 at 96.

[12] See L. Hamilton Krieger, 'The Content of our Categories: A Cognitive Bias Approach to Discrimination and Equal Employment Opportunity' (1995) 47 *Stanford Law Review* 1161–1248 at 1169. For an overview of the meaning of the 'intent' requirement in American disparate treatment law, see Sedler, n. 11.

[13] See Krieger, n. 12 at 1166–1167, 1183.

[14] It should be noted that there is more than one conception of causation in play in American anti-discrimination law: minimal causation (gender or race must have been one motivating factor among others) and necessity (the same decision would not have been reached had the factor been absent). For a very useful reconstruction of the concepts used in the Court's jurisprudence, see M. J. Katz, 'The Fundamental Incoherence of Title VII: Making Sense of Causation in Disparate Treatment Law' (2006) 94 *Georgetown Law Journal* 489–550 at 510–511. According to Katz (ibid. at 537) both standards are flawed: while the minimal causation (motivation) standard provides a windfall for plaintiffs in cases of overdetermination, the necessity standard is difficult to prove.

[15] Krieger, n. 12 at 1168. If the plaintiff would have been hired but for the fact that she is a woman many conceivable considerations on the part of the employer may have been relevant for the employer, for example, fear of impending maternity leaves, an allegedly greater propensity to socialize at the workplace, etc. The prohibited ground plays the role of a proxy and as a proxy the role of the cause. Alternatively, purposeful or intentional discrimination could also be seen as targeted at members of a certain sex regardless of whether the sex is a proxy for another trait. The defendant would then maliciously intend to inflict harm. It is conceivable, however, for discrimination to be 'a cause' in the pre-normative sense without being the 'but for' cause, that is, in cases of overdetermination in which a potential employer is relieved that she does not have to hire a person of colour simply because the

motive, intent and causation are confounded and liability is premised in the presence of unconscious discriminatory animus'.[16] In particular, protection from discrimination will succeed only if it can be shown that the defendant is liable of having perceived the plaintiff through the filter of some blurred, over-generalized, biased or stereotypical scheme *and* to have actually relied on that scheme to the detriment of the plaintiff.[17] In a similar vein, 'pretext' analysis[18] is geared towards uncovering the 'true reason' motivating the employer's decision, thereby drawing on certain standard assumptions to infer intent from evidence.[19]

The moralization of anti-discrimination law in the US is, in a sense, *entirely correct*, for it merely draws out what is already latent in the field. As I tried to point out above, distributive objectives become translated into the deontological idiom of the law (see p. 106 above). In the final event, this requires having recourse to non-normative intent in order to calibrate the application of anti-discrimination norms.

We shall see in the next chapter that anti-discrimination law becomes moralistic in the second sense, too, when questionable efforts are contemplated in order to enhance its thrust.

3. The Inscrutability of Intent

One might therefore wonder whether the official reluctance, on the part of the ECJ,[20] to take discriminatory intent in the pre-normative sense into account is not a shortcoming. The Court seems to fail to draw out what is inherent in this field of

person was not qualified enough. On such 'mixed motive' cases, see *Price Waterhouse* v. *Hopkins*, 490 US 228 (1989) and re-establishment of overdetermination as relevant by the United States Congress in 42 USC, sec. 2000e-2(m). See also Sedler, n. 11 at 101 n. 40.

[16] Krieger, n. 12 at 1172.

[17] Krieger, ibid. at 1174, 1176, reconstructs the underlying social theory of discrimination, which is used by the Court, in the following way:

> [...] [T]he assumption that statements reflecting stereotyped views betoken discriminatory animus makes sense if one understands discrimination as resulting from prejudice and further understands prejudice as comprising a cognitive component (stereotypes), an affective component (aversion or dislike), and a behavioral component (discrimination aimed at creating or enforcing social distance). If we believe that these three components necessarily function as inseparable parts of an integrated whole, then the presence of one can be assumed to evidence the others. [...] Seen in this way, prejudice, an attitude, causes discrimination, a behavior. Mediating between the two is conscious behavioural intention.

[18] This type of analysis had been introduced in *McDonnell Douglas Corp.* v. *Green*, 411 US 792 (1973). Roughly, it goes like this. First, the plaintiff must demonstrate that she is a member of the protected class, applied, and was qualified for the job and was rejected despite qualification. The position must have remained open after the rejection. Second, the defendant then must articulate legitimate, non-discriminatory reasons for action. Third, the plaintiff is given an opportunity for rebuttal and demonstration that what the employer said was a mere pretext, hence the decisive motive must have been discriminatory. Such cases are different from the mixed motive analysis introduced in *Price Waterhouse* v. *Hopkins*, 490 US 228 (1989), where the Court proceeded on the theory that the challenged conduct resulted from both legitimate and illegitimate motives.

[19] See Krieger, n. 12 at 1180.

[20] See Case C-177/88, *Dekker* v. *Stichting Vormingscentrum voor Junge Volwassen Plus* [1990] ECR 3941 at para. 17.

law. It will be seen, however, that what appears to be a shortcoming from one angle bespeaks sagacity from another.

It is a truism that actions admit of conflicting interpretations. Are we confronted with a case of discrimination on the grounds of aesthetics or on the grounds of sex if an employer hires merely slender women in their twenties with blonde hair? The question appears to beg the question. The sexual motive could scarcely be more blatant. Boo, what a sexist! This is the standard case of the guilty mind. The normative reversal marked by the antinomy applies with full force. This behaviour is so obnoxious that it *has* to count as discrimination on the grounds of sex.

But is there an objective way of telling why that has to be the case? The question concerns the determination of normative intent.

There are simple cases in which the association of one reason for action with another is merely inferential.[21] It does not amount to a valid defence against a murder charge to claim that one did not want to kill but merely to sever the head from the human body in order to kiss the person's lips. The inferential consequence makes x count as y. In cases of natural causation the inference is plain. Where social meanings are concerned matters are less obvious. As we have seen, it amounts to an amendment of protection on the grounds of sex when pregnant women are protected against preferences in favour of non-pregnant women. The 'but for' rationale does no more than merely aid interpretations to confront the question of what it really is that is meant by 'sex'. It cannot solve the interpretative question.

The attractive blonde is appointed to the job while male candidates are rejected: a clear case of sex discrimination. Would the case be equally clear if the woman had been equally well qualified as her contending male candidates and her looks been taken into account merely for reasons of customer satisfaction? It would amount to discrimination if we considered the reproduction of gender stereotypes relevant to answering this question. But why stop here? Would it also be an instance of sex discrimination if attractive blondes were preferred over unsightly women? The latter would also not be hired, alas, if they were men. Hence, this would not be a case of sex discrimination, extensionally understood. Pre-normative intention needs to be consulted in order to account for our intuitions. Evil attitudes and the influence of stereotypes cannot be ascertained by way of 'but for' causation.[22]

Inquiries into pre-normative intent are supposed to settle interpretative issues regarding normative intent. This is the core of the deontological inversion and of the antinomy that attributes to attitudes the same normative valence as to distributive objectives (see above p. 130). But intentions are elusive. One might wonder, therefore, whether pre-normative conventional standards would explain under which circumstances certain actions attain objective significance even against the express self-interpretation of agents. Even if there were such standards, which may duly be

[21] The following example is used by J. Gardner, 'On the Grounds of her Sex(uality)' (1998) 18 *Oxford Journal of Legal Studies* 167–187 at 180.

[22] Or consider a different example. Childbirth allowances, if they existed and were narrowly construed, would likely not be paid out to male homosexuals even if they decided to adopt. Would it make sense to call this *direct* discrimination on the grounds of sex?

doubted,[23] one would be reluctant to use them. The reluctance is owing to one of the most salient features of morality. Hegel summarized it in the following manner:[24]

The *right of the subjective will* is that whatever it is to recognise as valid should be *perceived* by it *as good*, and that it should be held responsible for an action—as its aims translated into external objectivity—as right or wrong, good or evil, legal or illegal according to its cognisance [*Kenntnis*] which this action has in its objectivity.

The second part of this statement is relevant to our problem. Agents rightly expect to have attributed to them as *their* deeds only actions that were—in one way or another—invested by them with certain significance. That is, they must have intended their actions *for their very own* reasons. They may still be guilty of having offended common understandings; but it is that, then, what they *really* did and not putting their mind to the act that is imputed to them (see the next section).

Owing to their social constitution, actions have countless effects. Did you vote for Tony Blair because you intended British soldiers to die in Iraq? Of course you did not, for there is only a contingent and no necessary association between your choice and this distressing effect. Indeed, it would be morally offensive to attribute to agents intentions that they did not have. It would be tantamount to denying them the status of self-determining persons. Since all action has countless effects (and consequently so-called 'side effects'), some of which can be reasons for action, it needs to be left to agents to determine which reasons they regard as decisive and which others they decide to discount.[25] Action takes place in the sphere of contingency. Agents can be self-determined only if they find respect for the reasons they have themselves recognized to be weighty enough to favour a certain course of action.

Hence, an employer hiring attractive blonde women may legitimately claim that his reasons—the high job qualifications of the applicants aside—are completely unrelated to sexuality. In fact, he may claim that the sheer allegation of sexism bespeaks the guilty mind of the accuser. The example, bland as it may seem, also demonstrates why morality is inexorably intertwined with hypocrisy. The indispensable relevance of the will acting for its own self-determined reasons constitutes the very possibility of dissimulation and concealment.[26] Morality and hypocrisy are twins. One cannot be had without the other. The agent's intent can never be established as a fact. In the words of Hegel:[27]

[23] For a strong skeptical argument, see J. Derrida, *Limited Inc* (Chicago, IL: Northwestern University Press 1988), 130.

[24] Hegel, n. 4 at 158, para. 132 (emphasis in the original). The matter is stated most clearly in the student notes taken by an anonymous student of Hegel's lecture class on the philosophy of law in the winter term of 1819/20. See G. W. F. Hegel, *Philosophie des Rechts*, ed. by D. Henrich (Frankfurt: Suhrkamp, 1983), at 106: 'Es ist das Recht des moralischen Willens, dass das, was ich als Zweck meines Handelns anerkennen soll, überhaupt als gut bestimmt sein muss. [...] Es kann mir eben deswegen eine Handlung nicht zugerechnet werden, insofern ich nicht weiss, ob sie gut oder böse ist.' On reflexive endorsement, see C. M. Korsgaard, *The Sources of Normativity* (Cambridge: Cambridge University Press, 1996), 104–105. This endorsement is decisive for post-conventional moral consciousness.

[25] See Hegel, n. 4 at 145, para. 118.

[26] See ibid. at 172, para. 140.

[27] See ibid. at 135–136 para. 106.

Human beings expect to be judged in accordance with their self-determination, and are in this respect free, whatever external determinants may be at work. It is impossible to break into this inner convictions of human beings; it is inviolable, and the moral will is therefore inaccessible. The worth of a human being is measured by his inward actions, and hence the point of view of morality is that of freedom which has being for itself.

It is impossible 'to break into' the inscrutable inwardness of conviction. Hence, every moral justification *is* also hypocritical, a pretext, a rationalization, an act of irony or cunning deceit.[28] This undecidability is constitutive of morality.

4. Conventional Understandings?

It may be argued, though, that it is not unreasonable to expect agents to understand the significance of their acts from the perspective of established pre-normative conventions. These conventions may not always be clear. At any rate, some conventions of respectful conduct need to be in place so that breaking them can attain the meaning of demeaning others.[29] The employer in my hypothetical example should not be surprised to be perceived by others as a roué.

The rejoinder is correct, but it is correct for the wrong reason. If an employer does not take into account whether acts offend the moral sentiments of other people he clearly fails to be a 'good' member of society. But the reason for failure is not that he has done something discriminatory, but rather that he offended common understandings. Anti-discrimination law protects from discrimination. Its purpose is not to reassure the self-righteous by reconfirming commonly held understandings of discrimination. Why should the moral significance attributed by others to acts, even if those others happen to be the majority, be of any relevance to those concerned with staying within the limits set by law? Even where the seemingly sex-driven employer is in a position to anticipate that his employment practice will enrage the purportedly progressive moral majority, why should their view of the act be of relevance to what the act *truly* is? The problem is not, hence, what people reasonably might abstain from doing because someone could take an offence; the problem is whether their acts *are* offensive or not.

This reply to the rejoinder may prompt the objections that leaving the determination of the moral significance of acts to the agent would be tantamount to surrendering to an imperfect world. It is more desirable, by contrast, to maximize the obligations for improvement and by denying agents the option to cut off the causal links connecting their acts with contingent results[30] or socially attributed

[28] For a succinct analysis, see C. Menke, *Tragödie im Sittlichen: Gerechtigkeit und Freiheit nach Hegel* (Frankfurt: Suhrkamp, 1996).

[29] See D. Hellman, *When is Discrimination Wrong?* (Cambridge, MA: Harvard University Press, 2008), at 55.

[30] A good example for the ludicrousness of extensional 'but for' causation is the case where retired persons are eligible for discounts, however, owing to a different retirement age for men and women non-retired men who are of the same age as retired women are ineligible to receive the discount. Sex is the 'but for' cause of unequal treatment. See the discussion in Gardner, n. 21 at 181.

meanings. Agents should not be allowed to claim in their defence that such consequences or meanings have not been their reasons for action. On the contrary, agents should be held responsible by virtue of action itself.[31]

The moralists' objection denies agents their autonomy. According to moralists, whoever acts becomes inextricably entangled in a network of social responsibility. Conversely, those abstaining from action—i.e., the moralists—retain a beautiful soul.[32] This is a hypocritical attitude, of course, for an agent who does not act cannot be a good person either.

As we shall see in the next chapter, those despairing of the inscrutability of intent assume that whoever acts from within a given structure that is infested with racism, sexism, homophobia, xenophobia, or Euro-centrism is prey to unconscious bias. For structural reasons, all acts are evil even when carried out unwittingly. People then come to be seen as mere puppets on the strings of bias. The principle remains that all agents are guilty; but the morally adulterated social structure does the intending for them. Ideally, this structure is revealed in tests of association whose impact on acts remains an open question.[33] The *potentia* is established without the *actus*.[34] The inscrutability of intent is reproduced, therefore, in the missing link between intention and action.

5. From Law to Casuistry

Pre-normative discriminatory intent cannot be ascertained propositionally. It is impossible to prove, that is, that a woman who did not hire a man abstained from doing so because she thought that men are disgusting creatures. It is impossible not because we all act in a multicoloured way, but because people rarely act with a clear state of mind.[35] Pinning down an intention, therefore, requires *moral evaluation*, that is, an act of attribution that is not an exercise of a cognitive capacity but an application of loosely connected moral standards.[36] Intention requires attribution, and such an attribution is not merely a statement *about* moral conduct but moral conduct *itself*. Since there can be no objective basis to draw on, relativity and

[31] See Hegel, n. 4 at 172, para. 140.

[32] See ibid. at 47, para. 14; Hegel, *Philosophie des Rechts*, n. 24 at 102. A more ample discussion of the beautiful soul is provided in Hegel's *Phenomenology of the Spirit*, trans. by A. V. Miller (Oxford: Oxford University Press, 1977).

[33] On the implicit association test, which is used to establish implicit or unconscious bias, see A. J. Lee, 'Unconscious Bias Theory in Employment Discrimination Litigation' (2005) 40 *Harvard Civil Rights-Civil Liberties Law Review* 481–503 at 483–486. See also https://implicit.harvard.edu/implicit/demo last visited 2 January 2010. The interesting matter about this type of theory is that if one were to deny the existence of unconscious bias one would likely be perceived to be in its grip.

[34] The idea is, apparently, that with the overwhelming evidence of bias 'there's got to be' an influence on action.

[35] I surmise that people very often do what they feel like doing, and what they feel like doing is inchoate and, in any event, different from the pointed and more clear-cut attitude that is required for there to be an 'intention'.

[36] I hasten to add that intent is as inscrutable as it is indispensable for talking meaningfully about human agency. See Derrida, n. 23 at 130.

conflict are the *reality* of raising discrimination claims. Morality is not a means of problem-solving. It is a means of creating conflict.[37]

The rest is casuistry, and casuistry is the domain of sophistry.[38] The standards developed by courts are law and, hence, 'external' in the sense that they are applied to agents regardless of the reasons for action they may have really endorsed. Agents become fully exposed to the harshness of social norms (*Sittlichkeit der Sitte*).[39] The conventions developed by courts, however, are not the happy end of the story. They are inexorably tied to the ontological commitments of morality, such as intent and animus. Their hollowness is reflected in attributions of intent that always have to reckon with deception, dissimulation, and misrepresentation. Consequently, they come in the form of statements such as 'we cannot but conclude that . . . ' or 'we think the defendant is honest'. Not surprisingly, practically the most important and not by accident most conflicted part of anti-discrimination law concerns the appropriate burden of proof.[40] Attributions of intent are governed by normative rules,[41] not by empirical regularities ('under condition x it is not an insult to suspect that A acted out of motive y, however, A should be given opportunity to show that what appears to be like acting out of motive y is indeed motivated by z').[42] In particular, the allocative aspect of such rules needs to be borne in mind, for they determine, from a distributive point of view, under which conditions a potential distributive agent is actually under an obligation to revise her plans.

6. A Minimalist Solution: Free-market Paternalism

The inscrutability of intent is the last stage in the transmigration of the indeterminacy of obligation.

For discrimination to count as an unlawful act, the imputation of discriminatory intent is inevitable. Obviously, this intent cannot be merely coextensive with the intent to treat differently, for the latter is manifest also in cases where unequal treatment is perfectly permissible. At any rate, on the basis of an intensional

[37] This basic paradox has been explored by Niklas Luhmann. See his 'Soziologie der Moral', in N. Luhmann and S. Pfürtner (eds), *Theorietechnik und Moral* (Frankfurt aM: Suhrkamp, 1978), 8–116 at 49–63; N. Luhman, 'Ethik als Reflexionstheorie der Moral', in *Gesellschaftsstruktur und Semantik: Studien zur Wissenssoziologie der modernen Gesellschaft*, vol. 3 (Frankfurt: Suhrkamp, 1989), at 459–444; N. Luhman, *Die Gesellschaft der Gesellschaft* (Frankfurt: Suhrkamp, 1997), at 1043.

[38] See Hegel, n. 4 at 172–173, para. 140.

[39] See F. Nietzsche, *Daybreak: Thoughts on the Prejudices of Morality*, trans. by R. J. Hollingdale (Cambridge: Cambridge University Pres 1997), at 10–12.

[40] See Ellis, n. 9 at 98–102; Katz, n. 14 at 516. See also D. R. Oritz, 'The Myth of Intent in Equal Protection' (1989) 41 *Stanford Law Review* 1105–1151 at 1134–1135, who observes that the intent requirement serves to allocate burdens of proof between the individual and the state.

[41] Their application is not controlled by truth conditions. See S. A. Kripke, *Wittgenstein on Rules and Private Language* (Cambridge, MA: Harvard University Press, 1982).

[42] On the burden of proof in cases of indirect discrimination, see C. Barnard, *EC Employment Law*, 3rd edn (Oxford: Oxford University Press, 2007), at 373–375. In fact, this is the solution suggested by Katz, n. 14 at 549: the requirement on the part of the plaintiff to show the existence of a minimal motivating factor and the opportunity on the part of the defendant that there was no relevance of the forbidden ground whatsoever.

interpretation of causation, the mere use of, or reliance on, an incriminated distinction is not in and of itself indicative of unlawful discrimination. The same observation holds true also with regard to the motive with which a distinction is used. A filmmaker may be relieved that no woman has a role to play in a movie set in a Trappist monastery. He may find dealing with actresses exceedingly distressing. He may choose to make films only about joyous and life-affirming homosexual Roman Catholic priests. If he does not hire any women to play a role in these movies he does not act for the wrong reason. He may invest every decision in the course of the production with his misogynistic zeal, but none of these acts will ever amount to sex discrimination. He does not act for the wrong reason, for his zeal does not harm any women. It is permissible, still, to produce such a movie. Reliance on a distinction is not at all sufficient to constitute discrimination. Disreputable motives do not suffice either.

Since, as I tried to point out above, normative guidance cannot be obtained at the distributive level, it seems that it would have to be found at the level of individual dealings. But at this level, the indeterminacy of intent translates *directly* into the indeterminacy of obligation. If it is unknown under which circumstances an act is truly aimed at evil, it is also unclear which acts truly *are* evil.[43] There is no objective way of telling good from bad by attending to subjective attributions. For some women, female beauty symbolizes female pride whereas for others, it is an heirloom of patriarchy. According to some, Muslims may not be hired for positions in which they are likely to encounter hostility because this is for their own good. Others find this outrageous.

It seems as though the 'wrong reasons' relevant for anti-discrimination law can only be pinned down by settling for the minimal solution suggested by the application of the proportionality principle (see above pp. 134–138). Anti-discrimination law is then a strategy of calibrating and strengthening market rationality. The reasons rejected by anti-discrimination law would be neither entirely objective (i.e., distributive) nor entirely subjective (i.e., intentional). They would be the reasons that are to be rejected by any *rational* agent.

The market is the medium where widely shared dislike of people (bias, stereotypes) translates into real economic disadvantage. This is the link targeted by anti-discrimination law. Following this link, it is possible to plot the contours of distributive objectives via deontological constraints on action. *Mere* dislike of someone—aversion—is a wrong reason for action. Deontologically understood, the reasons outlawed by anti-discrimination law are reasons *to dislike people* for the wrong reasons and to act on them in the context of market transactions.[44] This is to say, of course, that people may be disfavoured for the right reasons, for example, when they lack a sufficiently meritorious record of achievement. The neoliberal left, which endorses anti-discrimination law, believes that competitive forces are not strong enough to eliminate the influence of wrong reasons. Hence, anti-discrimination legislation is needed.

[43] See Hegel, n. 4 at 161, para. 134.

[44] See Gardner, n. 21 at 168: 'Being black or a women [...] reflects badly on no one. Those who tend to think that it *does* reflect badly are gripped by irrationality, often stemming from deficiencies of their own such as prejudice, gullibility, and superstition.'

According to Kelman,[45] an employer who is forced to employ a person who is disliked by his customers for arbitrary reasons is forced to internalize the social costs of combating discrimination. The employer ought to be seen as the agent of customers who suffer from irrational aversion. Protection from discrimination is a means of making sure that employees are treated according to standards of 'capitalist rationality',[46] which requires employers to take into account their 'net marginal product'.[47] Evidently, the perspective deemed relevant is that of market equality and the relentless commodification of persons as factors of production. In Kelman's opinion, anti-discrimination norms are market-perfecting.[48] Oddly enough, Kelman proceeds as though people had a claim to be treated as a marginal net product only, even though he abstains, rightly so, from assuming that everyone has a right to capitalist rational treatment.[49] The right to be free from discrimination is enforced by the employer acting paternalistically in the real interest of consumers. According to Kelman, the 'real' employer of a waiter is, indeed, the customer who should not want to suffer from irrational prejudice. Kelman even goes so far as to claim, without hesitation, that '[c]ustomers are duty-bound under anti-discrimination law to treat salespeople with whom they deal in an impersonal, capitalist, rational fashion (with regard only to their economic function, without regard to their status)'.[50]

This is a bold construction. Not only is the assumption of such an obligation nowhere warranted in the text of anti-discrimination statutes or directives, it also conflicts with the market rationality hailed by Kelman. On markets, consumers are under no obligation whatsoever to establish contact with salespersons they dislike. In fact, even assuming that they were obliged to overcome their sexist expectations regarding service personnel, such a duty would have to be balanced against their liberty interest to establish contact with whomever they please.[51] By default, customers may act out their prejudices, for even after anti-discrimination norms had been implemented, customers would be free to cease to request certain services after they have lost, for example, their prior 'sexy' aura. Following Kelman, one would have to assume that customers are under an *obligation* to consume, which is clearly absurd. Indeed, his position rests on a tacit moralism uncovered by Bagenstos.[52] First, it is unclear, for example, why the pleasure that an employer extracts from rewarding employees who are members of his favourite political party should be excluded from a welfare calculus. Second, Kelman's stern filtering out ('laundering') of sexually, racially, or nationally tainted preferences denies customers on moral grounds to have an affective component included into the 'embodied marginal net product' that Kelman claims employees to be. Clearly, Kelman thus

[45] See M. Kelman, 'Market Discrimination and Groups' (2001) 53 *Stanford Law Review* 833–896 at 847–848.
[46] Ibid. at 848.
[47] Ibid. at 835.
[48] See M. Kelman and G. Lester, *Jumping the Queue: An Inquiry into the Legal Treatment of Students with Learning Disabilities* (Cambridge, MA: Harvard University Press, 1997), at 221.
[49] For this charitable interpretation, see Bagenstos, n. 2 at 876–880.
[50] See Kelman, n. 45 at 848.
[51] See Bagenstos, n. 2 at 882.
[52] See ibid. at 887, 894–896.

does not define the marginal net product with reference to what customers *do* want but what they *should* want.[53] After all, he claims that the prohibition of discrimination 'destroys' the utility obtained from discrimination.[54] From a moral point of view, this may not be objectionable at all. But it does not demonstrate that discrimination is in conflict with 'capitalist rationality'.

7. Groupism and Reification

The laundering of preferences remains the work of intuition unless it is informed by an account of distributive justice. Anti-discrimination law, however, notoriously lacks such a distributive perspective.

Moral intuition is always prone to be led astray. Moreover, it is affected by an even deeper problem. The protected grounds of anti-discrimination law accept the ontological commitments created in the course of market dealings. People experience rejection on the basis of what they believe to be a widespread aversion towards, for example, women, Africans, Scientologists, Puerto-Ricans, Lutherans, Mexicans, Baptists, Americans, Sikhs, Central Europeans, homosexuals, Muslims, etc. The 'group identities'[55] thus created bear the reified[56] imprint of the market transactions, for markets allow participants to act out their whims. Anti-discrimination law promises to reverse the resulting negative distributive consequences.

The strategy of negating the negation on markets comes at a high cost.

First, it leads to the line-up of all those who have not been treated generously by nature or fate, that is, the plump, the unattractive, the disfigured, the ugly. They are widely disfavoured in a society that is spellbound by what cultural industries set out to be beautiful. The question arises, hence, who is to be admitted to the victim's club. Herein lies the explanation why even most high-minded scholars fear that an unlimited extension of prohibited grounds of discrimination would give rise to a *reductio ad absurdum*.[57] Whether or not a category becomes protected is a matter of political conflict, and not of logic.[58] The problem is exacerbated by instances of 'intersectionality',[59] that is, where disadvantage is suffered by those who happen to

[53] See ibid. at 896.
[54] See Kelman, n. 45 at 855.
[55] For a related analysis of the paradoxical constitution of 'communities', such as the 'gay community' or the 'deaf community', see N. Rose, *Powers of Freedom: Reframing Political Thought* (Cambridge: Cambridge University Press, 1999), at 177–178.
[56] See G. Lukács, *History and Class Consciousness: Studies in Marxist Dialectics*, trans. by R. Livingstone (Cambridge, MA: MIT Press 1971), at 92.
[57] See R. Post, 'Prejudicial Appearances: The Logic of American Anti-discrimination Law' (2000) 88 *California Law Review* 1–40 at 8; M. Bell, *Anti-discrimination Law and the European Union* (Oxford: Oxford University Press, 2002), 136–143 at 213: '[. . .] [T]here is a risk that where legislation attempts to encompass all grounds of discrimination it ends up mired in complexity or it is diluted by its generality.'
[58] See R. M. Unger, *What should Legal Analysis become?* (London: Verso 1996), at 89.
[59] For a classical instalment, see K. Crenshaw, 'Demarginalizing the Intersection of Race and Sex: A Black Feminist Critique of Anti-discrimination Doctrine, Feminist Theory, and Antiracist Politics' (1989) *University of Chicago Legal Forum* 139–167.

bear one and the other characteristic and who would not be disadvantaged if they were to bear only one.[60]

Second, anti-discrimination law is held captive by the social perspective of the market. The protected groups are 'groups' only from the perspective of market disadvantage. The group that one belongs to is the reflection of some instance of social devaluation. Anti-discrimination policy is basically committed to reversing its impact. The relevant gesture is often one of celebration.[61] The devalued needs to be appreciated as 'diverse' even if there is only very little to celebrate because, prejudice aside, the 'groups' are not so different from the mainstream.[62] All of this is odd, for there is no reason why somebody would have to be wonderful in order to be free from discrimination.

Third, there is something terribly disturbing about the idea of membership to a group if one does not share with one's fellows a common purpose or culture. I sense that heterosexual men do not feel that they belong to heterosexuals as a group. There is no common purpose shared with one another. There is no common objective associated with sexual orientation. All that heterosexual men have in common is a sexual preference for women. The case of Don Giovanni and Leporello aside, the pursuit of heterosexual objectives is not essentially dependent on the cooperation of fellow 'group members'.

The 'groups' relevant to the anti-discrimination universe reflect the commodified categories of consumption. I enjoy salmon prepared in whichever form. From the perspective of the market, I belong to the group of salmon eaters. 'Group' is understood here as a set. But I belong to this group as an individual. I am a member of the set of salmon eaters. My identity is in no manner dependent on the existence of other salmon eaters. My individual interest coincides with the individual interest of others only as regards the dissemination of product information. But it is information that is valuable to me in the privacy of my inner cravings. It is not the type of information whose value depends on being shared with others, such as the experience of reading a book in order to explore its meaning in a reading group. Such a group is defined by a common purpose because the purpose of learning from sharing ideas can only be pursued by the members jointly. Consumers do rarely share in pursuits. When push comes to shove, in a case of scarcity, they would not hesitate to compete against one another. The same is true

[60] Women wearing headscarves for religious reasons are a good example for that. See E. Holzleithner, 'Gendergleichheit und Mehrfachdiskriminierung: Herausforderungen für das Europarecht', in K. Arioli, M. Cottier, P. Farahmand, and Z Küng (eds.), *Wandel der Geschlechterverhältnisse durch das Recht?* (Zurich/St Gallen: Dike Verlag, 2008), 305–320. It does not seem to be the case that European employment discrimination law is really prepared for that type of issue. See J. Kenner, *EU Employment Law: From Rome to Amsterdam and Beyond* (Oxford: Hart Publishing, 2003), 394; E. Holzleithner, 'Mainstreaming Equality: Dis/Entangling Grounds of Discrimination' (2005) 14 *Journal of Transnational Law and Contemporary Problems* 927–958 at 945–947.

[61] See W. Benn Michaels, *The Trouble with Diversity: How We Learned to Love Identity and Ignore Inequality* (New York: Metropolitan Books, 2006), at 6.

[62] I, for one, find it doubtful whether there is, indeed, something like 'gay culture'. Indeed, the movement towards gay marriage indicates that it is infused with petit-bourgeois values. On the questionable merits of sustaining belief in a 'deaf culture', see Benn Michaels, n. 61 at 168–169.

of 'disadvantaged groups'. Their members contend for jobs. They do not act together or support each other. The protection of the right to equal treatment of one group member incidentally creates a public good for others. But the realization of any of the group member's goals does in no manner depend on the cooperation with others. It should not come as a surprise then, that it requires effort to alert members of 'disadvantaged groups' of their membership to that group.[63]

The recognition of commonalities is even more difficult to imagine across groups. Usually, members of different disadvantaged groups *do not* perceive to have in common the quality that they really share and which *in fact* accounts for the fact that they endure discrimination in the first place, namely, a lack of political and economic power. They do not share their experience of powerlessness and, consequently, fail to act on it. The lack of common experience is not ungrounded.[64] The encounters that upper-middle-class white women make with the glass ceiling is different from the exposure to racial prejudice suffered by impoverished immigrants.[65] Members of those groups simply do not experience one another as belonging to the same social world. Groupism and the 'diversity' of so-called 'cultures' are the epitome of a society drained of solidarity. The celebration of 'difference' is the effect of a society where solidarity is unknown to the powerless. It is the consequence of individualism.[66]

8. The Abstention from Terror

Moralism is inimical to moral autonomy, for it systematically invites attributing reasons for action to agents they themselves may have duly discounted. It represents the final destination of the voyages of normative intent, which was supposed to establish that doing x counts as doing y no matter what agents may think they are up to. Beyond that, once anti-discrimination law has passed through several stages of normative deficiency, it can be argued that it poses a threat to human autonomy because it wishes to go to the hearts, minds, and souls of people. If, as anti-discrimination law insinuates, the ill of social exclusion or stigmatization is rooted in unexamined attitudes towards others (prejudice or stereotypes), then the transformative effect of anti-discrimination law requires impregnating people's attitude towards others with tolerance and interpersonal bliss. Thus understood, anti-discrimination aspires to transforming the human will.[67] This aspect has given rise to the fear that anti-discrimination policies are merely heralding the advent of more intense forms of oppression.

Ever since the Jacobin *Terreur* of the French Revolution[68] and subsequent attempts to emulate the project of creating morally impeccable citizens by breaking

[63] See Rose, n. 55 at 178. [64] For similar observations, see Unger, n. 58 at 93.
[65] For a similar point, see Benn Michaels, n. 61 at 117.
[66] See Benn Michaels, n. 61 at 49, 143.
[67] On anti-discrimination law as a means 'to create liberals', see A. Koppelman, *Anti-discrimination Law and Social Equality* (New Haven, CT: Yale University Press, 1996), at 218.
[68] See Hegel, n. 4 at 390.

inherited habits and inclinations,[69] this policy objective has raised the spectre of authoritarianism,[70] if not totalitarianism.[71] In the case of anti-discrimination law such fears are ungrounded. It is intriguing, nonetheless, to examine briefly *why* this is the case and why anti-discrimination law would be, indeed, more effective if it were underpinned by violent terror.

It is erroneous to believe that one of the goals of anti-discrimination law, namely to affect personal dealings, in and of itself proves that it springs, at bottom, from some oppressive moral frenzy. In countless respects, the law affects quite permissibly the attitude with which we treat one another. A criminal defendant, for example, who is represented by an attorney stands a good chance of being treated with respect. If it were, indeed, as Koppelman has it, the core of the 'anti-discrimination project' to '[...] eliminate or marginalise the shared meanings, practices, and institutions that unjustifiably single out certain groups of citizens for stigma and disadvantage',[72] one could not but agree that this is a worthy and noble cause.

Nevertheless, the normative deficit of anti-discrimination law—its inherent lack of clarity with regard to what counts as unlawful discrimination—could be usefully cured through terror.[73] In its pure form, terror threatens subjects with physical extinction. A terror regime reckons with the omnipresence of the fear to reveal one's disloyalty or critical attitude towards the ruling nomenclature. People live under the constant threat of denunciation and impending attacks by terror's executioners. There are no clear rules laying down what it takes to avoid denunciation or investigation. Legality is unknown in the realm of terror. There is only the fear of being 'caught' and a profound lack of clarity with regard to what it takes to duck the bullet. Where terror rules, people are at pains to remain invisible and to display publicly, if they have to, their unflinching support.[74] Indeed, they compete with one another when it comes to excel in conformity. Terror removes difference from men and makes them endeavour to become the most perfect expression of the type of human being that society wishes to create.[75]

[69] See J. G. Fichte, *Reden an die deutsche Nation* (1808), *Sämmtliche Werke*, ed. by I. H. Fichte (Berlin: Veit & Comp., 1845–6), vol. 7, at 281, 297.

[70] It is exactly this spectre which had been raised in discussions in Germany. For an overview, see V. Winkler, 'Diskriminierungsschutz durch Recht: Anmerkungen zu einer ajuristischen Debatte' (2003) *Juridikum* 188–191 See also, without actually endorsing this misgiving, R. M. Hills, 'You Say you Want a Revolution? The Case against the Transformation of Culture through Anti-discrimination Laws' (1997) 95 *Michigan Law Review* 1588–1635 at 1589. For the American libertarian perspective, see D. E. Bernstein, *You Can't Say That! The Growing Threat to Civil Liberties from Anti-discrimination Laws* (Washington, DC: Cato Institute, 2003).

[71] In a totalitarian society, terror replaces law. See (with an eye to Arendt) R. B. Pippin, *The Persistence of Subjectivity: On the Kantian Aftermath* (Cambridge: Cambridge University Press, 2005), at 154.

[72] Koppelman, n. 67 at 8.

[73] For a classical phenomenology of terror, see H. Arendt, *The Origins of Totalitarianism*, new edn (New York: Schocken Books, 2004), pp. 598–603. The account given in the text above differs from Arendt, in particular as regards the relevance of fear.

[74] See F. Pohlmann, 'Moral und totalitärer Terror', in M. Junge (ed.), *Macht und Moral: Beiträge zur Dekonstruktion von Moral* (Opladen: Westdeutscher Verlag, 2003), 235–252 at 247.

[75] See Arendt, n. 73 at 600.

Fear permeates life from the public to the private sphere. Its omnipresence motivates self-censure and dissimulation all the way down to the intimate sphere. These defensive mechanisms compensate for the lack of guidance from rules. Socially shared standards of behaviour arise from constructive guesses undertaken by victims as to what it takes to be immune from persecution. The victims contribute to their own oppression—become, indeed, guilty of it—by creating norms governing their conformity.[76]

Evidently, terror is a useful means of filling a normative deficit. If nobody knows what the ideal society really would have to be like, the imaginative work can be delegated to the terrorized subjects. The emerging world will look petty, of course, for it will originate from the trifling fear of little people. Hence, a supplementary function could be played by terror even in the field of anti-discrimination law. If nobody can tell what an act of discrimination truly is then people orient their behaviour with regard to what they fear might infuriate others, in particular the censors employed in human resource departments. The fear of infuriation gives rise to a situation where certain acts are deemed problematic for no other reason than the systemic interpenetration of expectations.

Anti-discrimination law, of course, does *not* incorporate terror. The type of social exclusion suffered by discriminators is far too mild to instil fear of a sufficiently high proportion. The 'groups' protected are too divided and inhomogeneous to merge into a movement that could resort to terror as an effective tool.[77] The potential for terror, however, should make one suspicious of a reliance on 'conventions' discussed above. When conventions are not settled, drawing on them partakes of the insecurity involved in a situation of terror.

9. Conclusion

The consequences of the normative deficiency can be summarized as follows.

First, anti-discrimination law is congruent with the market mentality and does in no way transcend it. It is committed to a normative vision of market equality and unwittingly reflective of patterns of market exclusion by lumping disengaged individuals together in 'groups', which are in fact merely sets. Nowhere does anti-discrimination scholarship transcend the social imagery of the market by asking the question of what it is that these groups have in common—namely, their lack of social power—or what they could do jointly to overcome their situation. Indeed, anti-discrimination law is bedevilled by what Benn Michaels calls the 'illusion of inequality'.[78] The idea is that if only members of market societies ridded themselves of the wrong belief in the natural inequality between sexes, races, and ethnicities the world would be a much better place.

Second, in its inverted state, anti-discrimination law is based on a grandiose transformative vision—the creation of a society cleansed of prejudice and exclusion.

76 For related observations, see Pohlmann, n. 74 at 248–250.
77 See Arendt, n. 73 at 599.
78 See Benn Michaels, n. 61 at 106.

But it notoriously gives rise to small and unexciting results. The expectation is, indeed, that a large-scale social transformation might spring from the incremental accumulation of minor improvements, that is, protection from discrimination on a case by case basis, notably even through class action. The absence of vision for political action and the space carved out for litigation indicate a latent affinity to individualism. In fact, as will be seen per our discussion in the next chapter, recourse to pedagogic measures, re-education and mind-cleansing as a means of goal attainment[79] also manifests a shift from the collective assertion of interests towards supervised techniques of self-improvement, which are administered from above. The road leads from politics via management to training. I do not want to cast into doubt that pedagogic measures or 'diversity training' might help to enlighten employers and co-workers about their prejudice, ill-will, or the rights of others. But it cannot be denied, either, that supervised self-improvement on the part of the potential perpetrator does nothing to empower potential victims as a group.

Third, anti-discrimination law is sufficiently flexible to have, where necessary, protection from discrimination yield to the imperatives of economic rationality.[80] In fact, I speculated above whether it is not reduced, in practice, to an application of the proportionality principle. This is fairly obvious as regards the business necessity defences associated with indirect discrimination. As I tried to explain above (see p. 134) a similar observation can be made with regard to the identification of cases of direct discrimination.

In order to avoid misunderstanding, I should emphasize what I do not claim. I do not say that anti-discrimination law is the handmaiden of business interests. What I do say, however, is that anti-discrimination law can become a very blunt tool of social protection in the hands of a business-friendly judiciary. This, at any rate, seems to have been the American experience.[81]

Anti-discrimination law suffers from a profound normative deficiency.[82] One should not be surprised, hence, to realize that it has become the darling of neoliberal reformists in Europe.

[79] For references, see A. Somek, 'Catholic Concordance: Exploring the Context of European Anti-discrimination Law and Policy' (2005) 14 *Journal of Transnational Law and Contemporary Problems* 959–1006 at 1001–1005. Recently, the European Commission began offering a new programme of anti-discrimination and diversity management training. The sentence introducing the programme reads as follows. 'The European Commission recognized that training is one of the best methods to achieve change.' See http://ec.europa.eu/employment_social/local_employment/lla/fo/news.do?method=showNewsItem&newsid=1e27113d14cbcab50114d09d53400422&lang=en accessed 23 December 2010.

[80] For related observations, see T. Loenen, 'Indirect Discrimination: Oscillating between Containment and Revolution', in T. Loenen and P. R. Rodrigues (eds), *Non-Discrimination Law: Comparative Perspectives* (Amsterdam: Kluwer, 1999), 195–211 at 204. S. O'Leary, *Employment Law at the European Court of Justice: Judicial Structures, Policies, and Processes* (Oxford: Hart Publishing, 2002), at 148–149, 175.

[81] See Bagenstos, n. 2 at 40.

[82] This is particularly evident for the way in which age discrimination provisions failed to protect older workers against dismissals. Defendants usually succeed at justifying challenged practices as resting on factors other than age. See Sedler, n. 11, 102.

7

Moral Re-engineering: the Neoliberal Predicament

1. Introduction

The antinomy of anti-discrimination law goes back to the fact that, from a normative point of view, its distributive dimension is more fundamental than its deontological mode of realization. But since it can neither embrace a distributive pattern nor rest its faith on an extensional interpretation of direct discrimination, it needs to resort to pre-normative intent in order to ascertain the meaning of anti-discrimination norms. Distributive patterns and aiming at bad intentions compete for being the source of normativity. Unfortunately, the former is not and the latter cannot plausibly be such a source.

Interpretative tinkering with pre-normative intent motivates both to adjust the extension of prohibited grounds and to amend tacitly the set to which they belong. What is decisive is the resolve to control the doings of evil minds.

From the perspective of modern morality, however, pre-normative intent is inscrutable. Consequently, the real source of normativity is moral intuition, perhaps tempered by economic rationality, applied to singular acts. Anti-discrimination law is therefore destined to be the playing field of pervasive casuistry.

But this is not the end of the story. The normative deficit of anti-discrimination law culminates in a full-blown neoliberal predicament where attempts are made to overcome it without moving beyond the purview of pre-normative intent. It will be seen below, that attempts at radicalizing anti-discrimination law, if unheeded of the pitfalls of morality, fail, in particular, on the side of decommodification, that is, when it comes to making the life of people less dependent on the market mechanism.

The normative deficit of anti-discrimination law extends to efforts to overcome it by improving the moral perceptions of others at the pre-normative level.

2. The Micro-level Cousin of European Strategies

Aspirations to radicalize anti-discrimination law are manifest in the idea to make it more responsive to structural or systemic discrimination on the basis of isolating market rationality from the obscuring influence of misperceptions, such as prejudice and stereotype, and attendant practices of exclusion, stigmatization and subordination. This aspiration comes, to be sure, invested with a view of the social world that traces disadvantage back to the attitudes *tacitly* harboured by individuals who consequently find themselves encouraged to explore the darker quarters of their soul (i.e., their 'unconscious' or 'implicit' bias).[1] The existence of bias below the level of conscious recognition appears to be a widely accepted view among those who conceive of their work as belonging to the 'second generation' of anti-discrimination scholarship.[2]

In what follows, I should like to examine this neoliberal predicament. It comes to the fore where second-generation scholars desire to remedy the normative deficiency of anti-discrimination law without taking into account the constraints that they face owing to their adherence to the moral view of the world.

As pointed out above (see above p. 149), the predicament posed by the inscrutability of intent gives rise to the construction of a social ontology where not persons but unconscious structures of bias are seen to cloud the unadulterated perception of personal qualifications. I take this to be a fundamental premise of the so-called 'structural turn' of the 'second generation' of employment discrimination scholarship.[3] It is an attempt to take seriously the priority of indirect discrimination, at least as one of the major challenges of our age.[4] The structural turn is driven by the desire to overcome the constraints of the deontological make-up of the field by heightening self-observation to the point at which only collective re-education promises to offer reprieve from a world infested with distorted images and unexamined repulsion. This drive towards enhanced self-examination is most clearly reflected in the writings of Krieger[5] and Ayres[6]. It appears in the format of the exhortation to examine evermore conscientiously and studiously the way in which stereotypes and prejudice determine our perceptions of others. Since such stereotypes or prejudices are woven into the very fabric of society, they lead to a

[1] The author who arguably deserves credit for having initiated the discourse is C. R. Lawrence III, 'The Id, the Ego, and Equal Protection: Reckoning with Unconscious Racism' (1987) 39 *Stanford Law Review* 317–388 at 355–362, who argued that unconscious racism is part of the cultural fabric of society. In the meanwhile, it has grown into a cottage industry of its own. For overviews, see J. Armour, 'Stereotypes und Prejudice: Helping Legal Decisionmakers to Break the Prejudice of Habit' (1995) 83 *California Law Review* 733–772; J. Kang, 'Trojan Horses of Race' (2005) 118 *Harvard Law Review* 1489–1593.

[2] See C. Jolls and C. R. Sunstein, 'The Law of Implicit Bias' (2006) 94 *California Law Review* 969–996 at 970–971; see also S. R. Bagenstos, 'Trapped in the Feedback Loop: A Response to Professor Days' (2005) 49 *Saint Louis University Law Journal* 1007–1019 at 1009.

[3] For an overview, see S. R. Bagenstos, 'The Structural Turn and the Limits of Anti-discrimination Law' (2006) 94 *California Law Review* 1–47 at 2, 5, who identifies at least two defining features of the structural turn: first, the concern with unconscious and more subtle biases; second, the focus on discrimination that arises from interactions among workers at all levels of an occupational hierarchy.

[4] It has been observed that discrimination can work in many discrete ways today and hinder advancement and opportunity without the intervening of one particular decision to exclude a certain person. See T. K. Green, 'Discrimination in Workplace Dynamics: Towards a Structural Account of Disparate Treatment Theory (2003) 38 *Harvard Civil Rights-Civil Liberties Law Review* 91–157 at 105.

[5] See L. Hamilton Krieger, 'The Content of our Categories: A Cognitive Bias Approach to Discrimination and Equal Employment Opportunity' (1995) 47 *Stanford Law Review* 1161–1248.

[6] See I. Ayres, *Pervasive Prejudice? Unconventional Evidence of Race and Gender Discrimination* (Chicago, IL: University of Chicago Press, 2001).

paradoxical collectivization of individual responsibility that leaves the actual framework of social cooperation, i.e., the relations of production, unchallenged and in place. As a result, the point of decommodification is missed. What remains is moral hypertrophy.[7] Ironically, it is thought that the attainment of the high-minded moral goals of self-observation is best achieved through strategies of managed innovation,[8] incidentally matching the accelerated production methods of 'impatient capital'.[9]

With this characterization of the neoliberal predicament, the analysis comes to a full circle. We shall observe the recurrence, at the micro level of workplace organization, of a move to management that we encountered already for the macro level of European policy-making. Some of the same strategies that are supposed to guide intergovernmental and inter-societal policy learning are suggested to be used at the level of firms by those arguing the case for the second generation of anti-discrimination policy. There is reason to conclude, hence, that the move to informality and management is even particularly revealing about the internal normative weakness of anti-discrimination law.

3. A Strong Start

It is difficult to imagine an author with a sharper sense of the moral shallowness of anti-discrimination law, as practised, than Linda Hamilton Krieger.[10] First, she observes, quite perceptively, that American differential treatment jurisprudence, owing to its preoccupation with uncovering an intent that causes discriminatory behaviour, is based on the erroneous assumption that it is possible to determine the causal effectiveness of a forbidden ground from among a set of antecedent conditions.[11] From the outset, however, her observations reveal a moralistic concern with pre-normative intent. She argues that differential treatment jurisprudence invites—indeed, requires—the repeated commission of an 'attribution mistake' that correlates negative effects with a presumed or constructed cause: employment discrimination is caused by an act carried out by an 'invidiously motivated decisionmaker'.[12]

[7] See A. Gehlen, *Moral und Hypermoral: Eine pluralistische Ethik*, 5th edn (Munich: Aula-Verlag, 1986), 141–163. It means that everyone is everywhere and in every situation responsible to promote the good cause.

[8] See L. Sturm, 'Second Generation Employment Discrimination: A Structural Approach' (2001) 101 *Columbia Law Review* 458–568.

[9] For a powerful critique, see W. E. Scheuerman, 'Democratic Experimentalism or Capitalist Synchronisation' (2004) 17 *Canadian Journal of Jurisprudence* 101–127 at 126. For an attempt to formulate a reply, see S. Sturm, 'Gender Equity Regimes and the Architecture of Learning', in G. de Búrca and J. Scott (eds), *Law and Governance in the EU and the US* (Oxford: Hart Publishing, 2006), 323–360 at 330–331.

[10] The remark is not meant to exclude authors working from the same baseline of cognitive bias theory. See J. C. Williams and N. Segal, 'Beyond the Maternal Wall: Relief for Family Caregivers who are Discriminated against on the Job' (2003) 26 *Harvard Women's Law Journal* 77–162.

[11] See Krieger, n. 5 at 1204–1206, 1215–1216.

[12] Ibid., at 1216. See also S. Sturm, 'Race, Gender, and the Law in the Twenty-First Century Workplace' (1998) 1 *University of Pennsylvania Journal of Labour and Employment Law* 639–689 at 669–670.

But that is not how 'real discrimination' works. Evaluations that are important to career advancement are embedded into day-to-day interactions and decisions.[13] Therefore, anti-discrimination law, as practised, falls victim to a stereotype about the nature of discrimination.[14] Far from being exempt from the sphere it is supposed to govern, it becomes applied with a socially distorted image about how discrimination is brought about.[15]

It bears repeating, at this point, that it was found in Chapter 4 that what Krieger alleges to be an attribution mistake is constitutive of the very normativity of direct discrimination norms, for it is only through such attributions that pre-normative intent becomes divested of its ambivalence. This ambivalence is not least manifest in what I called, in the previous chapter, the inscrutability of intent. Eliminating from the horizon of anti-discrimination law the constitutive function of norms leaves it in an entirely moralistic state as a result of which it becomes impossible to pin down discrimination. What is taken to be 'real' discrimination, independent of norms, is a phantom chased by variously managed attempts at improving the performance of anti-discrimination strategies. In truth, instances of discrimination could not be ascertained were it not for the intervention of the moral intuitions of the beholder.

Aside from adducing an impressive array of psychological evidence to support her claim that in most instances discrimination arises from subconsciously biased cognitive processes, which remain unrecognized by current jurisprudence,[16] Krieger explains that anti-discrimination law is unable to take into account types of discrimination that do not stem from the unfair treatment of outsiders but rather arise from subtle intra-group favouritism.[17] In her opinion, anti-discrimination

[13] See Sturm, ibid. at 669.

[14] For similar observations, see B. Resnik, 'Unconscious Raising: Countering Stereotypes by Changing the Rules' (2005) *1 Regional Review* 33–37 at 33. For discrimination outside the employment discrimination context, such as retail discrimination, see Ayres, n. 6.

[15] L. Hamilton Krieger, 'Civil Rights Perestroika: Intergroup Relations after Affirmative Action' (1998) 86 *California Law Review* 1251–1333 at 1311. Krieger summarizes the stereotypical view in the following way:

> [D]iscrimination occurs when a sexist, racist, or otherwise bigoted person makes decisions about members of a targeted group. Because of his negative feelings towards or beliefs about members of the disfavoured group, the discriminator purposefully treats them unfairly. His negative feelings are likely to be expressed in racist or sexist comments. Even if the discriminator does not express these negative feelings, he knows of them and would admit them were he being honest. The kind of prejudice that leads to discrimination functions like a personality trait: it is something that exists inside the discriminator. It is relatively stable and expresses itself consistently over time and across different situations.

[16] See ibid. at 1326. See also A. Lawton, 'The Meritocracy Myth and the Illusion of Equal Employment Opportunity' (2000) 85 *Minnesota Law Review* 587–662 at 651–660.

[17] See Krieger, n. 15 at 1318–1320 on the importance of 'type I' discrimination (unfair treatment of outsiders and fair treatment of insiders) and the irrelevance of 'type II' discrimination (fair, 'by-the-book' treatment of outsiders and more favourable treatment of insiders). See also N. Dasgupta, 'Implicit Ingroup Favouritism, Outgroup Favouritism, and their Behavioural Manifestation' (2004) 14 *Social Justice Research* 143–169 at 162–163. According to Dasgupta, individuals who belong to socially advantaged groups typically exhibit more implicit preference for their in-group and a bias against out-groups than do members of socially disadvantaged groups. From a common sense perspective, this is not truly surprising. This finding reflects the realities of a hierarchical society.

law, as practiced in the US, helps to perpetuate practices of discrimination, as is shown in the recent reluctance of courts to treat word-of-mouth hiring practices as instances of discrimination even if they give rise to the exclusion of certain social groups.[18] Even worse, as biasing mechanisms remain undetected, adjudication is no less affected by inter-group bias than employment practice itself,[19] in particular, since the adversarial process invites presenting the opponent in a form that triggers the application of stereotypical expectations by members of the jury.[20] According to Krieger, the disparate treatment paradigm, applied in its traditionally stereotypical form and with its emphasis on colour-blindness, does not provide a remedial tool but is, indeed, part of the problem:[21]

> In short, from a cognitive process standpoint we cannot expect disparate treatment adjudications to be any less subject to subtle forms of intergroup bias than the decisions which give rise to them.

Furthermore, Krieger is well aware that, as a project, anti-discrimination law is prone to founder because of its embrace of its normative deficiency. Neither the precept of colour-blindness[22] nor the instruction 'not to discriminate' are adequate to the task of eliminating inter-group bias, which, according to Krieger, continues to pass unexamined and unabated precisely when such normative precepts are invoked.[23] Ironically, they have an adverse effect, for their use reconfirms the self-righteous attitude of neutrality, which is likely to reinforce subconscious bias and thus 'to exacerbate inter-group tension'.[24] Differential treatment jurisprudence is a blunt tool that fails to cut deeply into the structure of prejudice prevalent in society. Stereotypes are woven into the social processes we live by.[25] Normative precepts appealing to the good will of a possibly discriminating subject are bound to remain ineffectual.

The lower classes esteem members of the higher classes more than the other way round. It also does not come as a surprise that inter-group preferences are influenced by two different psychological forces: people's tendency to prefer groups associated with themselves as a confirmation of their high self-esteem and the tendency to prefer groups valued by the mainstream culture, which confirms, again, the sociopolitical order of society.

18 Word-of-mouth recruitment practices indirectly perpetuate the exclusion of certain groups if the insiders belong to a homogeneous group. Absent discriminatory intent, courts do not see such practices as violative of Title VII. See Krieger, n. 15 at 1326.

19 Ibid. at 1328, points out correctly that a judge or panel adjudicating how a reasonable employer would have acted in good faith does not bring to bear on the issue a social perspective that would be different from that of an employer.

20 See Krieger, n. 15 at 1327.

21 See ibid. at 1328.

22 See ibid. at 1277, 1285.

23 See Krieger, n. 5 at 1239.

24 Ibid. 1241. Apparently, Armour, n. 1 at 759–761, is more optimistic at this point because she believes that people can be trained in counteracting their automatic responses.

25 They are ingrained, in particular, in the culturally transmitted schemes we use to remove ambiguity from situations by looking at stereotypical factors, such as race. See Krieger, n. 5 at 1200; and Krieger, n. 15 at 1282. For example, European Americans are prone to attribute to male African Americans the dispositional quality to be more likely to engage in violent conduct than they are themselves. Many such attributions are made unconsciously.

4. The Law of Bias

These claims are bolstered, paradoxically, by a social psychology claiming that cognitive bias and stereotyping are *necessarily* concomitant to our entire social existence.[26] Whatever we perceive reaches the level of awareness already tainted with schemes[27] that complement missing information with what has been stored in a socially dispersed memory before.[28] Some of these schemes, if not most, include attribution preferences, which ascribe, for example, good attitudes to members of 'our' group and explain deviant behaviour on their part with reference to external circumstances rather than internal dispositions.[29] Through such schemes, which complement incomplete information and distort our perception of others through attribution preferences, we are socialized into taking for granted a distorted picture of social reality.[30] In particular, stereotypes, qua 'correlation constructs',[31] counterfactually link certain traits with dispositions (e.g., Pole = dishonest, thief). They operate as judgement heuristics for causal attribution and make it likely that responsibility will be attributed to a person rather than to a set of circumstances.[32] Stereotypes instruct people about what one had better expect from a certain type of person. Consequently, stereotypes are notoriously immune to revision in the light of experience. It lies in the nature of stereotypes that people cling to them even when confronted with countervailing evidence. Stereotypes are normatively resistant to learning.[33]

A major point of Krieger's analysis is that causal attribution preferences, peaked characterizations of minorities, and stereotypes affect social perception and judgement at a subconscious level. They cloud our view largely without our awareness and prior to the moment at which we reach a decision.[34] Implicit structures of knowledge influence decision-making profoundly. Krieger thus challenges the assumption that the addressees of anti-discrimination law could ever be thoroughly rational and fully self-aware persons.[35] Nobody can be that kind of person.

[26] See Krieger, n. 5 at 1190, 1198, where she asserts that our human cognitive organization predisposes us to stereotyping. See also B. J. Flagg, '"Was Blind, But Now I See": White Race Consciousness and the Requirement of Discriminatory Intent' (1993) 91 *Michigan Law Review* 953–1017 at 991.

[27] For a more general account of the role of schemes in structuring our interpretation of social reality, see H. Lenk, *Schemaspiele: Über Schemainterpretationen und Interpretationskonstrukte* (Frankfurt: Suhrkamp, 1995).

[28] For example, the more salient a trait is, the more there is a tendency towards polarized evaluations of out-group members. See Krieger, n. 5 at 1194.

[29] See Krieger, n. 5 at 1199–1204. See also P. C. Davis, 'Law as Microaggression' (1989) 98 *Yale Law Journal* 1559–1577.

[30] See ibid. at 1204.

[31] See ibid., 1195.

[32] See ibid., 1206–1207.

[33] See ibid., 1206.

[34] See ibid., 1207, 1209.

[35] See ibid., 1212–1216.

Interestingly, from a sociological perspective,[36] attribution preferences and stereotypes would count, emphatically, as part of the law of a society.[37] The law, accordingly, does not reside in a disembedded norm but in the persistence of expectations that people cling to even in the face of countervailing experience. Therefore, from a sociological point of view, Krieger is completely right in concluding that it would be a futile attempt to alter normative expectations through the issuance of norms. The normativity of such norms resides in their link with expectations that defy revision in singular cases. People experience themselves as socially *entitled* to expect good things from in-group folks and bad things from outsiders.

It should not come as a surprise that anti-discrimination norms, as Krieger observes, become assimilated to existing normative expectations up to the point at which the complacent comfort taken from colour-blindness hides from the view of the decision-makers the sway of cognitive bias.[38] This is, in her opinion, part of the normative fabric of American law. As pointed out above, Krieger leaves no doubt that American anti-discrimination law itself 'suffers' from a 'fundamental attribution error',[39] which is 'pervasive in Anglo-American culture'.[40] It locates the problem of discrimination within the individual decision-maker rather than in the environment in which decision-making is informed by subconscious social perceptions.

5. Changing the Law while Leaving the Market in Place

Krieger's project, therefore, is straightforwardly concerned with changing American law. She is aware, however, that changing the law requires more than, and something different from, the adoption of new rules. Or, more disturbingly, since the democratic process would obviously be infected by cognitive bias, too, there seems to be no democratic way of changing the law.[41]

Ordinarily, one might wonder at this point, whether the medium permitting the social reproduction of stereotypes poses the problem. The market, that is, facilitates interaction among strangers who are highly dependent on the use of abstractions and simplification. The indispensable use of stereotypes in dealing with strangers

[36] See E. Ehrlich, *Grundlegung der Soziologie des Rechts*, first published 1913, 4th edn ed. by M. Rehbinder (Berlin: Duncker & Humblot, 1989); N. Luhmann, *A Sociological Theory of Law*, trans. by E. King and M. Albrow (London: Routledge 1985), at 77–78.

[37] See Davis, n. 29 at 1576; I. F. Haney López, 'Institutional Racism: Judicial Conduct and a New Theory of Racial Discrimination' (2000) 109 *Yale Law Journal* 1717–1884 at 1806–1822.

[38] See Krieger, n. 15 at 1286.

[39] Ibid. at 1204–5 explains, with reference to the work of Fritz Heider, that the attribution error consists in overestimating the impact of stable, dispositional factors over situational factors in the attribution of causes of behaviour.

[40] L. Hamilton Krieger, 'Civil Rights Perestroika: Intergroup Relations after Affirmative Action' (1988) 86 *California Law Review* 1251–1333 at 1329.

[41] This observation about the implicit scepticism regarding democratic participation is confirmed in the most recent writings by Sturm. See Sturm, n. 9 at 329–330, where there is much talk of 'participation', but no mention of voting rights.

exercises, in turn, a homogenizing effect. In order to be able to appeal to the preferences of others or to invite their trust people bend themselves into the shape of stereotypical forms. The successful reproduction of cognitive bias depends on a *systemic* process of social construction where bias reaps reward through reconfirmation. Market participants, to be sure, have to signal to emotionally detached and potentially distrustful strangers that they possess ideal abilities and qualities, such as flexibility, adaptability, discipline, and endurance to work for distant rewards. These and more specific qualities are usually expected by personnel managers, who, consequently, whenever they interview business graduates, deplore the fact that their job applicants all look alike, express similar feelings, and seem to share the same interests and hobbies. The market gives rise to *real* abstractions. It encourages people to turn themselves into the puppets and buffoons they fancy to be in demand.

Insight into the sway that *real* abstractions exercise over people casts light on what might have been the final decommodifying mission of anti-discrimination law. The circle of stereotypization might be broken in an employment environment where people would have to be less afraid about 'not fitting in' and therefore also to resort less to the well-known social techniques of covering and ducking.[42] Such a decommodified setting *cannot* be created through anti-discrimination norms, for it requires the countervailing power of organized labour struggling for the accommodation of *imperfect employees* who are primarily concerned about, say, family, comrades, hobbies, or their sex life rather than business performance.

The neoliberal predicament can be encountered at exactly this point. Nowhere is the market as such put into question by proponents of the 'structural turn' and other members of the 'second generation' of anti-discrimination law. Differential power-relations are not perceived to pose the problem. The victims' contribution to their own oppression is entirely eclipsed. The normative deficit persists. Instead of embracing the road towards empowerment, the theory chooses 'culture' as a preferred target of moral cleansing.[43] Generally, for the second generation of anti-discrimination lawyers, the focus lies on organization and culture but never on the market.[44] It is as though the purity of the market needed to be rescued through 'de-biasing'[45] gullible folks from the corrupting influence of culture.[46] In Krieger's ideally de-biased world, people are apparently individuals, that is, they are who they are independent of the distorting influence of unconscious mental processes.[47] The real force underlying stereotypization is not taken into account.

[42] See I. Goffman, *Stigma: Notes on the Management of Spoiled Identity* (London: Penguin Books, 1990), at 127. K.Yoshino, 'Covering' (2002) 111 *Yale Law Journal* 769–939 at 865.

[43] See, for example, Sturm, n. 9 at 335.

[44] See Sturm, n. 8 at 468.

[45] See Jolls and Sunstein, note 2 at 977.

[46] Jolls and Sunstein, note 2 at 981, 984–985, are of course right in asserting that effective protection from direct discrimination and affirmative action programmes create situations in which, owing to the increase of members of the out-group, implicit bias becomes lessened, too. Mind that empirically the hypothesis did not hold true for Jews in twentieth-century Germany.

[47] It is a hallmark of neoliberal individualism to regard individuality not as a personal achievement but rather as a natural fact.

It is as though stereotypes were moral flaws that one happens to find in nature. Nor is—at any rate, not at a level going beyond instances of race and sex discrimination—the force of the market as a medium of interaction viewed as a problem. On the contrary, it is with Protestant vigour that Krieger and her associates conjure up the image of 'mental correction'[48] as the only tool effective enough to control cognitive bias 'through a careful process of re-engineering'.[49] Awareness-raising of colour and sex is deemed to be central to accomplishing this mission. But it is not all that clear what is implicated in the re-engineering of liberal subjectivity. One or the other clue, to be sure, is to be found in Krieger's writings. Decision-makers would have to be provided with a 'rich body of specific diagnostic information' or required to use 'less generalised, and more specific, preferably objective, criteria'.[50] In addition, in order to assert moral control over stable, subtle, and 'pernicious'[51] inter-group bias, monitoring practices might be instituted in order to make individual agents aware of, and responsible for, their evaluations.

To be sure, Krieger is much more sophisticated than her colleague, Oppenheimer,[52] who marches directly into the moralist trap by calling for a negligence standard of discrimination in order to make the non-self-observing more observant. Krieger perceives the moralism and rejects it.[53] Raising self-awareness does not suffice, for 'few employment decision-makers will perceive their decisions, whether biased or not, as lacking a reasonable, nondiscriminatory justification'.[54]

6. Businesses as Correctional Facilities

A somewhat clearer picture of how an employment anti-discrimination regime might work that would effectively target the influence of unconscious bias has been presented by Sturm.[55] It is in this context that the micro-level equivalent of European equality management can be encountered.

Ironically, in Sturm's proposal, the protection from discrimination emulates the design of a production process that is expected to be pregnant with innovation. The experimentalism of simultaneous or concurrent engineering has already been

[48] See L. Hamilton Krieger, 'Civil Rights Perestroika: Intergroup Relations after Affirmative Action' (1998) 86 *California Law Review* 1251–1333 at 1289. See also Dasgupta, n. 17 at 163.

[49] Krieger, n. 5 at 1216.

[50] Krieger, n. 48 at 1329–1330. See Resnik, n. 14 at 35–36.

[51] Ibid. at 1332.

[52] See D. B. Oppenheimer, 'Negligent Discrimination' (1993) 141 *University of Pennsylvania Law Review* 899–972 at 900.

[53] She also rejects the imposition of punitive damages for unintentional discrimination on the ground that there is a normative difference between unintentional and intentional discrimination. From a normative perspective, cognitive bias and disparate treatment go hand in hand. See Krieger, n. 5 at 1243.

[54] See ibid. at 1245.

[55] See Sturm, n. 8. See, in particular, her more recent work on how gender discrimination is to be avoided in the context of a special National Science Foundation programme. See S. Sturm, 'The Architecture of Inclusion: Advancing Workplace Equity in Higher Education' (2006) 29 *Harvard Journal of Law and Gender* 247–334.

transferred to processes of decentralized regulation by Sable and Cohen in an influential proposal that they introduced under the name of 'democratic experimentalism' and 'directly deliberative polyarchy'.[56] Simplifying a complex idea,[57] the basic thrust of the method is to encourage mutual learning, flexible adaptation of roles through processes of monitoring, benchmark-setting, and benchmark revision.[58] Sturm makes a remarkable effort at bringing these ideas to bear on the development of learning[59] anti-discrimination regimes. They are supposed to address the difficulty that, in order to increase its efficacy, protection from discrimination needs to cut deeply into the organizational structures and institutionalized practices of employment.[60] The core of the proposal consists of initiating self-regulation on the company level and to have only the processes—and not singular cases—monitored by courts.[61] The relevant accountability standards would be created, against the background of general norms, at the employment level and redefined and fine-tuned in processes of mutual learning and experimentation.[62] Workplace structures are the target of self-regulation in a regulatory environment, which is marked by the influx and circulation of expertise. In the words of Sturm:[63]

> 'Legality' emerges from an interactive process of information gathering, problem identification, remediation, and evaluation.

Upon closer inspection, it turns out that the normativity of rules becomes entirely replaced with management methods whose major legitimating factor is the appeal of innovation. In a sense, companies would not just be companies but also laboratories for the improvement of interpersonal dealings or, less euphemistically

[56] See M. C. Dorf and C. F. Sabel, 'A Constitution of Democratic Experimentalism' (1998) 98 *Columbia Law Review* 267–473; J. Cohen and C. S. Sabel, 'Directly-Deliberative Polyarchy' (1997) 3 *European Law Journal* 313–342; O. Gerstenberg and C. F. Sabel, 'Directly-deliberative Polyarchy: An Institutional Ideal for Europe?', in C. Joerges and R. Dehousse (eds), *Good Governance in Europe's Integrated Market* (Oxford: Oxford University Press, 2002), 289–342.

[57] I am using a euphemism for the fact that instead of being offered a description of how that might actually work, the reader not infrequently is fed with management and public administration jargon. See, for example, Sturm, n. 9 at 343:

> The prospect of benefiting from data gathering and monitoring increases the willingness to gather information necessary to identify problems and to share information with NSF. This is in contrast to a compliance framework, where failure prompts increased monitoring or sanctions and thus discourages genuine self-evaluation.

[58] The proximity to the Open Method of Coordination is fairly obvious. See S. Sturm, 'Gender Equality Regimes and the Architecture of Learning', in G. de Búrca and J. Scott (eds), *Law and Governance in the EU and the US* (Oxford: Hart Publishing, 2006), 323–360 at 323.

[59] The learning capacity is taken to be increased in competitive environments. The model is borrowed from the private sector. See Sturm, n. 9 at 327.

[60] See also Green, n. 4 at 145.

[61] See Sturm, n. 8 at 522, 556–564.

[62] See ibid., 560. As is explained by Sturm at 522:

> The structural approach to second generation problems calls for a dynamic and reciprocal relationship between judicially elaborated general legal norms and work-place generated problem-solving approaches, which in turn elaborate and transform the understanding of the general norm.

[63] Ibid. 433.

stated, correctional facilities where everyone is expected to do his creative bit in order to bring about a work organization that promises to strip all thoughts and sentiments of unconscious biases.

7. From Labour to Experts

Bagenstos correctly objects that it is not very reasonable to expect courts to intervene in order to rectify the structure of work organizations. Judges simply are not, and do not conceive of themselves as, management experts.[64] No less problematic, but even more revealing as regards the overall spirit of Sturm's proposal, is the role she accords to 'intermediaries'[65] or, more plainly, to experts who are supposed to assist management in creating a work structure that minimizes the influence of bias.

Sturm introduces their role in the attempt to escape the following dilemma. Judicially applied codes are either too far removed from concrete organizational structures in order to be applied without distortion or too minimal in order to make a difference. Legally enforced systems also invite strategic behaviour by employers, who find themselves discouraged from identifying and correcting problems.[66] By contrast, mere voluntarism is insufficient either, for a complete 'privatization' of responsibility for problem-solving would rob all employment law of its efficacy.

The solution to the problem of how the law can 'shape internal problem-solving processes without taking over the process of defining their features'[67] is seen to lie in increasing the involvement of nongovernmental organizations and professional networks. They are supposed to serve as the intermediaries at the interface of the legal system and business organization. Their intervention would bridge the gap between public and private, legal and non-legal, and coercive and cooperative.[68] Here is how Sturm characterizes these intermediaries:[69]

> These intermediaries are individuals and organisations who do not directly act for the state, but who have the authority to articulate and vindicate legal norms without directly deploying coercive state power. Their participation sets up regular occasions for evaluating and revising day-to-day practices. They are also connected to a broader community of practice that provides some form of accountability for the actions of the intermediary.

Evidently, their participation would be key to the success of the overall regulatory strategy. Intermediaries would draw on their contextual ('local') knowledge and establish linkages with broader pools of professional expertise.[70] Owing to their

[64] See Bagenstos,. 3 at 25.

[65] See Sturm, n. 58 at 325–326. They are called 'norm intermediaries' by Sturm, n. 9 at 329, because they are perceived to be 'carriers of ideas across organizational fields'.

[66] See Sturm, n. 8 at 522–523.

[67] Ibid. at 523.

[68] See ibid. at 524.

[69] Ibid.

[70] What Sturm has in mind here are transnational networks. See the revealing reference to the work of Slaugther in Sturm, n. 9 at 359 n. 87.

connections with professional communities, human resource managers or consultants would exercise sufficient influence on the structuration of the company's occupational framework without having to resort to legal sanctions.[71] Indeed, Sturm envisages them to be the major players in the problem-solving process while courts would be limited to monitoring how they cooperate with employees. Intermediaries would draw on broader information pools in order to develop benchmarks[72] for assessing the performance of specific workplace organizations. The courts would follow suit and use these benchmarks in adjudicating employment practice. Obviously, Sturm envisages this to be a process of guideline *production*:[73]

> This interactive, tiered system provides the infrastructure for identifying patterns within and across particular workplace contexts, earmarking effective problem solving and dispute resolution processes as benchmarks, and elaborating norms that emerge over time through this cumulative process.

Quite remarkably, the 'intermediaries' are expected to take exactly the space that was once occupied by collectively organized labour, precisely because labour always straddled the divide between public and private or cooperation and conflict. Under the auspices of neoliberalism, organized labour no longer exists. If labour were to take the place of those experts, the model would almost read like a socialist blueprint. The decisive influence on the organization of the workplace would lie in the hands of employees. But this is not the case. Despite all emphasis on 'grass-root participation' it is quite evident that the affected employees are perceived as 'outsiders' who are to be given a 'voice' and a little room for participation for the mere reason of 'information gathering'.[74] Members of the workforce communicate, but they do not vote. The decisions are arrived at on a different level. Second-generation anti-discrimination law does not empower. Labour is not at all likely to influence the result. On the contrary, lawyers, consultants, human resource professionals, and equal opportunity officers are not disinclined to accord priority to the interests of the organization and, hence, to 'subsume legal goals under managerial goals'.[75]

[71] See ibid.

[72] Benchmarks are used to attain a higher-than-average level of performance. Only superior performance is adequate. See W. H. Simon, 'Toyota Jurisprudence: Legal Theory and Rolling Rule Regimes', in G. de Búrca and J. Scott (eds), *Law and New Governance in the EU and the US* (Oxford: Hart Publishing, 2006), 37–64 at 49. Ever since antiquity, athleticism has rested on a culture of exaggeration, a celebration of the overload. It plays itself out in the maxim that on average *everyone* is expected to perform *above* the average level. For lucid comments on this paradox of competition, see P. Sloterdijk, *Nicht gerettet: Versuche nach Heidegger* (Frankfurt: Suhrkamp, 2001), 260. There is another paradox of competition that does not have to concern us here, according to which competition as a mode of social ordering can outperform other modes merely on its own terms. Competition is without competition only if competition is taken to be the norm. I owe this observation to Georg Lohmann.

[73] Sturm, n. 9 at 555. The regulation-output orientation is also evident in Simon, n. 72 at 57–59.

[74] See Sturm, n. 9 at 329–330.

[75] Lauren Edelman quoted in Bagenstos, n. 3 at 28.

8. From Law to Pedagogy

The emerging picture is disturbing. Questions of right and participation become transformed into issues of organizational *pedagogy*. The resolution of conflicts is notoriously seen to lie in better communication, more transparency, teamwork, closer bonding, more collegial leadership, or maybe even enrolment in anger management classes.[76] Pedagogicization is the shibboleth of the neoliberal belief in the concordance of labour and business interest. As we have already observed above, it is manifest, not least, in the Commission's newly developed penchant for diversity training programmes.[77]

The complicity of 'second-generation' ideas with neoliberalism can be observed also at a more general level. It is manifest in their preference for production-oriented 'experimentalist' models of regulation. Simultaneous engineering, independent monitoring, and benchmarking have been borrowed from strategies that were originally developed with the aim of enhancing business performance under accelerated and highly competitive conditions. Consequently, they introduce the genius of product flexibilization and customization into the sphere of norms. No longer is the creation of a certain degree of legal formality the objective. The relevant projects are rather enamoured with creating an output of 'rolling rules', that is, standards that are subject to readjustment from one situation to the next.[78] It is unnecessary to explain to whose benefit a 'rolling rule' would work so long as the rule-rolling 'intermediaries' are not representatives of labour. The neoliberal coup is thereby accomplished. Political and legal decision-making becomes 'synchronized' with 'the temporal dynamics of capitalism'.[79] Instead of meeting a defined objective, constant improvement counts as success.[80] This reflects the spirit of the old competitive maxim 'improve or die'.[81]

This particularly striking instance of the neoliberal predicament demonstrates also how attempts to overcome the normative deficit of anti-discrimination law inexorably remain affected by its paradigm. The lack of a normative orientation becomes pronounced in euphemistic terms, such as 'flexibility', 'experimentalism', and 'constant revision'. In them is reflected the world of human practice as

[76] For similarly critical observations, see Bagenstos, n. 3 at 29. On the risk of the cooptation of plaintiff lawyers, see ibid. at 32–34.

[77] See http://ec.europa.eu/employment_social/local_employment/lla/fo/news.do?method=showNewsItem&newsid=1e27113d14cbcab50114d09d53400422&lang=en accessed 23 December 2010.

[78] As has been succinctly observed by Scheuerman, n. 9 at 122: '[T]he traditional idea of the rule of law as requiring stable, general, and relatively clear norms is unceremoniously dumped.' Sturm's reply to this critique is remarkable (n. 9 at 333–334). Aside from bemoaning the lack of enthusiasm and mobility at the lower level (surprise?), she perceives the solution to lie in more research.

[79] Ibid. at 127.

[80] See Sturm, n. 8 at 560: 'Employers who are continually improving are in compliance.' See Simon, n. 72 at 57.

[81] R. Bork, *The Antitrust Paradox: A Policy at War with itself*, 2nd edn (New York: Free Press, 1993), at 95.

envisaged by the 'beautiful soul'. This type of moral consciousness is unable to determine what it takes to live up to a normative commitment in a singular case out of fear that the purity of the ideal becomes corrupted in the process of its realization. Its prevalence explains the excitement about permanent transformation, which serves as the equivalent of inaction; more precisely, it is the symbolic reconciliation of the fanatical activist[82] and the inactive bystander.

The normative deficiency of anti-discrimination law not only persists, but it becomes even more pronounced. It is not sufficient to demand from employers that they adopt 'reasonable' or 'adequate' structures for the protection from discrimination.[83] It ought to be known what it is that such structures are designed to protect. Rolling rules, I am afraid, are not part of the answer.

9. Ecstatic Self-observation

The extension of the normative deficit of anti-discrimination law to the efforts to overcome it are not only to be observed in the case of Sturm's remarkable proposal to supersede traditional legality with managerial expertise. It is also manifest on the 'ground floor', as it were, of cognitive bias theory.

Cognitive bias theory inherits from 'first-generation' anti-discrimination law the inscrutability of intent in modified form. Inscrutable intent is superseded with inscrutable bias. This matter is spelled out, with no reservation, by Krieger.[84] She admits readily that there is no way for an evaluating person to determine how much of her assessment of another person is attributable to cognitive bias. The submission leaves open, to be sure, whether a consortium of psychological experts would be able to arrive at a reasonably objective conclusion.[85] Krieger submits also that discrimination is rooted in subconscious inter-group attitudes which cannot be identified as if they were manifestations of an individual predilection for discrimination. According to Krieger, discrimination results from complex

[82] See Sturm, n. 9 at 329:

> New governance methods involve high energy, resource intensive, and sustained attention. Effective problem solving requires the capacity to determine the impact of current practices on affected individuals, and continually to renew the commitment to addressing those problems.

[83] See Bagenstos, n. 3 at 35:

> Unless we have an operating theory of what is wrongful about discrimination, we cannot know what kinds of 'second generation' conduct—decisionmaking actuated by unconscious bias, harassment, unequal distribution of favourable work assignments and so forth—should count as unlawful or improper discrimination. Without such a theory, courts have no ground on which to stand in assessing whether employers have done enough to mitigate the operation and effect of impermissible discrimination within their workplaces.

[84] See Krieger, n. 15 at 1290.

[85] What is more, the little effect that Krieger attributes to isolated disparate treatment litigation is another major reason why the solution for her problems would have to embrace an approach that puts indirect discrimination first. See ibid. at 1304.

cognitive processes that exhibit inter-group bias not consistently but randomly and intermittently. Strangely enough, against this background Krieger admits that '[w]e might not even be able to identify when discrimination has occurred'.[86] She goes on to explain that it is not to be expected that systems with cognitive bias give rise to consistent or statistically traceable patterns of 'outgroup discrimination'.[87]

This is an odd move. If unconscious animus cannot be observed easily, one would ordinarily consider 'substantial disparities in distribution' to be decisive in order to establish discrimination. Yet, caught in the predicament, Krieger deontologizes the notion of discrimination in order to identify a *transpersonal, collective force* that has all the qualities of aversion without being a manifestation of individual attitude. Part of the task of a new anti-discrimination law would be to 'enhance decision maker's awareness, motivation and control'[88] of this force.

The low expectation that Krieger has with regard to the observation of statistical patterns is consistent with her rejection of indirect discrimination (or 'disparate impact') as the foundational category.[89] She rests her hope on some modified form of disparate treatment analysis.[90] Her approach is supposed to uncover how meritocratic criteria can be affected by in-group preferences, for example, in the mode of weighing certain elements of successful job performance.[91] People tend to overvalue what they and their peers can do themselves or are likely to attribute failures to external circumstances rather than to stable dispositions.[92] But all these valuable insights do not remove from her analysis the basic normative deficiency. When is group bias unjustified? What if a preference for certain job performance

[86] See Krieger, n. 48 at 1313.

[87] Ibid.

[88] Bagenstos, n. 3 at 10. See Armour, n. 1 at 759–772; I. V. Blair, 'The Malleability of Automatic Stereotypes and Prejudice' (2002) 6 *Personality and Social Psychology Review* 242–261 at 255–256.

[89] At certain points, however, she appears to be willing to relativize this stance, for example, where she acknowledges that disparate impact cases could also result from 'in-group preferences'. See Krieger, n. 5 at 1244. See also n. 15 at 1308, 1332, where she praises disparate impact jurisprudence and affirmative action for providing more effective tools of combating discrimination.

[90] For a sceptical discussion of the practical implications, see C. A. Sullivan, 'Disparate Impact: Looking Past the Desert Place Mirage' (2005) 47 *William and Mary Law Review* 911–1002 at 951:

> [E]xperts will not only need to remind or convince the fact-finder that discrimination is still prevalent, but will also need to educate the fact-finder that social science research suggests that all of us—judges and jurors included—may be biased without knowing it. If Professor Green's theory is adopted, experts will also have to testify about how such biases are enabled by workplace structures and that this is likely to happen without manifesting itself in any particular employment decision. Without such testimony, a jury might erroneously believe that a woman and/or minority would not be more likely than their white male counterparts to be disadvantaged in a particular employment context. Without such proof, the sufficient evidence test may result in outcomes as bad as or worse than those decried under the McDonnell Douglas proof structure. One may be skeptical about the success of this enterprise on its own terms. Convincing a jury that everyone, including themselves, is prejudiced does not seem psychologically plausible in light of the deep commitment to egalitarian values that our society now embraces. But, even putting this foundational objection aside, the use of experts has its problems.

Expertise, it is explained further, may give rise to considerable hostility.

[91] See Krieger, n. 48 at 1299.

[92] See ibid. at 1295.

criteria expresses a certain cultural ideal? Imagine that only genteel British English is to be spoken by employees in a certain American department store. This would send out a message of sophistication, no doubt to the detriment of potential American employees. What would be invidious about a preference for British English, given that nowadays shopping is no longer about the acquisition of products but about creating a 'good experience' for customers? Krieger has no way of telling whether or not unlawful bias is in play, for she would have to admit that if running a department store with a British flair is not unreasonable then command of British English would be meritorious, even though British applicants are more likely to speak with the preferred intonation than African Americans who grew up in Detroit.

Krieger actually concedes that merit, far from being a neutral construct, is not free of 'inter-group' bias.[93] If that is, from a dialectical perspective, not an unsurprising result of her analysis, one begins to wonder what it is that becomes distorted, neutralized, or ignored owing to the interference of cognitive bias. If everything is biased, nothing is. Her analysis presupposes a merit-based norm that cannot be formulated unless one changes the perspective and endorses the cognitive bias of another group. The normative deficit makes itself felt again. I attribute (yes!) Krieger's reluctance to embrace a fully distributive perspective—according to which, by the way, the hypothetical example above would be resolved in favour of the fellows from Detroit—to the neoliberal predicament. Her analysis is spellbound by the quest for a morally and culturally purified market that promises to be cleansed of pernicious inter-group condescension.[94]

The sheer moralism of the ideal must strike one as peculiar. It is a very strange idea to ask people to abstain from disliking you. It is enough to demand that one not suffer any disadvantage. Remove the effect and the cause becomes irrelevant.[95]

10. Conclusion

The final truth about anti-discrimination law comes to the fore in the neoliberal predicament, which is manifest in attempts to defeat the normative deficiency without transcending the pre-normative horizon. Some such attempts identify

[93] See ibid. at 1302.

[94] Or maybe she would state the objective more modestly by saying that it is about diminishing the salience of inter-group distinctions based on race, sex, national origin, and religion. See Krieger, n. 22, at 1331, 1333. She reminds the reader of Bosnia and other instances of ethnic strife. I do not want to attribute to her the belief that anti-discrimination law could in fact be a means of overcoming division.

[95] In a similar vein, R. M. Unger, *What should Legal Analysis become?* (London: Verso 1996), at 95, observed:

> Prejudices about race and nationality, gender and sexual orientation, age and infirmity are not fictions; but they become immensely more potent when bound up with the institutionally based realities of economic and educational disadvantage, or social organisation and political demobilisation.

themselves, self-confidently, as the 'second generation' of anti-discrimination scholarship.

The approach of the second generation is based on the assumption that discrimination arises and exists as the result of the unconscious operation of biases against groups. Biases are a structural feature of social life. They do not originate in the minds of discriminators. Rather, individuals are socialized into relying on stereotypes and prejudice in their dealings with others.

The second generation seeks to entrust problem-solving not to general legislation, but to various management strategies for the improvement of relations among employees and to the administration of diversity training. Nowhere is the market seen as a source of the problem. Nowhere does organized labour enter the picture. The purity of the market economy remains unchallenged.

The persistence and aggravation of the normative deficiency is revealed in the inability on the part of second-generation scholarship to sketch out what unbiased and morally unadulterated dealings would amount to. The world without discrimination turns out to be an unpopulated utopia. The lack of a firm normative orientation is concealed in an exasperating praise of experimentalism and permanent revision.

The convergence with macro-level policy-learning processes, which were studied in Chapter 2, could not be more obvious. The second generation recommends moving from legislation to the management of permanent improvement and from compliance with norms to practical training.

The analysis has come to a full circle. The adoption of new governance strategies by anti-discrimination policy is the practical expression of a deep-seated normative deficiency. Their prevalence reveals the true significance of anti-discrimination law.

8

Beyond Inclusion

1. Introduction

The neoliberal predicament exposes the truth about anti-discrimination law. As a medium of social policy, it is powerless. Or, more adequately put, it stands for social policy in the state of disempowerment.

Anti-discrimination law's normative deficiency is both latent and manifest in moral intuitionism and casuistry. It remains latent, for the absence of distributive patterns and the inscrutability of pre-normative intent do not become salient so long as brave dispensations of moral judgements routinely generate streams of precedent that do not prejudice results. It is manifest, nonetheless, in the instability of the conceptual determinations, which were the subject of previous chapters.

The neoliberal predicament is, however, true to the distributive dimension of anti-discrimination law. It even lends it additional credence. It does so in a manner that reconfirms the importance of pre-normative intentionality. The second generation of anti-discrimination law wishes to bring so-called structural bias into focus. Quite remarkably, the very notion of structural bias embraces a synthesis of indirect and direct discrimination that tacitly accords priority to the former. The distributive perspective is thereby asserted. But it is introduced in a manner that entrenches the pre-normative point of view. Structural bias stands for the universal (unconscious) presence of bad attitudes. It is subjective in that it leaves a trace in individual reasoning processes; but it is supposed to be objective, too, for its influence is beyond individual control. It is in this manner that cognitive bias theory arrives at a formulation of indirect indirect discrimination.

Perspicuous by its absence, nonetheless, is the norm that would declare doing x to be tantamount to discrimination on the grounds of y. Rather, the normative deficiency persists in the form of managerial euphemisms as to how the influence of pervasive bias might be mitigated through the moral re-engineering of individual minds. The world of capitalism is to be given a moral makeover. Experimentalism is expected to do the trick. The alleged omnipresence of bias makes it impossible to imagine, though, what the morally purified social universe envisaged by the second generation of anti-discrimination law would look like. All that the would-be vanguard of anti-discrimination law does is to add another layer of employee observation. One must be disinclined to speak of progress here.

The following concluding observations begin with a very cursory sketch of a category that has over the years attained quite some prominence in anti-discrimination law. This category is accommodation.

It will be argued that accommodation requirements do not represent one more element in the deontological toolbox of anti-discrimination law but rather the law's very own means of drawing out its innermost aspiration. In principle, the embrace of accommodation reverses the deontological inversion of anti-discrimination law. The result of the double negation is not a mere affirmation of the distributive dimension but rather its transcendence into a broader agenda.

Not surprisingly, the limited personal scope of accommodation requirements is difficult to defend. With the recognition of accommodation, the emphasis of protection from discrimination shifts from conduct and distribution towards decommodification. Creating the conditions of a relatively more decommodified life presupposes the full range of social policy strategies whose capabilities have been impaired in Europe in the course of the ascendancy of anti-discrimination law.

Hence, one is bound to conclude, using old-fashioned philosophical language, that European anti-discrimination law is a self-contradictory project. It has deposed exactly that full-blown social policy which would be required for its own realization. Anti-discrimination law is social policy in the state of its disempowerment by competitiveness.

2. Accommodation

As a legal concept, 'accommodation' first appeared in the Americans with Disability Act.[1] It requires employers to make reasonable efforts in order to facilitate employment of persons with disabilities.[2] Similarly, Article 5 of Directive 2000/78/EC states that 'employers shall take appropriate measures, where needed in a particular case, to enable a person with a disability to have access to, participate in, or advance in employment, or to undergo training, unless such measures would impose a disproportionate burden on the employer'.[3] The inbuilt proportionality requirement with regard to what distributive agents may legitimately be expected to do indicates at least a family resemblance with anti-discrimination law.

[1] See para. 12111(9) and para. 12112(5A) of the Americans with Disabilities Act of 1990 (the ADA), 42 U.S.C. para. 12101 *et seq.* It needs to be said that in European labour legislation accommodation requirements date back to the nineteenth century. See L. Waddinton and A. Hendriks, 'The Expanding Concept of Employment Discrimination in Europe: From Direct and Indirect Discrimination to Reasonable Accommodation Discrimination' (2002) 18 *International Journal of Comparative Labour Law and Industrial Relations* 403–427 at 417–420.

[2] In fact, the failure to provide reasonable accommodation is part of what constitutes 'discrimination' according to para.12112(5A) of the ADA. The notion of 'disability' is defined in para. 12102(2) to mean a physical or mental impairment that substantially limits one or more of the major life activities of an individual, a record of such an impairment or being regarded as having such an impairment.

[3] It is understood by the ECJ that, in order to benefit from accommodation requirements, the disabled person must be capable of performing the essential functions of a post. See Case C-13/05, *Sonia Chacón Navas* v. *Eurest Colectividades SA* [2006] ECR I-6467, para. 49.

Nonetheless, it has been disputed, in the context of American anti-discrimination law, that accommodation requirements are part of anti-discrimination law.[4] In the resulting debate, the reasons why accommodation is, indeed, part of the universe of anti-discrimination law have been thrown into sharp relief.[5]

Clearly, protection from discrimination and accommodation serve the purpose of creating equal opportunity through market access.[6] They remove obstacles that arise because society has not done enough to ensure the participation of all.[7] Indeed, it is unconvincing to maintain that the root of the difference between anti-discrimination law and accommodation lies in the distinction between acts and omission. It is not true that abiding by anti-discrimination norms *merely* requires employers to abstain from certain acts. Compliance with anti-discrimination norms presupposes awareness of race, gender, or nationality disadvantage that might result from stereotyping and entrenched hiring practices.[8] The equivalence is clearly demonstrated in the case of a pregnant woman who (having become pregnant during her parental leave) wanted to return earlier from her parental leave. In order to avoid discrimination on the grounds of sex, the employer had to accommodate her even though she could not even work in her former capacity owing to her new pregnancy.[9]

The difference between accommodation and discrimination does not reside in the nature of conduct either. Both discrimination and failure to accommodate are most often instances of rational conduct. As Jolls explains:[10]

> Prohibitions on discrimination based upon customer or co-worker attitudes or upon correct employer beliefs about a particular group impose financial costs on employers, much as do accommodation requirements.

Moreover, charges that accommodation has been denied fit the very same deontological mould that is relevant to impute differential treatment to a discriminating subject, such as latent animus (aversion of disabled people), selective sympathy, or the reinforcement of systemic effects that give rise to 'self-excluding' behaviour on the part of the victim.[11] In particular, an employer's failure to accommodate may rest on a failure to appreciate the degree to which the accommodation of disabled

[4] See, most prominently, M. Kelman, 'Market Discrimination and Groups' (2001) 53 *Stanford Law Review* 833–896 at 837, 840, 892.

[5] See, in particular, C. Jolls, 'Anti-discrimination and Accommodation' (2001) 115 *Harvard Law Review* 642–699; S. R. Bagenstos, '"Rational Discrimination", Accommodation, and the Politics of (Disability) Civil Rights' (2003) 89 *Virginia Law Review* 825–923. See also S. R. Bagenstos, 'The Future of Disability Law' (2004) 114 *Yale Law Journal* 1–82 at 9.

[6] See Jolls, n. 5 at 696.

[7] Or, as Bagenstos would have it, accommodation requirements do not redistribute, they restore a just distribution. See Bagenstos, n. 5 at 862.

[8] See D. A. Strauss, 'The Myth of Colorblindness' (1986) 99 *Supreme Court Review* 99–134, at 111–114.

[9] See See Case C-320/01, *Wiebke Busch* v. *Klinikum Neustadt GmbH & Co. Betriebs-KG* [2003] ECR I-2041, paras 39, 41, 44.

[10] Jolls, n. 5 at 685–686.

[11] See Bagenstos, n. 5 at 867–868; 'The Future of Disability Law' (note 5) at 51–53.

persons is barely more expensive than accommodations made for non-disabled members of the workforce.[12]

Finally, it cannot be denied that protections from indirect discrimination (disparate impact) are functionally equivalent to accommodation demands.[13] A few examples, taken from Jolls,[14] may illustrate the point. Some US courts have held that employer policies that limit or deny leave time have an unlawful disparate impact on female employees. In effect, such judicial findings impose an accommodation requirement because even an unpaid pregnancy leave gives rise to real costs for employers. Ostensibly neutral job-selection criteria that disproportionately disadvantage a particular group may create disparate impact liability. Avoiding such liability would in turn require accommodations that benefit the affected group. Forcing an employer to eliminate an English-only policy, the employer may face additional costs resulting from poor workplace morale. Avoiding disparate impact liability may thus effectively be more demanding than fulfilling accommodation requirements, for it could affect adversely the productivity of the workforce.

Jolls observes correctly that disparate impact protection not only challenges the way in which candidates are selected for jobs, but also challenges the way in which jobs are defined or structured. In this respect, it resembles the 1990 Americans with Disabilities Act's (ADA) 'reasonable accommodations' provision.[15] Jolls argues convincingly that the distinction between selection procedures, on the one hand, and elements of the job, on the other, which has been invoked by some commentators in order to sustain the distinction between anti-discrimination and accommodation,[16] is untenable because the job-selection criteria will presumably continue to be relevant for assessing the employee's performance on the job.[17]

3. Unpacking the Meaning of Discrimination

One may wonder why accommodation requirements should merit special attention if what they amount to is but an application of the normative principle underlying anti-discrimination law in the first place. Indeed, they are not different, but special, for they reflect the law's own way of drawing out what it means to give adequate effect to this principle.

It bears emphasis, once more, that the twist inherent in anti-discrimination law's deontological realization gives rise to a flawed paradigmatic image of its point. The

[12] See ibid., 868.

[13] See also the discussion in Waddington and Hendriks, n. 1 at 424–425.

[14] On the following, see Jolls, n. 5 at 656–661.

[15] See ibid. at 669.

[16] It has been argued that while anti-discrimination rules are restricted to job selection criteria, accommodation requirements extend to the job definition itself. See P. S. Karlan and G. Rutherglen, 'Disabilities, Discrimination, and Reasonable Accommodation' (1996) 46 *Duke Law Journal* 1–41 at 9; S. Issacharoff and J. Nelson, 'Discrimination with a Difference: Can Employment Discrimination Law Accommodate the Americans with Disabilities Act?' (2001) 79 *North Carolina Law Review* 307–358 at 315.

[17] See Jolls, n. 5 at 670.

victim is supposedly identifiable on the basis of certain traits, such as sex or complexion. The discriminator aims at the victim as though it were a given target. This is a caricature of how the world where discrimination happens works. Usually, people experience situations of unequal treatment as situations that they cannot alter. Therefore, they decide to adapt. They may undertake efforts to pass as members of the preferred group (in the twentieth century, for example, by joining a political party) or cover up aspects of themselves which they fear to be stigmatizing (for example, religious beliefs). This is part of what it takes to engage in socially intelligent behaviour. The existence of intelligent behaviour explains why even societies that officially pride themselves in embracing 'diversity' may at the same time espouse a depressingly extreme level of uniformity. As an aggregate social phenomenon, discrimination against groups would not persist if it were not for the adaptive participation by its victims. Group members either adapt to unequal opportunities (for example, they try to pass as someone else) or decide to drop out of the 'race' and remain in their lower social station.

Not all are happy. A few do complain. Some experience extreme hardship and decide to revolt against the unequal allocation of the pains of adaptation. The question arises then—sometimes as a question concerning 'responsibility'—of who has to come towards whom. Do the structures of social cooperation have to reach out to those left behind or does it fall on the latter to 'improve'? Exemplifications of the problem abound.[18] Women who find themselves relatively disadvantaged when working in part-time jobs or when ineligible for higher termination payments would have had a choice not to procreate and not to assume caregiving responsibilities;[19] alternatively, they could have fitted their lives into the existing organization of full-time employment and delegated much of their maternal labour to nannies and maids; or women could have even tried to improve their performance as both professionals and caregivers. It is understood, of course, by anti-discrimination law that any of these alternatives would ask too much from women because it is reasonable to expect from employers to treat part-time and full-time employees alike. Migrant workers who struggle with language proficiency could have been expected, firstly, to stay at home or, secondly, to acquire a sufficiently high level of verbal communication skills so that their articulation problems would have lost salience. Again, allowing people to work in jobs where perfect language skills are unnecessary (e.g., as accountants or code writers) is a manner of accepting them as who they are. No improvements are necessary. Their way of being in the world is to be accommodated by this world.

These examples, facile as they may seem, demonstrate how protection from discrimination lifts from persons pressures of adaptation. These pressures range from ordinary learning and ducking all the way down to retreating from the scene

[18] For an intriguing discussion from a feminist perspective, see J. Williams, 'Gender Wars: Selfless Women in the Republic of Choice' (1991) 66 *New York University Law Review* 1546–1634.

[19] This is the message sent out by the ECJ in Case C-220/02, *Österreichischer Gewerkschaftsbund, Gewerkschaft der Privatangestellten* v. *Wirtschaftskammer Österreich* [2004] ECR I-5907, paras 46, 60. For purposes of equal treatment, it is not considered to be comparable to the fulfilment of the civic obligation of compulsory military service (ibid. at 64).

owing to the denial of opportunities. Whereas in the latter, most drastic, case the threat is one of exclusion, cases that concern passing or hiding involve the damage that market-based inclusion itself inflicts on human life.

Even most narrowly understood, protection from discrimination is about counteracting pressures of adaptation. If protection from discrimination on the grounds of nationality merely demanded that applications originating from a foreign country be reasonably considered it would still mean that foreigners do not have to travel in order to have a chance. Even though it may not be necessary to refer to one particular case for the sake of illustration, the *Coleman* case helps to explain why protection from discrimination without accommodation is empty.[20] While the ECJ extended protection from disability discrimination to a person who, without being disabled herself, is burdened with taking care of a disabled child, it withheld from that same person the benefit of accommodation of her special situation. The protection from discrimination was thereby rendered nugatory.[21]

Counteracting pressures of adaptation is the labour of decommodification. This focus on decommodification potentially reverses the normative twist of anti-discrimination law. The distributive perspective comes to the fore, however, still in a normatively deficient form and, hence, not patterned. But from the perspective of decommodification, the weakness can be turned into strength, for the question becomes what businesses may legitimately expect from people given whatever else is important to their life. Unlike mere distributive issues, this question cannot, not even on a philosophical level, be answered theoretically. It is a matter of political struggle whether and how forms of life assert themselves vis-à-vis the iron cage of capitalist rationality. Answers to this question are to be found in the full array of social policy, for there cannot be one single piece of legislation that would be capable of accomplishing this task. It requires, rather a *systematic effort* that is the response to, and actually part of, a form of life.

Accommodation, hence, marks the limit at which anti-discrimination law dialectically—i.e., through self-negation—reaches out beyond itself. The relation between the redistributive perspective and decommodification alters. The latter takes precedence over the former. The normative horizon of inclusive access to resources and opportunities is transcended in favour of a broader objective. Social policy becomes responsive to experiences of commodification and alienation. Whereas the former refers to life's dependence on the market nexus, the latter points to the resulting lack of self-realization and autonomy.[22] Not only are the lives that businesses prepare for people not truly wanted by them (think of the life of a check-out person), in many instances these lives are experienced as impossible to live, or only possible when lived in self-denial.

[20] See Case C-303/06, *S. Coleman* v. *Attridge Law and Steve Law* [2008] ECR I-5603.

[21] See ibid., para. 42.

[22] Deliberately, I abstain at this point to come up with a more sophisticated conception of alienation. For both elements mentioned in the text, see J. Elster, *An Introduction to Karl Marx* (Cambridge: Cambridge University Press, 1986), at 43–54.

This is the ill that should have been the target of anti-discrimination law had it been capable of its own realization.

4. The Persistence of the Deontological Perspective

Accommodation makes peoples' lives more independent from market forces. With the embrace of accommodation, unresolved distributive questions are thrown into sharper relief. This is evident, in particular, in the field of disability law where the question presents itself, repeatedly, of why employers—and not taxpayers at large—need to bear the costs for reversing the general ill of excluding people with disability from participation in society.[23] Remarkably, but not surprisingly, when judges are confronted with cumbersome distributive choices, existing accommodation requirements often become narrowly construed and assimilated into the deontological mindset of 'twisted' anti-discrimination law.

This matter has been beautifully demonstrated, for American law, by Bagenstos.[24] For example, the restriction of the scope of accommodation to 'job-related' adjustments is an attempt to respond to the challenge that it is far from intuitively clear to what extent an employer ought to invest disabled persons with the resources and equipment necessary to be a capable employee. Ironically, when confronted with this difficulty, courts seek refuge in assimilating accommodation to the deontological perspective of direct discrimination. Intuitively, it may seem evident that an employer failed to provide the necessary accommodations when his business establishment does not boast a wheelchair ramp. Such an omission smacks of ignoring people with disabilities. Intuition fails to do its work, however, where doubts remain as to whether the employer should also make efforts to facilitate or to enhance the employee's overall mobility. Employers would discriminate if they did not extend a benefit to a disabled person; the case would be different, though, if they did not modify the system of benefits such as to fit a disabled person's needs. Evidently, at the point at which anti-discrimination law has to prove its effectiveness it cannot embrace any distributive principles because it is devoid of a normative vision. In fact, the normative twist carries over into the understanding of accommodation. As Bagenstos explains:[25]

> So long as courts interpreting the accommodation requirement feel compelled to focus on the fault of individual employers, as opposed to that of society as a whole, that requirement will lack significant power to undo the deep-rooted structural barriers to employment for people with disabilities.

Moreover, the tenacity of the deontological comes to the fore in other line-drawing conundrums. Accommodation concerns all protected groups equally. Therefore,

[23] The question is all the more plausible that it is simply a matter of bad luck from the perspective of the employer to have a disabled person among the applicants for whom she needs to implement an accommodation. See Bagenstos, n. 5 at 52.

[24] See ibid., pp. 50–53.

[25] Ibid., p. 54.

the ominous question why this group rather than that group partakes of protection recurs vis-á-vis accommodation requirements. It is difficult to imagine a sound justification, for if accommodation is the revealed truth of protection from discrimination it is inconsistent to concede it only to one special group.

Kelman perceives the justification for drawing a line between disabled and less qualified persons in the goal of inclusion.[26] In his opinion, any alternative to accommodation would intolerably perpetuate 'social segregation' or 'widespread separation' of disabled persons as a group.[27] It is not clear, however, in which respect, as a social ill, segregation is so much more severe in the case of disability than in cases of the deprivation suffered by an underclass[28] or when it comes to those left out by a system of educational apartheid.[29] Apparently, a tacit appeal to the bad attitude manifest in the aversion of disabled persons is at work here.

When the deontological perspective becomes suspended the broad sweep of accommodation comes to encompass potentially all impediments to participation in markets that unduly compromise the integrity of one's life. Illness is an obvious case in point. From illness it is only a small step to respecting temper and moods or the fact that some people cannot but care about their families and friends or have a strong preference for living in a non-competitive work environment.[30] There are no a priori reasons for drawing the line at one point or another.[31] Kelman correctly observes that a person with a temporal illness or a strong preference for leading a family life is likely to be confronted with either dismissal or the urgent need to sacrifice leisure.[32] He also perceives clearly why the focus of accommodation, as practiced in disability law, is limited, for it does not include situations like these. Neither the frequently temporarily ill nor those who are more extensively occupied with their private life count for these reasons as 'disabled' from working in more prestigious or financially rewarding positions. They are ineligible for accommodation because they are not confronted with the type of long-term exclusion to be expected by those 'who are identified with social groups that are ordinarily excluded from the market realm, or are especially stigmatised when they see new instances of that historical exclusion'.[33] This difference begs the question. In an age

[26] On the distinctiveness of inclusion as a value in contrast to equality of opportunity and diversity, see H. Collins, 'Social Inclusion: A Better Approach to Equality Issues' (2005) 14 *Transnational Law and Contemporary Problems* 897–918 at 914.

[27] Kelman (n. 4 at 889) is consistent at this point and acknowledges that even those who are unquestionably disabled in a medical sense may not be entitled to benefit from accommodation law 'if they can avoid segregated status without accommodation.'

[28] See, for example, W. J. Wilson, *The Truly Disadvantaged: The Inner City, the Underclass, and Public Policy* (Chicago, IL: University of Chicago Press, 1987).

[29] Interestingly, the allocation of accommodation costs is taken by Kelman to be relevant to accommodation only if letting the employee pay would be experienced as a socially stigmatizing act (ibid., 888), from which ultimately follows that Kelman's is a recognition-based and not a distribution-based account of anti-discrimination.

[30] On the following see also P. Smith, 'Parental-status Employment Discrimination: A Wrong in Need of a Right?' (2002) 35 *University of Michigan Journal of Law Reform* 569–621.

[31] Taking commonsense judgements of individual responsibly into account as part of a hypothetical insurance scheme against impediments to social participation does not alter the fact that commonsensical responsibility judgements are unfounded. This is ignored by Dworkin.

[32] See Kelman, n. 4 at 889.

[33] Ibid. at 890.

where constant self-improvement and sycophancy are crucial to sustaining long-term employability it is difficult to argue awarding full protection to merely one group among many.[34] Kelman, indeed, is victim to a dogma of established equality law, which has been termed by Joshino the 'visibility' presumption.[35] This means that only those are eligible for protection from discrimination who belong to a socially highly perceptible group. It is a classical aberration involved in the deontological realization of anti-discrimination law.

5. Coda: the Wrong of Discrimination

I argued above (see p. 182) that recognizing the role of accommodation marks a shift from the distributive towards the decommodifying dimension of anti-discrimination law. The normative deficiency of the former is carried over into the latter. This is not disconcerting, for decommodification introduces a broader agenda that implicates a much wider array of social policy instruments than a piece of anti-discrimination legislation, let alone the administration of diversity training, would suggest. With the endorsement of accommodation, anti-discrimination law recognizes its limit. Even though internally inclining towards decommodification, protection from discrimination alone ultimately remains unable to achieve it.

Nonetheless, recognizing accommodation as indispensible for the realization of anti-discrimination law potentially reverses the deontological twist and *fully* reveals why discrimination is wrong.[36] In the case of people with disabilities this is obvious. By comparison with others, they would be expected either to make heavy investments in order to secure their capability to participate in social life or, if that were not possible, to continue to hide from society. The matter might appear less evident in cases that are falsely assumed to be the paradigmatic cases of discrimination, such as the firing of a person on the grounds of a sex change. But even in that type of case, it is clear that it would have been wrong to expect of a person who experiences the necessity to undergo a sex change to adapt to the employer's preferences. Anti-discrimination law protects, where an inequality arises, the most fundamental interest of people to stay who they are within society, even if that society is strongly inclined to force them into self-denial or to send them away.

Answers to the question under what circumstances it is wrong to force people into self-denial or to send them away are far from self-evident.

We expect those who are neither European citizens nor their dependents to apply for residence and work permits in order to be able to work in the Union. We sense that this is not unreasonable because we believe that, within limits, societies

[34] See Smith, n. 30.

[35] See K. Yoshino, 'The Assimilationist Bias in Equal Protection: The Visibility Presumption and the Case of "Don't Ask, Don't Tell"' (1998) 108 *Yale Law Journal* 485–571 at 496–497.

[36] On the following, see the discussion of three types of discrimination in A. Somek, *Rationalität und Diskriminierung: Zur Bindung der Gesetzgebung an das Gleichheitsrecht* (Vienna/New York, 2001), at 380–385. This perspective is often ignored in human rights law. I fully agree with Yoshino, on that point. See K. Yoshino, 'Covering' (2002) 111 *Yale Law Journal* 769–939.

are free to regulate membership. Of course, it is morally wrong to put people down because of their skin colour. If no further disadvantage follows from demeaning behaviour we are inclined to call the conduct insulting, but not discriminatory. But usually, victims of racism have no jobs and if they have jobs these jobs do not pay well. Again, the wrong of discrimination becomes fully exposed by asking what they would have to do in order to avoid disadvantage. In the worst case, it would imply withdrawing from social cooperation and finding another place where they are likely to fit in. Owing to stereotypes, people are not perceived as who they are but given the appearance that social standards expect these people to have. People feel constrained to show certain aspects of themselves and to hide others. Whoever benefits from adaptation to stereotypes may have bartered freedom for equal participation. In the worst instances of discrimination people are treated as though they were inexistent. They are alienated from society in the most elementary and also most brutal sense of the term.[37]

But in many cases the answers to the question whether adaptation presupposes self-denial will require public debate and political choice. For example, no judicial philosophy will be able to answer the question how much discipline and sacrifice may be legitimately expected from people in order to mitigate the impact of poor upbringing. Moreover, a variety of social and educational policy measures would be necessary to address the issue. Protection from discrimination is not adequate to this task.

6. Solidarity

Finally, we are once more confronted with the irremediable perplexity of anti-discrimination norms (see above p. 136). The recognition of discrimination presupposes self-assertion by the victims while the very existence of laws protecting from discrimination suggests that these victims lack the power to do so. This perplexity is re-confirmed by the fact that self-denial is the cure sought by the powerless against unequal treatment. Self-denial is the strategy with which the weak react to oppression. They try not to be a target. They go away and try their luck elsewhere.

Weakness is never a mere individual occurrence. Just as systemic discrimination is never the product of merely one agent, discrimination against individuals would not remain uncontested if the victim's peer did not enlist to their own oppression. Discrimination is a problem for members of 'groups' whose fellow members either do not fight for their interests or fail to realize that they have any.

The true remedy for individual disempowerment is a principle that has been forgotten by anti-discrimination law. It perceives the mutual support among and across groups as key to the realization of an autonomous life. Hence, even though it is difficult to imagine the distributive principle that would remove from

[37] For a brief reconstruction of discrimination from this perspective, see A. Somek, 'A Constitution for Anti-discrimination: Exploring the Vanguard Moment of Community Law' (1999) 5 *European Law Journal* 243–271.

anti-discrimination law its normative deficiency, it is not impossible to sketch the spirit that would animate more decommodified social arrangements. I surmise that they would espouse solidarity qua transcendence. It is different from solidarity qua identification, which is frequently encountered in contemporary political philosophy. I begin with a discussion of the latter and then turn to the former.

Solidarity as *identification* denotes something positive, for it reflects the ability of persons to put themselves into someone else's shoes. This positive attitude is expressed, however, in *negative form*; that is, it is directed *against* the realization in others of conditions that one would consider unwelcome oneself. Essentially, it materializes in assistance to others who happen to be in dire straits. Identification is possible inasmuch as others endure what one abhors. Consequently, solidarity evanesces quickly when the wants of others do not appear to be urgent enough. In some instances, the needs of others are then classified as 'expensive tastes'[38] for whose satisfaction, as long as they arise in others, nobody feels to have any responsibility.

The very notion 'expensive taste' reveals the *egocentrism* inherent in solidarity as identification. Tastes are considered inexpensive only inasmuch as I myself (or the great mass of others who are like me) experience a strong urgency of satisfaction. The less a situation is intuitively deemed alarming the more likely is solidarity qua identification to switch into a *path-dependent* mode. Generous gestures become settled against choices made by the subject of sympathy. The greater the scope drawn for individual responsibility, the more narrowly circumscribed the scope of solidarity.

Solidarity qua identification is therefore *systematically* vulnerable to being diminished through acts of *negative des-identification*. The latter may be triggered by simple parsimony or greed. Denials of assistance are notoriously rationalized with appeals to individual responsibility ('But thirty years ago they should have... '). It should not come as a surprise that the pursuit of neoliberal policies creates a high demand for morality. Lecturing people about what they should have done in order to avert their misfortune is the shibboleth of negative des-identification. It is supposed to fend off the claims made on those for whom life has gone well by those for whom it has not. Hence, the sparser this type of solidarity becomes, the more clearly is revealed its egocentric essence.

The morality of liberal disaffection comes with the mantra 'I was able to do it myself, so you should be able to do it yourself, too.'[39] Solidarity in the state of negative des-identification becomes tepid, herdish, and mean. Consequently, societies where solidarity has become weakened require 'identity politics' in order to upgrade the value of difference whenever those marked by difference are exposed to the risk of social exclusion. Well-meaning people have to transfigure immigrants,

[38] See W. Kymlicka, *Contemporary Political Philosophy: An Introduction*, 2nd edn (Oxford: Oxford University Press, 2002), at 72–75.

[39] For a more sophisticated analysis of this problem, see K. Günther, 'Zwischen Ermächtigung und Disziplinierung: Verantwortung im gegenwärtigen Kapitalismus', in A. Honneth (ed.), *Befreiung aus der Mündigkeit: Paradoxien des gegenwärtigen Kapitalismus* (Frankfurt: Campus Verlag, 2002), 117–140.

no matter how unsophisticated or even rearward their lifestyle, into an enchanting wellspring of the cultural enrichment in order to garner support for immigration-friendly policies. In a society sabotaged by resentment one is only allowed to be different so long as difference contributes to the common good.

By contrast, solidarity as *transcendence* goes beyond the bounds of the ego. Consequently, it involves *positive des-identification,* which could be characterized also as a form of identification that paradoxically involves self-transcendence. While negative identification reasserts the bounds of the ego in search of sufficient likeness in others—a likeness that is ultimately found wanting in 'irresponsible people'—positive identification elevates the ego to a grander sphere in which it conceives of itself as the realization of one possibility among many others. The ego is seen, then, as a contingent realization of alternate modes of being human and leading a life. The finitude of existence becomes aligned with the infinity of human potential. Des-identification is positive, in this case, since a dual negation of one's finite existence affirms community. Others with whom one identifies need not be sufficiently 'like' you, as in the case of sympathy, hence you negate the relevance of your own life, a negation that is negated in reaffirming a social world to which one belongs. The core idea, expressed by Humboldt[40] and approvingly, albeit somewhat mistakenly, referred to by Rawls,[41] is that one is dependent on others in order to realize *both* what one *is* oneself and what one *is not.* The relational dimension is not merely instrumentally valuable. Indeed, owing to interactions with others we are capable to discover and to assert who we are; what is more, however, through the individuation of others, which is mutually fostered, we *realize in others* what we ourselves are not able to accomplish ourselves. I make shoes and you make music. You could not compose the music that I enjoy if you had to make shoes. In community with others we partake of the wealth of experience created by others. Solidarity with others, thus, makes it possible to live with others without giving precedence to who one happens to be oneself.[42] Put in the terms accessible to the political idiom of modern liberalism, solidarity as transcendence treats *a whole social world as a public good.*

The realization of the decommodifying impulse inherent in anti-discrimination law would involve solidarity qua transcendence, for the latter incorporates the spirit of accommodation. It would also presuppose, however, reintroducing the full array of social policy strategies that have become eclipsed with the rise of anti-discrimination policy. What is more, it would require recovering solidarity from the reductions that it suffered at the hands of the latter.

[40] See W. von Humboldt, *Ideen zu einem Versuch die Grenzen der Wirksamkeit des Staats zu bestimmen* (Leipzig: Reclam, 1995), at 22–23.

[41] See J. Rawls, *Political Liberalism* (New York: Columbia University Press, 1993), at 320–321. In a typical Anglo-American preoccupation with work and production, Rawls assimilates the idea to that of a social union modelled on an orchestra.

[42] See R. M. Unger, *Law in Modern Society: Toward a Criticism of Social Theory* (New York: Free Press, 1976), at 206–207, where solidarity is characterized as the 'social face' of love.

7. Reversing Reductions

At the outset of this book I pointed out how anti-discrimination law commends itself as a strategy of reconciling competitiveness and solidarity. We are now finally in a position to realize that this reconciliation is tilted in favour of competitiveness. This is the case because it implicates a threefold reduction of solidarity.

First, solidarity is understood to be tantamount to a commitment to equality. As I tried to explain above, solidarity as transcendence may actually condone a great deal of inequality, for example, support of 'irresponsible' people by the ordinary guy. Maintaining a sheltered sector for the less energetic members of the workforce fits the same description. Reading solidarity as equality, by contrast, is consistent with a liberal view of social policy, according to which the latter is basically about taxes and transfers. Decommodification matters only insofar as people are guaranteed residual income in the case that they drop out of the race. It does not extend to tackling alienation. The bureaucratized capitalist economy creates tasks for people irrespective of whether these tasks can be meaningfully integrated into human life. This is not a direct concern of social policy inasmuch as it is concerned with equality.

Second, equality is, in turn, reduced to a matter that concerns equality of opportunity. Instead of providing, in particular, universal market-correcting access to decent housing, a good education, safe neighbourhoods, public transportation, cultural enjoyment, etc., equality of opportunity delivers equal access to hierarchical distinction. Conceivably, an egalitarian social policy, even if not concerned with mitigating alienation, might still be committed to creating a social space in which people encounter one another as not belonging to different social worlds. This type of social policy would target steep inequalities of income and boast a system of public education whose quality dwarfs offerings by the private sector. The creation of 'elite' institutions would definitely not be part of such a social world. The latter fits, however, perfectly well into the world of equality of opportunity.

Finally, the guarantee of equality of opportunity is given effect through protection from discrimination. Needless to say, there would be numerous alternative strategies for enhancing equality of opportunity, for example, financial transfers to needy students or the mixing of populations in cities through public housing projects.

Unsurprisingly, in an age where politics is little and economics is big a normatively feeble version of social legislation has come to prevail over more ambitious alternatives. The space thus created for competitiveness to nest into what remains of solidarity effectively submerges solidarity qua self-transcendence.

Anti-discrimination law is tailored to the interests of entrepreneurial selves who unluckily bear characteristics that are disfavoured on markets. It removes obstacles that these selves may encounter. It does not, however, in any respect challenge established social divisions and hierarchies. On the contrary, it is concerned with allocating professional and social prestige to members of (formerly) disfavoured groups. It takes established privileges for granted and promises to extend them to those who try hard. Overstating the point a bit, its ascendancy 'marks the degree to which the supposed left has turned into something like the human resources department of the right, concerned to make sure that the women of the upper middle class have the same privileges as the men'.[43] The problems faced by professional elites attain respectability when they can be cast in the format of race, sex, or sexual orientation discrimination. This respectability does not extend to those whose life is less productive and less achievement-oriented. The obstacles that a competitive society creates for them remain in place.

Of course, nobody can be against protecting people from suffering humiliating treatment. Nobody can be against diversity. Certain things can be done with anti-discrimination law. First, in cases of indirect discrimination it allows to challenge disparate impact by exposing the weak instrumental fit of employment practices. Second, it allows coming to the aid of people as long as judicial bodies intuitively agree that these have been wronged owing to the influence of evidently misinformed stereotypes or out of aversion of their race, sex, sexual orientation, or religion.[44] At the end of the day, the Sikh bus driver will be allowed to wear his turban on the job. This is not nothing. But it is at least debatable whether this is a grand social policy achievement. What anti-discrimination law cannot attain, however, is a synthesis of solidarity and competitiveness. Rather, owing to the normative deficiency the former becomes surrendered to the latter.

8. The Social Question in a Transnational Context

The suggestion that the presence of turban-wearing Sikh streetcar drivers in European cities may not represent a grand social policy achievement must appear unduly haughty and harsh. Does the author not realize what immense symbolic walls culturally homogeneous social worlds present for anyone who attempts to enter from the outside? Only someone who was born as an insider can be so adamantly ignorant and dismissive.

Engrained habits and local solidarities do indeed create walls that are built of spite and bigotry. But this realization does neither remove anti-discrimination law's normative deficiency nor alter the fact that Europe's social question arises at a different level.

The historical reason for inserting what is now 157 FEU Treaty into the agreement on the European Economic Community confirms that non-discrimination objectives were merely *contingently* related to the integration project. The article was supposed to forestall a competitive disadvantage for France, which had already adopted sex discrimination laws. The relation between anti-discrimination law and the common market was hence mediated by a concern with competitiveness. It was

[43] See W. Benn Michaels, *The Trouble with Diversity: How we Learned to Love Identity and Ignore Inequality* (New York: Metropolitan Books, 2006), at 114.

[44] See J. Gardner, 'On the Grounds of her Sex(uality)' (1998) 18 *Oxford Journal of Legal Studies* 167–187 at 168.

secondary that the comparative disadvantage resulted from the pursuit of a social objective. In other words, non-discrimination is not the European Union's social question.

The social question that is, by contrast, *intrinsic* to a transnational context was first brilliantly formulated by an author who was also vehemently opposed to recognizing its merit. Hayek,[45] indeed, expected such a context to be the nemesis of social policy. An international federal system which is *not* based on common sympathies would be politically disabled from pursuing redistributive policies at the federal level.[46] Above all, there would not be enough support among peoples to help each other out in times of crisis. No public expenditure would be wasted on rescuing inefficient businesses. What is more, such a federation would also motivate states to look to their left and right and to keep their social standards as low as possible in order to preserve the competitive edge of their businesses. Consequently, Hayek believed a federal transnational market society to be 'a necessary complement and the logical consummation of the liberal program'.[47]

Hayek's analysis reveals that the social question becomes self-referential in a transnational context. It is about whether, within such context, social policy will be generally asphyxiated or at least reduced to the level at which it merely prevents social disruption. Of course, no rational liberal society would leave its marginalized members completely to their own devices. Rather, it would use means-tested support in order to pacify the losers.[48] Sustainable pacification may require providing the underclass with even a sufficient share of games, porn, and drugs, which they may use in order to numb their unhappiness. Once they have been engrossed by media and anaesthetized by pharmaceuticals it will not likely occur to them that they could rebel against their station in an unequal society. A degenerate underclass is, no doubt, the hallmark of a smart liberal society.

In contrast to Hayek's premonitions, the founders of the European Community did not believe that the transnational system would either prompt or submerge the social question. Consequently, they did not see an inconsistency between creating a customs union and sustaining their own welfare states.[49] One explanation for their indifference is that the original six, with the possible exception of Italy, comprised a fairly homogenous set of social welfare states. What is more, before the revolution epitomized by *Cassis*,[50] the forces of negative integration did not impact severely on

[45] See F. A. Hayek, 'The Economic Conditions of Interstate Federalism', (1939), in, *Individualism and Economic Order* (Chicago, IL: University of Chicago Press, 1942), 255–272.

[46] Not by accident, the more recent developments in the case law of the ECJ have given rise to a renewed attention to Hayek's seminal contribution. See G. Majone, *Europe as the Would-be World Power: The EU at Fifty* (Cambridge: Cambridge University Press, 2009), at 66; F. W. Scharpf, 'The Double Asymmetry of European Integration, Or: Why the EU Cannot Be a Social Market Economy' (2009) 09/12 *MPIfG Working Paper* at 5.

[47] Ibid. at 269.

[48] For accurate observations along these lines, see A. de Swaan, 'The Receding Prospects for Transnational Social Policy' (1997) 26 *Theory and Society* 561–575 at 561–562.

[49] See Majone, n. 46 at 91–96, 123, 140

[50] See Case C-120/78, *Rewe Zentrale* v. *Bundesmonopolverwaltung für Brandwein* [1979] ECR 649 (*Cassis de Dijon*).

the Member States.[51] But even in the course of adapting to this change the social policies of the Member States experienced neither backlash nor defeat. Part of the explanation is that Member States with relatively higher regulatory standards were able either to halt further liberalization by the ECJ by endorsing harmonizing legislation or to tap opportunities of high-level harmonization where the ECJ sustained higher standards for health and safety or environmental and consumer protection.[52]

This is not to deny that subsequent enlargements increased inequalities among the working population of the Member States. Indeed, the matter has become most dramatic with the enlargements of 2004 and 2007.[53] With every enlargement the Union became socially more heterogeneous. Adopting, for the sake of exposition, a gross simplification made by Scharpf,[54] it can be said that the Union has now for decades been composed of Member States that embrace either of two different political economies. Market liberal states coexist alongside social market economies.[55]

Nevertheless, it was wrong to assume, as Hayek did, that social market economies, which are a very mixed bag by institutional standards, would not be able to compete with their more market liberal counterparts.[56] Sweden is the prime example of how well such economies can do.[57] Yet, the conditions for the success of social market economies are beginning to erode owing to a revolution in the ECJ's jurisprudence. The radical shift that is manifest in *Viking*,[58] *Laval*,[59] or *Überseering*[60] threatens to rob social market economies of their comparative advantage.[61] With these decisions, social market economies have come increasingly

[51] Höpner and Schäfer distinguish three phases of European integration. During the first phase, national welfare states were not affected at all. With the Community entering into the second phase, which is marked by *Cassis*, the mutual recognition principle was already piercing holes into the jurisdiction of Member States to regulate their markets. The third phase is entered as soon as Court and Commission effectively press for institutional innovation which would move all Member States more closely towards free market liberalism. See M. Höpner and A. Schäfer, 'Eine neue Phase der europäischen Integration: Legitimitätsdefizite europäischer Liberalisierungspolitik', in M. Höpner and A. Schäfer (eds), *Die politische Ökonomie der europäischen Integration* (Frankfurt: Campus Verlag, 2008), 129–156 at 135; M. Höpner and A. Schäfer, 'A New Phase of European Integration: Organized Capitalism in Post-Ricardian Europe' (2007) 07/4 *MPIfG Discussion Paper* 7–9.

[52] See Scharpf, n. 46 at 19.

[53] In particular, the differences in labour costs have never been that high before. See Majone, n. 46 at 132, 139.

[54] See ibid. at 25–26.

[55] For the sake of this brief exposition, the difference between 'social' and 'coordinated' market economies will be ignored.

[56] See Scharpf, n. 46 at 26.

[57] See S. Leibfried and H. Obinger, 'Nationale Sozialstaaten in der Europäischen Union: Zukünfte eines "sozialen Europas"', in *TranState Reprints* (Bremen: University of Bremen, 2008), at 22.

[58] Case C-438/05, *International Transport Workers Federation, Finnish Seaman's Union* v. *Viking Line* [2007] ECR I-10779.

[59] Case C-341/05, *Laval un Partneri Ltd* v. *Svenska Byggnadsarbetareförbudet* [2007] ECR I- 11767.

[60] Case C-208/00, *Überseering BV* v. *Nordic Construction* [2002] ECR I-9919.

[61] See M. Höpner, 'Usurpation statt Delegation: Wie der EuGH die Binnenmarktintegration radikalisiert und warum er politischer Kontrolle bedarf' (2008) 08/12 *MPIfG Discussion Paper* at 8; Scharpf, n. 46 at 27.

under pressure to give up what has been their major post-war achievement, namely the state-backed arrangements that lift life from the onerous entanglement by market forces. This case law, along with policy initiatives by the Commission,[62] has an asymmetrical impact on them.

This adverse effect is exacerbated by the Court's rulings on Union citizenship which force Member States to support nationals from other Member States without reciprocity.[63] It can happen that citizens from country A are to be given access to a social benefit or opportunity in country B even though neither the benefit nor the opportunity would be available for citizens of B in A simply because they are not provided there. Union citizenship is not counteracting but rather exacerbating the individualistic orientation of contemporary Union law. Social benefits are viewed as manifestations of government largesse which is subject to the constraint not to discriminate on the grounds of nationality. Such an attitude towards state-provided services bespeaks a tacit prevalence of consumerism; it even reveals a defective moral sense, since it ignores mutuality.

This development creates a major predicament. The Member States that are adversely affected avail of no outlet. The ECJ cannot be stopped through Treaty amendment, if only for the reason that any initiative for amendment would falter on divergent interests of the Member States. But even if amendments were possible it is difficult to imagine what a workable solution would look like.[64] The creation of a super court that is supposed to monitor the ECJ's case law would repeat the predicament inherent in Europe's divided political economies. The same obstacle arises with regard to potential opt-outs for the Member States which might be conceded by the Council in response to ECJ rulings. The social market economies no longer have a majority in the Council.[65] Their political economy appears to be a lost cause.

The Member States affected have every incentive, therefore, to form their own separate 'club' or even to withdraw from the Union. This is the upshot of Europe's social question. It may turn out to be the death knell of integration (and we did not even take Monetary Union into account). In her remarkable work, *On Revolution*, Hannah Arendt claimed that the social question sent the French Revolution to its doom.[66] Even though very much unlike the urgency of biological need that Arendt considered powerful enough to tear a polity apart, the social question in the transnational context may also turn out to be the one question over which the European Union may eventually founder.

[62] See Höpner and Schäfer, 'A New Phase', n. 51 at 12–17.

[63] See A. Somek, 'Solidarity Decomposed: Being and Time in European Citizenship' (2007) 32 *European Law Review* 787–818.

[64] They are discussed in Scharpf, n. 46 at 32–33.

[65] See M. Höpner, 'Warum betreibt der Europäische Gerichtshof Rechtsfortbildung?' (2010) 10/2 *MPIfG Working Paper* at 26.

[66] See H. Arendt, *On Revolution* (1963) (London: Penguin, 1990, repr.), at 62.

9. Conclusion

Neither rhetorical adjurations of European citizenship nor applause for anti-discrimination law point towards a common future. They are either beside the point or, as is the case for citizenship, part of the predicament. All that remains in such a situation is to explore whether there is a common inheritance that Europeans can draw upon in order to find a way out of their impasse.[67]

Unfortunately, access to this heritage has been severely distorted and curtailed by a most recent attempt of appropriation. During the last decade, Giddens[68] and New Labour proposed to reformulate social democracy on the basis of assimilating its agenda to the mindset of a market society. They gave their search for a middle path between laissez-faire and state intervention the name of the 'Third Way'.

Alas, the rhetorical success of their venture and the widespread attention that it received have rendered obscure, for members of our generation, the broader history and more daring ambition of precursors who ventured to find a Third Way in the past. But the misappropriation of a larger tradition by New Labour does not alter the fact that there is a whole variety of more ambitious projects waiting to be rediscovered.

First, and in contrast to Giddens' account, the Third Way has never been understood to be the middle way between laissez-faire capitalism and authoritarian socialism. Rather, it was supposed to offer an *alternative* to both. Its formulation has been the project of conservatives as well as democratic socialists. Among those contributing to the genre were pro-fascist authors such as Othmar Spann,[69] left-leaning social democrats such as Max Adler[70] or Otto Bauer,[71] Christian socialists such as Eduard Heimann[72] or proponents of a petit-bourgeois competitive society such as Alexander Rüstow.[73]

Second, the Third Way does not favour the unprincipled piecemeal social engineering so warmly recommended by Karl Popper.[74] The respective positions that claimed to have found the path were mutually exclusive. Eucken's competition-controlled ordered society[75] is incompatible with Adler's democratic socialism. What they share, however, is an aversion to dictatorship as well as to neoliberal de-politicization. Nonetheless, the Third Way, at least prior to Giddens, was never

67 For a related effort, see T. Judt, *Ill Fares the Land* (London: Penguin, 2010).

68 See A. Giddens, *The Third Way: The Renewal of Social Democracy* (London: Polity Press, 1998).

69 O. Spann, *Der wahre Staat: Vorlesungen über Abbruch und Neubau der Gesellschaft* (Leipzig: Quelle und Meyer, 1921).

70 See M.Adler, *Politische oder soziale Demokratie: Ein Beitrag zur sozialistischen Erziehung* (Berlin: Laub'sche Verlagsbuchhandlung, 1926).

71 See O. Bauer, *Bolschewismus oder Sozialdemokratie?* (Vienna: Verlag der Wiener Volksbuchhandlung, 1920).

72 See E. Heimann, *Reason and Faith in Modern Society. Liberalism, Marxism, and Democracy* (Middletown, CT: Welsyan University Press, 1961).

73 See A. Rüstow, *Die Religion der Marktwirtschaft*, new edn (Münster: Lit Verlag, 2001).

74 See K. R. Popper, *The Open Society and its Enemies*, 5th edn (Princeton, NJ: Princeton University Press, 1966) vol. 1 at 1–2, 157–160.

75 See W. Eucken, *Die Grundlagen der Nationalökonomie* (Berlin: Springer, 1965).

intended to mediate between the market and the state. Rather, it was based upon a rejection of both a laissez-faire system and Proletarian dictatorship.

Third, the legacy of the Third Way is with us even when its significance lies buried underneath its recent trivialization. This is revealed, quite significantly, in Žižek's commitment to a 'left Eurocentrism',[76] which he imagines to be a clear alternative to the two different authoritarian versions of capitalism that are currently rampant in the US and in China.

Finally, lest it be forgotten, it bears emphasis that this legacy has left an imprint on the constitution of the common market, too, since some Ordoliberals[77] were self-conscious defenders of a Third Way.[78] The 'social market economy' to which the EU Treaty makes a strange (and questionable)[79] *profession de foi* in Article 3(3) is an offspring of this quest.[80]

The European Union is confronted with a genuinely European predicament, that is, the social question, reappearing in a transnational guise. Anti-discrimination law is not a means to resolve it. The social question may tear the Union apart. The only way to maintain cohesion requires rediscovering a common intellectual template. Living up to its legacy, however, may very well require a profound reorientation of the European project.

[76] See S. Žižek, 'Taking on America', http://www.spiked-online.com/articles/00000006DA75.htm accessed 23 December 2010; S. Žižek, *The Ticklish Subject: The Absent Centre of Political Ontology* (London: Verso, 1999), 353.

[77] See D. J. Gerber, *Law and Competition in Twentieth Century Europe: Protecting Prometheus* (Oxford: Oxford University Press, 1988), at 261–265.

[78] Walter Eucken supported the Third Way. But he was not the only ordoliberal doing so. See A. Rüstow, 'Der dritte Weg', in his *Die Religion der Marktwirtschaft*, ed. by S. Tönnies (Münster: Litt Verlag, 2001), 41–100.

[79] See C. Joerges and F. Rödl, '"Social Market Economy" as Europe's Social Model?' (2004) 8 *EUI Working Paper Law*, No. 2004/8, at http://cadmus.eui.eu/bitstream/handle/1814/2823/law04-8.pdf?sequence=1, accessed 1 January 2011.

[80] See A. Müller-Armack, 'Das Konzept der Sozialen Marktwirtschaft—Grundlagen, Entwicklung, Aktualität', in D. Grosser, T. Lange, A. Müller-Armack, and B. Neuss (eds), *Soziale Marktwirtschaft*, 2nd edn (Stuttgart: Kohlhammer, 1990), 1–33 at 10 (quoting Alfred Müller-Armack).

Bibliography

Ackerman, B., *We the People*, vol. 1: *Foundations* (Cambridge, MA: Harvard University Press, 1991).

Ackerman, B. and Alstott, A., *The Stakeholder Society* (New Haven, CT: Yale University Press, 1999).

Adler, M., *Politische oder soziale Demokratie: Ein Beitrag zur sozialistischen Erziehung* (Berlin: Laub'sche Verlagsbuchhandlung, 1926).

Alber, J., 'Das "europäische Sozialmodell" und die USA' (2006) 34 *Leviathan* 208–241.

Alexander, L., 'What Makes Wrongful Discrimination Wrong? Biases, Preferences, Stereotypes, and Proxies' (1992) 141 *University of Pennsylvania Law Review* 149–219.

Amable, B., *The Diversity of Modern Capitalism* (Oxford: Oxford University Press, 2003).

Arendt, H., *The Human Condition* (Chicago, IL: University of Chicago Press, 1959).

Arendt, H., *On Revolution* (1963) (London: Penguin, 1990, repr.).

Arendt, H., *The Origins of Totalitarianism*, new edn (New York: Schocken Books, 2004).

Armour, J., 'Stereotypes and Prejudice: Helping Legal Decisionmakers to Break the Prejudice of Habit' (1995) 83 *California Law Review* 733–772.

Armstrong, K., 'The Open Method of Cooperation and Fundamental Rights: A Critical Appraisal', available at http://eucenter.wisc.edu/OMC/Papers/Rights/armstrong.pdf accessed 2 January 2011.

Armstrong, K. and Kilpatrick, C., 'Law, Governance, or New Governance? The Changing Open Method of Coordination' (2007) 13 *Columbia Journal of European Law* 649–677.

Ashiagbor, D., 'EMU and the Shift in the European Labour Law Agenda: From "Social Policy" to "Employment Policy"' (2001) 7 *European Law Journal* 311–330.

Ashiagbor, D., *The European Employment Strategy: Labour Market Regulation and New Governance* (Oxford: Oxford University Press, 2005).

Ayres, I., 'Alternative Grounds: Epstein's Discrimination Analysis in other Market Settings' (1994) 31 *San Diego Law Review* 67–87.

Ayres, I., *Pervasive Prejudice? Unconventional Evidence of Race and Gender Discrimination* (Chicago, IL: University of Chicago Press 2001).

Bagenstos, S. R., '"Rational Discrimination," Accommodation, and the Politics of (Disability) Civil Rights' (2003) 89 *Virginia Law Review* 825–923.

Bagenstos, S. R., 'The Future of Disability Law' (2004) 114 *Yale Law Journal* 1–82.

Bagenstos, S. R., 'Trapped in the Feedback Loop: A Response to Professor Days' (2005) 49 *Saint Louis University Law Journal* 1007–1019.

Bagenstos, S. R., 'The Structural Turn and the Limits of Anti-discrimination Law' (2006) 94 *California Law Review* 1–47.

Balkin, J., 'The Constitution of Status' (1997) 106 *Yale Law Journal* 2313–2374.

Balkin, J. and Siegel, R., 'The American Civil Rights Tradition: Anticlassification or Antisubordination' (2003) 58 *University of Miami Law Review* 9–33.

Barnard, C., *EC Employment Law*, 2nd edn (Oxford: Oxford University Press, 1999).

Barnard, C., 'EC "Social" Policy', in P. P. Craig and G. de Búrca (eds), *The Evolution of EU Law* (Oxford: Oxford University Press, 1999), pp. 479–511.

Barnard, C., 'Flexibility and Social Policy', in G. de Búrca and J. Scott (eds), *Constitutional Change in the EU: From Uniformity to Flexibility?* (Oxford: Hart Publishing, 2000), 197–216.

Barnard, C., 'Regulating Competitive Federalism in the European Union? The Case of EU Social Policy', in J. Shaw (ed.), *Social Law and Policy in an Evolving European Union* (Oxford: Hart Publishing, 2000), 49–69.

Barnard, C., 'The Social Partners and the Governance Agenda' (2002) 8 *European Law Journal* 80–101.

Barnard, C., *EC Employment Law*, 3rd edn (Oxford: Oxford University Press, 2007).

Barnard, C., 'Social Policy Revisited in the Light of the Constitutional Debate', in C. Barnard (ed.), *The Fundamentals of EU Law Revisited: Assessing the Impact of the Constitutional Debate* (Oxford: Oxford University Press, 2007), 109–151.

Barnard, C. and Deakin, S., 'A Year of Living Dangerously? EC Social Rights, Employment Policy, and EMU', in B. Towers and M. Terry (eds), *Industrial Relations Journal European Annual Review 1998* (Oxford: Blackwell, 1999), 355–372.

Barnard, C. and Deakin, S., 'Market Access and Regulatory Competition', in C. Barnard and J. Scott (eds), *The Law of the Single European Market. Unpacking the Premises* (Oxford: Hart Publishing, 2002), 197–224.

Bauer, O., *Bolschewismus oder Sozialdemokratie?* (Vienna: Verlag der Wiener Volksbuchhandlung, 1920).

Becker, G., *The Economics of Discrimination*, 2nd edn (Chicago, IL: University of Chicago Press, 1971).

Becker, G., *A Treatise on the Family* (Cambridge, MA: Harvard University Press, 1991).

Bell, M., 'Equality and Diversity: Anti-discrimination Law after Amsterdam', in J. Shaw (ed.), *Social Law and Policy in an Evolving European Union* (Oxford: Hart Publishing, 2000), 157–170.

Bell, M., *Anti-discrimination Law and the European Union* (Oxford: Oxford University Press, 2002).

Benn Michaels, W., *The Trouble with Diversity: How we Learned to Love Identity and Ignore Inequality* (New York: Metropolitan Books, 2006).

Bernstein, D. E., *You Can't Say That! The Growing Threat to Civil Liberties from Anti-discrimination Laws* (Washington, DC: Cato Institute, 2003).

Blair, I. V., 'The Malleability of Automatic Stereotypes and Prejudice' (2002) 6 *Personality and Social Psychology Review* 242–261.

Boni, S. and Manzini, P., 'National Social Legislation and EC Antitrust Law' (2001) 24 *World Competition* 239–255.

Bork, R., *The Antitrust Paradox: A Policy at War with itself*, 2nd edn (New York: Free Press, 1993).

Bratman, M. E., *Faces of Intention: Selected Essays on Intention and Agency* (Cambridge: Cambridge University Press, 1999).

Bröckling, U., *Das unternehmerische Selbst: Soziologie einer Subjektivierungsform* (Frankfurt: Suhrkamp, 2007).

Brown, W., 'Neoliberalism and the End of Liberal Democracy', in W. Brown, *Edgework: Critical Essays on Knowledge and Politics* (Princeton, NJ: Princeton University Press, 2005), 37–59.

Buchanan, J., *The Limits of Liberty* (Chicago, IL: University of Chicago Press, 1985).

Burchell, G., Gordon, C., and Miller, P. (eds), *The Foucault Effect: Studies in Governmentality* (Chicago, IL: University of Chicago Press, 1991).

Choudhry, S., 'Distribution vs. Recognition: The Case of Anti-Discrimination Laws' (2000) 9 *George Mason Law Review* 145–178.

Christensen, A., 'Structural Aspects of Anti-discriminatory Legislation and Processes of Normative Change', in A. Numhauser-Henning (ed.), *Legal Perspectives of Equal Treatment and Non-Discrimination* (Amsterdam: Kluwer, 2001), 31–60.

Cohen, G. A., *Self-Ownership, Freedom, and Equality* (Cambridge: Cambridge University Press, 1995).

Cohen, J. and Sabel, C. F., 'Directly-deliberative Polyarchy' (1997) 3 *European Law Journal* 313–342.

Collins, H., 'Discrimination, Equality and Social Inclusion' (2003) 66 *Modern Law Review* 16–43.

Collins, H., 'Social Inclusion: A Better Approach to Equality Issues' (2005) 14 *Transnational Law and Contemporary Problems* 897–918.

Coudenhove-Kalergi, R., *Die Wiedervereinigung Europas* (Vienna: Herold Verlag, 1964).

Craig, P. and de Búrca, G., *EU Law: Text Case and Materials*, 4th edn (Oxford: Oxford University Press, 2008).

Crenshaw, K., 'Demarginalizing the Intersection of Race and Sex: A Black Feminist Critique of Anti-discrimination Doctrine, Feminist Theory, and Antiracist Politics' (1989) *University of Chicago Legal Forum* 139–167.

Cusa, N. of, *De Concordantia Catholica* (*The Catholic Concordance*) (1443), trans. by P. E. Sigmund (Cambridge: Cambridge University Press, 1991).

Daly, M., 'Whither Social Policy? An Account and Assessment of Developments in the Lisbon Social Inclusion Process' (2007) 37 *Journal of Social Policy* 1–19.

Dasgupta, N., 'Implicit Ingroup Favouritism, Outgroup Favouritism, and their Behavioural Manifestation' (2004) 14 *Social Justice Research* 143–169.

Davidson, D., *Essays on Actions and Events* (Oxford: Oxford University Press, 1980).

Davis, P. C., 'Law as Microaggression' (1989) 98 *Yale Law Journal* 1559–1577.

de Búrca, G., 'EU Race Discrimination Law: A Hybrid Model?', in G. de Búrca and J. Scott (eds), *Law and New Governance in the EU and the US* (Oxford: Hart Publishing 2006), 97–120.

de Búrca, G. and Scott, J., 'Introduction: New Governance, Law and Constitutionalism', in G. de Búrca and J. Scott (eds), *Law and New Governance in the EU and the US* (Oxford: Hart Publishing 2006), 1–12.

de la Porte, C., 'Is the Open Method of Coordination Appropriate for Organising Activities at European Level in Sensitive Policy Areas?' (2002) 8 *European Law Journal* 38–58.

de Schutter, O., 'The Implementation of the EU Charter of Fundamental Rights through the Open Method of Coordination' (2004) 7/04 *Jean Monnet Working Paper*, available at http://www.jeanmonnetprogram.org/papers/04/040701.html accessed 2 January 2011.

de Swaan, A., 'The Receding Prospects for Transnational Social Policy' (1997) 26 *Theory and Society* 561–575.

de Tocqueville, A., *Democracy in America*, trans. by H. C. Mansfield and D. Winthrop (Chicago, IL: University of Chicago Press, 2000).

Deakin, S., 'The Many Futures of the Contract of Employment', in J. Conaghan, R. M. Fischl, and K. Klare (eds), *Labour Law in the Age of Globalisation* (Oxford: Oxford University Press, 2002), 177–196.

Deakin, S. and Reed, H., 'The Contested Meaning of Labour Market Flexibility', in J. Shaw (ed.), *Social Law and Policy in an Evolving European Union* (Oxford: Hart Publishing, 2000), 71–102.

Dean, M., *Governmentality: Power and Rule in Modern Society* (New York: Sage Publications, 1999).

Derrida, J., *Limited Inc* (Chicago, IL: Northwestern University Press, 1988).

Dinan, D., *Ever Closer Union: An Introduction to European Integration*, 2nd edn (Houndsmills: Palgrave Macmillan, 1999).

Donohue III, J. J., 'Advocacy versus Analysis in Assessing Employment Discrimination Law' (1992) 44 *Stanford Law Review* 1583–1614.

Dorf, M. C. and Sabel, C. F., 'A Constitution of Democratic Experimentalism' (1998) 98 *Columbia Law Review* 267–473.

Drysek, J. S., *Deliberative Democracy and Beyond: Liberals, Critics, Contestations* (Oxford: Oxford University Press, 2000).

Dworkin, R., *Sovereign Virtue: The Theory and Practice of Equality* (Cambridge, MA: Harvard University Press, 2000).

Ehrlich, E., *Grundlegung der Soziologie des Rechts*, first published 1913, 4th edn ed. by M. M. Rehbinder (Berlin: Duncker & Humblot, 1989).

Ellis, E., *EU Anti-discrimination Law* (Oxford: Oxford University Press, 2005).

Elster, J., *An Introduction to Karl Marx* (Cambridge: Cambridge University Press, 1986).

Enderlein, H., 'Wandel durch den Euro: Wie die Währungsunion die nationale Fiskal- und Lohnpolitik verändert', in M. Höpner and A. Schäfer (eds), *Die politische Ökonomie der europäischen Integration* (Frankfurt: Campus Verlag, 2009), 415–448.

Epstein, R., *Forbidden Grounds: The Case Against Employment Discrimination Laws* (Cambridge, MA: Harvard University Press, 1992).

Esping-Andersen, G., *The Three Worlds of Welfare Capitalism* (Princeton, NJ: Princeton University Press, 1990).

Esping-Andersen, G., *Social Foundations of Postindustrial Economies* (Oxford: Oxford University Press, 1999).

Eucken, W., *Die Grundlagen der Nationalökonomie* (Berlin: Springer, 1965).

Ferguson, N., *Collossus: The Price of America's Empire* (New York: Penguin Press, 2004).

Ferguson, N., 'The End of Europe?', available at http://www.travelbrochuregraphics.com/extra/end_of_europe.htm accessed 23 December 2010.

Ferrera, M., 'Towards an "Open" Social Citizenship? The New Boundaries of Welfare in the European Union', in G. de Búrca (ed.), *EU Law and the Welfare State: In Search of Solidarity* (Oxford: Oxford University Press, 2005), 11–38.

Fichte, J. G., *Reden an die deutsche Nation* (1808), *Sämmtliche Werke*, ed. by I. H. Fichte (Berlin: Veit & Comp., 1845–1846), vol. 7.

Fischer-Lescano, A. and Teubner, G., 'Regime-collisions: The Vain Search for Legal Unity in the Fragmentation of Global Law' (2004) 25 *Michigan Journal of International Law* 999–1046.

Fitzpatrick, B., 'Converse Pyramids and the EU Social Constitution', in J. Shaw (ed.), *Social law and Policy in an Evolving European Union* (Oxford: Hart Publishing, 2000), 303–324.

Flagg, B. J., '"Was Blind, But Now I See": White Race Consciousness and the Requirement of Discriminatory Intent' (1993) 91 *Michigan Law Review* 953–1017.

Flear, M. L., 'Neoliberalism, the Open Method of Coordination, and the Undemocratic Governance of Health' (2007, manuscript on file with the author).

Flear, M., 'The Open Method of Coordination on Health Care after the Lisbon Strategy II: Towards a Neoliberal Framing?' (2009) 13(1) *European Integration Online Papers* (*EIoP*), available at http://eiop.or.at/eiop/texte/2009-012a.htm accessed 2 January 2011.

Forsthoff, E., *Der Staat der Industriegesellschaft: Dargestellt am Beispiel der Bundesrepublik Deutschland* (Munich: C. H. Beck, 1971).

Foucault, M., *Ethics: Subjectivity and Truth*, ed. by P. Rabinow (New York: New Press, 1994).

Frankfurt, H. G., *The Importance of What we Care About: Philosophical Essays* (Cambridge: Cambridge University Press, 1988).

Fredman, S., 'Affirmative Action and the European Court of Justice: A Critical Analysis', in J. Shaw (ed.), *Social Law and Policy in an Evolving European Union* (Oxford: Hart Publishing, 2000), 171–195.

Fredman, S., *Discrimination Law* (Oxford: Clarendon Press, 2002).

Freeman, A., 'Anti-discrimination Law: A Critical Review', in D. Kairys (ed.), *The Politics of Law: A Progressive Critique* (New York: Pantheon Books, 1982), 96–116.

Freeman, A., 'Racism, Rights and the Quest for Equality of Opportunity: A Critical Legal Essay' (1988) 23 *Harvard Civil Rights and Civil Liberties Review* 295–392.

Freeman, A., 'Anti-discrimination Law: The View from 1989' (1990) 64 *Tulane Law Review* 1407–1441.

Fried, C., *Right and Wrong* (Cambridge, MA: Harvard University Press, 1978).

Fuchs, M., 'Free Movement of Services and Social Security—*Quo Vadis*' (2002) 8 *European Law Journal* 536–555.

Gamble, A., *Hayek: The Iron Cage of Liberty* (Cambridge: Polity Press, 1996).

Gardner, J., 'Liberals and Unlawful Discrimination' (1989) 9 *Oxford Journal of Legal Studies* 1–21.

Gardner, J., 'On the Grounds of her Sex(uality)' (1998) 18 *Oxford Journal of Legal Studies* 167–187.

Gehlen, A., *Moral und Hypermoral: Eine pluralistische Ethik*, 5th edn (Wiebelsheim: Aula-Verlag, 1986).

Gerber, D. J., *Law and Competition in Twentieth Century Europe: Protecting Prometheus* (Oxford: Oxford University Press, 1988).

Gerlach, R., 'Wozu noch Arbeitsrecht?' (2003) 2 *Juridikum* 103–106.

Gerstenberg, O. and Sabel, C. F., 'Directly-deliberative Polyarchy: An Institutional Ideal for Europe?', in C. Joerges and R. Dehousse (eds), *Good Governance in Europe's Integrated Market* (Oxford: Oxford University Press, 2002), 289–342.

Geyer, R. R., *Exploring European Social Policy* (Oxford: Polity Press, 2000).

Giddens, A., *The Third Way: The Renewal of Social Democracy* (Oxford: Polity Press, 1998).

Giubboni, S., 'Social Insurance Monopolies in Community Competition Law and the Italian Constitution: "Practical" Convergences and "Theoretical" Conflicts' (2001) 7 *European Law Journal* 69–94.

Giubboni, S., *Social Rights and Market Freedoms in the European Constitution: A Labour Law Perspective*, trans. by R. Inston (Cambridge: Cambridge University Press, 2006).

Goffman, I., *Stigma: Notes on the Management of Spoiled Identity* (New York: Penguin Books, 1990).

Goodin, R., *Utilitarianism as a Public Philosophy* (Cambridge: Cambridge University Press, 1995).

Green, D. P. and Shapiro, I., *Pathologies of Rational Choice Theory: A Critique of Applications in Political Science* (New Haven, CT: Yale University Press, 1994).

Green, T. K., 'Discrimination in Workplace Dynamics: Towards a Structural Account of Disparate Treatment Theory (2003) 38 *Harvard Civil Rights-Civil Liberties Law Review* 91–157.

Günther, K., 'Zwischen Ermächtigung und Disziplinierung: Verantwortung im gegenwärtigen Kapitalismus', in A. Honneth (ed.), *Befreiung aus der Mündigkeit: Paradoxien des gegenwärtigen Kapitalismus* (Frankfurt: Campus Verlag, 2002), 117–139.

Haas, E. B., 'The Study of Regional Integration: Reflections on the Joy and Anguish of Pretheorising', in L. N. Lindberg, S. A. Scheingold, and A. Stuart (eds), *Regional Integration: Theory and Research* (Cambridge, MA: Harvard University Press, 1971), 3–42.

Habermas, J., *Theory of Communicative Action*, trans. by T. McCarthy (Cambridge: Polity Press, 1984).

Habermas, J., *Between Facts and Norms: Contributions to a Discourse Theory of Law and Democracy*, trans. by W. Rehg (Cambridge: Polity Press, 1996).

Hall, P. and Soskice, D., 'An Introduction to Varieties of Capitalism', in P. Hall and D. Soskice (eds), *Varieties of Capitalism: Institutional Foundations of Comparative Advantage* (Oxford: Oxford University Press, 2001), 1–68.

Haltern, U., 'Pathos and Patina: The Failure and Promise of Constitutionalism in the European Union' (2002) 9 *European Law Journal* 19–38.

Hamilton Krieger, L., 'Civil Rights Perestroika: Intergroup Relations after Affirmative Action' (1988) 86 *California Law Review* 1251–1333.

Hamilton Krieger, L., 'The Content of our Categories: A Cognitive Bias Approach to Discrimination and Equal Employment Opportunity' (1995) 47 *Stanford Law Review* 1161–1248.

Hancher, L., 'Community, State, and the Market', in P. P. Craig and G. de Búrca (eds), *The Evolution of EU Law* (Oxford: Oxford University Press, 1999), 721–742.

Handler, J., 'The "Third Way" or the Old Way?' (2000) 48 *Kansas Law Review* 765–800.

Haney López, I. F., 'Institutional Racism: Judicial Conduct and a New Theory of Racial Discrimination' (2000) 109 *Yale Law Journal* 1717–1884.

Harvey, D., *A Brief History of Neoliberalism* (Oxford: Oxford University Press, 2005).

Haskovec, J., 'A Beast of a Burden? The New EU Burden-of-proof Arrangement in Cases of Employment Discrimination Compared to Existing U.S. Law' (2005) 14 *Journal of Transnational Law and Contemporary Problems* 1069–1106.

Hasnas, J., 'Equal Opportunity, Affirmative Action, and the Anti-discrimination Principle: The Philosophical Basis for the Legal Prohibition of Discrimination' (2002) 71 *Fordham Law Review* 424–542.

Hatzopoulos, V. G., '*Killing* National Health and Insurance Systems but *Healing* Patients? The European Market for Health Care Services after the Judgments of the ECJ in *Vanbraekel* and *Peerbooms*' (2002) 39 *Common Market Law Review* 683–729.

Hatzopoulos, V. G., 'Health Law and Policy: The Impact of the EU', in G. de Búrca (ed.), *EU Law and the Welfare State: In Search of Solidarity* (Oxford: Oxford University Press, 2005), 111–168.

Hayek, F. A., *Individualism and Economic Order* (Chicago, IL: University of Chicago Press, 1948).

Hayek, F. A., 'The Economic Conditions of Interstate Federalism', (1939), in F. A. Hayek, *Individualism and Economic Order* (Chicago, IL: University of Chicago Press, 1948), 255–272.

Hayek, F. A., 'Individualism: True and False', in F. A. Hayek, *Individualism and Economic Order* (Chicago, IL: University of Chicago Press, 1948), 1–32.

Hayek, F. A., *Law Legislation, and Liberty,* vol. 2 (London: Routledge, 1976).

Hayek, F. A., *Law, Legislation, and Liberty*, vol. 3 (Chicago, IL: University of Chicago Press, 1979).

Hayek, F. A., *The Fatal Conceit: The Errors of Socialism* (Chicago, IL: University of Chicago Press, 1988).

Hayek, F. A., *The Road to Serfdom*, new edn (London: Routledge, 2007).
Hegel, G. W. F., *Science of Logic*, trans. by A. V. Miller (London: George Allen & Unwin Ltd., 1969).
Hegel, G. W. F., *Phenomenology of the Spirit*, trans. by A. V. Miller (Oxford: Oxford University Press, 1977).
Hegel, G. W. F., *Philosophie des Rechts*, ed. by D. Henrich (Frankfurt: Suhrkamp, 1983).
Hegel, G. W. F., *Elements of the Philosophy of Right*, trans. by H. B. Nisbeth (Cambridge: Cambridge University Press, 1991).
Heimann, E., *Reason and Faith in Modern Society: Liberalism, Marxism, and Democracy* (Middletown, CT: Welsyan University Press, 1961).
Heimann, E., *Soziale Theorie des Kapitalismus: Theorie der Sozialpolitik*, 1st edn 1929, new edn ed. by B. Badura (Frankfurt: Suhrkamp, 1980).
Heller, H., 'Autoritärer Liberalismus?' (1933), repr. in *Gesammelte Schriften*, vol. 2 (Leiden: A. W. Sijthoff, 1971), 643–653.
Hellman, D., *When is Discrimination Wrong?* (Cambridge, MA: Harvard University Press, 2008).
Hepple, B., *Rights at Work: Global, European and British Perspectives* (London: Sweet & Maxwell, 2006).
Hervey, T., 'Thirty Years of EU Sex Equality Law: Looking Backwards, Looking Forward' (2005) 12 *Maastricht Journal of European and Comparative Law* 307–326.
Higgins, T. E. and Rosenbury, L. A., 'Agency, Equality, and Anti-discrimination Law' (2000) 85 *Cornell Law Review* 1194–1220.
Hill, S., *Europe's Promise: Why the European Way is the Best Hope in an Insecure Age* (Berkeley, CA: University of California Press, 2010).
Hills, R. M., 'You Say you Want a Revolution? The Case against the Transformation of Culture through Anti-discrimination Laws' (1997) 95 *Michigan Law Review* 1588–1635.
Hirschman, A. O., *The Passions and the Interests: Political Arguments for Capitalism before its Triumph* (Princeton, NJ: Princeton University Press, 1977).
Höffe, O., 'Transzendentaler Tausch: Eine Legitimationsfigur der Menschenrechte?', in S. Gosepath and G. Lohmann (eds), *Philosophie der Menschenrechte* (Frankfurt: Suhrkamp, 1998), 29–48.
Holmes, O. W., 'The Path of the Law', repr. in (1997) 110 *Harvard Law Review* 991–1009 (first published in 1897).
Holzleithner, E., 'Mainstreaming Equality: Dis/Entangling Grounds of Discrimination' (2005) 14 *Journal of Transnational Law and Contemporary Problems* 927–958.
Holzleithner, E., 'Gendergleichheit und Mehrfachdiskriminierung: Herausforderungen für das Europarecht', in K. Arioli, M. Cottier, P. Farahmand, and Z. Küng (eds), *Wandel der Geschlechterverhältnisse durch das Recht?* (Zurich/St Gallen: Dike Verlag, 2008), 305–320.
Honneth, A., *Leiden an Unbestimmtheit. Eine Reaktualisierung der Hegelschen Rechtsphilosophie* (Stuttgart: Reclam Verlag, 2001).
Höpner, M., 'Usurpation statt Delegation: Wie der EuGH die Binnenmarktintegration radikalisiert und warum er politischer Kontrolle bedarf' (2008) 08/12 *MPIfG Discussion Paper*.
Höpner, M., 'Warum betreibt der Europäische Gerichtshof Rechtsfortbildung Die Politisierungshypothese' (2010) 10/02 *MPIfG Working Paper*.
Höpner, M. and Schäfer, A., 'A New Phase of European Integration: Organized Capitalism in Post-Ricardian Europe' (2007) 07/4 *MPIfG Discussion Paper*.

Höpner, M. and Schäfer, A., 'Eine neue Phase der europäischen Integration: Legitimitätsdefizite europäischer Liberalisierungspolitik', in M. Höpner and A. Schäfer (eds), *Die politische Ökonomie der europäischen Integration* (Frankfurt: Campus Verlag, 2008), 129–156.

Höpner, M. and Schäfer, A., 'Grundzüge einer politökonomischen Perspektive auf die europäische Union', in M. Höpner and A. Schäfer (eds), *Die politische Ökonomie der europäischen Integration* (Frankfurt: Campus Verlag, 2008), 11–45.

Höpner, M. and Schäfer, A., 'Grenzen der Integration—wie die Intensivierung der Wirtschaftsintegration zur Gefahr für die politische Integration wird' (2010) *Integration* 33(1) 3–20.

Hunt, A. and Wickham, G., *Foucault and Law: Towards a Sociology of Law as Governance* (London: Pluto Press, 1994).

Hunter, R. C. and Shoben, E. W., 'Disparate Impact Discrimination: American Oddity or Internationally Accepted Concept?' (1998) 19 *Berkeley Journal of Employment and Labour Law* 108–15.

Huntington, S., *Who are We? The Challenges to America's National Identity* (New York: Simon & Schuster, 2004).

Hurley, S. L., *Justice, Luck, and Knowledge* (Cambridge, MA: Harvard University Press, 2003).

Illouz, E., *Consuming the Romantic Utopia: Love and the Cultural Contradictions of Capitalism* (Berkeley, CA: University of California Press, 1997).

Issacharoff, S. and Nelson, J., 'Discrimination with a Difference: Can Employment Discrimination Law Accommodate the Americans with Disabilities Act?' (2001) 79 *North Carolina Law Review* 307–358.

Jacobsson, K., 'Soft Regulation and the Subtle Transformation of States: The Case of EU Employment Policy' (2004) 14 *Journal of European Social Policy* 355–370.

Jepsen, M. and Serrano Pascual, A., 'The European Social Model: An Exercise in Deconstruction' (2005) 15 *Journal of European Social Policy* 231–245.

Jessop, B., *The Future of the Capitalist State* (Cambridge: Polity Press, 2002) 58–61.

Joerges, C., 'A New Alliance of De-legalisation and Legal Formalism? Reflections on Responses to the Social Deficit of the European Integration Project' (2008) 19 *Law and Critique* 235–253.

Joerges, C. and Rödl, F., 'The "Social Market Economy" as Europe's Social Model?' (2004) 8 *EUI Working Paper Law*, No. 2004/8, available at http://cadmus.eui.eu/bitstream/handle/1814/2823/law04-8.pdf?sequence=1 accessed 1 January 2011.

Jolls, C., 'Anti-discrimination and Accommodation' (2001) 115 *Harvard Law Review* 642–699.

Jolls, C. and Sunstein, C. R., 'The Law of Implicit Bias' (2006) 94 *California Law Review* 969–996.

Judt, T., *Ill Fares the Land* (London: Penguin, 2010).

Kagan, R., 'Power and Weakness' (2002) 113 *Policy Review*, available at http://www.uweb.ucsb.edu/thartman/files/127/Kagan–PowerandWeakness.pdf accessed 23 December 2010.

Kahan, A. S., *Aristocratic Liberalism: The Social and Political Thought of Jacob Burckhardt, Johan Stuart Mill and Alexis de Tocqueville*, 2nd edn (New Brunswick, NJ: Transaction Publishers, 2001).

Kang, J., 'Trojan Horses of Race' (2005) 118 *Harvard Law Review* 1489–1593.

Karlan, P. S. and Rutherglen, G., 'Disabilities, Discrimination, and Reasonable Accommodation' (1996) 46 *Duke Law Journal* 1–41.

Katz, L., *Ill-gotten Gains: Evasion, Blackmail, Fraud, and Kindred Puzzles of the Law* (Chicago, IL: University of Chicago Press, 1996).
Katz, M. B., *The Undeserving Poor: From the War on Poverty to the War on Welfare* (New York: Pantheon Books, 1989).
Katz, M. J., 'The Fundamental Incoherence of Title VII: Making Sense of Causation in Disparate Treatment Law' (2006) 94 *Georgetown Law Journal* 489–550.
Kelman, M., *A Guide to Critical Legal Studies* (Cambridge, MA: Harvard University Press, 1987).
Kelman, M., 'Market Discrimination and Groups' (2001) 53 *Stanford Law Review* 833–896.
Kelman, M. and Lester, G., *Jumping the Queue: An Inquiry into the Legal Treatment of Students with Learning Disabilities* (Cambridge, MA: Harvard University Press, 1997).
Kelsen, H., *Introduction to the Problems of Legal Theory*, first pub. 1934, trans. by B. Litschewski Paulson and S. L. Paulson (Oxford: Clarendon Press, 1992).
Kenner, J., *EU Employment Law: From Rome to Amsterdam and Beyond* (Oxford: Hart Publishing, 2003).
Kilpatrick, C., 'New EU Employment Governance and Constitutionalism', in G. de Búrca and J. Scott (eds), *Law and New Governance in the EU and the US* (Oxford: Hart Publishing, 2006), 121–151.
Koppelman, A., *Anti-discrimination Law and Social Equality* (New Haven, CT: Yale University Press, 1996).
Korsgaard, C. M., *Creating the Kingdom of Ends* (Cambridge: Cambridge University Press, 1996).
Korsgaard, C. M., *The Sources of Normativity* (Cambridge: Cambridge University Press, 1996).
Korsgaard, C. M., *Self-Constitution: Agency, Identity, and Integrity* (Oxford: Oxford University Press, 2009).
Koskenniemi, M., 'Constitutionalism as Mindset: Reflections on Kantian Themes about International Law and Globalization' (2007) 8 *Theoretical Inquires in Law* 9–36.
Koskenniemi, M., 'The Fate of Public International Law: Between Technique and Politics' (2007) 70 *Modern Law Review* 1–30.
Kripke, S. A., *Wittgenstein on Rules and Private Language* (Cambridge, MA: Harvard University Press, 1982).
Kristen, E., 'Addressing the Problem of Weight Discrimination in Employment' (2002) 90 *California Law Review* 57–109.
Krugman, P., 'The Euro Trap' *The New York Times* 30 April 2010.
Krugman, P., 'The Pain Caucus' *The New York Times* 31 May 2010.
Kymlicka, W., *Contemporary Political Philosophy: An Introduction* (Oxford: Oxford University Press, 2002).
LaRue, L. H., 'Discriminatory Intent' (1995) 1 *Race and Ethnic Ancestry Law Digest* 17–20.
Lawrence III, C. R., 'The Id, the Ego, and Equal Protection: Reckoning with Unconscious Racism' (1987) 39 *Stanford Law Review* 317–388.
Lawton, A., 'The Meritocracy Myth and the Illusion of Equal Employment Opportunity' (2000) 85 *Minnesota Law Review* 587–662.
Lee, A. J., 'Unconscious Bias Theory in Employment Discrimination Litigation' (2005) 40 *Harvard Civil Rights-Civil Liberties Law Review* 481–503.
Leibfried, S. and Obinger, H., 'Nationale Sozialstaaten in der Europäischen Union: Zukünfte eines "sozialen Europas"', in *TranState Reprints* (Bremen: University of Bremen, 2008).

Leibfried, S. and Pierson, P., 'Social Policy: Left to Courts and Markets?', in *Policy-making in the European Union*, 4th edn (Oxford: Oxford University Press, 2000), 267–292.

Lemke, T., '"The Birth of Bio-politics": Michel Foucault's Lectures at The Collège de France on Neoliberal Governmentality' (2001) 30 *Economy and Society* 190–207.

Lenk, H., *Schemaspiele: Über Schemainterpretationen und Interpretationskonstrukte* (Frankfurt: Suhrkamp, 1995).

Loenen, T., 'Indirect Discrimination: Oscillating between Containment and Revolution', in T. Loenen and P. R. Rodrigues (eds), *Non-Discrimination Law: Comparative Perspectives* (Amsterdam: Kluwer, 1999), 195–211.

Lohmann, G., *Indifferenz und Gesellschaft: Eine kritische Auseinandersetzung mit Marx* (Frankfurt: Suhrkamp, 1991).

Luhmann, N., 'Soziologie der Moral', in N. Luhmann and S. Pfürtner (eds), *Theorietechnik und Moral* (Frankfurt: Suhrkamp, 1978), 8–116.

Luhmann, N., *A Sociological Theory of Law*, trans. by E. King and M. Albrow (London: Routledge, 1985).

Luhmann, N., 'Ethik als Reflexionstheorie der Moral', in *Gesellschaftsstruktur und Semantik: Studien zur Wissenssoziologie der modernen Gesellschaft*, vol. 3 (Frankfurt: Suhrkamp, 1989), 459–444.

Luhmann, N., 'Inklusion und Exklusion', in *Soziologische Aufklärung*, vol. 6: *Die Soziologie und der Mensch* (Opladen: Westdeutscher Verlag, 1995), 265–274.

Luhmann, N., *Die Gesellschaft der Gesellschaft* (Frankfurt: Suhrkamp, 1997).

Lukács, G., *History and Class Consciousness: Studies in Marxist Dialectics*, trans. by R. Livingstone (Cambridge, MA: MIT Press, 1971).

Majone, G., 'Redistributive und sozialregulative Politik', in K. Jachtenfuchs and B. Kohler-Koch (eds), *Europäische Integration* (Opladen: Leske & Budrich, 1996), 225–247.

Majone, G., 'Europe's "Democracy Deficit": A Question of Standards' (1998) 4 *European Law Journal* 5–28.

Majone, G., *Europe as the Would-be World Power: The EU at Fifty* (Cambridge: Cambridge University Press, 2009).

Marshall, T. H., *Social Policy* (London: Heinemann, 1975).

Masselot, A., 'The State of Gender Equality Law in the European Union' (2007) 13 *European Law Journal* 152–168.

McCrudden, C., *Anti-discrimination Law*, 2nd edn (Aldershot: Ashgate, 2004).

McCrudden, C., 'The New Concept of Equality' (2003) 3 *ERA-Forum* 9–29.

McCrudden, C. and Kountouros, H., 'Human Rights and European Equality Law' (2006) 8 *University of Oxford Faculty of Law Legal Studies Research Paper*, 4–8.

Menke, C., *Tragödie im Sittlichen: Gerechtigkeit und Freiheit nach Hegel* (Frankfurt: Suhrkamp, 1996).

Menke, C., *Reflections of Equality*, trans. by H. Rouse and A. Denejkine (Stanford, CA: Stanford University Press, 2006).

Mill, J. S., *Considerations on Representative Government*, orig. edn 1861 (Amherst/NY: Prometheus Books, 1991, repr.).

Minow, M., *Not only for myself: Identity, Politics, and the Law* (New York: New Press, 1997).

Mohler, A., 'Der Weg der "Technokratie" von Amerika nach Frankreich', in H. Barion, E.-W. Böckenförde, and E. Forsthoff (eds), *Epirrhosis. Festgabe für Carl Schmitt*, 2nd edn (Berlin: Duncker & Humblot, 2002), 579–596.

More, G., 'The Principle of Equal Treatment: From Market Unifier to Fundamental Right', in P. P. Craig and G. de Búrca (eds), *The Evolution of EU Law* (Oxford: Oxford University Press, 1999), 517–553.

Mosher, J. A. and Trubek, D. M., 'Alternative Approaches to Governance in the EU: EU Social Policy and the European Employment Strategy' (2003) 41 *Journal of Common Market Studies* 63–88.

Mueller, D., *Public Choice III* (Cambridge: Cambridge University Press, 2003).

Müller-Armack, A., 'Das Konzept der Sozialen Marktwirtschaft—Grundlagen, Entwicklung, Aktualität', in D. Grosser, T. Lange, A. Müller-Armack, and B. Neuss (eds), *Soziale Marktwirtschaft*, 2nd edn (Stuttgart: Kohlhammer, 1990), 1–33.

Nagel, T., *The View from Nowhere* (Oxford: Oxford University Press, 1986).

Natali, D. and de la Porte, C., 'Participation through the Lisbon Strategy: Comparing the European Employment Strategy and Pensions OMC' (2009) 15 *European Review of Labour and Research* 71–91.

Newdick, C., 'Citizenship, Free Movement and Health Care: Cementing Individual Rights by Corroding Social Solidarity' (2006) 43 *Common Market Law Review* 1645–1668.

Niess, F., *Die europäische Idee aus dem Geist des Widerstands* (Frankfurt: Suhrkamp, 2001).

Nietzsche, F., *On the Genealogy of Morality*, trans. by C. Diethe (Cambridge: Cambridge University Press, 1994).

Nietzsche, F., *Daybreak: Thoughts on the Prejudices of Morality*, trans. by R. J. Hollingdale (Cambridge: Cambridge University Press, 1997).

Nozick, R., *Anarchy, State, and Utopia* (New York: Basic Books, 1974).

Offe, C., *Contradictions of the Welfare State*, ed. by J. Keane (Cambridge, MA: MIT Press, 1984).

Offe, C., 'Demokratie und Wohlfahrtsstaat: Eine europäische Regimeform unter dem Stress der europäischen Integration', in W. Streeck (ed.), *Internationale Wirtschaft, nationale Demokratie: Herausforderungen für die Demokratietheorie* (Frankfurt: Campus Verlag, 1998), 99–136.

Offe, C., 'The European Model of "Social" Capitalism: Can it Survive European Integration?' (2003) 11 *Journal of Political Philosophy* 437–469.

Offe, C., 'Sozialpolitik und internationale Politik: Über zwei Hürden auf dem Weg zum "Zusammenhalt" Europas' (manuscript on file with the author) (2004).

O'Leary, S., *Employment Law at the European Court of Justice: Judicial Structures, Policies, and Processes* (Oxford: Hart Publishing, 2002).

Oppenheimer, D. B., 'Negligent Discrimination' (1993) 141 *University of Pennsylvania Law Review* 899–972.

Oritz, D. R., 'The Myth of Intent in Equal Protection' (1989) 41 *Stanford Law Review* 1105–1151.

Patterson, D., *Law and Truth* (New York: Oxford University Press, 1995).

Perchal, S., 'Equality of Treatment, Non-discrimination and Social Policy: Achievements in Three Themes' (2004) 41 *Common Market Law Review* 533–551.

Pierson, P., 'Social Policy and European Integration', in A. Moravcsik (ed.), *Centralisation or Fragmentation? Europe Facing the Challenges of Deepening, Diversity, and Democracy* (Washington, DC: Brookings Institution, Council on Foreign Relations, 1998), 124–158.

Pinkard, T., *Hegel's Phenomenology: The Sociality of Reason* (Cambridge: Cambridge University Press, 1994).

Pippin, R. B., *The Persistence of Subjectivity: On the Kantian Aftermath* (Cambridge: Cambridge University Press, 2005).

Pogge, T., *World Poverty and Human Rights: Cosmopolitan Responsibilities and Reforms* (Cambridge: Polity Press, 2002).

Pohlmann, F., 'Moral und totalitärer Terror', in M. Junge (ed.), *Macht und Moral: Beiträge zur Dekonstruktion von Moral* (Opladen: Westdeutscher Verlag, 2003), 235–252.

Poiares Maduro, M., 'Striking the Elusive Balance between Economic Freedom and Social Rights in the EU', in P. Alston (ed.), *The EU and Human Rights* (Oxford: Oxford University Press, 1999), 449–472.

Poiares Maduro, M., 'Europe's Social Self: "The Sickness Unto Death"', in J. Shaw (ed.), *Social Law and Policy in an Evolving European Union* (Oxford: Hart Publishing, 2000), 325–350.

Polanyi, K., *The Great Transformation: The Political Origins of our Time*, 2nd edn (Boston, MA: Beacon Press, 2001).

Pollack, M. A., *The Engines of European Integration: Delegation, Agency, and Agenda Setting in the EU* (Oxford: Oxford University Press, 2003).

Popper, K. R., *The Open Society and its Enemies*, 5th edn (Princeton, NJ: Princeton University Press, 1966).

Post, R., 'Prejudicial Appearances: The Logic of American Anti-discrimination Law' (2000) 88 *California Law Review* 1–40.

Puntscher Riekmann, S., *Die kommissarische Neuordnung Europas: Das Dispositiv der Integration* (Vienna/New York: Springer Verlag, 1998).

Rawls, J., *A Theory of Justice* (Cambridge, MA: Harvard University Press, 1971).

Rawls, J., *Political Liberalism* (New York: Columbia University Press, 1993).

Raz, J., *The Morality of Freedom* (Oxford: Clarendon Press, 1985).

Raz, J., *Practical Reason and Norms*, 2nd edn (Princeton, NJ: Princeton University Press, 1990).

Reaumé, D. G., 'Discrimination and Dignity' (2003) 63 *Louisiana Law Review* 645–695.

Rebhahn, R., 'Grundfreiheiten versus oder vor Streikrecht' (2008) 22 *Wirtschaftspolitische Blätter* 63–69.

Reid, T. R., *The United States of Europe: The New Superpower and the End of American Supremacy* (New York: Penguin Press, 2004).

Resnik, B., 'Unconscious Raising: Countering Stereotypes by Changing the Rules' (2005) 1 *Regional Review* 33–37.

Rifkin, J., *The European Dream: How Europe's Vision of the Future is Quietly Eclipsing the American Dream* (New York: Tarcher/Penguin, 2004).

Roche, M., *Rethinking Citizenship: Welfare, Ideology and Change in Modern Society* (Cambridge: Polity Press, 1992).

Rödl, F., 'Transnationale Lohnkonkurrenz: ein neuer Eckpfeiler der "sozialen" Union?' in A. Fischer-Lescano, F. Rödl, and C. U. Schmid (eds), *Europäische Gesellschaftsverfassung* (Baden-Baden: Nomos 2009), 145–160.

Roemer, J., *Equality of Opportunity* (Cambridge, MA: Harvard University Press, 1998).

Rose, N., *Powers of Freedom: Reframing Political Thought* (Cambridge: Cambridge University Press, 1999).

Rubenfeld, J., 'The Anti-anti-discrimination Agenda' (2002) 111 *Yale Law Journal* 1141–1178.

Rüstow, A., 'Der dritte Weg', in A. Rüstow, *Die Religion der Marktwirtschaft*, ed. by S. Tönnies (Münster: Lit Verlag, 2001), 41–100.

Rüstow, A., *Die Religion der Marktwirtschaft*, new edn (Münster: Lit Verlag, 2001).

Sabel, C. F., 'Beyond Principal-agent Governance: Experimentalist Organizations, Learning, and Accountability', available at http://www2.law.columbia.edu/sabel/papers/Sabel.definitief.doc accessed 2 January 2011.

Sabel, C. F. and Simon, W. H., 'Epilogue: Accountability without Sovereignty', in G. de Búrca and J. Scott (eds), *Law and New Governance in the EU and the US* (Oxford: Hart Publishing, 2006), 395–411.

Sabel, C. F. and Zeitlin, J., 'Learning from Difference: The New Architecture of Experimentalist Governance in the European Union' (2007) C–07–02 *European Governance Papers.*

Santer, J., 'The State of the Union', Debate at the European Parliament, Strasbourg, 21 October 1998, available at http://www.lex.unict.it/cde/documenti/vari/98_99/jacquer_santer.htm accessed 2 January 2011.

Schaar, J. H., 'Equality of Opportunity—and Beyond' (1967), repr. in L. P. Pojman and R. Westmoreland (eds), *Equality: Selected Readings* (New York/Oxford: Oxford University Press, 1997), 137–147.

Scharpf, F. W., 'Die Politikverflechtungsfalle: Europäische Integration und deutscher Föderalismus im Vergleich' (1985) 26 *Politische Vierteljahresschrift* 323–356.

Scharpf, F. W., 'The Joint Decision Trap: Lessons from German Federalism and European Integration' (1988) 88 *Public Administration* 239–278.

Scharpf, F. W., 'Politische Optionen im vollendeten Binnenmarkt', in K. Jachtenfuchs and B. Kohler-Koch (eds), *Europäische Integration* (Leverkusen: Leske + Buderich, 1996), 109–122.

Scharpf, F. W., *Governing in Europe: Effective and Democratic?* (Oxford: Oxford University Press, 1999).

Scharpf, F. W., 'Democratic Legitimacy under Conditions of Regulatory Competition: Why Europe Differs from the United States', in K. Nicolaidis and R. Howse (eds), *The Federal Vision: Legitimacy and Levels of Governance in the United States and the European Union* (Oxford: Oxford University Press, 2001), 355–374.

Scharpf, F. W., 'The European Social Model: Coping with the Challenges of Diversity' (2002) 40 *Journal of Common Market Studies* 645–670.

Scharpf, F. W., 'Individualrechte gegen nationale Solidarität', in M. Höpner and A. Schäfer (eds), *Die politische Ökonomie der europäischen Integration* (Frankfurt: Campus Verlag, 2008), 89–99.

Scharpf, F. W., 'The Double Asymmetry of European Integration; Or: Why the EU Cannot Be a Social Market Economy' (2009) 09/12 *MPIfG Working Paper.*

Scheuerman, W.E., 'The Unholy Alliance of Carl Schmitt and Friedrich A. Hayek', (1997) 4 *Constellations* 172–188.

Scheuerman, W. E., 'Democratic Experimentalism or Capitalist Synchronisation' (2004) 17 *Canadian Journal of Jurisprudence* 101–127.

Schmidtz, D., 'Taking Responsibility', in D. Schmidtz and R. E. Goodin, *Social Welfare and Individual Responsibility* (Cambridge: Cambridge University Press, 1998), 1–95.

Schmitt, C., 'Starker Staat und gesunde Wirtschaft' (1932), repr. in *Staat, Großraum, Nomos: Arbeiten aus den Jahren 1916–1969*, ed. by G. Maschke (Berlin: Duncker & Humblot, 1995), 71–85.

Schnädelbach, H., *Hegels Praktische Philosophie: Ein Kommentar der Texte in der Reihenfolge ihrer Entstehung* (Frankfurt: Suhrkamp, 2000).

Schnapper, E., 'Two Categories of Discriminatory Intent' (1982) 17 *Harvard Civil Rights and Civil Liberties Law Review* 31–59.

Schubert, A., *Der Euro: Die Krise einer Chance* (Frankfurt: Suhrkamp, 1998).

Schumpeter, J., *Capitalism, Socialism and Democracy* (London: Routledge, 1992, 1st edn 1943).

Scott, J. and Trubek, D. M., 'Mind the Gap: Law and New Approaches to Governance in the European Union' (2002) 8 *European Law Journal* 1–18.

Sedler, R. A., 'The Role of "Intent" in Discrimination Analysis', in T. Loenen and P. R. Rodrigues (eds), *Non-Discrimination Law: Comparative Perspectives* (Amsterdam: Kluwer, 1999) 91–103.

Shoben, E. W., 'Disparate Impact Theory in Employment Discrimination: What's Griggs still Good for? What not?' (2004) 42 *Brandeis Law Journal* 597–622.

Shola Orloff, A., 'Gender and Social Rights of Citizenship: The Comparative Analysis of Gender Relations and Welfare States' (1993) 58 *American Sociological Review* 303–328.

Siegel, R., 'Equality Talk: Antisubordination and Anticlassification Values in Constitutional Struggles over Brown' (2004) 117 *Harvard Law Review* 1470–1547.

Simon, W. H., 'Toyota Jurisprudence: Legal Theory and Rolling Rule Regimes', in G. de Búrca and J. Scott (eds), *Law and New Governance in the EU and the US* (Oxford: Hart Publishing, 2006), 37–64.

Singer, P., *Practical Ethics*, 2nd edn (Cambridge: Cambridge University Press, 1993).

Sloterdijk, P., *Nicht gerettet: Versuche nach Heidegger* (Frankfurt: Suhrkamp, 2001).

Smith, P., 'Parental-status Employment Discrimination: A Wrong in Need of a Right?' (2002) 35 *University of Michigan Journal of Law Reform* 569–621.

Snyder, F., 'EMU Revisited: Are we Making a Constitution? What Constitution are we Making?', in P. P. Craig and G. de Búrca (eds), *The Evolution of EU Law* (Oxford: Oxford University Press, 1999), 417–475.

Somek, A., 'A Constitution for Anti-discrimination: Exploring the Vanguard Moment of Community Law' (1999) 5 *European Law Journal* 243–271.

Somek, A., 'On Supranationality' (2001) 5 *European Integration Online Papers* (*EIoP*), available at http://eiop.or.at/eiop/texte/2001-003a.htm accessed 2 January 2011.

Somek, A., *Rationalität und Diskriminierung: Zur Bindung der Gesetzgebung an das Gleichheitsrecht* (Vienna/New York: Springer, 2001).

Somek, A., 'Authoritarian Constitutionalism: Austrian Constitutional Doctrine 1933 to 1938 and its Legacy', in C. Joerges and N. Singh Ghaleigh (eds), *Darker Legacies of Law in Europe: The Shadow of National Socialism and Fascism over Europe and its Legal Traditions* (Oxford: Hart Publishing, 2003), 361–387.

Somek, A., 'Neoliberale Gerechtigkeit: Die Problematik des Antidiskriminierungsrechts' (2003) 51 *Deutsche Zeitschrift für Philosophie* 45–59.

Somek, A., 'Dogmatischer Pragmatismus: Über die Normativitätskrise der Europäischen Union', in S. Hammer, A. Somek, M. Stelzer, and B. Weichselbaum (eds), *Der soziale Rechtsstaat in Europa (*Festschrift *Theo Öhlinger)* (Vienna: WUV-Universitätsverlag, 2004), 41–67.

Somek, A., 'This is about ourselves, Or: What Makes Genetic Discrimination Interesting', in N. Stehr (ed.), *Biotechnology: Between Commerce and Civil Society* (New Brunswick, NJ: Transaction Publishers, 2004), 195–216.

Somek, A., 'Catholic Concordance: Exploring the Context of European Anti-discrimination Law and Policy' (2005) 14 *Journal of Transnational Law and Contemporary Problems* 959–1006.

Somek, A., 'Equality as Reasonableness: Constitutional Normativity in Demise', in A. Sajó (ed.), *The Dark Side of Fundamental Rights*, (Utrecht: eleven international publishing, 2006), 191–215.

Somek, A., 'Anti-discrimination and Decommodification', in D. Cinar (ed.), *Doing Justice to Diversity: Challenges and Visions* (Aldershot: Ashgate, 2007) (forthcoming; see http://www.euro.centre.org/data/1122641524_50805.pdf).

Somek, A., 'Solidarity Decomposed: Being and Time in European Citizenship' (2007) 32 *European Law Review* 787–818.

Somek, A., *Individualism: An Essay on the Authority of the European Union* (Oxford: Oxford University Press, 2008).

Somek, A., 'Und was fehlt eigentlich? Eine Anmerkung zu Europas politischem Erfahrungsraum', in C. Joerges, M. Mahlmann, and U.K. Preuß (eds), *'Schmerzliche Erfahrungen der Vergangenheit' und der Prozess der Konstitutionalisierung Europas: Rechts-, Geschichts- und Politikwissenschaftliche Beiträge* (Wiesbaden: Verlag für Sozialwissenschaften, 2008), 144–149.

Somek, A., 'Idealization, De-politicization and Economic Due Process: System Transition in the European Union', in B. Iancu (ed.), *The Law/Politics Distinction in Contemporary Public Law Adjudication* (Utrecht: eleven international publishing, 2009), 137–167.

Somek, A., 'The Argument from Transnational Effects I: Representing Outsiders through Freedom of Movement' (2010) 16 *European Law Journal* 315–144.

Somek, A., 'The Emancipation of Legal Dissonance' in H. Koch, K. Hagel-Sørensen, U. Haltem, and J. H. H. Weiler (eds), *Europe: The New Legal Realism* (Copenhagen: DJØF Publishing, 2010) 679–713.

Spann, O., *Der wahre Staat: Vorlesungen über Abbruch und Neubau der Gesellschaft* (Leipzig: Quelle und Meyer, 1921).

Stelzer, M., *Das Wesensgehaltsargument und der Grundsatz der Verhältnismäßigkeit* (Vienna/New York: Springer, 1991).

Stevenson, C. L., *Facts and Values* (New Haven, CT: Yale University Press, 1963).

Strauss, D. A., 'The Myth of Colorblindness' (1986) *Supreme Court Review* 99–134.

Strauss, D. A., 'The Law and Economics of Racial Discrimination in Employment: The Case for Numerical Standards' (1991) 79 *Georgetown Law Journal* 1619–1657.

Streeck, W., 'Competitive Solidarity—Rethinking the "European Social Model"', available at http://www.mpifg.de/pu/workpap/wp99-8/wp99-8.html accessed 23 December 2010.

Streeck, W., 'Neo-Voluntarism: A New Social Policy Regime?' (1995) 1 *European Law Journal* 31–59.

Streeck, W., 'Vom Binnenmarkt zum Bundesstaat? Überlegungen zur politischen Ökonomie der europäischen Sozialpolitik', in S. Leibfried and P. Pierson (eds), *Standort Europa. Europäische Sozialpolitik* (Frankfurt: Suhrkamp, 1998), 369–421.

Sturm, L., 'Second Generation Employment Discrimination: A Structural Approach' (2001) 101 *Columbia Law Review* 458–568.

Sturm, S., 'Race, Gender, and the Law in the Twenty-First Century Workplace' (1998) 1 *University of Pennsylvania Journal of Labour and Employment Law* 639–689.

Sturm, S., 'Gender Equality Regimes and the Architecture of Learning', in G. de Búrca and J. Scott (eds), *Law and Governance in the EU and the US* (Oxford: Hart Publishing, 2006), 323–360.

Sturm, S., 'The Architecture of Inclusion: Advancing Workplace Equity in Higher Education' (2006) 29 *Harvard Journal of Law and Gender* 247–334.

Sullivan, C. A., 'Disparate Impact: Looking Past the Desert Place Mirage' (2005) 47 *William and Mary Law Review* 911–1002.

Sunstein, C. R., *Our Partial Constitution* (Cambridge, MA: Harvard University Press, 1993).

Sunstein, C. R., *Free Markets and Social Justice* (Oxford: Oxford University Press, 1997).

Swan, P., 'American Empire or Empires? Alternative Juridifications of the New World Order', in A. Bartholomew (ed.), *Empire's Law* (London: Pluto Press, 2006), 137–160.

Szyszczak, E., 'The New Paradigm for Social Policy: A Virtuous Circle?' (2001) 38 *Common Market Law Review* 1125–1170.

Teubner, G., 'The Anonymous Matrix: Human Rights Violations by "Private" Transnational Actors' (2006) 69 *Modern Law Review* 327–346.

Trubek, D. M., Cottrell, P., and Nance, M., '"Soft Law," "Hard Law" and EU Integration', in G. de Búrca and J. Scott (eds), *Law and New Governance in the EU and the US* (Oxford: Hart Publishing, 2006), 65–94.

Trubek, D. M. and Mosher, J. S., 'New Governance, EU Employment Policy, and the European Social Model' (2001) 6 *Jean Monnet Working Paper.*

Trubek, D. M. and Trubek, L. G., 'New Governance and Legal Regulation: Complementarity, Rivalry, and Transformation' (2007) 13 *Columbia Journal of European Law* 539–564.

Unger, R. M., *Law in Modern Society: Towards a Criticism of Social Theory* (New York: Free Press, 1976).

Unger, R. M., *False Necessity* (Cambridge: Cambridge University Press, 1987).

Unger, R. M., *Democracy Realized: The Progressive Alternative* (London: Verso, 1996).

Unger, R. M., *What should Legal Analysis become?* (London: Verso, 1996).

van der Mei, A. P., *Free Movement of Persons within the European Community* (Oxford: Hart Publishing, 2003).

von Bogdandy, A. and Bast, J., 'The European Union's Vertical Order of Competences: The Current Law and Proposals for Its Reform' (2002) 39 *Common Market Law Review* 227–268.

von Humboldt, W., *Ideen zu einem Versuch die Grenzen der Wirksamkeit des Staats zu bestimmen* (Leipzig: Reclam, 1995).

von Mises, L., 'Liberalismus', in E. Becherath, H. Bente, and C. Brinkmann (eds), *Handwörterbuch der Sozialwissenschaften*, vol. 6 (Stuttgart: G. Fischer, 1959), 596–603.

von Parijs, P., *Real Freedom for All: What (if Anything) Can Justify Capitalism?* (Oxford: Oxford University Press, 1995).

Waddington, L. and Hendriks, A., 'The Expanding Concept of Employment Discrimination in Europe: From Direct and Indirect Discrimination to Reasonable Accommodation Discrimination' (2002) 18 *International Journal of Comparative Labour Law and Industrial Relations* 403–427.

Walker, N. and de Búrca, G., 'Reconceiving Law and New Governance' (2007) 13 *Columbia Journal of European Law* 519–537.

Walzer, M., *Thick and Thin: Moral Argument at Home and Abroad* (Notre Dame, IN: Notre Dame University Press, 1994).

Weatherill, S., 'After *Keck*: Some Thoughts on how to Clarify the Clarification' (1996) 33 *Common Market Law Review* 885–906.

Weber, M., 'Die protestantische Ethik und der Geist des Kapitalismus', in M. Weber, *Gesammelte Aufsätze zur Religionssoziologie*, vol. 1 (Tübingen: Mohr, 1920), 17–205.

Weber, M., *Gesammelte Aufsätze zur Religionssoziologie*, vol. 1, 7th edn (Tübingen: Mohr & Siebeck, 1978).

Weber, M., *Economy and Society: An Outline of Interpretive Sociology*, trans. by E. Fischoff, H. Gereth, A. M. Henderson, F. Kolegar, C. Wright Mills, T. Parsons, M. Rheinstein, G. Roth, E. Shils, and C. Wittich (New York: Bedminster Press, 1968).

Weiler, J. H. H., 'The Transformation of Europe' (1991) 100 *Yale Law Journal* 2403–2483.

Weiler, J. H. H., 'Federalism and Constitutionalism: Europe's *Sonderweg*', in K. Nicolaidis and R. Howse (eds), *The Federal Vision: Legitimacy and Levels of Governance in the United States and the European Union* (Oxford: Oxford University Press, 2000), 54–72.

Weiler, J. H. H., 'A Constitution for Europe? Some Hard Choices' (2002) 40 *Journal of Common Market Studies* 565–580.

Weiler, J. H. H., *Ein christliches Europa* (Salzburg: Anton Pustet, 2004).

Wickham, J., *The End of the European Social Model: Before it Began?* available at http://www.tcd.ie/ERC/observatorydownloads/Social%20Model.pdf accessed 23 December 2010.

Williams, J., 'Gender Wars: Selfless Women in the Republic of Choice' (1991) 66 *New York University Law Review* 1546–1634.

Williams, J. C. and Segal, N., 'Beyond the Maternal Wall: Relief for Family Caregivers who are Discriminated against on the Job' (2003) 26 *Harvard Women's Law Journal* 77–162.

Wilson, W. J., *The Truly Disadvantaged: The Inner City, the Underclass, and Public Policy* (Chicago, IL: University of Chicago Press, 1987).

Winkler, V., 'Diskriminierungsschutz durch Recht: Anmerkungen zu einer ajuristischen Debatte' (2003) 4 *Juridikum* 188–191.

Winterstein, A., 'Nailing the Jellyfish: Social Security and Competition Law' (1999) 20 *European Competition Law Review* 324–333.

Wodak, R., 'Critical Discourse Analysis', in C. Seale, G. Gobo, J. F. Gubrium, and D. Silverman (eds), *Qualitative Research Practice* (London: Sage, 2004), 197–213.

Wood, G. S., *The Radicalism of the American Revolution* (New York: Vintage Books, 1991).

Yoshino, K., 'The Assimilationist Bias in Equal Protection: The Visibility Presumption and the Case of "Don't Ask, Don't Tell"' (1998) 108 *Yale Law Journal* 485–571.

Yoshino, K., 'Covering' (2002) 111 *Yale Law Journal* 769–939.

Zeitlin, J., 'Social Europe and Experimentalist Governance: Towards a New Constitutional Compromise?', in G. de Búrca (ed.), *EU Law and the Welfare State: In Search of Solidarity* (Oxford: Oxford University Press, 2005), 213–241.

Zielonka, I., *Europe as Empire: The Nature of the Enlarged European Union* (Oxford: Oxford University Press, 2006).

Žižek, S., 'Taking on America', available at http://www.spiked-online.com/Printable/00000006DA75.htm accessed 2 January 2011.

Žižek, S., *The Ticklish Subject: The Absent Centre of Political Ontology* (London: Verso, 1999).

Žižek, S., 'What Does Europe Want', available at http://www.lacan.com/zizekslovenia.htm accessed 23 December 2010.

Index

Accommodation 18, 178, 183
as antidiscrimination law reaching beyond itself 178, 180, 182, 184
and protection from discrimination 179–180, 182
resolves normative twist 178, 182–183
Adaptability 14–15, 87, 95, 181, 186
Administrative authoritarianism 86, 165
Alienation 182
Americans with Disabilities Act 178
and Anti-Discrimination law 179–180
Animus 104, 150
Anti-discrimination Action Programme 58–59
Anti-discrimination law
absence of distributive patterns 17, 127, 132, 141
antinomy of 17, 113, 115, 159
and burden of proof 150
as moral equivalent to law and economics 15
deontological misreading 16–17, 91, 108, 111, 116, 126–127
deontological realization (translation) of 93, 106–108, 110, 151, 183
and entrepreneurial self 189
history 55
as an idol of supranationality 51
inverted appearance 16, 113
lack of formality 91, 171
and market access 51, 83, 137, 179
as moral purification of the market 15, 166, 174
and moralism 17, 82, 83
and neoliberal predicament 17, 159, 161, 166, 171, 174
and neoliberalism 13, 84, 91, 97
normative deficiency of 12–13, 17, 52, 90, 93, 104, 127, 131–132, 135–136, 141, 156–157, 159, 163, 166, 173, 190
its normative twist 115, 131, 146, 182
perplexity of 136, 186–187
as reconciliation of competitiveness and solidarity 3–4, 83, 170 n. 72, 189
its redistributive task 16, 89, 93, 99–103, 108–110, 113, 125, 182
its self-obfuscation 93
as social policy in the state of disempowerment 18, 136, 155, 166, 170, 177–178
systemic discrimination as target of 105–106, 113
its success 9, 59
Anti-discrimination policy 53–55, 63
and changing of attitudes 61, 82, 87, 155
see also New governance
Anti-discrimination principle 88–89, 135–136, 180–181
Attribution preference 164–164
as part of law of society 165
Austerity 35–36
Authoritarian liberalism 45–46, 50
Awareness-raising 58, 75, 82, 167

Beautiful soul 149, 171

Casuistry 4, 17, 134, 150, 159
Cognitive bias
see Unconscious bias
Communicative Action 71
Community Method 71–72
Competitiveness 3–4
Concordantia Catholica 61 n. 66, 64–65, 81, 171
Constructivism 19–20, 101
Consumer sovereignty 94, 107, 137, 152, 193
Cooperation 71 n. 149
Coordination 71 n. 149
Covering 166
Critical goods 4, 6
Cultural imperialism 98

Decommodification 18, 26, 28, 88, 90, 94, 113, 159, 178
and redistribution 89, 136–137, 182
and reversal of normative twist 182
Deontology 106
Direct discrimination 6, 16, 100, 126, 138
derogations 133–134
extensional interpretation 16, 118–119, 126–128
indirect indirect discrimination 101–103, 107, 177
intensional interpretation 16, 119–120, 127
special case of indirect discrimination 16, 113, 115–118, 123
systemic discrimination 106
Directly deliberative polyarchy 168
Disadvantaged groups 153–155, 157
Discourse 11, 69–71
Discrimination 180–181, 185
direct, *see* Direct discrimination
indirect, *see* Indirect discrimination
participation by victims 181, 186–187
and self-denial 136, 181, 185–186

Discriminatory intent
inscrutability 145–149
and intensional understanding of causality 121
normative 16, 103–104, 110, 126, 132, 155
pre-normative 16, 103–104, 110, 115, 127–132, 146, 149, 159
Distributive agents 106, 110, 126, 150, 183
Distributive justice 1, 93, 98–99
see Market equality
Diversity 96, 187, 190
Ducking 166, 181

Employability 9
Employment policy 9, 29, 38, 40, 75
concomitant with anti-discrimination agenda 21, 51
see European Employment Strategy
Enlargment of the European Union 192
Equal opportunity 3, 182
EQUAL programme 61–64, 81–82
Equality bodies 5, 54–55
Equality management 12, 92
macro level 13, 68, 83, 161, 175
micro level 13, 83, 91, 159, 161, 167, 175
Equality of opportunity 83, 179, 189
European citizenship 32–33, 193–194
European Employment Strategy 10, 40–43, 61–62, 68, 69 n. 129, 70,72, 75 80
and labour law 77
European social model 26–28, 59
Experimentalism 167, 172, 175, 177

Fictitious commodities 94 n. 5
Flexibilization 2, 40 n. 116
Flexicurity 8, 77
Forbidden grounds 5, 130
Fundamental freedoms 31, 47–48
and fundamental rights 49–50
as protections against discrimination 47
as protections against obstacles 47
their horizontal effect 49
Fundamental rights 78–79

Gender mainstreaming 10 n. 54
Good reasons 133, 138, 146
Governmentality 75 n. 181, 84

Harmonizing legislation 39
Human dignity 108
Human resources 9, 26–28, 55, 65–66, 75

Identity politics 187
Immutable characteristics 5, 15, 97
visibility presumption 185
Inclusion 2, 22, 40, 61, 70, 90 n. 31, 184
Indeterminacy 20, 128, 141, 150
Indirect discrimination 6, 16, 113–114, 173
as functional equivalent of accommodation 180
and proportionality test 117–118, 124, 133–134, 139
Individualism 86–87, 155, 158, 166 n. 47
In-group bias 164, 173
Innovation 168
Intergovernmentalism 45
Intermediaries 169–171
instead of workforce 170
Intersectionality 153

Joint decision trap 38
Juristocracy 57

Legal formality 91, 171
Legal Positivism 19
Legal scholarship 20
Liberal market economies 9, 192
Lisbon Strategy 10, 27, 43, 65–66, 68, 69 n. 131, 80

Mainstreaming 60 n. 57, 63
Margin of discretion 135
Market equality 93, 97, 110, 138, 157
Market rationality 85, 98, 151–152, 158, 182
and schizophrenia 137
Merit 174
Monetary Union 21, 35–36
Moral intuitions 149, 162, 177, 183
Moralism 142–143
see Anti-discrimination law
Morality 88–89, 127, 139, 146–147, 150
and hypocrisy 147
and neoliberalism 187

Natural Law Theory 19
Neoliberal left 14–15, 97, 98 n. 29, 151, 171, 190
contrast to neoliberal right 97
Neoliberal predicament 17, 159, 161, 166, 171, 174
Neoliberalism 13–14, 73, 75 n. 181, 84–86
apolitical 86–87, 158
contrast to classical liberalism 85
its illiberality 77
and morality 187
New governance 55–57, 64, 69, 74, 80–81
defies legality 75, 77 n. 191, 83, 92, 168, 172
holism 63, 68–70, 80
mobilization 63, 70–73
New Labour 194
Normative intent
See Discriminatory intent

Open Method of Coordination 40, 55 n. 20, 65, 68–69, 70 n. 143, 71, 73, 81, 168 n. 58
characterized 69 n. 131
Organized economies 8, 25, 28,
defined 44 n. 138
disadvantage in a transnational context 44–45, 192–193

Particularity 95–95, 97, 110
Pedagogicization 13, 158, 171
Postmodernism 19
Poverty 40
Pragmatism 74
Pre-normative intent
  see Discriminatory intent
Problem-solving gap 39
PROGRESS 58, 62
Proportionality Principle 79, 117, 134–135, 151, 158
Protocol on Social Policy 37
Psychoanalysis 90 n. 33

Quotas 110

Real abstractions 166
Redistribution 88, 99
Redistribution 2, 88–89, 93
  and decommodification 89, 185
Regulatory competition 34, 48, 190
Regulatory disarmament
  see Social policy
Renationalization 36
Responsibility 181, 184
Right answer 20

Schmidberger trap 49
Self-determination
  collective (among market participants) 95
  individual 147
Sheltered employment practices 16
Social and economic citizenship 76–77
Social dumping 39
Social legislation 1, 6, 38, 88, 100, 137
Social market economies 28, 192–193, 195
  see Organized economies
Social model 28
Social policy 3, 7, 11, 29–30, 50, 83, 178
  assimilation to internal market 7, 21, 32–34
  disarmament 21, 32, 36, 48–49, 52, 192–193
  domestication 21, 29–32, 38, 52
  subordination to economic policy 10, 14
  Union competence 36–38
Social Policy Agenda 64–65, 67
Social Policy Agreement 28
Social psychology 164
Social question 6, 21
  in a transnational context 7–8, 21, 51–52, 190–191
Social Welfare State 26–27, 41–43, 66 n. 111, 70, 73, 76, 78 n. 195
Solidarity 3, 30, 138, 155, 187
  as identification 187
  reductions of 188–189
  as transcendence 188
Spirit of the Age 14, 85
Stereotypes 164
Structural bias
  see Unconscious bias
Substantive economic due process 8, 47
Systemic discrimination
  see Anti-discrimination law

Technocracy 55, 57 n. 29, 167
Terror 155–157
Third Way 19, 194–195
Title VI of the Civic Rights Act
  see US American anti-discrimination law
Transnational Federalism 22, 191
  inverse competence structure 43–44
Transnational substantive economic due process 47, 52
Treating like cases alike 122–124
  and proportionality 125

Unconscious (structural) bias 18, 149 n. 33, 160, 163–165, 169, 172, 175, 177
  inscrutability 172
Underclass 184, 191
United States of America 91 n. 37
US American Anti-discrimination law 115 n. 8, 142, 158, 161, 183
US American Second Generation of Anti-discrimination Scholarship 160–161, 166, 174–175, 177
  moral hypertrophy 161
  moral re-engineering 167, 177
  productivist bias 167, 170
  structural turn 160, 166
  see also Neoliberal predicament
Utilitarianism 143

Visible characteristics 15

Wealth talent 95
Western Europe 25–26

Yielding 106, 108

Lightning Source UK Ltd.
Milton Keynes UK
UKOW030729181012

200775UK00006B/8/P

9 780199 693375